T0366922

KEEP ON BELIEVIN'

Music shapes our world more powerfully than any other cultural product. To fully understand America, we must learn the complex, diverse history of American musical life. The books in this series tell the stories of the artists, forms, and innovations that define the musical legacy of the United States and fashion its ideals and practices.

KEEP ON BELIEVIN'

The Life and Music of Richie Furay

Thomas M. Kitts

THE PENNSYLVANIA STATE UNIVERSITY PRESS | UNIVERSITY PARK, PENNSYLVANIA

Library of Congress Cataloging-in-Publication Data

Names: Kitts, Thomas M., 1955– author.
Title: Keep on believin' : the life and music of Richie Furay / Thomas M.
    Kitts.
Other titles: American music history.
Description: University Park, Pennsylvania : The Pennsylvania State
    University Press, [2023] | Series: American music history | Includes
    bibliographical references and index.
Summary: "Explores the life and career of American singer-songwriter,
    recording artist, and performer Richie Furay"—Provided by publisher.
Identifiers: LCCN 2022061270 | ISBN 9780271095233 (hardback)
Subjects: LCSH: Furay, Richie. | Buffalo Springfield (Musical group) |
    Poco (Musical group) | Rock musicians—United States—Biography. |
    Lyricists—United States—Biography. | LCGFT: Biographies.
Classification: LCC ML420.F899 K57 2023 | DDC 782.42166092 [B]—dc23/
    eng/20230106
LC record available at https://lccn.loc.gov/2022061270

The Pennsylvania State University Press is a member of the Association of
University Presses.

It is the policy of The Pennsylvania State University Press to use acid-free
paper. Publications on uncoated stock satisfy the minimum requirements
of American National Standard for Information Sciences—Permanence of
Paper for Printed Library Material, ANSI Z39.48–1992.

For my wife, Lisa

For our children:
Dylan, Holly, Hayley, and Julia

For my parents, Richard and Anna,
who encouraged my love of music

Contents

Illustrations

Preface

On August 6, 1970, I attended the Festival for Peace, a fundraiser for antiwar political candidates, at Shea Stadium in New York. There were many acts that I was anxious to see: Creedence Clearwater Revival, Steppenwolf, Janis Joplin, Johnny Winter, and many others. However, shortly after the performances began, in the blazing afternoon sun, a band called Poco took the stage. I had never heard of Poco. Their sound amazed me, a combination of rock and country, with one member playing a pedal steel guitar, which I don't remember if my fourteen-year-old self could identify. I had never heard anything quite like Poco. They were lively, fun, and riveting. I was especially impressed with their leader, Richie Furay. During my high school years, I saw Poco every chance I got, recruiting Poco fans from among my friends. I once coaxed one of my older brothers into seeing them in Central Park and, yes, he was suitably impressed.

As I began my research for this book, I was surprised to find many of my teenage opinions validated. In various music magazines, I used to look for Furay's name on the list of year-end polls for "best vocalist of the year." His name was never there. I just assumed that I lacked expert judgment. Certainly, Furay did not have the flash of Mick Jagger, the vocal pyrotechnics of Robert Plant, or the swagger of Rod Stewart, but certainly he deserved some recognition. During the course of this study, which necessitated listening and relistening to Furay's music, I was impressed time and time again by his vocals, particularly his phrasing, his clarity, his emotion, and his precision. Peter Knobler—an author and editor of *Crawdaddy* from 1972 to 1979—confirmed, "He has one of the great voices in rock and roll." Grammy Award–winning producer Val Garay, who has worked on albums with approximately 125 million worldwide record sales, said, "He's an amazing vocalist. . . . He has incredible range and incredible power. Just a great vocalist."[1]

I have long appreciated Furay the songwriter and his sense of melody, both for ballads and for high-energy country rockers often constructed off his tenacious riffs. However, through the course of writing this book, I became more and more impressed with Furay the lyricist. His lyrics are deceptively simple, repeatedly echoing the American plain style of the Puritans, Ben Franklin, Hemingway, Raymond Carver, and many others. Furay's lyrics are direct, exact, and highly polished. He does not waste words. Unabashedly, like many other American authors, Furay writes most often about his own life. You can bet that the "I" in any given Furay song is Furay himself. His lyrics, taken as a whole, tell his story: the pleasures and conflicts of being in a band, new loves and breakups, marital love and discord, the joys of parenthood, the struggle and ecstasy of spiritual conversion, and the realization of his own mortality. His story is that of an ever-optimistic American spirit, one who keeps on chasing dreams and "keeps on believin'."

Furay never attained the level of stardom of many of his former bandmates, like Neil Young, Stephen Stills, Jim Messina, Randy Meisner, Timothy B. Schmit, and even that of Poco after his departure. He never scored that one hit song or hit album that would have brought him widespread recognition in the music world. Although he may be widely acknowledged as one of the fathers of country rock, pop music critics and historians have undervalued and underappreciated his music. "Richie's probably one of the most underrated rock-folk, musician-singers," said Timothy B. Schmit of the Eagles, a band that—according to its cofounder, Glenn Frey—would not have been possible without Furay.[2]

My hope is that this book will bring greater recognition and appreciation to Furay, the pioneering country rocker, the vocalist, the songwriter and lyricist, the performer, and the artist.

A FEW EXPLANATIONS

I spend half the book on Furay's time in Buffalo Springfield and Poco, 1966–1973. While this period represents less than half his creative output and less than a decade in a career that encompasses more than five decades, Furay's years with Springfield and Poco represent both his formative work and his greatest work. He builds off of and, in some ways, responds to the music he created in those years in all his later music. Therefore, I considered those times worthy of greater exploration.

A second point: all references to charts, unless noted, come from *Billboard*.

Third, all biblical quotations are from the New King James Version of the Bible (NKJV), Pastor Furay's translation of choice because of its accessibility and its closeness to the King James edition. In addition, Pastor Chuck Smith, founder of the Calvary Chapel movement and mentor to Furay, approved of the NKJV.[3]

Acknowledgments

Many people have helped and supported me with *Keep on Believin'*. I thank my dean at St. John's University, Glenn Gerstner, who granted me generous research support and course reductions so I could concentrate on this book. Larry Pitilli, a good friend and colleague, answered all my technical questions on music. Randy Ortiz, another good friend and colleague and a Grammy Award winner, patiently explained the mechanics of recording. Other friends helped me think out my concepts and direction: Steve Hamelman, Nick Baxter-Moore, Wayne Robins, and Robert Tomes. The late Bill Keogan, an expert librarian, procured needed source materials for me while finding other relevant materials. I am also very appreciative of my chair Kathleen Marks, Kevin James, and Luca Iondoli, also at St. John's, and Ryan Peterson at Penn State University Press for his enthusiasm and patience. I am very grateful also to Kenneth Womack, the series editor of American Music History at PSUP, who welcomed my project with enthusiasm.

I thank my friend Mark Volman of the Turtles and Flo and Eddie. In many ways, this project began with Mark. A few years back, I asked Mark if he knew Richie Furay. "Sure. We lived with each other for a while in Laurel Canyon, and we talked each other through our recoveries from hip surgeries." Mark put me in contact with Richie.

Richie's manager, David Stone, was helpful in numerous ways, especially in helping me contact many of my interviewees and providing encouragement. I am, of course, grateful to those I interviewed: Dickie Davis, Val Garay, George Grantham, Nels Gustafson, Bob Harmelink, Furay's sister Judy Hugli, Peter Knobler, Geoff Mayfield, Randy Meisner, Jim Messina, Leanne Meyers, Mitch Rose, Timothy B. Schmit, Scott Sellen, and Kenny Weissberg. That they all were so open and generous with their time and responses is a testament to the love they bear Richie.

Richie Furay himself was spectacularly cooperative. We exchanged many emails, and he submitted to some dozen lengthy interviews, answering all my questions—if his memory allowed. He shared intimate details with me about his life and music and tolerated even the most ridiculous or detailed questions with patience. He provided me with photos and helped put me in contact with bandmates, friends, and family. I also thank Nancy Furay for her patience, as I delayed several outings with my extended interviews of her husband. It was an honor to get to know Richie and to share a lot of laughs in the process.

Other than Richie, the other person most responsible for helping me during this undertaking has been my wife, Lisa, who generously gave me all the time I needed to write and research. She excused me from household chores, shopping trips, and our favorite activities, like days on the beach at our Florida retreat. I am also appreciative of our children: Holly, Dylan (who helped with some fact finding), Hayley (who transcribed several interviews for me), and Julia. They and their partners (Simon, Devin, Gio, and Anish, who helped with formatting the manuscript) always seemed to appear at the right time to provide me with some relief and reenergizing laughter. I am grateful to them all.

CHAPTER 1

"We Were the Dreamers"

Richie Furay and Yellow Springs

Throughout its history, Yellow Springs, Ohio, Richie Furay's birthplace, has been developed by visionaries and dreamers with big plans and faith in the human spirit. Men like Elisha Mills and his son William, Robert Owen,[1] Horace Mann, the Rev. Moncure Daniel Conway, and Arthur Morgan sought to establish enterprises in Yellow Springs that would serve not only the immediate community but also the world community. Each hoped to construct a new paradigm, a new "city upon a hill."[2] They found their inspiration not so much in the Bible or in the religious rigor of John Winthrop but in the do-goodism of Ben Franklin and an American idealism that transcends economics, religion, gender, and race. Some enterprises worked out better than others, but throughout the years, a series of altruistic and optimistic experiments, perhaps best exemplified by Antioch College, have left an imprint of openness and hope on the village and its inhabitants.[3]

The village was named after an actual yellow spring, now a featured attraction of Glen Helen Nature Preserve and about a mile from the Humanist Center in the middle of town. Shawnee chiefs and warriors like Tecumseh, Blue Jacket, and Black Hoof bathed in its restorative waters. The first white settler, Lewis Davis of Dayton, Ohio, arrived in 1803 after purchasing land from Congress as part of US westward expansion, and he built a home near the yellow spring (which has an ocher tinge from its high iron content). Davis traded with the Shawnee and opened a tavern to host white guests who visited the mythical spring. In 1826, Elisha Mills purchased land near the spring and began promoting his "water cure spa, just a day's ride north of Cincinnati."[4] As a boy, Richie Furay hiked with friends to the yellow spring to play cowboys and Indians. "It was a wonderful place to go and play and pretend we were out in the wild," he recalled.[5]

William—or "Judge"—Mills, son of Elisha Mills, bears the title "the father of Yellow Springs."[6] Although not a sworn-in judge, Mills reconciled many private disputes among residents and worked tirelessly to develop Yellow Springs. While he was involved in several businesses, his greatest contribution came in the mid-1840s when he convinced the Little Miami Railroad Company to place a stop in Yellow Springs instead of Clifton, at the time a far more prosperous community, just five miles away. When funding faltered, Mills traveled at his own expense to Boston and New York to lobby investors. The first passengers disembarked in Yellow Springs in 1846. The result was that Yellow Springs flourished and Clifton floundered. Unfortunately, Mills lost most of his wealth in the Panic of 1857 and struggled financially until his death in 1879. His obituary in the *Xenia Torchlight* celebrated his many contributions to Yellow Springs and his "ardent hopefulness,"[7] a trait Mills has in common with many Yellow Springers, including Richie Furay.

Antioch College

At a meeting in Dayton, Ohio, in 1850, the Christian Connection, a loose collection of various religious denominations, passed a resolution to found a college for men and women that, despite some disagreement, would be nonsectarian. To procure the college's location in Yellow Springs, Judge Mills, who had studied the classics at both Kenyon College and Miami University of Ohio, donated $30,000 and twenty acres of land. Antioch has had a profound effect on Yellow Springs. In many ways, the college stands as a symbol of the town's idealism and hopefulness. In 1853, at the formal inauguration of Horace Mann, Antioch's first president, over three thousand attendees arrived from across the country. "Dreams ruled the day," wrote Yellow Springs journalist Diane Chiddister in 2003.[8]

Antioch would be only the tenth US college to admit both men and women, following the first, Oberlin College, Ohio, by only sixteen years. Among its first ten faculty members was Rebecca Pennell, Mann's niece and the first woman professor in the United States to have the same rank and pay as her male counterparts. Mann's feminism was, however, limited. He did not grant women students the same rights and privileges as their male counterparts, and he discouraged the commingling of the sexes. Male and female students, for example, could not leave campus together unless accompanied by a faculty member and, in what sounds particularly odd today, women were not permitted to memorize texts or speak extemporaneously—unwomanly practices in the mid-nineteenth century. Furthermore, Mann, for all his liberality, considered the day's feminists as extremists, "the ultra sorts," and considered feminist thinker Margaret Fuller, who knew Mann's wife, as bothersome.[9] Not particularly fond of the Fuller family, he thought that Margaret "had the disagreeableness of forty Fullers."[10]

Mann and Mills were both abolitionists, who agreed that Black people should have access to higher education at Antioch. It was a controversial decision, one that affected enrollment and fundraising—a constant problem in Antioch's history. In the mid-1850s, Mann's admittance of two Black women students caused one trustee to resign and withdraw his children from the college. A few years later, Antioch issued a formal policy stating that no student should be rejected because of his or her race or gender, a policy that the college clung to despite opposition. In 1863, approximately a dozen students left when two Black women enrolled. In the previous year, the Rev. Moncure Daniel Conway, a Cincinnati minister who admired Mann, had brought escaped slaves from his father's plantation to dwell in the safety of Yellow Springs.

Over the years, Yellow Springs has proven more racially tolerant than most communities, which is not to say it has been without incident and demonstration. In 1942, students and faculty from Antioch and nearby Wilberforce University, a historically Black college, led a successful protest at the Little Theatre (now the Little Art Theatre) to remove the restrictions that allowed African Americans to sit only in the last two rows. A year later, in 1943, Antioch increased its efforts to recruit African American students by offering scholarships to non-white students. One recipient was Coretta Scott, whose future husband, Martin Luther King Jr., delivered the commencement address at Antioch in 1965. In 1946, a year after Furay's birth, Dr. William Anderson, a music professor, became the first African American professor to chair a department outside of the nation's historically Black colleges, a position he held until 1965, and in 1959, Jim McKee was appointed police chief of Yellow Springs, the first African American to hold that position in a predominantly white community in the United States. He remained chief until his retirement in 1993.

Perhaps the most noted racial protests occurred outside Gegner's Barbershop beginning in 1960. That August, the *New York Times* reported that proprietor Lewis Gegner had been found guilty of violating an ordinance against discrimination as he refused to serve African Americans, claiming that he lacked the expertise to cut their hair.[11] Over the next several years, intermittent protests occurred, including one with over six hundred participants led by former Antioch president Arthur Morgan. On March 14, 1964, another large protest turned into a near riot. Police chief Jim McKee ordered that tear gas and fire hoses be used to disperse the crowd. He later called it "the worst day of my life."[12] Richie Furay found himself in the midst of that protest: "I remember getting caught up in it. I had just been hanging out. [It was] the first time I ever got a taste of tear gas. It was quite a feeling, to say the least."[13] Finally, in June, Gegner closed his shop and vowed never to cut hair in Ohio again.

To be clear, African Americans have long been attracted to Yellow Springs because of its reputation for racial tolerance. In the 1940s, particularly after World War II, Yellow Springs had its historically steepest growth spurt. Its population rose from 1,640 in 1940 to 2,896 in 1950, an increase of 76.6 percent with over 400 African Americans comprising 14 percent of the population.[14]

If Antioch promoted racial tolerance, it also inspired new solutions and progressive educational and societal projects. In 1921, after a shutdown because of financial constraints, Arthur Morgan, an engineer, was installed as president and found the college "in its usual state of poverty-stricken idealism."[15] Yet Morgan saw not only a challenge but also an opportunity to develop a college to match his vision. "I believe it is near enough dead," he wrote, "to start over in the form I dream of."[16] Morgan pushed forward with fundraisers, public relations events, and a cooperative education program that combined work off campus with a rigorous liberal arts education. By his second year, enrollment had sprung from approximately fifty to four hundred students, the faculty from six to forty-five, and the budget to half a million dollars. Additionally, Morgan founded the Antioch School, an alternative elementary school, still in existence, which seeks "to emphasize the joy of living" and to tap into "[the] spirit of action, of daring and adventure, so nearly universal in youth."[17] Morgan remained as president until 1936, when Pres. Franklin Roosevelt tapped him to head the Tennessee Valley Authority. Yet his influence on Yellow Springs continued. In 1940, he founded Community Service, Inc. (CSI) "to promote family life and small towns—the world's classic small communities—as the best hope for a rational human future" in a rapidly urbanizing America.[18] CSI is still headquartered in Yellow Springs. Morgan died in 1975 in Xenia, Ohio, approximately ten miles from Antioch College.

As Richie Furay put it, Yellow Springs "looked very much like Mayberry," the idyllic fictional town of *The Andy Griffith Show* (1960–68), "but it was quite a progressive community, thanks in part to the presence of Antioch College."[19] Antioch's influence would be more potent at some times than other times

—depending on enrollment and solvency—but Yellow Springs has maintained a progressive spirit and openness. In 1979, for instance, Yellow Springs became the smallest municipality to pass an ordinance prohibiting discrimination based on sexual orientation. However, in some ways, as Richie's sister Judy says, "The town was sort of divided" between the more longtime residents and the college community.[20] That is not to imply that there was tension so much as a lack of socializing between the two groups who, like the African Americans and whites, coexisted rather than mingled. The acclaimed actor John Lithgow, who moved to Yellow Springs after his father, Arthur, took a professorship at Antioch, wrote that, in contrast to the other residents, the college personnel "teemed with pinko bohemians and tweedy anarchists."[21] However, in a town where "everything is in walking distance," the groups interacted daily and mostly got along well.[22] Lithgow's brother David, for example, hung out at times with Judy, as David's best friend Dan McGregor, son of Antioch's president, had a crush on Judy's girlfriend. Rod Serling, who created the *Twilight Zone* TV series, was a student at Antioch, who participated in its work-study program and lunched regularly at the counter at Furay's Drug Store, where he usually ordered a cheese sandwich and Coke and became friendly with the Furays. "I saw hippies, bohemians, and jeans all the time," said Judy,[23] not a usual experience for most Midwestern small-town residents in the 1950s or 1960s.

In fact, Richie's love for performing took root when—in 1956, at ten years of age—he appeared as an extra in *Much Ado About Nothing*, a production of Antioch's Shakespeare Under the Stars. In 1952, Professor Lithgow had founded the festival, which hired professional actors for the main roles and used Antioch students or Yellow Springers in minor roles or as extras. The festival brought international attention to both Antioch and Yellow Springs. After the first season, Queen Elizabeth II wrote a congratulatory letter, and the *New York Times* would consistently send their leading theater critics, including the legendary Brooks Atkinson, to review the productions. "That's one of the things that made me want to be an actor," said Richie, who—at college and later in New York and Los Angeles—considered acting as a career.[24]

Yellow Springs Today

That bold liberal spirit, that openness, that trust in dreams and people that early Yellow Springers embodied is very much visible in the streets of Yellow Springs today. Xenia Avenue, the town's main street, flies as many rainbow as

American flags and features as many boutiques, tie-dye shops, and art studios as convenience stores and barbershops. A lively music scene, interrupted by the coronavirus pandemic in 2020, offers a diversity of live music; everything—from jazz to bluegrass to chamber music to rock—plays in bars, cafés, coffee shops, and clubs. In addition, there is a Yellow Springs Community Band, a Yellow Springs Ukulele Club, and the World House Choir, which performs to inspire "our communities toward justice, diversity, and equality."[25] Twice a year, a street festival features two performance stages and, annually, the PorchFest calls on local musicians to play on porches, front yards, and patios within a half-mile radius of downtown. (Coincidentally, Furay performed two livestream back porch sessions from his home in Colorado to raise funds for music-related organizations during the COVID-19 pandemic.) A quick survey of the internet finds Yellow Springs referred to as "retro-hippie," "Ohio's hippie enclave," "a little hippie haven," and the "cutest hippie town ever."[26]

Comedian and actor Dave Chappelle, a resident of Yellow Springs, interviewed live on CNN during New Year's Eve 2019, placed Yellow Springs "deep in the heart of Trump country, but the town . . . is like an itty-bitty Bernie Sanders island in the Trump Sea."[27] In 2018, Richie and Judy sold the Xenia Avenue properties they had inherited to Chappelle. In the 2020 presidential election, while Pres. Donald Trump won Ohio with 53.7 percent of the vote, Joe Biden scored 92 percent of the vote in Yellow Springs.[28]

The Furays of Yellow Springs

Paul Richard Furay was born on May 9, 1944, in Dayton, Ohio, as Yellow Springs had no hospital. At that time, with D-Day or the Normandy Invasion, a crucial turning point of World War II, still a month away, the outcome of the war was in doubt. Yellow Springs, like the rest of America, was preoccupied with the war effort: over two hundred young Yellow Springers had enlisted; the local post office promoted defense stamps; community leadership conducted air raid drills; local stores, like the town beauty shop, boasted of saving aluminum; and residents dutifully participated in rationing and shopping with coupons for sugar, canned goods, meats, cooking oil, and more. In late June and early July 1943, Yellow Springs held the Little Peace Conference in Bryan High School, which focused on supporting veterans upon their return to the community, and Antioch College welcomed several Japanese American students onto its campus as part of a national program that permitted students to leave internment camps to enroll in participating colleges.

Several days before Richie's first birthday, Germany surrendered uncon-ditionally, and Japan followed that August. America and Yellow Springs celebrated. It had been a tumultuous half century for Americans, which began with the assassination of Pres. William McKinley in 1901, followed by signifi-cant labor unrest, World War I, the chaotic and freewheeling 1920s, the Great Depression, and then World War II. When the war ended, a tired America sought stability, tranquility, and prosperity. It was time for family, home, and hearth, which was barely disturbed by the Korean War (1950–53), sometimes called "The Forgotten War" or "The Unknown War" for its limited media cov-erage and its limited hold on the American consciousness.

Many Americans remember the late 1940s and 1950s as a time of content-ment. The economy thrived; TV sets and new appliances proliferated, making homelife more comfortable; and a car culture developed, hastened by the High-way Act of 1956 and emerging suburbs. When Richie was two and his sister Judy five, the Furay family participated in the new middle-class prosperity. Their father, Paul Furay, bought the drugstore he had managed, turning Fin-ley's Drug Store into Furay's Drug Store, and he took the family on summer vacations, driving to destinations in Michigan, Florida, and Virginia, for exam-ple. These vacations formed some of Richie's fondest youthful memories.

After purchasing the drugstore, the Furays moved from North Winter Street, less than a mile outside of town, to 616 Xenia Avenue, in the center of town and little more than a five-minute walk to the drugstore. The Furays lived upstairs and rented the bottom floor, which housed two shops. While their parents worked long hours at the drugstore, particularly their father, young Richie and Judy were looked after by their paternal grandmother, who favored Richie. She did some cooking, but a housekeeper cleaned. Richie and Judy would have lunch at the drugstore's counter or, if it was crowded, they took their lunches to the back room, with Richie reading one of the latest comic books. Later in the afternoon or on their way home from school, the children might return for milkshakes, ice cream, or other treats. Paul Furay was extremely gregarious, always smiling as he interacted with customers, whose names and children's names he knew. It's a practice that Richie absorbed and adopted for his career as a musician and pastor. When possible, Richie would spend time after or before a show or service to make himself available to fans and congregants. In March 2015 at the New York City Winery, for example, Richie walked from table to table welcoming early-arriving guests. Furay's mom, Naomi or "Snookie," was also outgoing, only slightly more reserved than her husband, but was primarily responsible for the accounting. "She was in the back a lot," recalls Judy, "with her big old-fashion adding machine on the desk with the big handle that you pulled and her big ledger book, which must have been two inches thick. I remember her sitting there for hours looking for a penny."[29]

Paul spent most of his day at the drugstore, where he employed a staff of about half a dozen. He left home at about 6:00 a.m. and finished his day as late as 10:00 p.m., trying to find time to return home during the day or for an occasional dinner in the evening. "We didn't get to spend a lot of time together," said Richie. "It was the sad part of my growing up. My dad was very intent on providing for the family and making provisions for us."[30] The store was open Sundays, which meant Paul would spend at least part of his day there. Judy explains, "It was a very small town with two drugstores. [Our dad] had to be at the top of his game. It was competitive. I remember a man came in and asked him for a pair of red shoestrings and he was a customer of the other drugstore. My dad said, 'We don't have them right now.' The man turned to go out and my dad said, 'If you come in tomorrow, I'll have them for you.'"[31] Getting those shoestrings required a trip to a supplier in Springfield, which would add an extra hour to Paul's already long day. Snookie spent more time with the children. She volunteered with Judy's Brownie and Girl Scout troops, and she helped coach Richie's little league teams. Always a gifted athlete, she had played basketball and tennis when she was younger, and she golfed into her eighties.

Paul's lack of time with this family was typical for fathers in the 1950s. The evening family dinner, for example, has been much mythologized in American popular culture, especially in the television shows of the 1950s and 1960s, like *Ozzy and Harriet*, *Father Knows Best*, and *Leave It to Beaver*. As the *New York Times* reported in 1990, that "celebration of the breadwinner's return . . . has been clouded by selective memories and myth . . . and few methodical surveys. . . . Even [in the 1950s], for many families who experienced divorce, poverty, shift work or any number of other factors, this [family dinner in TV land] was not a reflection of their lives."[32] Similarly, at that time, fathers especially were expected to be strict disciplinarians and strong heads of households, but neither Richie nor Judy recalls ever being severely disciplined, and most of the time their mild-tempered father and mother handled things quietly. The family attended services on Sunday at the local Methodist church, where Snookie sang in the choir and Richie and Judy attended Sunday school. There was the usual sibling rivalry between Richie and Judy, but nothing especially intense, and Richie remembers looking up to his sister. He followed her path to Bryan High School, where their parents had been sweethearts, and then to Otterbein College.

In 1955, Paul, who was not a pharmacist, and Snookie sold Furay's Drug Store to Carl E. Lowe, who operated Lowe's Drug Store until his retirement in 1973. Snookie, who had an especially astute business mind, convinced her husband to sell only the business and not the building, thus generating additional income. The couple invested in a new venture, Furay's Gift Shop, and constructed a long building in a vacant space, a large alley at 241 Xenia Avenue, closer to their home. The successful business was more of a mini–department store than what we might consider a gift store today. They sold everything from jeans and books to housewares, sporting equipment, and jewelry. Their father carried his people skills into the gift store. "The kids sometimes called him Captain Kangaroo; he kind of looked like him; his hair was gray. . . . He had a mustache, and in the back where we had a little shoe department, he had a rocking horse for kids," recalls Judy, who worked alongside her parents in the store. "He was a very well-liked person. I remember one day he let Mike DeWine [Yellow Springs native and future US senator and governor of Ohio], take a swing with a baseball bat in the store."[33] Although Paul still worked long hours, he made an effort to spend more time with his son, who was moving into his teen years. Richie recalls a favorite memory of demonstrating his little league pitching skills to his dad: "I don't know how fast I was throwing, but I was stinging his hands."[34] There was no anger in the pitches, only a son showing off for his father's approval and acknowledgment.

Tragedy Strikes

Judy remembers the day clearly:

> I was going to be a junior and Richard was going into eighth grade when our father died. . . . The whole thing was really a shock. He was forty-five. They brought him down on a stretcher one Sunday morning . . . the day of the Coffman [mom's family] reunion. Richie went to the reunion with an aunt, and I stayed home. My mom barely made it to the hospital before he died. It was that quick. Somebody at the reunion, an older cousin, came up and told Richard that his father had just died; it was a real shock. . . . It was a real shock to the whole town. . . . He knew everybody in the town, was friends with everybody.[35]

On that August 1957 morning, Richie awoke to paramedics attending to his father. His mom had called an ambulance when her husband complained of chest pains. Paul had suffered a ruptured aortic aneurysm, almost impossible to treat. The easygoing father was much beloved by the community, and his viewing was rumored to be one of the most heavily attended in Yellow Springs. Richie was not only saddened but also confused. At thirteen, he was ill-equipped to handle a parent's sudden death. While the family regularly attended church, they were not overly attentive to religion and scripture and, therefore, did not find the guidance and comfort in the Bible that Richie would find in later years. Furthermore, in the 1950s, mental health therapy was not commonly where middle-class families turned for help. In his confusion, Richie did not rebel or demonstrate anger. He just carried on and avoided confronting his grief. Perhaps aware of his mom's and sister's struggle, he did not want to be an annoyance, and perhaps he felt instinctively the need to be a man modeled after his father, which meant staying composed and strong. On the other hand, Judy's schoolwork would be affected: "I held it inward. My English teacher said, 'If you don't participate your grade will go down.' But I couldn't. I was still in shock. He died in August and school started in September."[36] Judy experienced nightmares for some time.

Snookie was intent on remaining strong, insistent that, as Richie writes, her children "could look toward the future with optimism."[37] However, both she and her daughter found their home on Xenia Avenue too full of memories and reminders. Although Richie had hoped to remain in the central location with his backyard basketball court, Snookie decided to move less than a mile away to Spillan Road. Grandma Furay did not make the move as the new home was smaller and the children were now in their teens. Snookie continued to run the variety store and take the children on summer vacations to, among other places, Washington, DC, Colorado (where later Richie would reside for most of his life), and California, where Richie flew in a plane for the first time and insisted that they tour the television home of Ozzie and Harriet.

Richie was a fairly stable teen, occupied by an intense interest in sports and music. Perhaps too he recognized that his father's death did not allow him the luxury of rebellion. His teenage angst expressed itself in occasional beers with friends and an outburst now and then. Both Richie and his sister remember his slamming and shattering the dashboard of the family car over his frustrations with acne. His sister laughed as his mom threatened him idly with military school. "I was pretty straight and narrow, I guess." He recalls one friend from high school of whom he was warned: "Now this is one of those guys that you don't want to be associated with because he is really a rebel. Stay away from him." Richie remained friends with the "rebel," who went on to become a dentist.[38]

Sports and Music

Like most American boys in the 1950s, sports were important to a young Richie Furay. He particularly liked basketball and baseball. He and his friends spent long days playing basketball on the Furays' small black-topped court, which his parents had constructed for him. Initially, basketball was Richie's favorite sport but, in time, baseball replaced basketball, largely because Richie's short stature proved a disadvantage—as an adult he would stand five feet, nine inches. His height may have kept him off the high school varsity, as he had to be content on the reserves. But even before then, baseball took over his boyish fantasies. He simulated games by pitching a rubber ball off the outside entrance to his basement as he imagined facing the day's stars like Willie Mays, Hank Aaron, and Mickey Mantle. He would turn imaginary double plays mimicking his favorite infielders, Johnny Temple and Roy McMillan, from his favorite team, the Cincinnati Reds. "Man, I would stand out there for hours and bang a ball against that thing and pick up grounders. . . . Then my cousin and I—there was a big open field next to our house—would go and hit flies to one another." When he was a little leaguer, his uncle took him to see the Reds play: "My mouth just dropped. I mean I never saw green grass like that in my life. It was a whole different world."[39] Richie played second base on his high school team and dreamed of a career in the major leagues.

Richie was a decent student, but when his focus was not on sports it was on music. When he was eight years old, he placed a guitar at the top of his Christmas list. That Christmas morning, he awoke and raced to the tree and saw a gift wrapped in a peculiar shape that could only be a guitar. His heart soared, only to plummet when he unpackaged the "puke green" toy guitar replete with cowboy scenes.[40] He sped to his parents' bedroom and spared them none of his disappointment. He would not be appeased until his parents agreed to drive to Springfield, some twenty minutes from Yellow Springs, to buy him a real guitar. Before long, Richie held a Gibson ES295, a hollow-body electric guitar, first sold in 1952 and deemed a classic after Scotty Moore played it on Elvis Presley's first four Sun singles.[41] Richie also insisted on lessons. "Every Monday night my mom, he, and I would drive to Springfield and he took music lessons at Morelli's," Judy said. "We would sit and wait for him. His hand couldn't even go around the neck. But he loved it."[42]

He remained persistent and diligent as he struggled through beginning songs like "The Rustic Dance." "I mean from the time that I was a little kid . . . when my parents gave me a guitar . . . all I wanted to do was play music."[43] After a few months, Richie and three friends formed a quartet and earned a dollar each when they performed at a senior citizens' home. Curiously, Richie's father placed a condition on his son's guitar lessons: Richie must learn the trumpet in high school. Richie followed through and made it up to second chair, first trumpet in the high school band, which suggests he was fairly good but lacked the leadership qualities of first chair. He never played trumpet during his professional career.

While still in junior high, Richie was invited by a group of high school students to join their vocal group. He sang with the Barons until the end of his freshman year, at which time the other Barons graduated. While they performed only sporadically, Richie was Little Anthony to their Imperials as he sang lead to their backing *oohs* and *aahs*. They performed doo-wop songs of the day, like "Teenager in Love," "16 Candles," "In the Still of the Night," and some Frankie Lymon and the Teenagers songs.[44] When the band played high school dances, the underaged Furay and his girlfriend, Diane Bingham or "Bubbly," were allowed entrance. Richie wrote his first song, "Bubbly," for Diane, but no one, says Richie, has ever heard it except for the two young teens. The first song that Richie wrote and recorded was Buffalo Springfield's classic "Sad Memory," also about an early girlfriend: "I was head over heels about this girl in college, and thought she was the one. But she wasn't." And with characteristic optimism, "I always want to believe that there is hope out there and there's something better right around the corner," and then, referring to his wife, Nancy, "and there was."[45]

While his mother sang in the choir, neither parent played an instrument, and neither was more than a casual music listener. Snookie's favorite singer was Kate Smith, "The First Lady of Radio," who had a big, booming voice and was best known for her signature recording of Irving Berlin's "God Bless America." Paul preferred what Richie called the "deep country" of Eddy Arnold and Porter Wagoner.[46] Judy, three years older than Richie, listened to the popular teen hits of the day and especially liked the Platters ("The Great Pretender," "Twilight Time"). She and her friends listened to Wingy Wing, or WING-AM, out of Dayton, which Richie would listen to as he grew into his teen years. A very young Richie, however, gravitated toward music. Judy remembers: "We had an old jukebox in the drugstore, a great big fancy thing. It was huge, four feet by three or four feet. When those records got old [Dad] brought them home. I had no interest in them, but Richard did. [Before he could read], he had every single record memorized by their labels."[47] As Richie puts it, "That's definitely where my musical ambition started. Just with the store, those little records [my dad] brought home, and the radio."[48]

FIG. I
Fifteen-year-old Richie
Furay takes the stage
at a high school dance.
Courtesy of Richie
Furay.

Highlights of the "Leap Year Lope"

For Christmas one year, Paul gave Snookie a Revere reel-to-reel tape recorder, which Richie hijacked and carted off to his room, where he taped his favorite songs off Wingy Wing. In those early teen years, he loved the vocal harmonies of the Five Satins, the Del Vikings, the Drifters, and the Dovells as well as the rockabilly rhythms of Eddie Cochran, Gene Vincent, Buddy Holly, and Carl Perkins. But his first musical hero was Ricky Nelson. In 1957, Nelson began performing on *The Adventures of Ozzie and Harriet*, often at scenes staged at high school dances, as he became the first teen idol to use television to promote a slew of hits, beginning with "Teenager's Romance," "Be-Bop Baby," and "I'm Walkin'." In time, young Richie noticed that Nelson had a dazzling guitar player in James Burton, who would inspire many 1960s guitarists and play an important sliding dobro on Furay's "Child's Claim to Fame" from *Buffalo Springfield Again* (1967). Also, in 1957, a Yellow Springs resident, twenty-four-year-old Brien Fisher, appeared on *American Bandstand* to perform "Fingertips," a gentle rockabilly original. Neither Richie nor Judy remembers the appearance. But the harmonies and the rockabilly rhythms from these years would have a strong impact on Furay's future music.[49]

As a high school student, like many young Americans, Richie was captivated by the new folk music, especially the Kingston Trio, who would inspire much of the folk boom that ran from the late 1950s into the mid-1960s. As a freshman, in 1958, he heard the trio's #1 *Billboard* hit, a rendition of a traditional folk song, "Tom Dooley." Richie was hooked. "They really took off and struck a chord with me. . . . I really loved that band. [They] had a tremendous influence on my life."[50]

From 1958 through 1962, the Kingston Trio released seventeen albums, five of which reached #1 on the *Billboard* charts. Two reached #2, three peaked at #3, one at #4, two others in the Top 10, and the remaining four positioned between #11 and #18. In later years, the Greenwich Village folkies and other "purists" favored Woody Guthrie and Pete Seeger, and many derided the Kingston Trio for their showbiz flair and commercialism, citing their uniform appearance, their clean-cut collegiate look, and their lack of grit and political angst. But the trio's influence was substantial. In the late 1950s and early '60s, guitar and banjo sales soared with many young people taking lessons to learn the simple folk style and chords. Before heading to college, Richie, who had stopped playing his guitar while in high school, started playing again. But he traded in his Gibson for a Martin D-28 acoustic guitar, the one he would use to write many songs. Still, he longs for the classic Gibson: "It was a beautiful Gibson. I wish I had it now."[51]

The Imprint of Yellow Springs

It is difficult to measure the influence of Yellow Springs on Richie Furay, a third-generation Yellow Springer who lived there for his first twenty years. Like those founders and the subsequent builders of Yellow Springs, Richie possesses an "ardent hopefulness," and he is, undeniably, a dreamer. In fact, he has written and sung consistently about dreams throughout his fifty-year career, from his lead vocals on Neil Young and Buffalo Springfield's "On the Way Home" ("When the dream came . . . ," 1968), to Poco's "What A Day" ("I've got to dream," 1969), to his solo album *I Still Have Dreams* (1979), right through "Heartbeat of Love" ("You've taken me beyond every dream," 2006) and "Hand in Hand" ("You are the girl of my dreams," 2015). I asked him in 2015 if he was still a dreamer: "Sure! I am very blessed that I am able to still do what I do, at the level that I do it, and, I, I have dreams and I have aspirations. . . . I'm 71 years old. Am I going to see all of those dreams fulfilled? I don't know, but it keeps the creative juices flowing."[52] However, like many of the Yellow Springers mentioned above, not all Furay's dreams have come true.

Of course, his upbringing, particularly the influence of his parents, has strongly shaped Richie's enduring optimism. Both Richie and Judy describe their parents as "optimistic," "pleasant," and "upbeat."[53] Similarly, Richie and his music are generally buoyant, energetic, and hopeful, as he "keeps on believin'." I spoke to him when, at age seventy-five, he was recording his country-covers album. He could barely contain his boyish enthusiasm: "It's really going to be good! It's amazing how good it's certainly going to turn out! I'm getting ready to go to LA tomorrow to finish up some vocals and then we go to Nashville again in March to finish up some more of the background vocals and then [Val Garay will] be mixing it."[54] And, on another occasion, "I can't wait for you to hear the 'Pickin' Up the Pieces' that we did in Nashville in November. We did it Bakersfield! We didn't do it Nashville,"[55] referring to the different styles of country music from those two cities.

But in the fall of 1962, work on his twenty-first studio album, as either a solo artist or band member, was a long way off. Furay instead ventured off to Otterbein College in Westerville, Ohio, still clinging to dreams of a professional baseball career. However, in addition to his glove, he carried a Martin D-28.

CHAPTER 2

"Consequently, So Long"
Otterbein College and Greenwich Village

In the fall of 1962, Richie Furay arrived at Otterbein College in Westerville, Ohio, about seventy miles from Yellow Springs. "When I went to college. I didn't know what I wanted to do. I thought I'd be a baseball player." That dream was dashed soon after arrival: "These guys [at Otterbein], man, they were so far ahead of me. I was not as good as I thought I was, and I thought I had better pursue something else. . . . Maybe I'll be an actor." On his application, Richie had indicated that he was interested in acting, so the college matched him with a roommate who was a first-semester acting major. Soon he and his roommate auditioned for the campus production of *The Pajama Game*. Richie was confident he would land a good part—perhaps the lead. After all, the eighteen-year-old reasoned, he had a good voice, performed well with the Barons, and had theatrical experience with Shakespeare. (Yes, the extra role when he was ten.) His ego was again wounded when he saw the audition results: "You know how they put the list up with who made the lead and who was going to be what part? Pat McGinnis, my roommate, was going to play the lead. I'm looking up and down the list for my name and then I saw that one of the side-cast characters is Richie Furay. It was like, 'Oh boy, maybe this isn't going to work either.'"[1] Furay performed in the chorus.

Richie had another idea. He signed up for the freshman student talent show. Accompanying himself on his Martin D-28, he belted out "They Call the Wind Mariah," a Broadway show song, written by Alan Lerner and Frederick Loewe for *Paint Your Wagon* (1951), but which Furay had learned from the Kingston Trio's performance on . . . *from the "Hungry i"* (#2, 1959). Fellow freshman Bob Harmelink, who performed with his barbershop quartet, recalled that Richie "brought the house down." Not only did Richie win first prize, but he was asked to sing the song again. "From then on," according to Harmelink, "he was the star of the campus."[2] More importantly, Richie saw his future that night: "I thought . . . all of a sudden, I'm a folk singer."[3]

During his second semester, Richie, along with Harmelink, pledged to a fraternity—Lambda Gamma Epsilon or the Monks, so called because they had a large percentage of members training for the ministry or majoring in theology, along with members of the football team, who led the fraternity to a drinking record at the South Heidelberg, a bar in Columbus, Ohio. At the time, Richie was not much interested in beer drinking, theology, or the Bible—although some dozen years later the Bible would consume him. Richie pledged because some of its members were enthusiastic about the current folk music. As part of his and Harmelink's initiation, sophomore Nels Gustafson called on the pair to serenade Nels's girlfriend over the telephone. As the unremembered song progressed, Nels joined in with his deep, rich voice. They not only impressed the coed, but they also impressed themselves. Their harmonies blended so smoothly and expressively that they decided to form a trio called the Monks. They performed on and around campus at various events, usually for free, as they developed their craft and learned how to please audiences. Richie always sang lead, Bob high harmony, and Nels bass. They covered the Kingston Trio; Peter, Paul, and Mary; and the folk hits of the day, like the Highwaymen's "Michael Row the Boat Ashore" (#1, 1960) and Dylan's "Blowin' in the Wind" (1963).

Richie, however, was the only one thinking about a career in music, and he was anxious to learn from the more experienced Bob and Nels. Bob grew up in a musical household. "I started singing at the age of five with my family. There were six of us: The Harmony Harmelinks. My mom was a concert violinist, and my dad was a singer in a champion barbershop quartet. My mom established the first women's barbershop quartet in Ohio." Nels's training in harmony came as a member of the Warren Boys Choir from Warren, Pennsylvania, a prestigious youth choir that toured the United States. Harmelink did most of the musical arrangements for the trio and especially helped Richie develop his vocal skills in harmony. "I think I stretched Richie," said Harmelink.[4] Importantly, Bob and Nels persuaded Richie to try out for Otterbein's A Capella Choir, selective in its membership of some fifty singers, mostly music majors with previous experience in choirs. Richie agreed but only when he heard that the choir, during his sophomore year, would tour the East with several days in New York City, home of Greenwich Village, the epicenter of the current folk revival.

Richie passed the audition and enrolled in a necessary and demanding class that included music theory and training in vocal harmony. "I don't have any idea how I made it."[5] Richard Chamberlain, the choirmaster, taught the class and worked his students: "He was a military kind of guy; you got there on time, and you worked hard."[6] Nels added that he was "extremely tough, very much a professional who molded that choir."[7] The choir performed a well-rounded program spanning German choral songs, hymns, Negro spirituals, traditional folk songs, and more. Most were performed a cappella with a few songs accompanied by an organ. The only one of the Monks who had a solo was Nels with "Wayfaring Stranger." Richie was in the tenor section. "His voice was totally different from a choir voice," said Bob.[8] Richie benefited significantly from the experience. He learned vocal techniques like how to breathe properly and sustain high notes, he improved his abilities to read music and arrange harmonies, and he widened his musical scope. "This was clearly a moment of destiny."[9]

The A Capella Choir hit the road in the spring of 1964—almost without Richie. On the night before Christmas break of his sophomore year, Richie and some friends attended a party in nearby Dublin, Ohio. Richie woke up sick the next day, and he knew he was suffering from more than a hangover. He had a pain deep in his stomach and a fever that kept rising with alternating chills and sweats. He made it back to Yellow Springs, where, twice, a doctor misdiagnosed Richie with a stomachache or a bad case of flu and sent him home, where his condition worsened. He had to be rushed to a hospital in Springfield, where he passed out and where it was discovered that his appendix had ruptured. Richie spent two weeks in the hospital, where he sang for other patients. His long recovery process resulted in his missing his final exams, which, at that time, most colleges scheduled after the new year, and his sitting out the upcoming semester. Richie, however, did not want to miss the choir's trip to New York with the possibility of performing with the Monks in the same venues as Dylan and Peter, Paul, and Mary had. But if he were not matriculated at Otterbein, he couldn't participate in the tour. Richie talked with the choirmaster. Perhaps persuaded by Richie's earnestness, motivation, and work ethic, Chamberlain, a by-the-book taskmaster, yielded to the driven Furay—that is, as long as Richie would attend the twice-weekly rehearsals. Every Tuesday and Thursday Richie would drive from Yellow Springs to Otterbein. Nels and Bob were shocked to see Richie at the first rehearsal: "The standard was very high," said Nels. "For Richie to get back in [after his illness], that was saying something."[10]

Richie was on the bus when the A Capella Choir left Otterbein with stops in Pennsylvania, Delaware, Maryland, and New York City. The choir performed in churches that were associated with the college, which is affiliated with the United Methodist Church. Local families hosted choir members with Richie, Nels, and Bob generally assigned to the same host. Richie had his guitar, and the Monks would perform for their hosting families—rehearsals for what they hoped would be performances in New York.

New York

In late March 1964, the A Cappella Choir arrived in New York City, where they spent about a week. Best of all, they had a Saturday night free, which the Monks used for a visit to Greenwich Village. Nels, with his over-six-foot frame and deep voice, managed to talk house managers into allowing the Monks to perform onstage at the Four Winds and the Cafe Wha?, where Dylan had been fired after being late for the third time.[11] With some choir members in the audiences, the Monks were well received. At the end of their set at the Four Winds, Richie approached the manager, John Hopkins, who agreed to schedule the Monks for some dates in the summer. Excited, Richie told the other Monks about the offer and all agreed to return in June. Richie, however, implied that the gig came with a salary, which it did not. Instead, Hopkins promised that the Monks could pass the basket. That is, like at the other basket houses in the Village, the night's earnings would depend on the generosity of the patrons. Richie held on to that secret until after the Monks returned a few months later.

Euphoric over their coffeehouse success, the Monks boarded the bus back to Ohio. While Bob and Nels completed the semester at Otterbein, Richie, realizing that he would need to fund his New York dream, took work at Morris Bean and Company, a tire castings manufacturing plant, where he worked the 3:00 p.m.–11:00 p.m. shift. Richie, thin—or "scrawny"—at about 125 pounds and weakened from his illness, was assigned to work with a stocky but muscular partner, Ronnie Sams.[12] The work required heavy lifting and could be dangerous. Sams took one look at Richie and complained unsuccessfully to his foreman. Slowly, however, Ronnie warmed up to Richie, respecting his perseverance, and the two became friends. On one occasion, Richie injured his finger, almost catastrophically, when he and Ronnie poured melted aluminum into a tire casting. He pulled his finger on his fret-playing hand from the container with the aluminum just in time to prevent it from being crushed. His finger had to be heavily bandaged.

Greenwich Village—Summer 1964

In June 1964, Sams drove Richie to the airport in Dayton for his flight to New York. Richie carried his Martin D-28 guitar and the Revere tape recorder that he had seized from his mom several Christmases ago. Bob and Nels arrived a week or so later. All their parents had mixed reactions to their summer in New York, but ultimately all proved supportive. Bob, a biology major, turned down an opportunity to work in a laboratory at The Ohio State University campus at Wooster. His mom, a schoolteacher as well as a performer, called him "crazy" and then added, "Have fun in New York."[13] Richie's mom was "definitely not happy. She wanted me to do something more concrete, more legitimate, than going to New York to be a folk singer. That was a hippie thing. It just wasn't the normal route that somebody would take if they were going to have a life." But before he left, she gave him Arthur Frommer's *New York on $5 a Day*. "My life was going to be playing music. I was pretty much determined," added Richie.[14] Nels said that Richie was the "driving force in getting us to New York. He was the highest motivated to be successful in music."[15] Bob added, "Richie saw this as his life's work. I saw it as a summer fling. And maybe, just maybe, I might get lucky and hit the big time. It was not at all, 'I'm going to make it or die here.'"[16]

By the time the Monks arrived, the Greenwich Village folk scene, which had peaked the previous year, was in decline. The electric pop and raved-up blues of the Beatles and the British Invasion some six months earlier had replaced folk as the dominant pop music form. Ian Tyson of Ian and Sylvia commented, "The Beatles shut us down. . . . It was over. Over. . . . All us folkies were just standing there with egg on our faces."[17] As Richie said, "It was winding down. It wasn't like the era of Peter, Paul, and Mary and Bob Dylan in the streets of New York."[18] Not only had British Invasion acts begun to take over the charts, holding four of the Top 10 places on *Billboard*'s Hot 100 singles chart for the week of July 4, 1964, but electric guitars and amplifiers had started to appear in the windows of Bleecker Street music shops, replacing the acoustic Martins. To be clear, however, the Village in 1964 was still an exciting place for a young musician. The folk-music scene, albeit in decline, was still active, with musicians creating original music, interested record labels, music publishers, a radio show every Saturday night (*Oscar Brand's Folksong Festival*), supportive publications like *Sing Out!* and *Broadside*, and the *New York Times*, which covered the scene regularly through future Bob Dylan biographer Robert Shelton. And there were still plenty of venues. Within short walking distance of where the Monks shared an apartment, Native American singer-songwriter Roland Mousaa once "counted 37 coffeehouses."[19] The major clubs, like the Village Gate, the Gaslight, Gerde's Folk City, and the Bitter End, featured established performers, while smaller clubs, with capacities of maybe forty people, showcased new performers, like the Monks, and passed the basket. On weekends, folk musicians would meet in Washington Square Park and play for locals, suburbanites, and tourists. "We'd go over there and practice," said Nels. "On Sunday afternoons it would be a big hootenanny."[20]

The Monks may have been enjoying their adventure, but they were barely surviving economically. They relied on cheap, not always healthful food: pizza, egg rolls, bouillon cube soup, or maybe a free burger at one of the clubs. However, they were getting better—that is, more shameless—at soliciting crowds for contributions to the passing basket. One night they might rely on partial truths about being poor college students, but on other nights they would just fabricate stories: "We got kids at home and this is our only means of support."[21] If they saw guests start to leave, they would hustle up to them with the basket. It could often be embarrassing for musicians, especially when customers might give nothing or respond rudely. As Paul Nelson wrote, "The life-style for a musician in those days shifted rapidly from ecstasy to embarrassment; from acute depression to severe good times."[22]

If food was less than plentiful, the Monks' living accommodations were far from lavish. Upon arrival, they spent a few days with a fraternity brother in Bedford-Stuyvesant, whose church had hosted the A Cappella Choir that spring. Bed-Stuy was a frightening place for three young white college students from middle America. As Fred Shapiro wrote in the *New Yorker* in the summer of 1964, "The Bedford-Stuyvesant ghetto is bigger than Harlem, more heavily populated, and tougher."[23] They then spent a night in Central Park and a few nights in a Bowery youth hostel, a large room with cots, where they had heard that someone had been murdered the previous week. For safety, they kept their belongings in a locker at either the Port Authority Bus Terminal or Grand Central Station, depending on the source.[24] Finally, the Monks found an apartment for sublease. Andrea "Bunky" Skinner and her partner Jake, later of the Fugs, were going on tour, and the trio moved into the sixth-floor walk-up on the corner of Bedford and Grove streets in the Village.[25] Importantly, the apartment gave the Monks a safe place to sleep and rehearse, which they sometimes did on the rooftop. They recorded themselves on the Revere, fastening the mic, which "kept falling off," to a broom or mop handle, and stood around and sang, listening to the playback and refining their sound.[26] At night, they took the short walk to the Four Winds to play their sets. On weekends they might do four or five twenty-minute sets rotating with three or four other acts as patrons rotated between clubs. Their set consisted of folk songs like Dylan's "Don't Think Twice It's All Right," the Kingston Trio's "The Seine," Peter, Paul and Mary's "Autumn to May" and "Very Last Day," Ricky Nelson's "Lonesome Town," and folk standards like "Samson and Delilah." They also worked in a couple of original songs, Nels's "Valley Road" and Richie's "Hear Our Song" and "The Ballad of Johnny Collins," a derivative ballad about a Civil War soldier. Civil War ballads were popular during the folk revival. "We just were trying to go with the mood of the day," said Harmelink. "We didn't do very many protest songs at all. Mostly just fun folk, exciting harmony stuff."[27]

After a good basket take, the Monks might celebrate with a steak dinner at Tad's, a very low-end steakhouse. Food critic Robert Sietsema described Tad's as "rough and tumble steak consumption. . . . The taste was all blood and minerals, the fat was more like gristle, and, thin as it was, the steak required a bit of sawing to dismantle." The food may not have been very good, but there was a lot of it. The steak dinner included a large baked potato or helping of mashed potatoes, a tossed salad, and Tad's [in]famous "grease-sodden" Texas toast, which Sietsema describes as "half of a demi-baguette that's been split longitudinally, griddle-toasted, and brushed with garlic-scented fat of uncertain provenance."[28] Yet to the Monks and many poor and young New Yorkers it was a treat. The price of a steak dinner at Tad's in 1964 was about $1.25, or the equivalent of about $10.00 in 2020. When they arrived back at the apartment, they shared a common New York City tenement experience. They grabbed rolled-up newspapers, flicked on the light, and attacked the scattering cockroaches.

Au Go-Go Singers

After just a few weeks in the Village, the Monks met Ed E. Miller, an entrepreneur from the garment industry who was dabbling in music. In May, he had scored a #6 hit with "Don't Let the Rain Come Down (Crooked Little Man)," a song performed by the Serendipity Singers and adapted by Miller and Ersel Hickey from the English nursery rhyme "There Was a Crooked Man." Miller was scouting for talent for his upcoming musical, a loose history of folk music in America, to be staged in the Village. He needed a large group, like the nine-piece Serendipity Singers, but they were on the national stage as a result of their hit single. Miller combined the Monks with the four-piece Bay Singers, composed of female vocalist Jean Gurney and three male vocalists: Roy

Michaels, a banjoist; Fred Geiger, a guitarist; and stand-up bassist Mike Scott. But he still needed another female vocalist and hired Michaels's girlfriend, Kathi King. Then he recruited the final member, a very talented young guitarist and vocalist named Stephen Stills. Richie and Stills became fast friends. "I met Richie and really liked his guitar and I really liked Richie," said Stills.[29] Stills played Furay's Martin D-28 whenever he could. With the ensemble complete, Miller scheduled rehearsals.

On July 14, Miller began rehearsals for *America Sings* with music director Bert Carroll— who cowrote "Wear My Ring Around Your Neck," a #2 hit for Elvis in 1958—and with staging by Marvin Gordon. The play would open the following week, on July 21, and hopefully settle in for a long run at the Players Theatre, next to Café Wha?. Each of the nine performers received $50 (equivalent to $420 in 2020) a week during rehearsals and $75 ($630 in 2020) a week during performances, big money to the youths. Six of the cast performers were under twenty-one, including Richie, Harmelink, and Stills, so their parents had to cosign their contracts. Bob and Nels decided to skip the fall semester at Otterbein, a decision Richie had reached before he had arrived in New York. To promote the show, Miller crammed the ensemble into an open vehicle; no one remembers whether it was an open limousine, a trolley, or "something like a wagon."[30] As they rolled through the Village streets, they would sing a few songs from the show and yell, "Come see us! *America Sings*!" It was an old technique. Jazz bands had done the same thing in Harlem years earlier, and, a few years later in 1975, the Rolling Stones performed "Brown Sugar" on the back of a flatbed truck as they cruised down Fifth Avenue in the Village. Unlike the jazz bands in Harlem or the Stones, the Au Go-Gos found the promotion to be, as Bob put it, "hokey" and "Mickey Mouse."[31] Nels tells of another strategy for selling tickets. Once the show was up and running, members stood in front of the theater's kiosk hawking tickets. Once Nels, in full stage makeup and costume, was on duty when someone approached him and handed him a booklet, "Hope for Homosexuals." When Nels was less than responsive, the man taunted and then pushed Nels. A patrolman on horseback saw this, hurried to Nels's defense, and knocked the harasser unconscious. Nels looked on in shock.

America Sings! opened with a sound collage. Over "Pick a Bale of Cotton," members entered in choreographed movement or dance, one or two at a time, and sang a line from a well-known folk song: "Swing Low, Sweet Chariot," "Nobody Knows the Trouble I've Seen," or "Ezekiel Saw the Wheel," among others. Furay entered singing "Frog Went a-Courtin'." The show would proceed with a series of traditional folk songs ("Greensleeves," "Oh Shenandoah"),

Negro spirituals ("Motherless Child"), sea shanties ("Drunken Sailor"), bluesy folk songs ("Scarlet Ribbons"), bluegrass numbers ("Bowling Green"), and songs made famous by recent folk acts, like the much-recorded "Lonesome Traveler" (Weavers, Lonnie Donegan, Tarriers), the Kingston Trio's "Tom Dooley" and "M.T.A.," and Billy Edd Wheeler's "High Flyin' Bird." The finale featured a rousing rendition of Guthrie's "This Land Is Your Land"—controversial stanzas omitted. The show flopped and closed after two weeks. With the folk boom winding to a close, it is probable the timing was off. In addition, the production might have been a little schmaltzy if not inauthentic, especially for the Village, and its refusal to include protest songs made it seem dated. However, good things resulted for the cast.

Howard Solomon, the owner of the Café Au Go Go, caught *America Sings!* He was impressed enough to offer the ensemble steady work at not only his Bleecker Street club but also at other clubs throughout the United States. Solomon, who named the group the Au Go-Go Singers, wanted to be more competitive with the Bitter End, the club across the street, which featured the Bitter End Singers. "We saw the Bitter End Singers every chance we got," said Harmelink. "We considered them a competing band. They were more be-bop, more showy with dance and costumes. More put together. More professional than us. . . . One of the girls was named Nancy Priddy [on whom Stephen Stills had a crush]. . . . Stephen wrote [Buffalo Springfield's] 'Pretty Girl Why' for her."[32] After additional rehearsals, Solomon scheduled the group to open for pianist-comedian Vaughn Meader, who, famous for his impersonations of President John F. Kennedy, was now rebuilding his career in the aftermath of Kennedy's assassination.

Shortly after the Au Go-Gos were formed, Furay and other group members, including Stills, Bob, and Nels and a rotating population, took an apartment on the ground floor of 175 Thompson Street.[33] It was a large open room, "like a flophouse," said Harmelink. The roommates rehearsed during the day and performed and saw acts in the evening. They were immersed in the Village scene. The excitement of those months was still fresh in Harmelink's voice over fifty years later: "The village was great. It was a community. As an entertainer, you could get into any club. Just tell them I'm with the Au Go-Go Singers. 'Oh come on in, there's a place in the back here.' That's how we saw Buffy St. Marie, Odetta, and Richie Havens, who was amazing, played everything with one big thumb over the top of the guitar. Amazing."[34] They learned stage techniques from musicians and groundbreaking comedians like Bill Cosby, Flip Wilson, and Richard Pryor. Stills echoed Harmelink: "Yeah, I met Freddie Neil, Tim Hardin, John Sebastian, Cass Elliot, Richie Havens—the list goes on and on.

I even met Richard Pryor when he was just starting out. I took in all of the influences by osmosis, I guess."[35] They befriended Peter Torkelson (later, Peter Tork of the Monkees), Gram Parsons, who lived across the street, and Charlie Chin, who would play banjo on the Springfield's "Bluebird." "There were so many really creative people in the Village then," remembers Stills.[36] At the end of a night, the Au Go-Gos would head back to their apartment and watch comedian Soupy Sales on TV. "We loved him," says Harmelink.[37] The next morning, "at some ungodly hour," they would awake to the clopping of a horse, the click-clacking of rolling wheels, and the shouts of a peddler, "Fa-rui-t!"[38]

Ed E. Miller stayed involved with the Cafe Au Go-Go Singers and booked them for a short tour of the borscht belt in the Catskill Mountains, where they played clubs and resorts like the legendary Grossinger's, once opening for Tony Bennett. In addition, Miller got them a date at Gracie Mansion, the residence of the mayor of New York, who in 1964 was third-term mayor Robert F. Wagner. But Miller's biggest contribution to the singers had come earlier, when he had persuaded Hugo Peretti and Luigi Creatore from Morris Levy's Roulette Records to see *America Sings!* The two cousins, songwriters and producers with creative control at Roulette, were impressed enough to sign the cast to a recording contract. At the end of the summer, the Au Go-Go Singers entered the studio with Hugo and Luigi as producers. The pair had worked with Jimmie "Honeycomb" Rodgers, Perry Como, Sarah Vaughan, Sam Cooke, and Etta James and had scored an impressive resume of hits, but mostly bland pop fare. If they weren't sanitizing R&B songs for white artists, they were depleting the energy of soul artists. Barney Hoskyns called their production of Georgia Gibbs's smash "Dance with Me Henry (Wall-flower)" "soulless bowdlerizing of Etta James's lubricious 'Wallflower,'" and he lamented their work with Sam Cook as "saccharine, string-saturated atrocities." To Hoskyns, they were "magnificent scammers" with "even less taste than all the other pop scammers."[39] Still, within three months of arriving in New York City, Richie was entering a recording studio for the first time.

They Call Us Au Go-Go Singers

The recording sessions for *They Call Us Au Go-Go Singers* took just a few days, which was common at that time. In their role as producers, Hugo and Luigi mostly stayed in the booth, interacting very little with the musicians. The producers, with some input from Miller, selected the songs to be recorded, a dozen folk songs with only three coming from *America Sings!*: "High Flyin' Bird," "This Train," and "Lonesome Traveler." Most of the dozen tracks on the album are competent, even energetic, renditions of standard folk songs, but ultimately the album is ordinary and predictable. The vocals and harmonies are all fine, but there is nothing unique, no edge. The album, unintentionally, looks backward at a folk scene passing rather than ahead to the emerging electric folk music. Indeed, "The House of the Rising Sun," a traditional folk ballad but recorded by the Animals with electric guitars, held the #1 spot on the *Billboard* charts for three consecutive weeks beginning September 5 and held a spot in the Top 10 from August 15 until October 3, 1964. *They Call Us Au Go-Go Singers* was released a few weeks after "Rising Sun" began its drop.

The opening track and single from the album was "San Francisco Bay Blues" by Jesse Fuller, who had first released the song in 1955 and, over the years, saw it performed and recorded by many of the Village folkies, including Ramblin' Jack Elliot (first version, *Jack Takes the Floor*, 1958), the Tarriers (*Gather 'Round*, 1964), and Richie Havens (*Mixed Bag*, 1966), and then later by rock musicians like Hot Tuna (1990), Paul McCartney (1991), and Eric Clapton (1992). Fuller, a one-man band, played a twelve-string guitar, harmonica, or kazoo, used one foot to tap a cymbal, and used his other foot for the fotdella (a string bass he had invented). He said of "San Francisco Bay," "That's a song that got me so much money."[40] But not much from the Au Go-Gos' flopped single. The song concerns a singer whose "baby" left him because of his "bad" treatment. Brokenhearted and broke, he longs for her return and "a brand new day" when they can walk side by side "down by the San Francisco Bay." But the Au Go-Gos emphasize the hopefulness too much with their light breezy rhythms, joyful harmonies, and misguided, even silly, logotomes: After the line "wanna lay me down and die," they sing "ba trinka trinkle" (0:22, and again at the 1:24 mark); with lyrics suspended, soprano Kathi King sings "ba ba ba bap" over the men's "aah aah . . . ," ending the break with a mocking "wah-wah-wah-wah" (00:45–00:59); the song concludes with "ka-drinka drink, ka-drinka drink." The song sounds similar to past hits by large folk groups like "Walk Right In" by the Rooftop Singers (#1, 1962) or Ed E. Miller's own "Don't Let the Rain Come Down." But the time for large folk groups was fading rapidly.

Stephen Stills sings lead on two of the album's tracks and Richie one. Stills sings a Miller composition, "Miss Nellie," an inane and outdated tale about "a brave young Englishwoman" who discovers a man lying on the sand with an "arrow in his belly." Although the "injuns kept a comin' with their little drums a-drummin'," Miss Nellie, "who wasn't made of jelly," picked up the wounded man's gun and shot the Indians, "one by one," until the Calvary rescued her. The chorus of "Run, run, Miss Nellie, run run" (repeated several times) suggests that with some electric instruments and some revisions to the lyrics, the song, without much difficulty, could have been reworked into a Beach Boys cars song. Stills's lead vocal on "High Flyin' Bird" marks the highpoint of the album—and illustrates just how far ahead of the others Stills was. His voice is husky, gritty, and strong and grows more powerful and bluesy as the song progresses. The singer sees a high-flying bird, reflects on his "free and easy" flight, and compares it to his life and his father's, who was a miner and tried his whole life to fly or lift himself up, only flying at death. The singer contemplates his own life as "rooted like a tree," with his "sit-down, can't fly . . . gonna-die blues." Flight serves as a metaphor for freedom—freedom unhindered by life's pressures and human misery. The more the singer contrasts the bird's unfettered flight with his and his father's oppressed groundedness, the more the singer's anger intensifies, heard in the bluesy and angry vocals of Stills, only nineteen at the time of the recording. Stills delivers a powerful performance, enhanced by the contrasting vocals of Gurney and King, which soar above (see 00:39–00:43, 00:48–00:54, 00:59–1:03 and elsewhere). The performance remains one of the most moving renditions of the Wheeler song, surpassing the original release of Judy Henske and Wheeler's own 1967 recording and standing alongside Richie Havens on *Mixed Bag* (1966) and Jefferson Airplane's live (1967) and studio (ca. early 1966) performances.

Furay's developing tenor can be heard on harmonies throughout the album, but he takes the lead on Tom Paxton's "Where I'm Bound." The ballad, recorded by Paxton earlier that year as "I Can't Help But Wonder Where I'm Bound," concerns an uncertain and unhappy rambler who has difficulty with commitments and individual purpose. Furay's almost breathy vocals emphasize the sadness of the singer, but he sounds a bit too self-pitying. Richie's expert phrasing, a hallmark of his vocal style, had yet to be realized. The Furay who would sing his and the Springfield's "Sad Memory" three years later is barely recognizable here. Interestingly, Harmelink, picking up on studio chatter, believed that Roulette may have had plans for Richie: "I think they wanted Richie to be the next Jimmie Rodgers." Hugo and Luigi had produced Rodgers's "Honeycomb" (#1, 1957), "Kisses Sweeter Than Wine" (1957, #7), and "Secretly" (#3, 1958), but that had been years ago. "Where I'm Bound" may have been Richie's tryout. Interestingly, on the last verse of "Where I'm Bound," Gustafson stepped up to the microphone and whistled along with Richie's melody lines. "No one told him to do that. He just inserted himself in that song during one of the verses. And they kept it."[41]

Sales for *They Call Us Au Go-Go Singers* were poor. Harmelink recalls a release party that Roulette had scheduled. Excited and expecting many guests, Harmelink practiced signing his autograph. "I think I only signed twenty copies," he said.[42] The album was re-released in 1999 with a bubble sticker added to the front cover: "First Recordings of Stephen Stills and Richie Furay."

On to Texas

They Call Us Au Go-Go Singers may not have sold the way anyone had hoped, but Roulette tentatively scheduled a recording for a second album in January 1965. However, Solomon, along with Hugo and Luigi, made a significant change. They fired Ed E. Miller, whose role had been diminishing since the end of *America Sings!*, and hired Jim Friedman, an accomplished musical director who came recommended by Cass Elliot of the Mamas and the Papas. Friedman saw the talent in the group: "They had "a miraculous sound. . . . They were singing harmonies that were incredible."[43] Under his direction, the Au Go-Gos became more skilled and more innovative with "a jazzier feel . . . edgier than what we'd been doing."[44] More specifically, Friedman said he introduced the group to "modern chording, counterpoint, and dissonance."[45] However, he did not appreciate their repertoire or their stage act. "They had no direction and were trying to sing this medley [that] had all the phony folk songs of the era—'Charlie on the MTA,' 'Tom Dooley'—all the current fake folk songs."[46] He also noticed their awkward choreography and onstage "gimmicks": "I told them to stand still and sing. . . . No more dancing."[47]

The Au Go-Gos would rehearse in Friedman's apartment, crowded around his piano. Richie remembers:

> Jim would be playing the piano, and he would have this song that we were all supposed to learn. And he'd say, "Richie, I want you to sing this," and he would play the part out on the piano and I would get it in my head, and then, "Bob, I want you to sing this," and then to one of the girls, "Jean, you sing this, and Steve you sing this." I couldn't believe how it all fit together. This guy was hearing this all in his head. He was just an amazing talent! . . . He was a great guy . . . a kind of father figure to us. He took us under his wing.[48]

On several occasions, Stills has noted that he benefited from "a lot of good training" from Friedman, and in the early days of the Springfield, he called

AU GOGO SINGERS

FIG. 2 The Au Go-Go Singers on stage in Texas in late fall 1964. Richie Furay is center stage with (*far left*) Bob Harmelink and (*far right*) Stephen Stills, with Nels Gustafson behind Stills. Courtesy of Robert Harmelink.

Jim "his biggest musical influence."[49] After Friedman revamped their stage act, Solomon scheduled the Au Go-Gos for a six-week tour of Texas with mostly extended gigs in three supper clubs. (See fig. 2.) The first stop, after their long train ride, was the Petroleum Club in Beaumont (November 4–14), followed by the Tidelands Inn in Houston (November 17–29), and then the Caravan in Austin (about December 1–12). They also did a local TV show in Houston and, just before heading home, a short performance and autograph session at a Montgomery Ward department store.

The Au Go-Gos were well received throughout Texas. Friedman, who traveled with the group, organized a set to appeal to older, more conservative audiences. They opened with the collage from *America Sings!*, then other songs from that ill-fated play (e.g., "Shenandoah"), a few cuts from their album ("San Francisco Bay Blues," "Pink Polemoniums"), and a few newer songs worked up with Friedman ("Underground Railroad," "In the Hills of Shiloh," both cowritten by Shel Silverstein and Friedman). In Houston, where they opened for deadpan comedian Jackie Vernon, Maxine Mesinger called the Au Go-Go Singers "great folk singers . . . bright, fresh, [and] young," and in a newspaper clipping, G. C. calls the singers "a lively and accomplished group" and "a musically sophisticated crew," referring to individual songs and performances as "invigorating," "splendid," "impressive," and "beautiful." G. C. and Mesinger both commented that it was difficult for Vernon to follow the Au Go-Gos.[50] Thus, believes Nels, "Vernon hated us. . . . Jackie Vernon didn't interact with the band on the Texas tour. He just ignored us. A bunch of college kids, what did we know?"[51]

In Austin, John Bustin, hailed as "the Dean of Austin Entertainment," was "pleasantly surprised" that the ensemble was not "a rowdy rock 'n' roll unit but a folk singing ensemble of considerable taste and style . . . one of the freshest and most appealing acts to grace the Caravan stage in quite some time." He goes on to say that they entered "drifting on stage," one member at a time, each singing a line from a different folk song. "They create the kind of zesty entertainment that should sky-rocket them right on up into the folk-music galaxy." Bustin might have found the clean-cut youngsters especially appealing and "very personable" because he had just been to Los Angeles, where at the Whisky a Go Go his ears had been "assaulted" by "what must have been the most raucous band on the entire West Coast."[52]

In Texas, however, the Au Go-Go Singers began to fall apart. "Jim Friedman sowed discord in us," says Harmelink. "He said, 'Howie's not treating you right. He couldn't even fly you down here. You had to ride a train. And here you are. You have no way to get back home.' He really planted the seed that he had a better manager for us."[53] Friedman intimated that waiting in the wings were Jack Rollins and Charlie Joffee, partners who managed Woody Allen and Harry Belafonte. On December 2, the same day as Bustin's review, all nine members signed a letter, drafted by Friedman, declaring their contract with Solomon "null and void" for "misrepresentation of facts" concerning the Texas tour, specifically citing food allowances, which "do not exist."[54] In effect, the letter fired Solomon. "We gained a lot of experience in Texas, but we didn't make any money. We were scraping to get by."[55] Solomon paid the nine members and Friedman $500 a week, but they had to pay for all costs, including lodging, food, travel, and laundry.

The letter upset Solomon. He called Texas, where an unsuspecting Harmelink picked up the phone: "'What's the meaning of this? You guys are listening to the wrong person. If you go through with this, you will never sing in New York again. I have lawyers too.' He scared me," related Bob. "I had just turned twenty and was getting threatened by someone in New York City."[56] Nels, serving as the representative of the group, decided to call Roulette Records. He complained that they were not getting the benefits originally outlined in the tour agreement. "I don't remember who I spoke to, but I said, 'This is unacceptable.' The guy on the phone demanded, 'Do what you have to.' I said, 'No, I don't think so.' He said, 'Do it or when you get back to New York you'll end up in the East River.' . . . They were a tough bunch to say the least."[57] The Au Go-Gos completed the Texas tour.

Back to New York

The Au Go-Gos trudged back to New York via rail and, after Christmas break, reconvened. In one of Solomon's last acts as manager, he booked the Au Go-Gos on Rudy Vallee's *On Broadway Tonight*, a nationally broadcast TV show with seemingly all of Yellow Springs, Ohio, tuned in. Solomon, however, realized the folk boom was done and handed the band over to Friedman and new managers Rollins and Joffee, who immediately arranged auditions before one of the most successful talent agencies in New York. The agency was excited about working with the Au Go-Gos—until they heard they were under contract with Roulette Records. "Why didn't you tell me you were with Roulette; that's Mafia."[58] Friedman scheduled a meeting with Morris Levy, who refused to release them from their contract.

In addition, Kathi King, their wonderful soprano, felt the stress of performing. At the slightest onstage glitch, she would storm off. Furthermore, Pres. Lyndon Johnson had escalated the Vietnam War, and the draft threatened the singers. Gustafson received a call from his sister who worked for the military in Washington, DC: "Nels, if you don't get back to college, you'll be singing in Vietnam."[59] He borrowed money and returned to Otterbein. Harmelink realized the curtain was crashing down on his musical dream when Stills berated him during rehearsal: "Nels had left; Kathi was not there any longer. Stills, Freddie [Geiger], and I were harmonizing, and I hit a chord that was a barbershop chord. Stephen looked at me like, 'What? Where did that come from?' It was a hokey sound to him. His mind was way beyond that. He was making arrangements that were just revolutionary. . . . I thought, 'This isn't going to work.' I think Stephen wrote me off. That look he gave me. We never sang [together] again."[60] With that, Bob returned to Otterbein and the A Cappella Choir. Stills and Furay, however, would not let the draft deter their fledgling careers. Stills received his draft notice first. He rehearsed acting insane before the draft board, but much to Stephen's surprise he discovered that he was "as deaf as a post," and he was rejected.[61] Furay then received his notice and he, too, decided he would act insane. Genuinely frightened and nervous, with shaky hands and chewed fingernails slightly bloodied, he met the sergeant and stared out the window as if in a daze, not making eye contact. Furay said it was better than his audition for *The Pajama Game*.[62] The sergeant may have been suspicious and told Furay that the board would call again in six months—and the sergeant kept his promise.

With Kathi out and Nels and Bob back in college, the Au Go-Gos disbanded. The four remaining Bay Singers asked Stills to join them on a brief tour of coffeehouses in Canada, where they billed themselves as the Company and where, in Fort William, Northern Ontario, Stills met Neil Young. After the tour, Stills, anxious to go electric, headed directly to the West Coast. Richie remained at the Thompson Street apartment for a few more weeks. He took a few acting classes, auditioned for a couple of television shows, and tried to sell encyclopedias door-to-door. He was still committed to music, but he needed money. He found a job through his cousin, an executive at Pratt & Whitney, an aerospace manufacturer in East Hartford, Connecticut. Richie distributed precision tools to the workers from the tool crib. He had been dating Ann Gurney, whose sister Jean was in the Au Go-Gos, and moved in with the Gurney family in Wilbraham, Massachusetts. Whenever he could, Richie headed back to the Village, keeping sharp by playing, for instance, at Hoot Night at the Bitter End on Mondays.

In the summer of 1965, Richie invited Gram Parsons up to the Gurneys' home in Massachusetts. Gram brought something he wanted Richie to hear: *Mr. Tambourine Man*, the first album from the Byrds, whom Gram would join in 1968. Richie had heard the title track, which was a #1 hit. But when he listened to the album, he knew he had to resume music full time, and he had to contact Stills, except Furay did not know Stills's whereabouts. "The way I reached out to Stephen was through his dad. The address that I had was in El Salvador. I sent him a letter: 'How do I get a hold of Stephen?' But a response never came, and I was getting very discouraged and then finally my letter came back and it said, 'You don't have enough postage.' So I had to send the letter again."[63] Meanwhile, as Furay waited, Neil Young was in New York and, at Stephen's direction, had looked up Richie. In late 1965, Young met Richie in his former apartment on Thompson Street, where friends had assumed the lease. Neil shared a few songs with Richie, which Richie recorded on his Revere tape recorder. Furay was especially impressed with "Nowadays Clancy Can't Even Sing." Young taught Richie the song, which Furay performed as a solo folkie in the Village.

Meanwhile, Furay waited to hear from Stills.

CHAPTER 3

"What a Day"

Laurel Canyon and Buffalo Springfield

"Hey, come on out to California," said the voice on the other line. "I got a band together. All I need is another singer and we're ready to go. I'm in Los Angeles." Richie's response was immediate: "I'll be right there."[1]

In early February 1966, Furay boarded a plane for Los Angeles with his Martin D-28 guitar and his Revere tape recorder, anxious to team with Stephen Stills and to escape the New York City winter for the sun and palm trees of Southern California. Over the past two years, the epicenter of the pop music scene had shifted to Los Angeles, the home of the Byrds, the Beach Boys, Phil Spector, the Wrecking Crew, Gold Star Recording Studio, the Capitol Building with its record-stack design, the Sunset Strip, Ciro's, the Whisky a Go Go, the Hollywood Bowl, and *American Bandstand*, which had moved from Philadelphia two years earlier. Furay and Stills, who had arrived about six months earlier than Richie, in August 1965, were following in the footsteps of other Village folkies like the Mamas and the Papas, who were now "safe and warm . . . in LA" with "California Dreamin'" climbing the charts, peaking at #4 about a month after Furay's arrival. Furay reasoned that this new band with Stills could not fail. Stills was not only an extraordinary talent, but he also shared Richie's ambition, urgency, and obsessive work ethic.

Furay hurried to the LAX pickup zone, where he expected to greet Stills and ride off into folk-rock music stardom. As Richie waited for Stills, he watched fast, lavish cars stop to gather their stylishly dressed passengers. Time passed and no Stephen. Richie grew anxious, realizing he was in a strange city with no friends, family, or acquaintances. He removed his suit jacket, then his tie, and walked to the nearby pay phone several times to make frantic calls to the number he had for Stills. His confidence in the plan began to wane. He thought of Stills's previous attempt to go electric before he left New York. "He was trying to do a take-off on the Lovin' Spoonful," says Richie. "I'll tell you what: Pratt & Whitney Aircraft [where I worked at the time] sounded better to me than that band, and so I went back to work up there."[2] Finally, Stills arrived in a car driven by Richard "Dickie" Davis, a friend who Stills had met in Houston while touring with the Au Go-Go Singers and who did miscellaneous jobs at the Troubadour, not yet the prestigious club it would become. Davis, who would play a major role with Buffalo Springfield and Poco, recalled, "I took one look at Richie in his Brooks Brothers suit and crew cut, and I thought right then nothing was going to happen."[3] But if Davis was disappointed, so was Richie. He asked Stills about the band, only to find that Stills had just added its second member: Richie himself. Furay was not amused. "Oh brother," he thought, "have I made a mistake now."[4]

Davis changed his mind when he heard the two jam at Stephen's apartment: "They were really good. It had aspects of the Everly Brothers. . . . They had a really good harmony and they obviously knew each other musically very well. . . . I thought, 'Things might work out if [Furay's] hair gets a little longer and he loses that jacket.'"[5] Richie remained annoyed at his friend's ploy. He had left his girlfriend, his job, and a musical community in which he was comfortable, despite its dwindling numbers. Always both a dreamer and pragmatist, the twenty-one-year-old called his mom in Yellow Springs to ask her to contact Rod Serling, their former customer at the drugstore, to see if he would recommend an acting school. Richie's sister Judy remembers Serling's advice: "Tell him to go home and forget about it."[6]

Living and Practicing with Stills

Furay moved into Stills's small one-bedroom apartment on Fountain Avenue near North Fairfax in West Hollywood, at the foot of Laurel Canyon. Stills had the bedroom and Richie slept in the only other room, an all-purpose room. Since arriving in Los Angeles, Stills had collaborated unsuccessfully with Van Dyke Parks, and he had auditioned for *The Monkees*, a new musical sitcom for television, but lost the part to his friend and fellow transplanted Village folkie Peter Tork. He explained that his call to Richie was "only half a lie. . . . I needed him."[7] Perhaps to exact a little passive-aggressive revenge on his roommate, Furay often slipped out in the mornings and used his savings for breakfast at Thriftimart, a supermarket with counter service, a luxury Stills could not afford.

Furay and Stills are very different personalities. Richie is more measured, more conservative and pragmatic in his lifestyle. Richie may have smoked marijuana from time to time and taken amphetamines and cocaine when on tour, but he was never a heavy drinker and never indulged in LSD or heavier drugs. Despite an extramarital affair in the early 1970s that almost ruined his marriage, Furay has never been a womanizer: "The groupie part of it was never a huge thing, but marijuana and cocaine, yes."[8] Stills was more reckless. "Stephen went where the action was," said Bob Harmelink, who not only lived in the apartment on Thompson Street but also roomed with Stills when the Au Go-Go Singers toured Texas. "He was really a party boy and a ladies' man."[9] Stills could also be obnoxious and arrogant. Davis, who shared his apartment with Stills for a while, said, "Stephen was a difficult roommate. I mean I couldn't have been more delighted when there was a place next door for him to go"—the apartment that Stills would share with Furay.[10] But Stills could be very charming and kind. As Harmelink and Davis both point out, he was not mean-spirited. Although Richie can be stubborn and uncommunicative, he was the newcomer and recognized Stills's superior talent, so he yielded to him on musical and other issues.

In the approximately one year since Richie had played with him, Stills had made significant strides as a guitarist, vocalist, and songwriter. "At that time, Steve was way beyond a lot of people," says Richie. "He really had good phrasing . . . good from-the-gut music singing. I learned a lot from Steve."[11] As the two began playing and harmonizing, they knew something was, indeed, happening. They sat no more than a foot from one another in the all-purpose room and learned Stills's impressive new songs, many of which appear on Buffalo Springfield's first album. "We learned all of the harmony parts," recalls Richie. "We did the Lennon-McCartney thing. . . . That's how we learned to phrase together."[12] Rarely going out—Stills had no money and Richie guarded his—they practiced for long stretches of time. Unfortunately, the tapes that Richie made on his Revere have been lost with time, but we can hear what they sounded like on demo tracks recorded a few months later and released on *Buffalo Springfield, Box Set* (2001), Disk 1, particularly "Baby Don't Scold Me," "Neighbor Don't You Worry," and "We'll See."

Barry Friedman and Neil Young

Before Richie arrived, Stills had found a patron in Barry Friedman, no relation to Jim Friedman from the Au Go-Go Singers. Only three years older than Stills, Friedman had been working in the entertainment industry since he was ten years of age, when he actually produced variety shows at a theater in Los Angeles. He had since worked as a circus performer, photographer, radio producer, assistant television producer for *Chucko the Clown*, publicist for the Beatles' 1964 Hollywood Bowl concert, and, in July 1966, producer of a Michael Nesmith track on the Paul Butterfield Blues Band's classic album *East-West*. Anxious to manage Stills, Friedman encouraged him to audition for the Monkees and to work with Van Dyck Parks. At one point, he told Stills, "Look Stephen, if you want to put a band together I'll help you do it."[13] He directed Stills to list the musicians in his dream band. Two of the names were Richie Furay and Neil Young.

After hearing Stills and Furay sing together, Friedman stepped up his efforts. He arranged for each to sell a song to Columbia Screen Gems for $100 each. Richie sold "Loser," which has never been recorded, and Stephen sold "Sit Down I Think I Love You," which appeared on the Springfield's first album and was later covered as a single, peaking at #36, by the Mojo Men, and then as a single by the Executives, who had a minor hit with it in their native Australia. Both Stills and Furay had signed away writer's royalties with the sale. "Barry was a go-getter," said Richie, and neither he nor Stills trusted him fully.[14] Stills asked Dickie Davis "to keep an eye on things for us." Davis acknowledged that "Barry was a bit of a huckster," but added, "I saw no problem with the way he was dealing with them," which proved correct.[15]

Friedman, who a couple of years later would change his name to Frazier Mohawk, lived in an ornate rented house down the road from Stills and Furay. The grand living room featured stained glass windows, a huge fireplace that took up most of one wall, and a large bathtub in its middle, encircled with tiles of the Don Quixote story. While the house had only one bedroom, the property held four small guest houses, one of which was occupied by the folk duo [Tom] Mastin & [Mike] Brewer, who later found some success with Brewer & Shipley ("One Toke over the Line"). The duo was working with a rhythm section of Jim Fielder (who later played bass with Buffalo Springfield before joining Blood, Sweat & Tears) and drummer Billy Mundi (later of Zappa's Mothers of Invention and Rhinoceros). Stills and Furay tried to recruit Fielder and Mundi, but Friedman insisted they remain with Mastin & Brewer, who were professionally further along.

In the meantime, Stills was trying to locate Neil Young. In March 1966 the search led him to a phone number for Ken Koblun, a bassist who had played with Young in various bands and whom Stephen had met in Canada and Richie had met in New York with Neil. Koblun had just finished a series of dates with his new band, 3's a Crowd. Just as he had done previously with Richie, Stills persuaded Koblun to come to California to join his exciting new band. Koblun accepted the offer but was disappointed when he saw the "band" had only two members and no scheduled gigs. In an effort to impress him and persuade him to stay, Stephen and Richie informed their new recruit about the recent sale of their songs, feted him at dinner at Pioneer Chicken (a fast-food restaurant with bright orange deep-fried chicken), and arranged for a sleepover in Friedman's giant room. Koblun was not sufficiently impressed. After just a few days in Los Angeles, Koblun, with Richie and Stephen fast asleep near him in Friedman's large room, made his escape. "Steve, I can't make it," read the note he left behind.[16] He was soon back on stage with 3's a Crowd.

Within days of Koblun's leaving, Stills and Furay signed individual management contracts with Friedman and his friend Chuck Kaye, who had purchased their songs on behalf of Screen Gems. To save money, Stephen and Richie moved in with Friedman, who allotted each $1 a day for food. Then, on Wednesday, April 6, one of the most significant meetings in rock-and-roll music history occurred—a story with more variations than participants. However, for certain, Furay, Stills, and Friedman, driving in a van, had a serendipitous meeting with Neil Young and Bruce Palmer, riding in Young's hearse on Sunset Boulevard. Young writes that they hopped out of their vehicles in the middle of the street to hug one another; Friedman says they turned the corner, stopping in front of a liquor store; Palmer says they pulled into a parking lot.[17] There are other minor conflicts, but, clearly, no one has inflated the story for dramatic effect or self-aggrandizement. But memories can be unreliable, and details from one memory conflated with those from other memories. I asked Richie about the conflicting details:

> Yeah, well, the version I'm going to tell you, right now, is the true version. Stephen and I were with Barry Friedman . . . we had gone someplace down on Sunset, and we were going east, back to his house. Bruce and Neil had been in Los Angeles a couple weeks and they couldn't find us in the scene any place. We weren't going down to the Whisky [a Go Go] or going here or there. They figured they were never gonna find us, so they were on their way west of the 405 to head up to San Francisco. And that's when we got into a traffic jam right in front of this little restaurant called Ben Frank's, and there Neil was, man, in a 1953 hearse with Ontario license plates. It was like, "Who else could that be?" And we got together in the parking lot.[18]

Richie makes at least one minor error, which might be typical of each version. Neil arrived in Los Angeles on April 1, just five days, not "a couple of weeks," before the encounter. As Young explains, "Buffalo Springfield was a mirage. . . . Only those who were there know what happened and we're not too sure."[19]

After the laughter, back smacks, hugs, and giddiness, the five headed to Friedman's house. In the grand room, Richie and Stephen showcased their work to Young and Palmer. Young was impressed: "Richie was a natural vocalist, and they were really great. They sang like birds together." When they launched into Young's composition, "Nowadays Clancy Can't Even Sing," which Neil had taught Richie in New York some sixteen months earlier, Young "added a little guitar and a high voice here and there." At that moment, Young knew, "This was going to be good."[20] However, they still needed a drummer, and Mundi agreed to sit in with them for a couple of days.

A confident Friedman got busy. He immediately rented living space for them and a small theater for rehearsals in the infamous Hollywood Center Motel, a cheap and sleazy motel convenient for sex workers and those down on their luck. In his search for a drummer, he telephoned Jim Dickson and Eddie Tickner, comanagers of the Byrds, who recommended Walter Milton Dwayne Midkiff, otherwise known as Dewey Martin. Martin, an experienced drummer, had worked with stars like Carl Perkins, the Everly Brothers, Patsy Cline, Roy Orbison, and the Modern Folk Quartet, and, until a few days before the call, had been drumming for the Dillards, managed by Dickson and Tickner. The Dillards had just decided to drop their electric instruments and return fully to their bluegrass roots, making a drummer expendable. Martin was irked when he was asked to audition for an unnamed band. "I didn't have to audition for Orbison or Patsy," he noted.[21] Martin strutted into the motel's theater as they rehearsed "Go and Say Goodbye." "I knew I had never *ever* heard a vocal sound like that. And I just took to it."[22] Martin was the third Canadian to join the band. But he claimed that he was also a soulful vocalist in the style of Otis Redding and Wilson Pickett and he expected to sing a song or two. The band agreed, and in those early days Martin sang Pickett's "Midnight Hour," the only cover ever in the Springfield setlist and sometimes introduced jokingly by Furay: "It's time for the Top 40 portion of our program."[23] Friedman's call also produced more than a drummer. Stills, Furay, and Young had only acoustic guitars. Dickson and Tickner volunteered the now useless electric guitars of the Dillards. Now all the band lacked was a name.

Buffalo Springfield

Like the meeting on Sunset Boulevard, details vary about how the band took its name. According to Neil Young, he, Van Dyck Parks, and Stills saw the steamroller as they were "walkin' along" outside Friedman's home, and "either me or Stephen said, 'Buffalo Springfield.' I think it was me, but I can't swear to it." Stills, however, remembers the full band "walking across the street, and Richie [said], 'Wow, that's really cool.' And we all just gave a collective 'wow!' because [Richie and I] had been finding-the-name game for about a month." Parks contends otherwise: "I thought of that name." He said he entered Friedman's house and told Dewey, "Your name is on that sign, on that road leveler." Stills responded to Parks with laughter: "In his dreams."[24] What is certain is that a construction crew was repairing Fountain Avenue in front of Friedman's house. A steamroller, unattended, had a plate that identified its manufacturer: Buffalo Springfield. The musicians unscrewed the plate and positioned it on the mantel over Friedman's enormous fireplace. They all agreed that Buffalo Springfield would be their name. Young, to this day, insists that there be no *the* before *Buffalo Springfield*. Coincidentally, the headquarters for the Buffalo Springfield Roller Company, which endorsed the band's use of its name, was located in Springfield, Ohio, where Richie first took guitar lessons as a boy and where his father secured stock for his inventory. A replica of the plate absorbs the cover of *Buffalo Springfield, Box Set*, and another hangs on Furay's home garage.

Buffalo Springfield, the name, is rich in implication. With the Beatles and the British Invasion still dominating the charts, the name evoked the power of America in all its complexity, competitiveness, and amplitude. *Buffalo*, or the American bison, recalls the Old West with its chaos, rugged individualism, and large animals grazing on the plains, mirrored in the wistful ballads of Young and Furay, or that same herd stampeding in a mad rush, reflected in the blazing guitar interplay of Stills and Young. Furthermore, the band often favored cowboy-Indian attire. At the same time, the city of Buffalo suggests a toughness and perseverance, a blue-collar town that endures harsh winters. Springfield, more suggestive of Springfield, Illinois, than the Ohio location on the plate, is the capital city in the Land of Lincoln, Lincoln's home for some twenty-four years just prior to his presidency, hence conjuring thoughts of freedom, fairness, intellectualism, and Midwestern pragmatism. Buffalo Springfield, name and band, asserted its Americanness, creating a distinct body of work as bountiful and diverse as the American landscape and population. Unfortunately, like America, the band could be impatient with its high expectations, and, like Americans, the band members had energetic individualist impulses that fractured communal solidarity. However, in April 1966, Buffalo Springfield synthesized into a powerful unit, ready to take on the pop music world. "Whether or not we were the best musicians didn't matter," added Furay; "we had magic, and we all knew it . . . undeniable magic."[25] Buffalo Springfield was about "love and chemistry," said Young. "Everybody was the same; we were all in a band together. That gave an urgency to the music."[26]

That chemistry, that "magic," galvanized the Springfield. Within five days of the Sunset Boulevard meeting, the band played their first gig, on April 11, 1966, at the Troubadour's Hoot Night, basically an open mic event. Within ten days, based on the recommendation of Byrds bass player Chris Hillman and a Dickson and Tickner visit to a rehearsal, the Springfield opened for the Byrds before an audience of ten thousand at San Bernardino's Swing Auditorium and continued in support of the Byrds for six more dates that April. Less than a year earlier, Furay had listened to the Byrds' first album with Gram Parsons in the home of the Gurney family in Wilbraham, Massachusetts.

The Whisky a Go Go

After the brief tour with the Byrds, Dickie Davis asked Chris Hillman to recommend Buffalo Springfield to Elmer Valentine, an owner of the Whisky a Go Go and a hard-nosed self-described "crooked cop" who had fled Chicago.[27] Impressed with their audition, Valentine hired the Springfield to be the Whisky's opening act from May 2 through June 18—supporting the Grass Roots, Johnny Rivers, Love, Them with Van Morrison, and the Doors—with a few days off to open once again for the Byrds. It is hard to overestimate the importance of the Whisky shows. Without climbing in and out of tour buses, the Springfield polished their setlist, sharpened their ability to play together, and practiced during the day with the opportunity of showcasing themselves in the premier club on the exploding Los Angeles scene. Buffalo Springfield was dynamic at the Whisky. Stills and Furay were up front singing, with Richie positioned center stage and flanked on one side by Stills and the other by Young, who would quickly gravitate toward the rear to be near Martin and Palmer. Young did not sing much at the Whisky shows but "generated all sorts of commotion on his guitar" as he played off the lead guitar of Stills[28]—the only band on the Sunset Strip with two leads. Bruce Palmer, usually with his back to the audience, perfected his bass patterns, weaving in Motown runs or thick and raw Stax grooves, while Martin, a no-frills drummer, pounded a steady beat and entertained the crowd with his kooky facial expressions and his vocal performance of "Midnight Hour." Buffalo Springfield locked in a groove at the Whisky with the musicians challenging, pushing, and nurturing one another.

Looking back, the band believed they peaked at the Whisky, though they were less than a month old when the residency began. "The first week at the Whisky was absolutely incredible," said Stills. "That's when we peaked, and after then it was downhill." Young agrees, claiming the Springfield "reached our peak at the Whisky," while Furay elaborates: "The Whisky was as good as we ever were, as dynamic as we ever were, as close as we ever were, as unified, because we were working every day. . . . We were tight, we were good, and we felt we were good." Martin said, "We cast a spell on people.[29] Indeed, lines formed around the corner to see Buffalo Springfield as much as the headliners. That spring, according to Kenny Weissberg, the Springfield unseated the Byrds as "the ultimate Southern California house band. The Whisky was their roost and the faces in the crowd were more than repeaters, they were season ticket holders."[30] Word spread among industry insiders.

Offstage, the band spun in a whirlwind. With each show came more frenzy, more distractions, more groupies, more drugs, more invitations to parties, more potential managers, and more record labels promising stardom. The band also had some money, each earning $120 a week at the Whisky, or about $1000 in 2020 value. Starry-eyed, naive, and susceptible to rock-and-roll tempters and opportunists, the band believed their moment had arrived. Friedman directed Davis, who did "whatever needed to be done" for the Springfield, to look over the record deals from the many offers—increasing, it seemed, daily.[31] An excited Davis verbally accepted an initial offer from Dunhill, who had produced hits for the Mamas and the Papas and the Grass Roots. But Elektra, who had signed Love, made an offer, and then Warner Bros. committed $10,000 to the band, double what Dunhill had offered, only to be outdone when ATCO, a subsidiary of Atlantic, countered with $12,000—a very large advance for the time. A confused Davis sought advice from acquaintances Charlie Greene and Brian Stone, who he knew had worked with Sonny & Cher. Greene and Stone seized the opening and wooed the Springfield into a management contract.

Despite all Friedman had done for the band, the Springfield believed they needed new management, one with more insider experience, more music contacts, and more clout than Friedman. Greene and Stone entered at the opportune moment. The slick pair of New Yorkers or, as Harvey Kubernik called them, "two rascally East Coast PR flaks" and "gimcracks,"[32] impressed the band with their long black limousine, abundant pills, and inexhaustible supply of marijuana and their stories, mostly exaggerated, of their work with Sonny & Cher. Greene's smooth talk, sleek dress, and stylish haircut complemented the quiet demeanor and business attire of Stone, which, to the band, suggested business acumen. "Pretty much from the beginning," said Davis, "Greene and Stone looked like a problem to me. It was my idea but I regretted it."[33] When journalist Chris Hodenfield told legendary producer Jerry Wexler that he had talked with Greene, Wexler grinned; "Did he tell you how he created Sonny and Cher from pure mud? How he shaped them with his hands and *breathed* upon them?"[34] One important point that Greene and Stone neglected to tell the Springfield was that Sonny paid them $250,000 to buy out their contract. As Chris Hillman said, you had to count your fingers after shaking hands with Greene and Stone.[35]

In short order, Greene and Stone signed Buffalo Springfield and worked out the details with ATCO, Sonny & Cher's label. Friedman was furious. He was being pushed aside and made it clear that he preferred Elektra: "If they'd signed with Elektra it would have been a different story, I think. Elektra was more nurturing and [founder and CEO] Jac Holzman had a great understanding of music and musicians. His approach was damn near religious." At this point, Friedman had only individual contracts with Stills and Furay, which the new managers bought out within a few months—at gunpoint, according to Friedman. "And that was the last I saw of The Buffalo Springfield," he said. "Charlie more or less said that if I came back around, I'd be dealt with. It was scary as hell."[36] The band would regret abandoning Friedman—to whom they dedicated their second album. As John Einarson summarizes, Friedman was their "nurturer, provider, [and] supporter."[37] Neil Young wrote, Buffalo Springfield "made a lot of bad and inexperienced decisions, starting with losing Barry Friedman."[38]

At first, Greene and Stone seemed to pay immediate dividends. They invested in the band, setting them up in apartments, renting a car for each of them, doling out cash advances, and purchasing new guitars and equipment. Furay selected a twelve-string Gibson ES-335 in partial imitation of Roger McGuinn: "We kind of modeled ourselves after the Byrds, but I didn't want to do a [twelve-string] Rickenbacker and be just like [McGuinn]." Furay used the twelve-string throughout his days with the Springfield, but rarely afterward. "I pretty much put it on the shelf."[39] While with the Springfield, Richie had two twelve-strings stolen, an occupational hazard. The managers also arranged for the band to be one of the opening acts for the Rolling Stones on July 25 at the Hollywood Bowl, where the Springfield performed four songs.

The First Single

In the summer of 1966, confident if not arrogant, Buffalo Springfield entered the prestigious state-of-the-art Gold Star Studios, recording home to the Beach Boys and Phil Spector. They were poised, they believed, to take their place among rock's hierarchy, recognizing their only competitors as the Beatles, the Byrds, and the Rolling Stones—the three major influences on them. The Springfield combined the folk-rock feel and the Americanness—or, later, the Americana—of the Byrds with the harmonies of the Beatles and the intensity of the Stones. All they had to do was capture their sound on vinyl.

Initially, Buffalo Springfield hoped that Jack Nitzsche would produce the album. Nitzsche had worked as an arranger and conductor for Phil Spector and had played several instruments and helped with arrangements on *Aftermath*, the Rolling Stones' recent release. However, Greene and Stone convinced the band that the two of them could produce the album. After all, they told the Springfield, they had produced hits for Sonny & Cher, who, a year earlier, had a #1 with "I Got You Babe," followed by a #8 with "Baby Don't Go"—although how much they did for the duo, especially in the studio, is debatable. The credits on Sonny & Cher's first album, *Look at Us*, which features "I Got You Babe," read "York-Pale Production / Subsidiary of Greene and Stone Enterprises." Then, three lines below, "Arranged and Produced by Sonny Bono." Still, the Springfield believed they had the songs, the arrangements, and the sound all worked out at the Whisky. The producer simply had to tape it. Certainly, Greene and Stone would be fine.

As Buffalo Springfield entered the studio in mid-1966, rock music—with the rise of the album—was asserting itself as an art form. Within approximately the last half year, the Beatles had released *Rubber Soul* (December 1965) with *Revolver* awaiting release (August 1966); the Byrds had delivered *Turn! Turn! Turn!* (December 1965) followed by *Fifth Dimension* (June 1966); Love had released their eponymous first album (March 1966); the Stones, *Aftermath* (April 1966, UK; July 1966, US); the Beach Boys, *Pet Sounds* (May 1966); Frank Zappa and the Mothers of Invention, *Freak Out!* (June 1966); and Bob Dylan would soon release *Blonde on Blonde* (July 1966). Buffalo Springfield was eager to be in the conversation. But with rock journalism in its infancy and free-form FM radio still almost a year away, the band knew a hit single

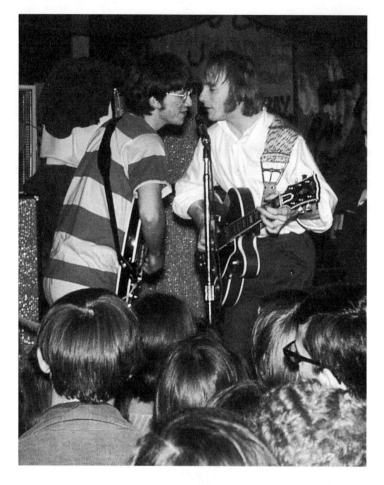

FIG. 3 Richie Furay and Stephen Stills at the Cellar, Arlington Heights, IL, May 13, 1967. Photo by Douglas E. Slowiak (with thanks to Jackie Ripley).

was their fastest path to recognition.[40] In July, the Springfield recorded the A- and B-sides to their first single. The A-side, they thought, would be "Go and Say Goodbye," backed by "Nowadays Clancy Can't Even Sing." Stills and Furay had been playing "Go and Say Goodbye," a Stills composition, since Richie's arrival on the coast. A quick-tempo folk-rock song with strong country leanings and a heavy Beatles influence, the song features lead vocals sung in unison by Stills and Furay, much as Lennon and McCartney had done on such up-tempo Beatles songs as "I Want to Hold Your Hand" and "Please Please Me." As Richie said, "We modeled ourselves, at least vocally, after the Beatles."[41] The phrasing of Stills and Furay is exact and potent, especially in the chorus. They effectively blur the opening words of the second line, "Is it you don't . . ." only to lengthen each of the following words, "want to see her cry." Their unison lead vocals are showcased on two other Stills compositions on the first album: "Sit Down I Think I Love You" and "Don't Scold Me," which, at the 1:56 mark, in a kind of homage to the Beatles, quotes the main riff from "Day Tripper." (See fig. 3.)

The perspective of "Go and Say Goodbye" resembles "She Loves You" and "You're Going to Lose That Girl," two songs in which the Lennon-McCartney protagonists warn and advise male friends about possible impending breakups. In "Go and Say Goodbye," the friend has presented the Stills-Furay character with a letter intended for his soon-to-be ex-girlfriend. The song is the protagonist's response, in which he angrily tells the friend, "You really should know better" than to send a letter. He advises the friend to "face her with the trouble / Even though it's hurting like a curse." In the chorus, the protagonist softens his tone, appeals to his friend's sense of fairness, and addresses him with increased understanding and affection: "Brother, you know you can't run away and hide." In the bridge (0:56 mark), as in "You're Going to Lose that Girl," the key shifts and the voices rise as the protagonist grows frustrated with the friend's resistance to his advice: "Tell me why . . . It's a lie." Very succinctly, in 2:19, Stills establishes a recognizable situation (one friend asking another for love advice), creates a dramatic scene with rising tension, and, with the repetition of the chorus at the end, relieves the tension—although we cannot be certain what the friend decides. The directness and brevity with which Stills tells the story is a hallmark of his lyrical style with the Springfield.

Musically, "Goodbye" puts its folk-country roots up front with a twelve-beat intro that features Stills on acoustic guitar picking a variation of "Salt Creek" (sometimes "Salt River"), a traditional fiddle tune performed by Doc Watson, among others, and taught to Stills by Chris Hillman. On the fifth beat Young enters with his Gretsch hollow-body electric guitar to pop out high-register riffs, approximating a steel guitar. Throughout the song, Young continues the steel-guitarlike riffs above the vocals and the acoustic guitars while Palmer plays off a pumping-country bass pattern and Martin drives the song with an insistent but warm snare. Just past the midpoint, Stills rings out a solo with a wonderful bluegrass feel. Its catchy chorus and the storyline would seem to give it hit-single potential. As the lead track on *Buffalo Springfield*, it announces an energetic new band, one highly skilled and inventive. It remains one of Furay's favorites, "a song I've loved ever since the first time I heard it, sitting in the little apartment we shared on Fountain Avenue in Los

Angeles."[42] He recorded it again with Poco on *A Good Feelin' to Know* (1972), infusing rock beats into the country feel, and, later, in a purer country version on *Alive* (2008), reprised on *50th Anniversary Return to the Troubadour* (2021) with the addition of harmonica solos by Jack Jeckot.

"Nowadays Clancy Can't Even Sing" is more meditative and darker than the vigorous and assertive "Go and Say Goodbye." It is a complex song with enigmatic images inspired by a fellow student in Young's high school:

> Many people . . . tell me they don't understand "Clancy." They can't figure out all the symbols and stuff. . . . Clancy is just an image, a guy who gets come down on all the time. He was a strange cat, beautiful. Kids in school called him a "weirdo," 'cause he would just whistle and sing "Valerie, Valera" [an upbeat German folk song] in the halls. After a while, he got so self-conscious he couldn't do his thing anymore. When someone as beautiful as that and as different as that is actually killed by his fellow men . . . like taken and sorta chopped down—all the other things are nothing compared to this.

Young also said he projected some of his hurt emotions after a breakup with a girlfriend who apparently cheated on him.[43] With Young's guidance above, the song becomes clearer. The "I" in the song, the protagonist, reflects on his own misery, his own crushed spirit, and wallows in self-pity until he considers Clancy, in whom he finds ironic inspiration. Singing, in the song, may represent living fully, but it is also, literally, singing. Unlike Clancy, the singer still has "the feeling to keep him[self] alive," but "havin' [the feeling] and sharin' it ain't quite the same." He tells of his battle to create the song we hear. Even though someone has been "stomping all over [the singer's] face," deafening his voice by "putting sponge in the bells [he] once rung," and tying his free-roaming "gypsy" spirit, nothing, realizes the narrator, can be worse than losing the will to create and sing as Clancy has. But the singer struggles with "writing this song," "trying to tune all the bells [he] once rung," and with "pencil and paper just counting the score," or writing the music. But, at the song's hopeful completion, he is "singing the meaning of what's in [his] mind." Thus, through his therapeutic creative process, the singer surfaces from his depression.

Furay delivers a captivating and poignant vocal performance, alternately tortured, frustrated, angry, and self-pitying—and always distressed. It is the voice of a protagonist desperately but optimistically trying to lift himself from his darkness and confusion. His imbalanced emotional state is reflected in the music, in the alternating time signatures of 4/4 and 3/4, with the 4/4 measures featuring a two-chord progression of Gmaj7 and Dmaj7, picked with a slight tremolo effect, at the beginning of each verse with some thin guitar lines underneath and Young's gentle bluesy harmonica on top. In the 3/4 measures, Stills backs Furay on vocals emphasizing the desperation as chords are slashed and cymbals crash. "Clancy" reveals the work of an introspective and daring young songwriter, who is self-revealing while also being obscure and concealing. However, the protagonist of the song, like Young himself, may be somewhat inscrutable even to himself.

With both songs completed, Greene and Stone rushed the masters to Ahmet Ertegun, cofounder and president of Atlantic. Ertegun, well-respected and well liked by musicians, was anxious both to recoup his hefty investment in the band and to introduce Buffalo Springfield to the world. To be sure, the band's music excited him: "The songs they wrote didn't resemble anything that anybody else was doing. They also had three outstanding lead singers who were also great guitar players. . . . They were one of the greatest rock 'n' roll bands I've ever heard in my life."[44] Within a couple of weeks of recording sessions, Ertegun rushed out a single, but he decided to make "Clancy" the A-side with "Goodbye" the B-side. The impact of the decision was disastrous. Not only did the single flop, but Stills was also upset. He had expected *his* song to be the A-side, the first single. As Richie put it, "Buffalo Springfield was Stephen Stills's band. Steve was the heart and the soul of the Springfield. Not Neil, not me, not anybody else."[45]

Ertegun's decision has been second-guessed ever since. "Clancy" is an introspective song, rather melancholy, lyrically complex, and without a very radio-friendly chorus, not crafted, it would seem, for AM radio, car listening, or sing-alongs. While "Goodbye" might have had the catchy chorus and told a relatable story, its country flavor might not have made it palatable to the Top 40 audience. Country-rock was a few years off. But, of course, hit singles are always difficult to predict. Who would have thought the novelty song "Winchester Cathedral," recorded during the same month as "Clancy," would be an international hit for the New Vaudeville Band? If we look at the songs in the Top 10 during the week of "Clancy's" release, we find an eclectic lot: "Wild Thing," The Troggs (#1); "Hanky Panky," Tommy James and the Shondells (#2); "Little Red Riding Hood," Sam the Sham and the Pharaohs (#3); "The Pied Piper," Crispian St. Peters (#4); "I Saw Her Again," Mamas and the Papas (#5); "Hungry," Paul Revere and the Raiders (#6); "Summer in the City," Lovin' Spoonful (#7); "Sweet Pea," Tommy Roe (#8); "Mother's Little Helper," Rolling Stones (#9); "Somewhere, My Love," Ray Conniff and the Singers (#10). None approach the lyrical sophistication of "Clancy."

Furay was surprised by the choice of single and still, over fifty years later, is emphatic: "I can't believe Ahmet made that big a mistake. Because ['Clancy'] was not the song. The song that should have been released was 'Do I Have to Come Right Out and Say It?'"[46] The gentle Neil Young ballad is an internal monologue in which the lovestruck singer practices his appeal to the woman who is "overworking [his] mind." The simple, direct lyric, delivered delicately by Furay, captures the singer's nervousness and intimidation and might have been a more suitable single. Young agrees that either "Come Right Out" or "Go and Say" would have been "a much better choice."[47] Love ballads have a familiarity. The Association, another band on the Los Angeles scene, recorded "Cherish," a ballad about unrequited love, at about the same time the Springfield recorded "Clancy." Released a few weeks after the Springfield's single, "Cherish" held the #1 spot on *Billboard* for three weeks, from September 24 to October 14, 1966. Interestingly, Valiant, the label, was reluctant to release the single, claiming it sounded "old and archaic."[48] Maybe Ertegun was too eager to brandish his innovative new band.

The Album

Without a hit single, *Buffalo Springfield* drew little attention at its initial release on December 5, 1966. It featured seven songs by Stills and five by Young, with Furay singing lead on four, Stills on three, Young on two, and Stills and Furay in unison on three. Furay, much like George Harrison, would have to wait for the second album to place a song although he had recorded demos for "Sad Memory" and "Can't Keep You Down," an early form of "Do You Feel It Too," which he later recorded with Poco, and "My Kind of Love," dropped from the album at the last minute for Young's "Flying on the Ground Is Wrong." Richie did not push. "All I know is that when we got started Neil and Steve were so prolific that I couldn't find a place for one of my songs."[49] As the first album reveals, the quality of their writing was high. Stills contributed "Hot Dusty Roads," a bluesy shuffle; the ferocious "Leave," with blistering lead work from both Young and Stills; and "Sit Down I Think I Love You," which Stills and Furay sing together with such certitude as to add drama and edge to the folk-rock arrangement, which includes a Stills garage-rock fuzz solo followed by Young's high-register, cleaner solo.

Young's songs, like "Clancy," are introspective and brooding. In 1970, Young said, "[My songs] are about my feelings. . . . Most of them are about . . . frustration."[50] Young, an epileptic, wrote and sang "Burned," about having a seizure: "Crashed and my ears can't hear a sound / No use runnin' away . . . it's so confusin'." To be sure his vocals, which made Young nervous, kept pace with the fast rhythm, the band gave him amphetamines, "to get [him] loosened up."[51] The band's second single, "Burned," failed to chart. Two other songs suggest his fragile psyche. "Flying on the Ground," a moderately slow ballad, sung tenderly by Richie, reveals insecurity, fragmentation, and imbalance: "I'm in pieces on the ground. . . . Sometimes I feel like I'm just a helpless child / Sometimes I feel like a king." In "Out of My Mind," Young meditates on fame, which he both desires and fears. The thumping and ominous intro with a tremolo guitar riff signals the singer's dark meditation but also, in hindsight, forecasts the anguish that would surround the band. Young, only twenty-one at the time and on the threshold of success, sings in an uncanny world-weary voice, frightened of what might lie ahead. The taste of stardom at the Whisky and his brief time in the studio with his bandmates and Greene and Stone worried him "out of [his] mind" that he could lose his authentic artistic self, or "what I'm living for." The singer feels entrapped by the demands of stardom, represented in the opening lines by screaming fans who cluster around his limousine. It's a poignant moment that portends the difficulty Young would have committing to the band. In 1970, he said, "I never wanted to be in a group. . . . I came out here . . . to make it as a single artist and all of a sudden I was in this group and the group was so good I couldn't believe it. And it was fun."[52] At first. According to Stills, "Buffalo Springfield was a happy band"—until the recording studio. (See fig. 4.)[53]

Problems

Buffalo Springfield recognized immediately that Greene and Stone were not technically competent to produce a record. Furay noticed that they didn't know how to operate the console board, and Stills remembers the very first session and hearing Greene's voice over the talkback: "'[The song's] too long. Play it faster.' . . . Neil and I looked at each other and said, 'I think we better learn how to work this shit.'"[54] Young writes, "We did not know much about making records and neither did they."[55] The Springfield found out what most music insiders knew: Greene and Stone did not produce Sonny & Cher; Sonny produced Sonny & Cher. The Springfield had no choice but to hope their music would overcome the deficiencies of their producers—which it may have, but not completely.

FIG. 4 Buffalo Springfield "noodling" for the photographer. *Left to right*: Bruce Palmer, Stephen Stills, Neil Young, Dewey Martin, and Richie Furay. Photograph permission of Pictorial Press Ltd. / Alamy.

Davis recalls listening to the finished album with the band: "We went up to a friend's house in Laurel Canyon. Steve Saunders had a really good sound system . . . state-of-the-art stuff." They played the album. "It was god-awful. I remember the feeling in that room as we were listening. Everything sunk."[56] Stills found the sound "appallingly fast. . . . This doesn't sound like us. . . . It sounded really fast and perky." He noted that the "vocal harmonizings in the background [were] too loud."[57] As Davis pointed out, the band sounded fine in the studio. The problem was with the mix. Harmonies were too loud or not loud enough, Palmer's bass was consistently too low in the mix, and, overall, it sounded flat. They asked Ahmet Ertegun to let them remix the album with Barry Friedman, but it was too late. "The truth is," Stills said, "we never got on record what we sounded like live. Man, we were the Stones onstage."[58]

Unfortunately, no official live releases of the Springfield exist. However, bootleg recordings, even of poor quality, do corroborate Stills's comment. "Pay the Price" and "Don't Scold Me" seem ordinary on the album, almost lifeless, compared to the raging live recordings.

The band might have found only some comfort in the review of *Buffalo Springfield* in *Crawdaddy!* Paul Williams called it "a lovely, moving experience" before noting that "the production job on this LP is sadly amateurish. The bass is under-recorded, the drums misunderstood, and the guitars tend to tinkle when they want to ring. On stage, the Springfield have a deceptively full sound. . . . They project a richness and a fullness which is more satisfying than one could possibly imagine. It's a delicate balance, however, and it wasn't achieved in the recording studio. . . . But the album, despite it all, is beautiful. Every track on it will entrance you at one time or another."[59] Stills remains bitter about the production. When he walked into rehearsals for the Springfield reunion shows in 2010, the album was playing. He demanded they turn it off. "I can't listen to that!"[60]

In 2018, Neil Young remastered all Buffalo Springfield albums for release in a box set, *What's That Sound? Complete Albums Collection.* The sound is, indeed, much improved and clarified. As one fan commented in response to AllMusic's 4.5-of-5-star review, "I can finally hear all instruments."[61] However, even on the original release, the quality of the songs, the lead vocals, the harmonies, the lead guitar lines, and the guitar interplay result in a significant achievement. In 2020, *Rolling Stone* ranked *Buffalo Springfield* #12 on its list of best albums of 1966, behind *Aftermath* (#1), *Blonde on Blonde* (#2), and *Pet Sounds* (#2), but ahead of *Ray's Mood* by Ray Charles (#13); *Soul Sister*, Aretha Franklin (#14); and *Fresh Cream* by Cream (#19).[62]

CHAPTER 4

"Merry-Go-Round"

Confusion in the Springfield

Sunset Strip, a 1.5-mile stretch of Sunset Boulevard from Crescent Heights Boulevard on the east to Sierra Drive on the west, was the fun zone for the Hollywood glamour set from the late 1920s into the 1950s. Tuxedo-clad stars, movie producers, and gangsters frequented the posh nightclubs with high-end food, gambling, and entertainment. Rising stars, directors, producers, and gossip columnists sought to affirm their status with published photographs from clubs like the Trocadero, which was featured in the original *Star Is Born* (1937); the Mocambo, where Frank Sinatra made his Los Angeles debut and which exhibited live exotic birds in aviaries along its walls; and Ciro's, designated "celebrities only" and seemingly camouflaged by its plain exterior. By the end of the 1950s, the glitz and glamour were gone. The clubs had closed and only locals and a few tourists dined on the Strip. By the mid-1960s a younger group began to colonize the area with its cheap rents and available venues. As the influx increased, locals grew uneasy at the sights and sounds of loud electric guitars, long hair, far-out dress, and drug use. One day, after his crew cut grew out, Furay entered Thriftimart for his usual furtive breakfast but was denied service. He never returned.

One July afternoon in 1966, Neil Young experienced a much more horrific incident. As he drove his '57 Corvette, provided by Greene and Stone, he saw the police confronting Dickie Davis on a parking violation. Young pulled over to help the often hot-tempered Davis. When Young did not produce a driver's license, the police turned their attention on him and decided to haul him to the police station. One officer called the musician a "a filthy animal." Young countered by telling the officer he looked like an "insect, a grasshopper." Young was tossed into a cell, but before his release without charges, the officer "beat the shit out of [him]." Brian Stone filed and eventually won a lawsuit on Young's behalf, citing Young's "lacerations, head injuries, and a broken bridge in his mouth."[1]

Throughout 1966 tensions increased between the recent arrivals and longtime residents, who watched their neighborhood turn into a huge hippie hangout, especially at night, when the clubs were open and young people cluttered the streets. The older residents and business owners, excluding, of course, those who catered to the counterculture, lobbied the police to enforce loitering laws and a decades-old curfew law for those under eighteen. They wanted to stop the Strip from becoming Greenwich Village west. The young people organized a protest for the evening of November 12, 1966. Over a thousand demonstrators took to the streets to protest the curfew and the forced closing of Pandora's Box, which authorities targeted as a hub of delinquent disorder. That evening the police arrested approximately three hundred demonstrators. It marked the beginning of the Sunset Strip Curfew Riots, also known as the Hippie Riots, which continued through December.

On the weekend of November 12, Buffalo Springfield was playing a series of gigs in the San Francisco Bay Area, which included the Fillmore Auditorium, the Avalon Ballroom, and clubs like the Gay 90's and The Ark in nearby Sausalito. Stills had been struggling to write an antiwar song, but the song was not coming together until he turned his attention to the riots near his home.

"For What It's Worth (Stop, Hey What's That Sound)"

Once Stills shifted his attention to the protests on Sunset Strip, he finished "For What It's Worth" in fifteen minutes.[2] Over the years, the song has established itself as an enduring protest classic, occupying a place on most "greatest" lists: for example, #3 on *Rolling Stone*'s "Readers' Poll: The 10 Best Protest Songs of All Time" (2014) and #10 on Pop Dose's "Greatest Protest Songs of All Time" (2017). It has earned a place on Hardeep Phull's *Story Behind the Protest Song: Reference Guide to the 50 Songs That Changed the 20th Century*, and David Browne compares it to "We Shall Overcome" for its ongoing relevancy.[3] Like "We Shall Overcome," which has been sung at pro-union rallies and civil rights marches, "For What It's Worth" has a vagueness, a lack of specificity, that makes it adaptable to most protest situations. Indeed, at its release, most listeners thought it was about the Vietnam War. Over the last fifty years, powerful cover performances have been recorded by a diverse range of artists including, in the 1960s, the gospel and soul group the Staple Singers and pop star Cher; in the 1970s, Afropop singer Miriam Makeba and teen idol David Cassidy; in the 1980s, punk band Plain Wrap and alternative rock band Icicle Works; in the 1990s, the hip-hop, electronic dance band Oui 3 (who created their own verses); and sampled by hip-hop artists Public Enemy (which featured Stills re-singing a verse and chorus halfway into the song); in the 2000s, two heavy metal artists, Ozzy Osbourne and Queensrÿche; and in the 2010s, *American Idol* alumna Haley Reinhart, rapper Jay Rock, and punk band Anti-Flag. In 2020, Stills performed an inspiring rendition with singer-actor Billy Porter at the 2020 Democratic National Convention. Interestingly, Richie Furay has been performing the song since 2013, when a promoter, booking his tour of Japan, mandated it in the contract.

A significant part of the song's effectiveness and the logic behind its unfixed details lay in its narrative voice. The singer in "For What It's Worth" is an innocent observer. Like Huck Finn, he is perceptive but unaware of the circumstances and cultural implications unfolding before him. The song's title, with its "little me" dismissiveness, reflects a self-effacing commentator who, in his inexperience and modesty, seems to say, here is my unassuming observation, "for what it's worth." He stands apart, neither protester nor counterprotester, but he will, as Stills said, "spread the news like the minstrels in the fifteenth century."[4] In the opening lines, the singer, or the minstrel, notes with uncertainty: "There's something happening here / But what it is, ain't exactly clear"—"ain't" further indicating his lack of sophistication. Stills signals his concern in the worried tone of the vocals, and Young sounds a subdued but definite alarm, a two-note ominous riff that rings a high E note on the first beat followed by a high B on the third, supported underneath by a plucked E chord and Martin's bass drum, mic'd to approximate a heartbeat. This arrangement backs all four stanzas. In line three the singer is startled to see "a man with a gun," presumably a police officer, which he may not have noticed immediately, as the gun, not the uniform, usurped his consciousness. Stanza one, thus, establishes the narrative voice and the impending danger.

In the chorus, the hook, the innocent observer reacts to the gravity of the situation and calls on listeners to pay attention. The time of innocence, indicated by "children," is over: "I think it's time we stop / Children, what's that sound? Everybody look what's going down." The melody quickens and backing vocals by Furay and Young add urgency and intensity, both of which will increase in the following stanzas and choruses. In the second stanza, the singer fears the "battle lines being drawn." He begins to side with the "young" demonstrators, who are only "*speaking* their minds" (italics mine)—an implication of nonviolence in contrast to the patrolman's gun. The stanza closes angrily as the singer notes "the resistance" to their expressing themselves, an anger intensified by Furay's harmonizing with Stills for the closing two words ("from behind"). The second chorus further intensifies the drama as Young adds a guitar run, the first of a series of bursts throughout the song. Low in intensity at first, the runs increase in volume and emotion.

In the third stanza, behind Stills's lead vocals, Young and Furay add *oohs* and *aahs* as the drama rises with "a thousand people in the street / singing songs" and holding signs that "mostly" say, "Hooray for our side." The image of the protesters is not derogatory, but emphasizes their youthfulness and naivete, which severely contrasts with the police and the portentousness of the stanza's opening line, "what a field day for the heat." The police, or "the heat," it seems, look forward to breaking up the protest with force and making arrests—anything to keep the demonstrators from "speaking their mind." After the third chorus, the singer makes his most astute observation, as Stills and Furay sing in unison to warn of paranoia, which can "creep" into hearts and psyches and then "strike deep" in a sudden, desperate, and disproportionate act. After this verse, Young plays a grinding staccato-like riff, which flies upward and fades away, suggesting a mind slipping into the irrational. The implication is that the police, "the man," will crush the young protesters from an irrational fear, for "step[ping] out of line" and challenging social codes. The song ends with Furay and Stills repeating the chorus three times with Stills breaking the melodic contours with passionate expression, signaling a warning about the escalating tensions not only on Sunset Boulevard but also in America with, in 1967, its expanding polarities between young and old, hawks and doves, and Blacks and whites, and other tensions that have infused the American psyche then and now. "For What It's Worth," not unlike a poem from William Blake's *Songs of Experience*, depicts the paranoiac fear of the empowered to silence all challenges to its authority. The song's continued relevance stems, in part, from its awareness of this paranoia and the inherent optimism in protest.

Like all things Buffalo Springfield, there is uncertainty as to the details of how the title was derived. Charlie Greene said he suggested the title while riding in a limousine after Stills said, "Let me play you this song for what it's worth." Furay's account is that Ahmet Ertegun had gone to Stills's house to hear new songs when Stills said, "I have another one, for what it's worth."[5] Either way, on December 5, the day *Buffalo Springfield* was released, the band rushed into the studio to record "For What It's Worth." Over the Springfield's objections, Greene and Stone produced the record. Backed with "Do I Have to Come Right Out and Say It," the single, with Ertegun's added parenthetical "(Stop, Hey What's That Sound)," was rushed out in California by the end of December to capitalize on the tension on the Strip, and then released nationally in early January. "For What It's Worth" first appeared on the *Billboard* charts on January 28, at #90, and steadily climbed to its peak position, #7 on April 1, fading away on May 6 after a fifteen-week run. The Springfield had a hit! Ertegun decided to re-release *Buffalo Springfield* in March with the hit as the opening track and dropping "Baby Don't Scold Me." The re-release fared little better than the initial release, reaching only #80 on the album charts.

New York City—January 1967

In the closing days of 1967, Buffalo Springfield flew to New York City for a ten-day engagement in support of Mitch Ryder and the Detroit Wheels at Ondine's, located on East 59th Street in the shadow of the Queensborough Bridge (now the Ed Koch Queensboro Bridge), also known as the 59th Street Bridge, as in Simon and Garfunkel's hit "The 59th Street Bridge Song (Feelin' Groovy)." Ondine's was among New York City's hippest clubs. Andy Warhol and his friends were frequent patrons, and the Doors made their highly successful New York City debut there, just weeks before the Springfield arrived. To warm up for the dates, the Springfield played the Night Owl Café, barely a five-minute walk from Stills and Furay's old apartment on Thompson Street.

Overall, the engagement did not go well. Despite its high profile, Ondine's was small, tiny by Los Angeles standards, and the Springfield had trouble balancing their sound. In addition, the band, staying in tight quarters, passed colds and sore throats to one another, which, predictably, had a drastic effect on their vocals and dispositions, especially performing as many as three sets a night. "It was quite hard to get it together," said Furay.[6] One evening, things went very wrong. Richie tells the story:

> It was a two-tiered stage. Stephen and I and Neil were on one level. Neil may have even been on the second level. Bruce and Dewey were definitely on the second level. Bruce kept hitting Stephen's head with his bass because he was always playing with his eyes closed, and he never knew what he was doing as he was rocking out and grooving to the music. He kept messing up Stephen's cowboy hat, knocking it off. . . .

Stephen threaten[ed] him: "If you do that one more time, I'm going to punch you out." Well, he did it one more time and he punched him out.[7]

For the third set that evening Stills played bass. Young's assessment that "we bombed out in New York," however, may be severe. Ertegun called the performances "exciting" and "mind boggling."[8] And there were some high points, like jams with Odetta and Otis Redding, who joined Dewey for a duet of "In the Midnight Hour," which brought the house down.

While in New York, Buffalo Springfield recorded new songs, including Young's "Mr. Soul," "the definitive take of the song," says Young. "That's the real Buffalo Springfield," Young continues. "Really a unified [collaboration]— everybody had their idea, and we all did 'em, and it worked." This was the kind of sound and feel the Springfield hoped to achieve on the first album. Unfortunately, that recording was lost or unplayable until 2001, with the release of the box set. Young called that take "better than all the other [released] versions combined."[9]

Those January recording sessions marked the beginning of the end for Greene and Stone. "Mr. Soul" was, in fact, their last credited production for the Springfield. In the studio, Greene lost patience with Stills's disparaging remarks and punched him out. The management team stayed on until the end of the year, at which time the band bought out their contract. On balance, the pair—absolute hustlers, shady characters, and big talkers—nonetheless believed in Buffalo Springfield and labored to take them into stardom. However, they failed in an important duty of a rock band manager: easing tension and interpersonal conflicts. The feuding between Stills and Young had been on and off since the early days at the Whisky. Furay said that while their clash has often been "blown . . . out of proportion," it was real.[10] "There was turmoil in the band all along," said Furay, and the managers did not know how to mediate the disputes. Instead, with Stills and Young, "they would not put one against the other, but they would definitely play one against another." They would appease each of their egos by telling each separately that the Springfield depended on him more than any other member. "You're the guy," they would tell each of them.[11] In truth, however, it is doubtful whether anyone could have reconciled the disagreements between the young but large egos of the irascible Stills and the uncommunicative Young, or as Bruce Palmer called the pair, "two spoiled little brats."[12] But where Greene and Stone especially failed the band was in the studio. They were not producers, and they should never have been behind the console.

Bruce Palmer

During the final days of the New York sessions in mid-January, Bruce Palmer was arrested on drug charges—for the second time. The first time was in early September 1966 and forced him to miss two or three gigs, with Jim Fielder filling in for him. This time was different. The Canadian was deported and away from the band for four months. With "For What It's Worth" rising in the charts, the band had recording sessions planned and a heavy touring schedule, including television shows. Buffalo Springfield scurried for replacements. For *Hollywood Palace*, a nationally broadcast variety show, Dickie Davis pretended to play bass with his back to the audience, seated on a runway slightly stage left to the lead singer's microphone. The Springfield performed "For What It's Worth" followed by the recently recorded "Mr. Soul." During Young's solo in "Mr. Soul," Davis was surprised to find Young right in front of him. "Neil walks down the runway and walks up to me and plays the solo from 'Mr. Soul' to me. I'm bopping along and I'm hoping I look like a bass player." It was caught on camera.[13] After the filming, the Springfield borrowed Love's Ken Forssi for a three-day, eight-set run at Gazzarri's on Sunset Strip, before hiring old friend Ken Koblun for the next dozen dates or so. In mid-February, Springfield roadie Miles Thomas took on the role of bassist for a performance on *The Smothers Brothers Show*. Jim Fielder then signed on from mid-February until the end of May for some fifty dates and session work. Fielder can be heard on "Everydays," which appeared on *Buffalo Springfield Again*, and "Pretty Girl Why" on *Last Time Around*. Palmer played on six of the ten tracks on *Buffalo Springfield Again*.

Palmer's deportation dealt a severe blow to the band's sound. Over the years, listeners have generally undervalued Palmer, as they frequently do bass players or drummers who do not compose or sing lead. But as Young wrote, "Bruce was the element that made us unique. . . . He was a complete original. He played like Motown, but he had an added flair that was totally Bruce. . . . A genius player. . . . After we lost him, we were never the same. It was the beginning of the end, right there."[14] Palmer not only helped to establish and hold down the groove for Stills's and Young's guitar interplay, but he also could be funky, as in "Leave," and surprising, as in "Mr. Soul," when—perhaps as a tribute to Otis Redding, whom he jammed with at Ondine's—he added a run lifted from "I Can't Turn You Loose" at the 1:24 mark. Dickie Davis recalls how other bassists admired Palmer: "When Buffalo Springfield first started playing at the Whisky a Go Go, the other musicians in town used to call going to see the Springfield, going to see Bruce. . . . He played pretty thrilling bass.

He could add some basslines in places where other people just kept this standard rhythm." Young writes, "Musicians would just stand there slack-jawed, watching and listening to him play." Davis also notes something else about Bruce in those early days: "At the time, poverty really weighed on him. Bruce didn't have any bass strings. . . . He used other people's discarded bottom E strings and strung four of them on his bass. . . . He still played beautifully and sounded great."[15] After his deportation, Palmer returned to the band at the beginning of June 1967. However, his drug intake increased, and he became more and more frustrated with Young and Stills. When he was arrested in late January 1968 and scheduled again for deportation, the Springfield fired him. Jim Messina was hired as his permanent replacement.

"Chemistry is the big thing in any group," Young understated, and Palmer was an essential element in the fragile chemistry of Buffalo Springfield.[16] Unlike his bandmates, he never sought the spotlight and never complained about any lack of attention from fans or managers. He never lobbied for one song or another, either in the studio or on stage, content to play what the others decided. His quietness led some to see him as inscrutable, even mystical, "the mystery man of the Buffalo," as one writer stated. Richie said he could be "quirky," but Davis said most of the time he was "very gentle, easy to get along with, unassuming." However, as Davis added, "he had another side and occasionally I encountered it," noting a time when during a disagreement Bruce "punched me in the face."[17] Palmer was also irresponsible. He neglected his wife and children, and he was careless if not reckless in his drug intake, favoring marijuana and LSD, which led to sloppy performances on stage and in the studio. When he was straight, his musicianship and personality made him an excellent fit for the Springfield. As Furay says, "The original chemistry—Dewey, Bruce, Stephen, Neil, and me—was as unique as you can get and it was impossible to duplicate that." In 2012, Young wrote, "If we hadn't lost Bruce, the sky would have been the limit for Buffalo Springfield . . . we would probably still be together today (if we had all lived)."[18] Palmer died of a heart attack in 2004 at age fifty-eight.

Neil Young

With Palmer's deportation, Neil Young started to pull away from Buffalo Springfield. Young's bandmates had long been skeptical about his commitment to the band. Stills noted that Young "never played a team sport in his life, so he [couldn't] make that kind of commitment." Dickie Davis, touted in one article as the "sixth" Buffalo, remarked, "I think Neil always thought of himself as an individual and was just using the band as a way to move his individual career ahead."[19] Still, in early May 1967, when Young informed the Springfield that he was leaving, the band was irate. They had just had their first hit, Palmer was due back within a month, they were getting national bookings, and they had started making some money, $1000 a show (equivalent to about $8000 in 2020). In 1969, Young told the *Toronto Daily Star* what his bandmates had long understood: "I never wanted to be in a group. . . . I came out to [Los Angeles] to make it as a single."[20]

Several recent events and band decisions may have prompted Young's announcement. Recently, Young had begun recording with Jack Nitzsche and members of the Wrecking Crew, and he felt bolstered by the just-completed "Expecting to Fly," which would appear on *Buffalo Springfield Again*, even though no other members of the Springfield played on the track. Moreover, Young was upset when the band decided to release Stills's "Bluebird," not "Mr. Soul," as the next single. "Mr. Soul" is a powerful record, but Stills and the others argued that it recycled the dominant riff of "Satisfaction," and thus sounded too similar to the Rolling Stones' hit. Besides, Young's high-pitched nasally voice had not yet proven radio friendly. "Burned," their first single featuring Young as lead vocal, had failed to chart. "Bluebird" peaked at a disappointing #58.

Furthermore, just prior to Young's announcement, the Springfield was booked for an appearance on *The Tonight Show Starring Johnny Carson*, the most popular late-night talk show in America. The band was excited, except for Young. In 1995, Young told *Mojo*, "Actually, the reason I initially left the group was because I didn't want to do [that show]. I thought it was belittling. . . . That audience wouldn't have understood us. We'd have been just a fuckin' curiosity to them."[21] The Springfield had to cancel the performance. But the most compelling reason for Young's resignation was that he felt too pressured. The tension with Stills was sometimes unmanageable, resulting at times in physical altercations, especially maddening after his relatively tranquil sessions with Nitzsche. In addition, the pressure of being in a band that was supposed to rival the Beatles weighed on him. "I just couldn't handle it toward the end. My nerves couldn't handle the trip." He denies that a solo career beckoned: "It wasn't me scheming on a solo career, it wasn't anything but my nerves. Everything started to go too fucking fast. . . . I needed more space. . . . I just wasn't mature enough to deal with it. I was very young." In a telling statement to his father, years after the group broke up, he said, "I should have been happy [in the Springfield], but it was the worst time of my life."[22]

If we look at Young's songs from the first and second Springfield albums, they reveal a questioning and even tortured psyche—from "Clancy" and "Out of My Mind" to "Mr. Soul," "Expecting to Fly," and "Broken Arrow," whose fragmented production and jarring movements and images reveal cluttered and confused personae. In "Mr. Soul," Young's singer "drop[s] by" for a psychological wellness check. He addresses his "soul" with an ironic lyrical lightheartedness ("my head is the event of the season") delivered in end and internal rhyme ("*down* on a *frown*" for example), indicating that the singer is locked into an impenetrable private internal world. Through the song, Young questions the significance of fan attention, the depth of his art, and the possible changes fame will work on him. "Expecting to Fly," with Nitzsche's guidance, receives an effective baroque production, complete with strings, English horn, and choir, and reflects Nitzsche's work with producer Phil Spector on such classics as the Righteous Brothers' "(You're My) Soul and Inspiration" (1966) and Ike and Tina Turner's "River Deep—Mountain High" (1966). In the song, Young comes close to apologizing or explaining his decision to leave the Springfield, personified by "babe," a soon-to-be ex-lover. Young is now "expecting to fly" in much the same way the Springfield had expected "to fly" into stardom. The singer wonders if he could "ever wave goodbye," but in recent months he has "stumbled" and "fumbled" and needs to leave as "the love . . . was gone." He expresses his gratefulness and love to his bandmates: "If I never lived without you / Now you know I'd die," and, "If I never said I loved you / Now you know I'd try." These four lines, which begin the closing stanza, are typical of Young's ambiguity and indirectness— in song and in life. Note, for example, the double negative here. Dickie Davis summarized what most irritated the band about Young: "Neil would just disappear, and you didn't know where he was, and he wouldn't answer your phone call."[23]

Young performed with Buffalo Springfield until the end of May. Palmer returned in the first week in June to take over for Fielder and, after a few dates as a foursome, the band added Doug Hastings from the Daily Flash to replace Young, an impossible task. At the Monterey Pop Festival, David Crosby supported the band on rhythm guitar and backing vocals. (See fig. 5.) Young continued recording with Nitzsche, but the results were mixed and could not live up to "Expecting to Fly." Furthermore, Young could not get ATCO to release him from his contract. Regardless, Young planned to move to England with Nitzsche and Denny Bruce, a manager and future producer. One day the three were riding in Nitzsche's car when "Mr. Soul" played on the radio with the deejay referring to Young as a former member of Buffalo

FIG. 5 Richie Furay with Buffalo Springfield at the Monterey Pop Festival, June 1967, with Dewey Martin on drums and David Crosby filling in for Neil Young. Photo by Henry Diltz.

Springfield. "That snapped something in his mind," Bruce said. "You could see Neil thinking. And all of a sudden we're not moving to England and he's back in the fucking group."[24] This after Nitzsche had sold his house and the three had moved in together "expecting to fly" to London imminently. After the Springfield performed a six-day run at the Fillmore in San Francisco, with Muddy Waters and Richie Havens, they dismissed Hastings, and Young rejoined them on stage on August 12.

Young's commitment to any group has only been temporary and in the moment. He would be an off-and-on again member of not just the Springfield, but also Crosby, Stills, Nash & Young and Crazy Horse. "Neil has proven that he isn't a team player," says Richie, who has been frustrated by Young many times over the years. "He's a genius, an enigma," Stills says.[25] Perhaps, with Bob Dylan, he epitomizes rock and roll's Emersonian individual: "I shun father and mother and wife and brother, when my genius calls me," wrote Ralph Waldo Emerson in 1841. "I would write on the lintels of the door-post, *Whim*. I hope it is somewhat better than whim at last, but we cannot spend the day in explanation. Expect me not to show cause why I seek or why I exclude company."[26]

However, a recording contract did call, and Ertegun demanded a second Buffalo Springfield album with Neil Young.

Buffalo Springfield Again

With their first album, Buffalo Springfield had a unified objective: to transfer their sound on stage to vinyl. However, no such unified effort or objective marked their approach to their follow-up album. Furay said that "the very first Buffalo Springfield record is the only group record. With the second record, people started to bring in other people. . . . Neil and Steve, in particular, would go off to experiment with other musicians."[27] *Buffalo Springfield Again* was recorded over nine chaotic months with Palmer and Young absent from gigs and sessions and with eight producers or coproducers earning credit. (Generally, band members, except Palmer, received production or coproduction credits on songs they wrote and sang, with additional coproduction credits going to Greene and Stone for "Mr. Soul," Nitzsche for "Expecting to Fly," and Ertegun for "Everydays" and "Bluebird.") The fracturing of the Springfield is reflected not only in these credits but also in both the lack of unison lead vocals by Stills and Furay, three on the first album, none here, and Young's ambitious "Broken Arrow." "Broken Arrow" assembles musical fragments like Dewey Martin's singing the opening lines of "Mr. Soul" to a backing track of screaming crowds, parts of "Down Down Down" (a Young-Springfield track unreleased until the box set), a ballpark organ, and a light jazz segment featuring a clarinet. These elements are held together by the recurring refrain of a somber image of an Indian holding a broken arrow, a sign of peace or, in certain contexts, surrender. Young said, "It's just an image of being very scared and mixed up," like both composer and band.[28] "Broken Arrow" marks a fitting close to the musical collage that is *Buffalo Springfield Again*.

At *Again*'s release in November 1967, the two most important rock music magazines issued lukewarm reviews, noting the album's eclecticism but also its lack of cohesion or a trademark group sound. An anonymous reviewer in *Rolling Stone* wrote, "This album sounds as if every member of the group is satisfying their own musical needs," resulting in "a musically and vocally interesting album" but "no blend. . . . It is simply a very good, but not great, second effort by a highly talented group." Albert Bouchard in *Crawdaddy!* thought that *Again* lacked originality, sounding at times like the Beatles, the Byrds, the Association, Moby Grape, and Richie Havens, and found songs like "Mr. Soul," "Good Time Boy," and "Rock & Roll Woman" derivative.

But, he concludes, *Again* "is so filled with so many different kinds of beautiful music . . . that you'll really love it if you aren't hung on originality. . . . Every song is . . . well-structured and carried out." John Gabree, in *Downbeat*, sneered that Buffalo Springfield may be skilled in different musics, but the group "never emerges with a sound of their own. They are almost the Bobby Darins of groups . . . the album lacks focus." Tom Phillips in the *New York Times* was more enthusiastic but tentative, finding the album "one of the most varied and weird and beautiful things I've heard."[29] New standards for evaluating the rock album may have influenced critics' response to *Again*.

By 1967, the album had become the benchmark by which to judge the artistic achievement of rock artists. Exhausted with albums featuring a couple of hit singles, maybe a few decent tracks, and always filler, critics and fans expected major rock artists to make a sonically, if not thematically, cohesive statement throughout the album. Rock artists, too, expected it of themselves and either rose to the challenge to take their place among the elite or, if still producing only singles, remained in the lower tiers of pop. After years of producing hit singles for the Beach Boys, Brian Wilson took his inspiration for *Pet Sounds* from the Beatles: "*Rubber Soul*," he said, "is a complete statement, damn it, and I want to make a complete statement, too!"[30] Therefore, the diversity of sounds and arrangements on *Buffalo Springfield Again* might have put off some critics, who viewed the album as a loose collection of songs, a kind of compilation. However, *Again*'s accomplishment lies in its ability to juxtapose various forms and sounds, innovative and traditional, into a statement about what rock and roll, always a hybrid music, is and can be. The album works because there are no weak tracks. There are the ferocious rock and roll of "Mr. Soul" and the softer California rock, with sweet harmonies, of "Rock & Roll Woman"; elaborate productions like the psychedelic "Expecting to Fly" and Stills's "Bluebird," ethereal and mysterious, with strong folk-rock rhythms that lead us into what Greil Marcus would call "the old, weird America"[31]; the light soulfulness of the jazzy "Everydays" and the Everly Brothers–influenced "A Child's Claim to Fame"; the Stax funk of "Good Time Boy"; the blues-rock of "Hung Upside Down"; and the experimental art rock or quasi-psychedelic "Broken Arrow." *Again* is a musical collage of America, at once taking us back and leading us forward.

Over the years, *Again* has come to be considered a pop music masterpiece. Robert Christgau, the self-proclaimed dean of American rock critics, lists the album as a required holding for a basic record library, and Colin Larkin ranks it #165 on the *Virgin All-Time Top 1000 Albums*. Similarly, Robert Dimery places it on his list, organized alphabetically by decade, of *1001 Albums You Must Hear*

Before You Die, and, in 2020, *Rolling Stone* ranked *Again* #2 on the "Highest Rated Albums of 1967," behind only Elvis Presley's *How Great Thou Art* and ahead of other classics like *Sgt. Pepper's Lonely Hearts Club Band*, Dylan's *John Wesley Harding*, and two albums by Jimi Hendrix (*Axis: Bold as Love* and *Are You Experienced*).[32]

Furay the Songwriter—"A Child's Claim to Fame"

Furay had been experimenting with writing songs since high school. While he placed no songs on the Springfield's first album, he found a home for three of his songs on *Again*, two that audiences at a Furay show still expect to hear today: "A Child's Claim to Fame" and "Sad Memory." "A Child's Claim" is the first of many songs in which Furay would couch angry words in sweet melodies, a pattern many listeners have missed over the years, believing Richie to be too cheerful a songwriter. Peter Knobler, author and former editor-in-chief of *Crawdaddy!*, commented: "I met them in 1970 backstage at the Fillmore East, and we did an interview. I remember my first question—because as an interviewer, you want to establish right away that this is not the normal sort of 'what's-your-favorite-color' interview. . . . So what dawned on me was . . . if you listen to Richie sing, it's happy, happy, happy. If you listen to the words, it's not so happy. . . . He said, 'You know, you're absolutely right.' . . . And we started talking about it, and the interview went perfectly well."[33] On "A Child's Claim to Fame," Furay sings in a weary voice of his frustration with Neil Young, his indecisive and uncommunicative bandmate. "He was in [the Springfield], he was out, he was in, and he was out. He wasn't at Monterey. We were gonna do the *Johnny Carson Show* and he didn't show up to get on the plane that day."[34]

In the title, Furay refers to Young as a child, who is stuck in "make believe" and explains his actions with a "lullaby" (alibi?), which can no longer "pacify" the singer. The cause of the disruption, according to Furay and the song, is Young's ego and self-centeredness, which seem to give him a childish, even self-delusional, "claim to fame." Young might disagree by citing many of his Springfield songs, like "Out of My Mind," "Broken Arrow," and "Mr. Soul," the track just previous to "A Child's Claim," all of which are filled with self-doubt, self-questioning, and Young's fear of fame. After the brief instrumental intro, Furay begins the song with "well," a kind of sigh as if to say, "here we go again." Throughout the song, he extends the long vowels to voice his exasperation: *goes, day, why, I, lies, lullaby*, and more. To suggest the endless pattern of Young's continued noncommitment, Furay ends the song with a repetition of the first stanza: "Well, there goes another day . . ."

An early example of a country-rock ballad, "Child's Claim" has a moderate tempo with Richie holding down the rhythm on acoustic guitar with Palmer on bass and Martin on drums—Martin might have felt he was back in Nashville, where he had honed his chops with Carl Perkins, Patsy Cline, and Charlie Rich. Stills and Young add a gentle potency, playing off one another and trading solos as one of Richie's early guitar heroes, James Burton, emphasizes the countryness of the song with his dobro fills and solo from the 1:28–1:44 mark. Ironically, "Child's Claim" was produced by Young, who—with Stills and Furay—sings harmony and who called in Burton to overdub his dobro when Richie was not there. Furay did not meet Burton until almost fifty years later. "Child's Claim" was a staple in the Springfield's repertoire. They performed it at Monterey just before they recorded it. Furay said the song, which was engineered by future Poco member Jim Messina, served as "a sort of blueprint for Poco."[35]

In 2011, Buffalo Springfield performed "Child's Claim" on their reunion tour. Young surprised Richie in Santa Barbara: "I start the lick [*imitates guitar*]," says Richie, "and, [*imitating Neil Young*] 'Hey, stop! Stop! Did you write that song about me?' Five thousand people, you know, out there in the audience and Neil stops the song and . . . I'm stunned. 'It's like, um, well, well, yeah, maybe, I mean, yeah!'"[36] The Springfield never really discussed lyrics with one another: "I don't remember getting into any real deep discussions about what we wrote. . . . A lot of the songs back then were pretty simple, and you could pretty much understand them. But as I go back and listen to them, Neil's songs had deeper meanings to them, like 'Flying on the Ground Is Wrong.' I probably should have asked him what some of these songs were about [especially since I sang lead on some of them]."[37] In the case of "Child's Claim," Young seemed to recognize the song was about him, if not immediately then soon after. On the Springfield's next and last album, *Last Time Around*, he saves his only lead vocal on the album for "I Am A Child," an apparent rebuttal to "Child's Claim" or an answer song in the country music tradition of Hank Thompson's "The Wild Side of Life" (1952) answered by Kitty Wells in "It Wasn't God Who Made Honky Tonk Angels" (1952), or Hank Locklin's "Please Help Me I'm Falling" (1960) with a response by Skeeter Davis in "(I Can't Help You) I'm Falling Too" (1960). Like those songs, "I Am a Child" imitates the original form of the initial song. Young uses the same country ballad form as Furay's "Child's Claim," the same image of a child, and the same technique of concluding the song by repeating the first stanza.

Young begins "I Am a Child" with a waah-waah harmonica, perhaps mocking what he perceives as the whining of Furay and, for that matter, Stills. Young then sings, without apology and almost insolently, "I am a child"—the lack of the contraction (*I'm*) adding emphasis. He relishes his innocence, noting that his addressee(s) "can't conceive of the pleasure in my smile." He concludes stanza one with, perhaps, sarcasm, "It's lots of fun to have you there." The chorus, however, is direct and biting. "I gave to you," Young sings, his voice still soft and masking bitterness, "now you give to me." Young might be referring to his overall contribution to the band or, more specifically, the songs he wrote that Furay sang. Somewhat arrogantly, he sings that he would like to see what "you" (could refer to Furay and Stills) learned from me and tests his addressee(s) with a rather abstruse question. "What is the color when black is burned?" His sarcasm is more direct in verse two: "You make the rules, you say what's fair / It's lots of fun to have you there." In short, "I Am a Child" is a biting response cloaked in a tender melody, soft voice, and easy rhythm.

"Sad Memory" and "Good Time Boy"

"'Sad Memory' was an accident," says Furay. "I had no plan on recording it when I went to the studio that day. . . . The guys were late. Stephen and Neil hadn't showed up. I'm sitting there with the engineer and I said, 'Well, let's go ahead and get a sound on my acoustic guitar.' So I started playing the song, and while I was just playing through the song, Neil came in and heard it and said, 'We gotta record that one.'" The only two musicians on the record are Neil and Richie. No overdubs, nothing else needed. They left it alone to capture the full emotion and poignancy of a sad memory. Richie explains its inspiration: "It's a break-up song. Basically, I was in love with a girl in college, and I'm telling you, man, if that relationship would have continued on, I may not have headed off to New York to be a folk singer."[38]

The positioning of "Sad Memory" on the album, between the rocking blues and fuzztone guitar of "Hung Upside Down," the opening track to Side Two, and the spirited "Good Time Boy" accents its sparse production and raw emotion. "Sad Memory" begins with a gentle strum on Richie's acoustic guitar and, after a slight pause, his vocals—a highlight on an album of highlights—wistful but strong and never melodramatic. He re-creates an ambivalent memory of holding hands and strolling in the summer shade and breeze with his girlfriend. But the girlfriend breaks off the relationship, and the singer draws in the listener, seeking support and understanding: "Did you ever love a girl? Who walked right out on you?" As the singer tries to move on and "forget the past," the memory haunts him, and the song concludes by repeating the opening line: "Soft winds blow in the summer night." Furay's vocal performance is supported by Young's bluesy guitar runs, which enter at the 1:24 mark to underscore the melancholy of the singer. In addition, the echoey sound of Young's guitar adds a haunting effect, reflecting, so it seems, the deep recesses of the singer's torn psyche. The arrangement and production, simple and uncluttered, yield full command to Furay's impressive vocals. When Buffalo Springfield performed "Sad Memory" in Oakland during their reunion tour, Young introduced the song: "This is a sad story. . . . I love this song."[39]

"Good Time Boy," Richie's third song on *Again*, represents the only light-hearted moment of the album. Furay wrote the song for Dewey Martin, a very different voice and personality from his own. Martin fancied himself an R&B singer in the style of Otis Redding and Wilson Pickett and enjoyed a boisterous and rollicking night on the town; Martin, indeed, was the "Good Time Boy" in the song or "good ol' Dew," as he sings. The track is a pastiche of the Stax sound, inclusive of Palmer's funky bass, a lively horn section provided by the American Soul Train from Louisiana, and Martin's raw, snarling vocals with his breaking of melody lines, soulful grunts, stutterings like "now-now-now-now," and ad libs like "sock it to me" and "groove it on me now." In performance, "Good Time Boy" replaced Martin's cover of "Midnight Hour" and his lead vocals on "Nobody's Fool," another Furay original, which Richie would rearrange and record twice with Poco.[40] "Good Time Boy" gave Martin a new opportunity to showcase his front man talent, as he would step out from behind the drums, yielding his kit to Stills.

Rodney Bingenheimer, a Los Angeles deejay, said, "Dewey was always the friendliest and most fun of the band," while Jim Delehant described him as a "sharp dresser" and "classic cut-up," who loved pranks and stylish dress. Mark Volman of the Turtles remembers that Dewey liked to "showcase his jackets as much as his voice."[41] Martin, however, could be tiring, overly talkative, and obnoxious, especially after ingesting amphetamines. Young said, "He was one of the reasons the group broke up. We just couldn't hack him anymore. . . . [He] just bugged the hell out of us. If he hadn't been a darn good drummer the group wouldn't have had him." Stills sometimes had problems with Martin's drumming, believing Martin sometimes pushed or rushed the beat. Furay, who had Martin serve as his best man at his wedding, deflected

Stills's statement. He simply said, "[Dewey] just had this positive attitude on life, and I loved that."[42]

As the Springfield's "merry-go-round" year of 1967 drew to a close, Furay was optimistic about the band's future. After all, the original band was back together—after some additional difficulty with Palmer just before Christmas; Greene and Stone were gone; *Again* was highly accomplished; "Expecting to Fly" had just been released as a single, and additional recording sessions and high-profile gigs were scheduled for the new year. Richie expressed his hopefulness in the absolutely bubbly lyrics and rhythms of "What a Day," which the Springfield would record in January with Stills singing lead. "It's a good morning and I'm feeling fine," wrote Richie, who calls on the listener (his bandmates?) to "smile" as "a frown would be passé . . . it's such a wonderful day." Unfortunately, Furay's hopefulness for the band would be short-lived and, coincidentally, the Springfield's "What a Day" would not be released until the box set in 2001.

CHAPTER 5

"Anyway Bye Bye"

The End of Buffalo Springfield

The first two singles following "For What It's Worth," "Bluebird" (#58) and "Rock & Roll Woman" (#44), failed to crack the Top 40. The group hoped that "Expecting to Fly," their first single since the release of *Buffalo Springfield Again*, would fare better and provide momentum for a band hoping for a better 1968. Entering the charts on January 13, at #99, "Expecting to Fly" climbed only one notch the following week, to #98, before falling into pop singles oblivion. Neil Young was crushed and the band deflated.

For the last few months, Bruce Palmer's drug use had been becoming more and more problematic, and Palmer was losing patience with Stills and Young. "I was sick and tired of [Stills's and Young's] antics, the dueling that was constant between Stephen and Neil."[1] How much Stills and Young fought is open to speculation. Certainly, at times, it turned physical. Dickie Davis, who took over as manager for Greene and Stone, put it this way: "Yeah, well, they occasionally got along. They mostly fought. I remember one time in Seattle [March 1967] at some club they actually came to blows. I used to tell people that Neil was at a disadvantage because he had a hollow-body guitar and Stills had a solid-body guitar, which gave him an advantage in a fight. They were at each other a lot."[2] Nancy Furay remembers them tossing chairs at one another backstage, but Richie said, "They could clash a little bit, but a lot of people have blown that out of proportion. If there were two guys that were like brothers, it was Stephen and Neil."[3] Jim Messina, who would play a vital role in the Springfield in their last year, said, "Those two really did make some great music together. And I never saw them fuss or fight or even talk bad about one another. Maybe they did in other circles."[4] In 1999, Young explained, "That was all blown out of perspective. You got to remember we were 21, 22, or 23 years old, whatever we were, and under an immense amount of pressure, everything happening at once. We reacted like normal people. A couple of guitar players."[5] In 1970, Stills dismissed the issue: "Neil is just about my best friend in the whole world."[6] About all we can say with certainty is that the two young, ambitious musicians had an intense, competitive, and often volatile relationship that helped produce great rock and roll.

Palmer Out, Messina In, Young Out, Young In

The evening of January 26, 1968, proved disastrous for the Springfield. After a concert at the University of California, Irvine, Stills and Young had to be pulled apart by Martin during a backstage scuffle. That night, on the way home from the concert, Bruce Palmer was busted again for drugs—twice. The first time he was pulled over for speeding when the police officer discovered he had no license, but he did have an open bottle of alcohol, marijuana, and an underage girl. Released on bail, Palmer planned to spend the night at the Tropicana Motel in West Hollywood, a favorite haunt of rock stars in the 1960s and 1970s and about a fifteen-to-twenty-minute walk to the Troubadour. Palmer called the police to complain about the guests below him. The officers came to his room instead and found him in possession of marijuana. Palmer was detained and then deported within a couple of weeks.

The Springfield sought a permanent replacement for Palmer. Curiously, no band members wanted any of the musicians who had previously filled in for Bruce—neither Jim Fielder, Ken Koblun, nor Ken Forssi. Stills and Furay remembered Mike Scott from the Au Go-Go Singers and flew him in for an audition, but, as Richie says, "the chemistry wasn't right."[7] Scott, who arrived in a suit, was still an East Coast folky playing stand-up acoustic bass. Jim Messina, only twenty-one at the time, requested an audition and was hired. Messina, a gifted engineer, had been working in studios since he was fifteen and leading bands as a guitarist playing mostly surf music. When Messina was seventeen, in 1965, Tutti Camarata hired him as a sound engineer at Sunset Sound Recorders, especially to work with younger musicians. In the summer of 1967, he was assigned to the Springfield, working on about half of the tracks as an engineer on *Again*, including Furay's "A Child's Claim to Fame" and Young's "Broken Arrow." Messina thought the gig with the Springfield was temporary. He had just been offered a job as a producer for A&M Records, founded by Herb Alpert and Jerry Moss, but the job would not start for three months. "So I told them I would temporarily work with them as their bass player."[8] Messina proved reliable, compatible, and a very capable player.

The Springfield played a few gigs with Messina in early February and, then, with no dates scheduled until March, they returned to the studio to complete a third album. Young, however, failed to show for the sessions and, in his typical fashion, failed to communicate with the band. Furthermore, Stills was becoming less committed to the band. Fed up with the drama and problems, he had begun playing with other musicians, including Jimi Hendrix, Eric Clapton, Al Kooper, David Crosby, and Buddy Miles. "I could definitely see the end coming," he said.[9] But anxious to recoup his recent advance, to remove Greene and Stone, Ahmet Ertegun insisted on a third album. With Young absent and Stills with little interest, it was left to Furay and Messina to assemble a cohesive album from completed tracks and fragments. At the end of February, the pair traveled to New York to play the album for Ertegun and other ATCO executives. The album was promptly rejected. They would have to try harder.

With Young out of the band, Buffalo Springfield did photo shoots as a quartet for a new album cover and then promo pictures for an April tour in support of the Beach Boys. Within days of completing the photo sessions, Young decided to rejoin the band and the photos were redone. "I was going crazy, joining and quitting and joining again. . . . So I'd quit, then I'd come back 'cause [the music] sounded so good. It was a constant problem"[10]—especially for his bandmates.

Drug Bust

Buffalo Springfield was booked to play two nights, March 22–23, with Jefferson Airplane and Canned Heat, to inaugurate the Kaleidoscope, a new club on the Sunset Strip. On March 19, while the band was rehearsing in the home of Susan Haffey, Stills's girlfriend, with whom he was living, the police responded to noise complaints from neighbors and told the band to quiet down. On the following evening, after repeated noise complaints, the police interrupted a post-rehearsal jam session with the Springfield and Eric Clapton. This time, as the door opened, the officers were greeted by a gust of marijuana smoke. Stills reacted quickly and fled through the bedroom window, and he made his way to the home of Dennis Wilson. In total, the police arrested approximately fifteen attendees, including Furay, Young, Messina, and Richie's wife, Nancy. It was a humiliating experience for Nancy and Richie, who were forcibly showered, deloused, and placed in a cell. Nancy's mom read about it in the newspaper the next day when a coworker showed her the article. Minutes before the bust, Richie and Nancy had left with Martin, but the couple returned to ask Messina about a meeting Richie had planned for the next day. Ultimately, Furay and the others received "slaps on the wrist," found guilty of disturbing the peace, but Clapton faced deportation.[11] Furay testified on Clapton's behalf, and Clapton remained in the States. On the poster featuring caricatures of musicians for *Echo in the Canyon* (2018), Andrew Slater's documentary on the Los Angeles music scene, the drug bust is referenced in a drawing of Stills halfway out a window with a police officer tugging at his jeans and waving a baton.

Immediately after the arrests, Young quit the Springfield—for the third time. Ertegun persuaded Neil to remain until all commitments were fulfilled, including the April tour with the Beach Boys and a few post-tour dates. The executive hoped that the tour, with its steady gigs and forced togetherness, would reignite their enthusiasm for both the music and one another and that the group would move into the future. While the Springfield had to cancel the two gigs at the Kaleidoscope that weekend, they did perform on Sunday evening at the new club for a hastily arranged benefit for the Radio Strike Fund, which supported striking deejays at free-form progressive rock FM stations in Pasadena and San Francisco. Along with the Springfield, the show featured Jefferson Airplane, Steppenwolf, Quicksilver Messenger Service, and others, with, according to Pete Johnson in the *Los Angeles Times*, each "act in top form." But the critic asserted that the Springfield "stole the show," leaving "no doubt that it is the best American group to emerge in the last couple of years."[12] In one of their new songs that evening, Young may have delivered his final notice to the band. Accompanying himself on piano, he sang "Birds": "When you see me fly away without you. . . . It's over. It's over."

Problems continued for the band. During the last week in March, after a performance in Fresno, Dickie Davis found himself in an argument with Dewey Martin over who would drive a rental car. Martin tossed the keys somewhere in the parking lot, and Davis quit. It was his last straw. Davis had been with the band since the very beginning, when Stills picked up Furay at the airport in 1966. Davis was on the payroll and took care of tasks large (helping procure a record contract) and small (chauffeuring them to gigs). In late 1966, while playing in the San Francisco area, where Stills completed "For What It's Worth," the band was broke. "There was no money for food, so I thought, I'll call my parents. . . . They sent me $300 and we went out and bought food and we ate. . . . I thought of myself as one of them."[13] Before the Springfield, Davis had worked on stage lighting in clubs on Sunset Strip. He had no experience as a manager when he replaced Greene and Stone, and the band thought of him more as a friend than someone to provide career direction. He also had a temper that, along with his sarcasm, could aggravate situations, as he did once with Bill Graham of the Fillmore West and East. Davis, however, was always well-intentioned. "My whole focus on everything I did was to advance the band. . . . I would have done anything to keep that group together. . . . They were five unique pieces that fit really well."[14] Significantly, Davis helped broker the separation from Greene and Stone and helped the members gain their publishing rights.

The End

"This is it, gang," Stephen Stills announced to five thousand fans in the Long Beach Sports Arena on May 5, 1968. Then, for over a minute, the guitarists tuned their instruments—a constant practice between songs that irritated former member Bruce Palmer[15]—before opening their last show with "Rock & Roll Woman." Excited fans rushed the stage, and an arena official stopped the song to exhort them to return to their seats, threatening to end the performance. A bootleg recording of the event, staticky and unevenly balanced, nonetheless reveals the band's live sound with their beautiful vocal harmonies, fierce guitar interplay, and relentless energy. The Springfield may have been "scared" and "tense," as Young declared, but they performed a commanding set, concluding with an almost twenty-three minute version of "Bluebird."[16]

Within days, Stills was in the studio with Mike Bloomfield and Al Kooper for what resulted in *Super Session* by Bloomfield, Kooper, and Stills, a #12 album. Young mapped out *Neil Young*, his first solo album, which failed to chart. As Young began recording in August, Furay and Messina initiated rehearsals for Poco. In the fall, Martin had assembled a group of musicians and hit the road as Buffalo Springfield, which angered the others. After a lawsuit, he added *New* before *Buffalo*, which promoters generally ignored. In the 1980s Bruce Palmer formed the Springfield, and after Martin joined, they rechristened the band Buffalo Springfield Revisited, with promoters often using small font size for *Revisited* or even dropping it altogether. In the 1990s Martin went out as Buffalo Springfield Again. Furay filed a cease-and-desist order in 1992, but Martin used the name for a few more dates in 1994 before stopping. Asked about the court order served on the best man at his wedding,

Richie said it was misleading for Martin to use the name. "It should have been left alone. I mean we were what we were."[17]

But in 1968, as spring turned to summer, Furay and Messina were left to deliver a Buffalo Springfield album to ATCO.

Last Time Around

Buffalo Springfield's final album was more of a compilation than even *Buffalo Springfield Again*. "*Last Time Around* was pieced together by Jim Messina because neither Steve nor I gave a shit. . . . We just didn't want to do it, y'know. It's weird," said Young.[18] Messina, with Furay's help, was left to sift through tapes to find enough quality material for an acceptable album. The project required overdubs and cutting and pasting. Furay worked alongside Messina but was little help in the mechanics of production. "I have to tell you that I wish that I had paid a little more attention to what was going on," said Richie, "because I'm still, to this day, not very comfortable [with the technological process of making records]. . . . I don't even have a little studio in my own home."[19] Messina was grateful for Furay's presence: "Richie was very sweet to be there because otherwise nobody else would've been there. I would've been doing it all on my own. He was there to give me some moral support, to answer questions if I needed them answered."[20]

Last Time Around succeeded against all odds. It was released at the end of July to very favorable reviews. Barry Gifford in *Rolling Stone* raved: "As a final testament to their multi-talent, the Buffalo Springfield have released *Last Time Around*, the most beautiful record they've ever made." In the *New York Times*, Ellen Sander praised the album and the band, calling their previous albums "quietly beautiful" and "consistently overlooked and underrated," and added that *Last Time Around* "is perhaps their finest, albeit their parting, hour. . . . The entire album has a fresh, natural feeling about it." Robert Christgau defined the album as "Buffalo Springfield's beautiful farewell album" with its "country elements . . . incorporated into a total style."[21]

Despite the reviews, Neil Young was not only displeased with the album, but he was also unappreciative of Furay's and Messina's efforts, which prevented a costly settlement with ATCO. "It was such a disgraceful mess," he said, "that I can't bear to listen to it again. . . . The mixes are incredibly awful." Reminded of Young's comments, Furay laughed sarcastically: "That was his choice. . . . If he wanted to be there, he could have been there."[22] With no hit single, no supporting tour, no interviews or media appearances, and little promotion from ATCO, *Last Time Around*, pushed by fan devotion and positive reviews, reached a #42 chart position, the band's highest.

Last Time Around features twelve tracks: five composed by Stills, three by Furay, two by Young, one by Messina, and another by Furay-Young (but mostly Furay). The only song Young sings is, tellingly, "I Am a Child," his response to Furay's "Child's Claim to Fame." Revealing of the Springfield's state of flux during the recording sessions, only one track, "On the Way Home," features all members (i.e., either Palmer or Messina), and seven tracks feature only one or two members ("Four Days Gone," "Carefree Country Day," "Special Care," "The Hour of Not Quite Rain," "Questions," "I Am a Child," "Kind Woman"). The opening track, "On the Way Home," a brisk folk rocker, sung by Furay and written by Young, represents, as the title suggests, another statement of farewell from the capricious but ingenious singer-songwriter-guitarist. Unusual for a pop song, the words of the title do not appear in the lyrics. Young's singer explains that "when the dream came," the beginning days of the Springfield, the fast pace of being in a promising rock-and-roll band drove him dizzy, "insane . . . like a smoke ring day when the wind blows." After he considers himself from the perspective of his bandmates ("I saw myself as you knew me"), perhaps thinking of "Child's Claim," he ends with a proclamation of love and a plea for understanding: "And I love you / Can you see me now? . . . And I love you / Can you feel it now?"

"On the Way Home" is an exciting production. It begins with the falsetto harmonies of *whew-whew-whew* (marking the speed of the Springfield's short journey), which feed into a driving rhythm powered by Martin's no-frills drumming and Palmer's percolating bass. Along the way, the track features brief ethereal strings (1:34–1:42, 1:56–2:06), acoustic guitar fills and vibraphone taps by Stills, and carefully placed *whews*, *aahs*, *oohs*, and *I-love-you*s. Furay's spirited vocal performance slightly elongates key words: "dream," "eyes," "insane," and "wind," among others, to merge melody and meaning. It all comes to a dramatic stop at 2:25. Messina, engineering the session, recalls that the band had grown exhausted with multiple takes: "It was about 10 o'clock at night, and I said, 'Why don't you guys come back in tomorrow around 11 or 12 and I'll have this done.'" Messina arrived early the next morning: "I edited the tapes together, so that all the verses and choruses were where they needed to be and they were in time." In the days before digital recording, such editing was tedious and required surgical precision. Messina stretched out a tape in an Editall Block, cut the tape with a razor at the precise spot, then attached it to the master, which he did many times to get the opening track to *Last Time Around*. "Then, I believe we took and added some overdubs and voices to it."[23] In the fall, Ertegun released it as a single, but it stalled at #82. Well into the 2010s, the song remains in setlists by both Furay and Young.

By *Last Time Around*, the Springfield had three gifted songwriters, all unique in their approach. Young looked within and wrote introspective songs about his self-concerns, confusion, and anguish. ("I'm in pieces on the ground.") Especially in the Springfield years, he used songs to journey through himself. His songs were a way for him to analyze himself and figure himself out. He often presented distinctive but abstruse images and innovative means of expression. He experimented more freely than the others with production ("Expecting to Fly") and song structures ("Broken Arrow"). On the other hand, Stills used existing song structures from a variety of genres, which he synthesized with his rock-and-roll sensibility. Young and Furay could be straight country whereas Stills approached country and other forms from a rock perspective—compare "Child's Claim" and "I Am a Child" with the country-rock of "Go and Say Goodbye." Stills's lyrics, direct and crisp, looked outward, away from the self, at a world gone wrong ("For What It's Worth") or at people who might have disappointed his singers. On "Pretty Girl Why," from *Last Time Around*, Stills uses a melancholy soft jazz, almost lounge rhythm, to pose a question—"Pretty girl, why not love me?"—and to plead for her to give "the minstrel boy . . . peace amidst the horror" of his battle with unrequited love. In "Questions," also on *Last Time*, he asks his lover, "Where are we goin', love? / What are *you* feelin'?" (Stills combined "Questions" with "Carry On" to form the opening track to CSN&Y's second album, *Déjà vu*, 1970). While the "I" in Young's and Furay's songs generally represent the composer himself, the "I" in a Stills song is more likely a character who may or may not be a mask for the composer. On "Special Care," a pounding blues rocker, Stills presents an angry, perhaps paranoid singer who rails first at someone in the window and then at a person on the corner: "You there, do you think I'm . . . playing the fool? . . . Would you like to shoot me down?" At the conclusion, the song mocks the concept that "all men are created equal" and suggests that if we do not care for the "forsaken" (homeless, mentally disabled, etc.) that they will "burn your house down." Stills plays all instruments on the track (guitars, bass, organ, piano) except for drums, which he leaves to Buddy Miles.

As "Special Care" suggests, Stills's songs were more socially conscious than either Young's or Furay's. (In the future, near and distant, Young would write political songs: "Ohio," 1970, and "Living with War," 2006). Two other songs on *Last Time Around* reveal both the political and the genre-exploring Stills. In "Four Days Gone," which Barry Gifford called "one of the best tracks the Springfield has ever done,"[24] Stills demonstrates his efficiency in creating a short slice-of-life drama with a convincing character, tension, and social implication, all in under three minutes. "I ran into a draft dodger," said Stills, "and wrote that song 'Four Days Gone' about him."[25] The singer, not a draft dodger but a deserter, has been AWOL for four days, hitchhiking to escape the "government madness" and to meet his girlfriend and settle, presumably, in Canada. "Parched and dry" in a car with an older couple who has provided him with soup, he is nervously polite and apologetic about not sharing his name. With his fear dramatized in Stills's brittle, almost quivering, voice, he asks to be dropped off at the next turn. In 1968, at the song's release, listeners would have recognized the backdrop of the Vietnam War, which was pervasive in the consciousness of the young. Between 1963 and 1973, tens of thousands of American draft dodgers and deserters struggled to get to Canada to avoid the Vietnam War.[26] With "Four Days Gone," Stills voices a note of sympathy for deserters and draft dodgers and, thereby, a quiet protest to the war. The song, out of the folk-music tradition, would not have been out of place performed in a basket house in Greenwich Village when Stills and Furay were performing there. In a demo released on *Buffalo Springfield, Box Set*, Stills delivers a moving performance accompanying himself only on piano. On *Last Time*, the song is amplified, but only slightly, with a steady backbeat and cymbal tap, a slashing guitar chord, and piano, leaving the vocals suitably high in the mix.

In "Uno Mundo," Stills unleashes a fiery, almost joyful Latin-flavored rhythm with congos and maracas to express a cynical worldview: "Uno mundo, somebody's dreaming . . . fanciful scheming." He alludes to problems around the world: "Asia is screaming" (1968 was the deadliest year of the Vietnam War), "Africa's seething" (perhaps a reference to the large-scale famine in Biafra and Nigeria at the time), and "America bleeding" (the Vietnam War, civil unrest). "Uno Mundo" undercuts the cheerful optimist of the previous summer. "The Summer of Love makes me laugh," said Stills. "It's preposterous. . . . If you're on acid or smoke a lot of pot, everything seems more important. I think that's (exactly) what we saw happen."[27] As well as the hippie movement, Stills could have had in mind the *Our World* broadcast, which on June 25, 1967, became the first live satellite television program seen by over 400 million viewers in twenty-four countries. Showcasing artists and performers from around the world—including the Beatles, who debuted "All You Need Is Love"—the implication was clear: people can transcend politics to create peace and solve problems.[28] Stills, whose father served for many years in the Navy, absorbed Latin music in his youth while spending time in New Orleans, Florida, and Costa Rica, where he graduated from high school.

Throughout his career, he would return to those rhythms for inspiration and exploration. Among many examples are "Suite: Judy Blue Eyes" (1969), "Love the One You're With" (1970), "Dark Star" (1977), "Panama" (1994), and "Spanish Suite" (1979, released 2005). "There's an edge of salsa under all of my rhythms," says Stills.[29]

Furay's lyrics, like Stills's, are polished and economical. But rather than tell stories, Furay generally tries to capture and transmit a feeling, an emotional moment in time, as in "Sad Memory" or "What a Day." Unlike Young's, Furay's lyrics, at least while in the Springfield, are not self-probing, and unlike Stills's, never political and not as detailed in their storytelling; instead, Furay only suggests a scene. Compare, for example, "Go and Say Goodbye" or "For What It's Worth" with "Merry-Go-Round" or "Kind Woman." Furay's music relies on traditional rock and roll, country, and folk ballads. "In the Hour of Not Quite Rain" is a notable exception, inspired by what might be called classical pop, but its orchestration owes as much to the arranger as to Furay. In future years, Furay experimented with merging forms, like rock and roll with devotional music ("Seasons of Change," 1982) or country with classical pop ("Crazy Eyes," 1973). While all three of these writers would grow and evolve, all wrote songs with the Springfield that would remain in their setlists for over fifty years.

"It's So Hard to Wait" is one of the few elusive lyrics in the Furay catalog. Despite his cowriting credit, Young had only minimal input on the song, "toss[ing] in a line or two."[30] The song seems to be a plea from the heartbroken singer to an ex-lover, calling on her to "love me enough to begin." The singer tells her not to be "alarmed" if he stares at her and repeats the recurring line of the title, "it's so hard to wait." But wait for what? Her return? A new love? His love sickness to pass? His emotional immobility? Could the song be about the Springfield in some way? In 2020, Furay looked over the lyrics for the first time in years: "I'm not sure what I was writing about [or] what that song was even about."[31] The song is best read as an expression of overwhelming and paralyzing sadness. The effective arrangement and vocals turn a mediocre song into a very good record. By *Last Time*, Furay had developed into a confident singer who relied on his natural vocal tones, to which he added different colors and shades for expressiveness. On "So Hard," for instance, he slows the melody to convey despair before slipping into a heartfelt falsetto. Gone are the mannered tones that could be heard in parts of "Clancy" and "Do I Have to Come Right Out and Say It." With the sparse arrangement and the use of clarinet and saxophone, suggested by Messina, the track has the feel of an old-time jazz-pop ballad.

"In the Hour of Not Quite Rain" has its origins in a radio contest. Program director Ron Jacobs of KHJ or "Boss Radio," which had the largest share of the Los Angeles area teen market at the time, pitched an idea to Greene and Stone: "You Write the Words. . . . Buffalo Springfield Writes the Music. . . . And a Hit Is Born!" The winning lyricist would receive $1000 plus royalties. Greene and Stone approved the contest without informing the band. "It may have been a good publicity stunt," says Furay, but "it didn't fit the dynamics of the band at all."[32] Approximately fifteen thousand entries were submitted. Young and Stills simply ignored the contest. Since Palmer and Martin did not write at the time, the task fell to Richie. "Bruce picked out the lyrics and being a kind of quirky guy, he picked out 'In the Hour of Not Quite Rain,' and that left me pretty much the one to try and write the music." Written by Micki Callen, a teenager from suburban Los Angeles, the winning lyrics are heavy-handed, a bit grandiose in their effort to create a dark atmosphere, but typical of work from young aspiring writers. Furay approached the task with a Midwestern pragmatism and integrity: "You make a commitment, you go through with it."[33] He constructed a slow, shuddering melody, which challenged his vocal range, and with the help of Jeremy Stuart's orchestration—which included quivering strings, a droning cello, an oboe, a triangle, a French horn, drums, and well-placed cymbal crashes—created a successful mood piece of foreboding and eerie solitude. The arrangement owes a debt to the Beach Boys' *Pet Sounds* and the Beatles' *Sgt. Pepper's Lonely Hearts Club Band*. The high notes and falsettos of the melody lines were difficult enough for the twenty-four-year-old Furay, but unattemptable for a seventy-four-year-old. In Los Angeles in 2018, before a Wild Honey Orchestra and Friends benefit concert and tribute to the Buffalo Springfield, Furay, one of the "friends," was asked what he would sing. He good-naturedly responded, "I certainly won't be singing 'In the Hour of Not Quite Rain.'"[34] Our Truth, a duo including twin sisters Corinna and Isabelle Cott, performed the song with the full orchestra that evening.

On the expansive four-CD *Buffalo Springfield, Box Set*, released in 2001, compiler Neil Young omitted "In the Hour of Not Quite Rain," apparently believing it was not Buffalo Springfield enough, which angered fans who wanted all the official releases. He also left off "Carefree Country Day," Jim Messina's lazy, humorous country rhythm about a singer who is "buckin' time" and getting by "haulin' on junk . . . what a wonderful way." The song, which Gifford in *Rolling Stone* called "the best track on the album," features Messina's fat, slow, thumping bass line that at 1:20–1:28 features three glissandos that humorously mirror the lethargy of the singer. As Gifford wrote, it "has the most relaxed country flavor this side of Jack Elliott."[35] Furay had little explanation for the omissions: "I don't think Neil likes those songs. . . . But I know why 'Carefree Country Day' was not included. Neil didn't feel that Jimmy was an enough part of the band. But the song was on the last record. . . . And it was a testimony to Jimmy, putting things together for us, to make that last record a doable product. But Neil was calling most of the shots [on the box set]."[36]

"Merry-Go-Round" and "Kind Woman"

In Furay's "Merry-Go-Round," the singer is mesmerized by love at first sight, which has him "upside down on a merry-go-round. . . . What in the world did you do to make me love just you?" The song uses a rising and falling, almost sing-song melody line and carnival musical atmosphere with bells, a calliope, and a harpsichord to reflect his happy instability. He hopes for "not your standard [or] neighborly" love, but a love much deeper and more sustaining. In the song, Furay recalls his earliest days as a nervous suitor of his future wife, Nancy, whom he first saw from the stage at the Whisky a Go Go. She had come with her then-boyfriend, a member of the Leaves, a popular LA band, and returned to see the Springfield with friends. In "Merry-Go-Round," Furay sings that she was "straining [her] eyes to see, just steady on me." From the stage, the performer returned the stare: "I'm telling you, I couldn't wait for Stephen's 'Sit Down, I Think I Love You' to come into the set. I would sing it and gaze down on her."[37] Finally, he worked up the courage to speak to her, but only from his car as she stood with friends. The next day Nancy left for a three-month stay in Hawaii, where she thought she might move. After her return and Richie's dogged determination, Nancy and Richie married on March 4, 1967, less than a year after he first spotted her in the audience. Together, well over fifty years later, they have four daughters and thirteen grandchildren.

Over the years, Richie's favorite theme has been love: first love, falling in love, longtime love, breakups, love problems and dilemmas, love for friends, love for nature, and love for God. He has probably written more love songs for his wife than any of his contemporaries. However, none of his love songs has proven more enduring than "Kind Woman," the final track on *Last Time Around*. As Messina listened to the tapes, Stephen Stills approached him: "Listen, Richie wrote this amazing song called 'Kind Woman.' Try not to let that one slide. It's just too damn good."[38] The high point for Furay, not only on the album but also in his time with the Springfield, comes in his simple, two-verse declaration of love and plea for love in return. Written after his marriage, "Kind Woman," like "Merry-Go-Round," draws on Furay's initial impressions and feelings for Nancy, to whom he regularly dedicates the song in performance. For Richie it was, as he titles a song on *Hand in Hand*, "Love at First Sight" (2015). The lyrics to "Kind Woman" reveal a nervous singer stumbling for the right words ("mmm") to convey his love:

> I got a good reason for loving you
> It's an old-fashioned sign
> I kinda get the feelin' like mmm you know when
> I fell in love the first time.
>
> [*chorus*] Kind woman
> Won't you love me tonight
> The look in your eyes
> Kind woman
> Don't leave me lonely tonight
> Please say it's all right
>
> Remember once before you're hearing
> The old folks say
> Love's an ageless old rhyme
> But nowadays you know the sayin' depends so much on
> The kind of woman that you find
> [*Repeat chorus.*]

In the chorus, Furay's singer pleads for her love in return. To be clear, he is not crafting a carpe diem seduction, a possibility eliminated by his tender vocals, the pedal steel guitar, the uplifting piano fills, and several key words and phrases, like defining her only as "kind" (hardly a sexually charged description) and referring to "an old-fashioned sign," the wisdom of "old folks," and love as "an ageless old rhyme"—hardly the language of seduction on the Sunset Strip in 1968. Besides, Furay is rarely ironic, wry, or anything but direct in his lyrics. Instead, through these words and references, he emphasizes the sincerity of his love, an "old-fashioned" love resulting in homes and families. To underscore the point, Furay aims for an old-time feel in the music, much as he did in "It's So Hard to Wait," but here the music is traditional country. The kind of musical setting we might hear in a couple of Furay's country heroes like Buck Owens in "Only You (Can Break My Heart)" (1965) or George

Jones in "Walk Through This World with Me" (1967). Dickie Davis remembers that during the Springfield days, "Richie sang George Jones stuff sitting on a couch, and he was really good at it."[39]

After recording the basic track in February 1968, Furay and Messina realized that "'Kind Woman' was more country than 'A Child's Claim to Fame,' which," Richie said, "was more bluegrass."[40] However, for a more complete country sound, the track needed a pedal steel guitar. On the advice of Springfield roadie Miles Thomas, they flew in Rusty Young from Colorado, who was excited about playing on a Buffalo Springfield album: "I idolized that band. . . . It was the Beatles and the Springfield for me."[41] The future member of Poco added steel guitar fills to punctuate the verses and a solo from 2:20–2:54, featuring some bluesy sharp-edged lines, never, as Furay said, falling into a "cry-baby pedal steel" or "weepy cliché."[42] Along with several songs on the Byrds' *The Notorious Byrd Brothers* (January 1968), "Kind Woman" was one of the first rock songs to use a pedal steel guitar. The country-rock era was germinating.

For years, Furay was troubled by the musical timing of "Kind Woman." In 2006, for *The Heartbeat of Love*, he re-recorded the song: "In the original recording, there are some out of time measures. . . . When we were recording it . . . the bass player [Richard Davis, no relationship to Dickie] had no problem playing it, but the [forgotten] piano player stumbled every time over those little tricky 5/4 measures that would come into it. He used to play it 3/4 and there's all of a sudden a 2/4 or something in there, and so I wanted to record the song in time, in straight 6/8, 3/4 whatever."[43] Messina who, as of 2019, often included "Kind Woman" in his solo sets, prefers the original time. For *Heartbeat*, says Richie, "We put it in time, in straight 3/4 time." The re-recording combines country with gospel-like background vocals from Kenny Loggins, Neil Young, Mark Oblinger, Richie, and his daughter Jesse, a fine country singer in her own right, with pedal steel by veteran session musician Dan Dugmore, fiddle by Nashville veteran Hank Singer, who opens the song and solos near the end, and a guitar solo from Young from approximately the 2:50 mark to 3:05. "It took forever to get that guitar solo," says Richie:

I waited for probably eight or nine months for Neil to do it. It was so funny 'cause after I called Stephen about singing on [the album, which he did. Stills] said, "Well, have you called Neil to ask him to sing on it? . . . Why I bet he would really like to do something." I'm thinking, well, 40 years ago I couldn't get him on "Kind Woman" so maybe I could get him on it today. Then he just dragged his feet and it was so exhausting, the waiting. The album was finished, and all I'm doing is waiting on Neil to put, what, 15 seconds of guitar solo on this song. Finally, after I couldn't get a hold of him, I called Elliot [Roberts], his manager, and I said, "Look, let's just take a pass on this, and let it go." He said, "No, Neil really wants to do it. He's in Hawaii now. When he comes home he'll do it." And so he did it, and I listened to it over the phone and I thought, "Yeah, yeah, this is really cool, man. Send it out."[44]

Furay finally received the tape from Young:

When [Neil] sang his parts, they were beautiful. The guitar parts he played were beautiful. But . . . when I first heard his solo, the pickups to the solo weren't right. I was like "Where did this come from?" They were bad. I mean the whole solo was great, but it was just about the first five or six notes. I went in and replayed them. My buddy John Macy [coproducer of *Heartbeat* with Furay] and I set up a little amplifier. I brought my Gretsch guitar in and played the notes. If you listen to it now, you can't hear that there's been any editing or any difference. I doubt that Neil even knows it.[45]

Young's solo is, indeed, as Richie says, about fifteen seconds (2:50–3:05) and "beautiful," rich, slow country-blues played on low register strings, not unlike Duane Eddy's guitar on B. J. Thomas's "Rock & Roll Lullaby" (1972). More often than not when artists cover their own material or when alternative versions are released, the unfamiliar versions drive listeners back to the original. Not this one. "It's now the definitive 'Kind Woman' version for me," declares Richie.[46] After years of clinging to either the Springfield's or Poco's "Kind Woman," listeners, because of personal histories and associated memories, may have difficulty agreeing with the singer-songwriter.

When Buffalo Springfield united for the Bridge School benefit in 2010, Young invited Furay to come out a day ahead of the others so the two could become reacquainted and play some songs. One of those songs was "Kind Woman." "Neil was afraid because he was thinking that we're going to do it like the Springfield. I said, 'No, just do it like we played it on *Heartbeat of Love*. It's all in time.' After that there was nothing else for us to talk about . . . as far as music. He was afraid that the rest of the band wasn't going to be able to play it because of the out-of-time measures."[47]

Rock and Roll Hall of Fame

In 1997, Tom Petty inducted Buffalo Springfield into the Rock and Roll Hall of Fame. Petty profiled the Springfield well:

> They were fringe and paisley. They were the city and they were the canyons. They were the Sunset Strip and the Whisky a Go Go. They were three great voices and they were poets. They were electric and they were an absolutely new acoustic. They were ominous and they were a country morning. They were Cuban heels and moccasins. They were Gretsch guitars and Fender amps. They were dueling guitar solos, one fluid and bluesy, the other fuzzy and angry. They were beautiful harmonies. They were a psychedelic orchestra. . . . They were immeasurably influential, and they begot many more groups that would make more silver and gold music throughout the decades to follow.[48]

Furay heard of the Springfield's induction in a message on his answering machine from Neil Young: [*Imitating Neil Young*] "Hi, Richie? This is Neil and I'm so happy to hear that we're going to be inducted into the Rock and Roll Hall of Fame together. I'm so proud of you, and I'm so happy that we're going to do this together." Plans were set in motion for a public performance of the Springfield at the ceremony, thirty-nine years and one day since their last performance in Long Beach in 1968. However, as May 6, 1997, approached, the reunion fell apart. As Furay says, "I got a fax from [Neil] one day that told me he wasn't coming, and he didn't show."[49] In a statement through his record label, Young announced that he was protesting that performers "are forced to be on a TV show, for which they are not paid, and whatever comments they would like to make, dirty laundry they would like to air, thanks they would like to give, are all subject to the VH-1 editor." Young said he accepted the honor "in the name of Rock and Roll."[50] Furay has another explanation: "I think that there were jealousies and . . . that may have been the reason that [Young] didn't show up. . . . One of the other guys [Stills] was inducted twice that night."[51] Indeed, Stills was inducted on the same night as part of Crosby, Stills & Nash. Young, who was inducted as a solo artist in 1995, may have been upset that it was not Crosby, Stills, Nash & Young. In a humorous moment during the Springfield's acceptance speeches, Stills quipped to Furay: "So, Rich, he quit again." Not so incidentally, Young inducted Paul McCartney into the Hall of Fame at the ceremony just two years later. For his part,

Furay called his induction "the honor of a lifetime," placing him, as he said, in the company of "musical immortals."[52]

At the end of the evening, the plan called for members of the Springfield to join Petty and others for a jam on "For What It's Worth." Furay had a dilemma. He was anxious to play with his old friends but as a Christian pastor at the time, he knew that a small number of his congregation were upset with his continuing rock-and-roll performances. Pastor Richie decided to play, that is, until a piece of salmon interfered with his plans. "I had ordered steak. Then Tom Petty who was sitting right next to me . . . ordered salmon. I thought, 'Oh man, that looks really good.' I asked if they would go back and get me salmon. So they brought me out salmon."[53] As the night passed, Richie grew sicker and sicker until he had to scramble up to his hotel room before the jam.

Reunion and Box Set

After years of speculation about a Buffalo Springfield reunion, the five original members met for a rehearsal in the home of Stephen Stills in Encino, California, in July 1986. Film footage shows Stills and Young in control as they work out a tentative arrangement to a new hard-rocking song of Young's called "Road of Plenty," which he would later record and which evolved into "Eldorado" (*Freedom*, 1989).[54] The rehearsal went so well they planned to play again in about a month. Stills, Furay, Palmer, and Martin arrived and waited and waited. No Young. After some time, they tracked him down in a studio, where Young was mixing recent recordings. He had no intention of going to the rehearsal. Thoughts of a reunion ended.

Over the years, Young has consistently expressed interest in a Buffalo Springfield reunion. As early as 1970, he said, "I would like to do another couple of concerts with the original Buffalo Springfield, the original. I think we could get everybody together, I'd love to do that, it'd be fun."[55] In 1973, asked about a reunion, Richie was practical: "It's all up to Neil Young right now."[56] Three years after failing to appear at the Rock Hall's induction ceremony, Young released "Buffalo Springfield Again" (*Silver & Gold*, 2000). With wistful nostalgia in a beautifully warm melody, Young blames the breakup of the Springfield on the band being "young and wild" in a scene that just "ate us up." But he yearns "to see those guys again / And give it a shot." He then speculates, "Maybe now we can show the world / What we've got." Before the song fades, he adds, "But I would just like to play again for the fun we had,"

FIG. 6 Richie Furay and Neil Young during Buffalo Springfield's 2011 reunion tour. Photo by Vincent Rodriguez.

before ending with an affectionate and plaintive three-word chorus, "Buffalo Springfield again."

Both before and after the induction ceremony and the recording of *Silver & Gold*, Young worked on *Buffalo Springfield, Box Set*. According to *Billboard*, it took Young about a decade to complete, working alongside production coordinator Joel Bernstein. Young summoned Stills and Furay to his studio to listen to tapes. Stills said, "It was so emotionally draining. It's like revisiting your childhood."[57] Young made some odd decisions on the 2001 release, like leaving off the two tracks from *Last Time Around*; omitting an extended version of "Bluebird," previously released on a compilation (*Retrospective*, 1969); excluding any live material, presumably because of poor sound quality; and repeating several tracks on more than one of the CDs. Reviews were overwhelmingly positive, though most mentioned the omissions. Ben Edmonds called Buffalo Springfield "a great American band" with an "overabundance of talent," noting that this collection gives an opportunity to "linger . . . over the magic they made."

On *AllMusic*, Richie Unterberger praises the collection with 4.5/5 stars but, "as good as it is," he writes, it "could have been one of the greatest rock box sets of all time," but for the "bizarre repetition[s]" and absentee tracks—calling "Not Quite Rain" "one of Richie Furay's best moments." He concludes, "If only a saner approach . . . had been employed."[58]

Young was not finished with Buffalo Springfield's catalog. In 2018, he remastered and re-released the band's studio albums in another welcomed box set, the *What's That Sound? Complete Albums Collection.*

Reunion Tour

In 2010, Neil Young asked the surviving members of Buffalo Springfield to reunite on October 23 and 24 for two benefit shows for the Bridge School at the Shoreline Amphitheatre in Mountain View, California. The Bridge School, founded by Peggy Young, Neil's ex-wife, serves students with severe speech and physical impairments. Their son Ben, who has cerebral palsy, attended the school. With Palmer and Martin deceased, the band recruited veterans Rick Rosas on bass and Joe Vitale on drums. "The way that came down is Stephen picked the drummer and Neil the bass player," said Furay.[59] Their sets, the same on both nights, included a dozen Springfield songs spanning their three albums, with Young's "Rockin' in the Free World" as an encore.

Furay, Stills, and Young so enjoyed their time together, on and off stage, that they decided to reunite for a 2011 tour, again with Rosas and Vitale. They played six shows in California during the first week in June 2011 before traveling to Tennessee for a Saturday night set at the Bonnaroo Music and Arts Festival. Reviews all along the way were overwhelmingly positive. In *Rolling Stone*, David Fricke said Buffalo Springfield "played like a band genuinely reborn: thrilled to be on stage again, determined not to let their songs or legacy down." He cited their "jubilant fraternity in the close-harmony, especially by Young and Furay in the soft vocal rain at the end of 'On the Way Home.'" (See fig. 6.) Reviewing the show in Oakland, Jim Harrington was especially impressed with Stills and Young: "Watching these two studs lock horns . . . never fails to impress." In the *Los Angeles Times*, Mikael Wood noted how the band paid little heed to nostalgia and instead "tore through material from its three studio albums . . . with the kind of abandon not often seen on the back-from-the-dead circuit."[60]

Furay said the tour "was a great time . . . really wonderful." But something peculiar happened at Bonnaroo. "After every show before Bonnaroo," Furay said, "we would get together and everybody would say, 'Hey man, it was fun tonight. We had a great time. You did this and it was so cool,' and then after Bonnaroo we never even saw each other. We went to our own buses, and that

FIG. 7 Buffalo Springfield, 2011. Photo by Vincent Rodriguez.

was it, man. . . . It was very surreal."[61] That night, Neil decided to withdraw from the thirty-date second leg of the tour, which was to begin later that summer and extend into the fall. Yes, Young quit again. And, again, Furay and Stills were incensed. "We didn't go to all that trouble for seven shows," Stills said. "That's what impetuosity will do for you. . . . When Neil is involved in anything you need a seatbelt." They even talked of recording a new Springfield album. "That's where some of these songs [for *Hand in Hand*, Furay's 2015 solo album] come from. . . . And the part that got me was that [*imitating Neil Young*] 'I don't want to play any of those old songs.'" Stills continued: "[He] ruined my financial planning. Also, 150 people got laid off that were supposed to work on the tour." Furay agreed, "I don't want to play games. There were people that were working with us that turned down huge jobs because they thought we were going on the road together. Joey [Vitale, drummer] and Rick [Rosas, bassist] both turned down huge jobs."[62]

Young explained, "I have to be able to move forward. I can't be relegated. I did enough of it for right then." Yet, surprisingly, he hinted at a Springfield future: "There is the seed of something great still there. It's worth exploring again." In time Stills's and Furay's anger subsided, "Working with Neil is a privilege, not a right," said Stills. "Life goes on, man," said Furay. "You can love Neil or hate him. I appreciate him. He has obviously established himself as one of the most significant music icons of our time," said Furay.[63]

A Final Word on Furay and the Springfield

"When Buffalo Springfield were inducted into the Rock and Roll Hall of Fame, I was thinking, 'Will people think that I just rode in on Stephen's and Neil's coattails?' Did I have a contribution? I found out that when we . . . did our reunion that my contribution was as significant as anyone's."[64] Furay sang lead or co-lead on fifteen of the Springfield's thirty-five recordings released while the band was extant. (Stills sang lead or co-lead on sixteen, Young on just six, and Messina one). As the third songwriter, Furay contributed seven songs to the final two albums (none on the first); he sang harmonies, and with his rhythm guitar, he—along with Palmer and Martin—built the foundation for the guitar interplay of Young and Stills, especially important on stage during long jams. Furthermore, on stage, Furay was the most animated, the most natural showman. As Young said, "We played in such a way that the three of us were basically huddled together behind while Stills and Furay were always out front. . . . [Richie] had a way of tiptoeing across the stage with feet turned inward which got the girls screaming."[65] Dickie Davis commented on Richie's stage presence: "You should have seen Richie on stage at the Whisky. He was a powerhouse. He was so excited, so happy, and so powerful. He would dance on his toes from one side of the stage to the other while singing and playing the guitar. Richie was incredible. I had never seen anything like it."[66] Importantly, Richie's personality helped to stabilize the band's chemistry as much as possible. He was easygoing, a team player, and pragmatic, "a sweet guy and a real pro."[67]

CHAPTER 6

"Pickin' Up the Pieces"

Poco

For the last two years, Richie Furay had been consumed by all things Buffalo Springfield. As the days of the band drew to a close, he struggled with his next career move. One day, in April 1968, while the Springfield were on the road with the Beach Boys, Furay rode in a taxi with Jim Messina. The two had grown close, and the Springfield's bassist had a suggestion: "Hey, instead of going in a folk-rock direction . . . why don't we try to put country music with rock 'n' roll?"[1] Furay hesitated but soon agreed and committed to developing a new band around the sounds of "Child's Claim to Fame" and "Kind Woman." Messina had spent his early years in Texas, moved to California with his parents when he was about ten, and returned to Texas during summers to visit relatives. "I grew up listening to Bob Wills and the Texas Playboys . . . Spade Cooley and Hank Thompson, Johnny Cash, and Chet Atkins."[2] Furay, for his part, was a fan of not only George Jones, but also the Bakersfield Sound of Merle Haggard and Buck Owens, and in his teen years he listened to the rockabilly of Eddie Cochran, Gene Vincent, and Ricky Nelson. The pair shared visions for the new band. Messina's was more idealistic: "We wanted to instill positive feelings through our music, a positive note in society."[3] Furay's was more commercial and measurable: "Our ambition is to conquer both the country and the Top 40 markets simultaneously. We want to take the rock form over to the country side, and have them dig us."[4]

Country-rock was very much in its infancy in the summer of 1968 when Poco, or Pogo as they were first called, formed. Certainly, over the previous few years, bands had experimented with country sounds. The Beatles had recorded "I Don't Want to Spoil the Party" (1964) and covered Buck Owens's "Act Naturally" (1966), and the Lovin' Spoonful had a Top 10 hit with "Nashville

Cats" (1966), which used a pedal steel guitar. With the term "country-rock" not yet in popular usage—it would be another year—Jon Landau investigated the trend in *Rolling Stone*, in September 1968, as Pogo rehearsed in Furay's living room. As Landau pointed out, Dylan's hit album *John Wesley Harding* (December 1967) had inspired groups to pursue a more country sound. He cited the Springfield's *Last Time Around*, with the "straight country" of "I Am a Child" and "Kind Woman," and the Byrds' *Sweetheart of the Rodeo*, which is the band "doing country as country" leaving "just enough rock in the drums to let you know that they can still play rock and roll."[5] Landau fails to mention what many consider the first country-rock album, *Safe at Home* (March 1968) by the International Submarine Band, which featured Gram Parsons, Furay's friend from Greenwich Village who turned Furay on to George Jones. However, the album was only mediocre and attracted little attention. As Chris Hillman, who played with Parsons in the Byrds and Flying Burrito Brothers, explained, "Gram had not quite developed into the soulful guy he was going to be."[6] Parsons joined the Byrds before the release of *Safe at Home* and was a strong force on *Sweetheart of the Rodeo*, now regarded as a classic but a flop at its August 1968 release, peaking at #77. But country-rock was taking hold on the LA scene. Between 1968 and 1970, country-rock bands proliferated: the Nitty Gritty Dirt Band, Dillard & Clark, Hearts & Flowers, Shiloh, Rick Nelson's Stone Canyon Band, Michael Nesmith and the First National Band, and Pogo.

The first Furay-Messina recruit was Rusty Young, who played pedal steel on "Kind Woman." Furay and Messina insisted a steel guitar be an integral part of their sound. Most of the other bands, including the Byrds, would hire a steel guitarist for their recorded work only. Young joined immediately when he heard he could play dobro, banjo, and mandolin as well as steel guitar. He said his role was to add "color to Richie's country-rock songs." However, as a result of his experience in Boenzee Cryque, a Denver-based psychedelic rock band, he had developed a way for the pedal steel to fit a more rock sound. "I pushed the envelope on steel guitar, playing it with a fuzz tone, because nobody was doing that, and playing it through a Leslie speaker like an organ, and a lot of people thought I was playing an organ."[7] Young then suggested George Grantham, the drummer from Boenzee Cryque, who could also sing high harmonies. They flew Grantham in for an audition, and he clicked immediately. Importantly, Furay commented, "There was no danger that his ego would run amuck."[8] After the dysfunction within the Springfield, Furay and Messina were as focused on band chemistry as musicianship, seeking only compatible and fully committed members. It could be why Dewey Martin, disruptive at times in the Springfield, was not considered for Pogo. "I can't tell you why Dewey wasn't really considered," said Furay, "other than things were moving fast and that's how they all turned out."[9] (In over twenty-five hours of interviews, Furay rarely, if ever, spoke negatively of anyone.) The invitation overwhelmed Grantham: "I was so thrilled, man. . . . I was in the throne. I was in Richie's house with Jimmy and Rusty rehearsing for a record. I couldn't believe it all."[10]

The four members auditioned two bass players: Randy Meisner and Timothy B. Schmit. Grantham called Meisner a "shoo-in." Young and Grantham had known Meisner for a while. "He was the first one we thought of," said Grantham.[11] Randy, who was from Nebraska, would hang out with the pair when his band, the Poor, played Colorado. Schmit had learned of the opening from Cathy Patrick, a friend of the Springfield whom Schmit had met in Los Angeles while his band—the New Breed, later Glad—were in town. "I think I took one of my bandmate friends with me," said Schmit. "I did my little audition. I sang with them. I played a little bit. . . . It was thrilling because these guys could really sing. I'm sort of a natural harmony singer. So it was a really easy fit."[12] Schmit returned a couple of days later for a second audition. The band decided on Meisner, largely on Young's insistence. Richie sensed "definite friction" between Young and Schmit, mostly coming from the steel guitarist. "I think we just kind of gave in to Rusty's feelings on that and went with Randy."[13] With the Vietnam War in full escalation, the band was also concerned with Schmit's draft status. He was a college student, and dropping out could lead to a draft notice. Schmit returned to Sacramento, wrote Furay a thank you note, and enrolled for the fall 1968 semester at Sacramento State College (now Sacramento State University). "I was devastated. I thought I had blown my single chance of getting out of Sacramento and really doing what I wanted to do."[14]

Richie thought briefly about adding a keyboardist to the band. He invited Gregg Allman, an acquaintance, to audition. One morning as Young arrived at the rehearsal, he heard a Hammond organ. "They've replaced me," he thought.[15] But Furay thought it might be "fun" to experiment with the combination of a pedal steel and organ. But Allman only played with the band for a couple of days. "It happened quickly," said Furay. Allman was gone "before we had a chance to really make any kind of effort to see what a band would sound like with him in it." Furay seems to remember his brother Duane calling him about a potential band.[16]

As the band rehearsed in September, Gram Parsons—who had left the Byrds, at this point, and returned to California after living in England with

Rolling Stone Keith Richards—was interested in joining Pogo or merging it with his new band. "We actually had discussions about putting one band together," said Richie. "The thought was who would you let in and who would you leave out. He was already working with Chris Hillman and Sneaky Pete [Kleinow, steel guitarist], Chris Ethridge, and the rest of the guys in the [Flying Burrito Brothers], and I got Rusty and Jimmy. How were we gonna make one band out of this thing?"[17] Young remembers that Parsons then asked about joining Pogo, and Richie invited him to audition. "It didn't work out," said Young, "because he didn't like Jimmy Messina. . . . Jimmy was our friend and Gram was a little strange, so we told Gram that we would stick with Jimmy." Indeed, Messina saw an "edge" to Parsons. "Even back then it was destructive. It came across when we were auditioning him," said Messina. "I felt he would have been a disruptive element, and Richie naturally sensed that."[18] Furay could not extend an invitation to his friend: "I saw him as a very self-destructive person, a very talented guy, but never sure of himself in the way that maybe a lot of self-destructive people are."[19] Unlike the other members of Pogo, Parsons, who had offered Furay acid in New York, was a heavy drug user who would die at age twenty-seven, in 1973, after a lethal combination of morphine and alcohol.

The band rehearsed daily from August into October, crafting their sound and developing a setlist. "We rehearsed day and night," remembered Grantham. Richie would bring in an original song in one stage of composition or another. "We'd listen to it," said Grantham, "and we'd put our two cents in, what we could contribute and what we thought about the song and we'd work with it."[20] They built the harmonies: Meisner on top, Richie in the middle, and Grantham on the bottom. Messina, on lead guitar, and Young would work out guitar parts and guitar interplay, and perhaps come up with the intro to the song. "Rusty and I were the ones who created the grooves, the licks, and the motion, that kind of stuff," said Messina. "If you listen to the music with Rusty and me, we pretty much were the bowsprit to the boat in terms of energy and musicality and Richie and Randy or [later] Timmy or George at the time were doing most of the vocals."[21] Furay and Messina were coleaders. Furay, as Meisner put it, was "more the artist" and Messina, as he defined himself, more the "craftsman," i.e., more the technical expert, formulating the precise sound and arrangements.[22] The coleaders complemented one another, and each member of the band was fully invested and confident. "Each one of those guys, Rusty, George, and Randy," said Messina, "was just perfect for what we wanted to accomplish. It just felt right."[23] Meisner alluded to the positive collaborative spirit: "All this talent, all sharing with each other."[24] Richie understated the closeness of the members, both musically and personally: "I thought of us as a pretty close-knit band." Pogo was not only workshopping their sound but also pioneering country-rock, and people were taking notice, even in rehearsals. "Glenn Frey [cofounder of the Eagles in 1971] sat in my living room at 2300 Laurel Canyon Boulevard," said Furay, "when I was rehearsing Poco for the first time. He definitely heard something there that he liked."[25]

However, before they could proceed, the band needed a manager. Furay convinced Messina that they should hire Dickie Davis, who had worked with the Springfield in a variety of capacities, including manager, just before its breakup. Richie seemed to hire him as much out of friendship and loyalty as for his managerial skills. Under the best of circumstances, managing a band is onerous and complicated. Managers have to be students of the industry. They are expected to direct bands on finding, retaining, and expanding their audience; to arrange profitable, or at least cost-effective, tours; and, as part visionary, to recognize new musical trends and help construct the band's response. As part therapist, managers need to soothe wounded artistic egos and resolve internal personnel conflicts, often needing to keep their talent emotionally measured, representing the calm voice of reason in negotiations with sometimes unfair record label executives, promoters, fans, and members of the press. Certainly, Davis was dedicated to the band and the members all liked him. However, he might not have been the best choice for a fledgling band seeking large-scale success. Davis did not have the national contacts or networking skills necessary to expand his local contacts, and he had a volatile temper that led to problems. But he got right on the initial tasks: booking gigs, promoting the band within the industry and the press, and negotiating a record deal. But first, the band had to have a name.

By October the band was ready for a performance, but they still had not agreed on a name. Davis suggested Pogo. He reasoned that the four letters would be "really big on a marquee. When you got the Jefferson Airplane on a marquee the letters are only like four inches tall, but if you have a four-letter name the letters will be twelve inches tall. . . . And I liked Pogo because he was a comic book character that I really loved when I was a kid."[26] Walt Kelly had created *Pogo*, the comic strip, in the 1940s, but in the late 1960s, it had developed an audience among the counterculture for its satire, targeting such issues as segregation, environmental destruction, and the Vietnam War. Pogo, the title character, was a possum who dwelled in a swamp with other permanent and visiting anthropomorphic residents and visitors. In 1969, Kelly described Pogo as "reasonable, patient, softhearted, naïve, [and] friendly."

He would rather "spend his time fishing or picnicking, [but] his kind nature often gets him reluctantly entangled in his neighbors' escapades."[27] The name was fitting, especially for a band who showcased positive energy and country rhythms. Furay defines the music as he sings the opening lines from their first album: "It comes from the backwards of meadows and memories." In 1969 interviews, he called their music "rural rock" and alluded to country music as "white soul music," a term he had heard from Gram Parsons.[28]

Back at the Troubadour

Like Buffalo Springfield, Pogo debuted at the Troubadour on a Monday Hoot Night, where they performed five songs on, most likely, October 14, 1968. They were invited back to the club for a full set on October 24, but Furay, not completely satisfied with the name Pogo, billed the band as R.F.D, an abbreviation for Rural Free Delivery. It was probably inspired by the popular TV series *Mayberry R.F.D.*, a spinoff from *The Andy Griffith Show*, set in the small idyllic Southern town. Some thought the abbreviation represented Richie Furay's Dream, which in October 1968 would have been apt. They returned as Pogo for an extended engagement opening for Biff Rose, November 19–December 1, and then again, opening for the Nitty Gritty Dirt Band, December 6–9. As with the Springfield, the buzz was immediate and reviews positive. After R.F.D's October 24 appearance, Michael Etchison of the *Los Angeles Herald-Examiner* wrote that the band did "something between country and rock, authentically both." He went on to write that they were well-rehearsed, which "the packed house appreciated," and cited their "rich high harmonies" and Rusty Young's steel guitar, especially "amazing" to be heard playing a "hard rock solo on 'Short Changed.'"[29] Young, whose musicianship was commended frequently in early reviews, seemed to be immediately achieving one of his objectives: "I'll do whatever it takes to make the pedal steel popular, to show people that it can fit into everything, that it's not just for Hawaiian music."[30] After Pogo opened for Biff Rose, Pete Johnson wrote in the *Los Angeles Times* that "the singing combination of Furay and Meisner is terrific . . . melt[ing] together in delightful harmonies and separate for strong solos. . . . Pogo is one of the tightest groups I have seen," and he celebrated their "originality, diversity and togetherness."[31] By the end of 1968, Pogo had played some twenty-five shows to enthusiastic audiences.

Fans and record label executives clamored around the band. "It was terrific!" recalled Furay. Grantham said, "I was just overwhelmed. It was like an answer to my prayers and dreams."[32] Clive Davis, president of Columbia Records, was anxious to sign the band, but Furay was still under contract to Davis's rival Ahmet Ertegun at Atlantic/ATCO. Ertegun, on the other hand, wanted to sign another new group, Crosby, Stills & Nash, but Nash, as a former member of the Hollies, was under contract with Columbia. David Geffen, who was working with CSN at the time, suggested a solution: a trade, like "kids swapping baseball cards that just happened to be worth millions of dollars," as Clive Davis wrote.[33] Ertegun and Davis would simply trade the rights to the two musicians. CSN were now free to sign with Atlantic, and Pogo with Epic, a subsidiary of Columbia. A letter dated January 15, 1969, between Atlantic and Epic finalized the terms of the deal. Both bands got right into the studio. While recording, Pogo gained some noteworthy publicity. A cover story in *Rolling Stone* on the country influence on rock touted Pogo as one of the "four . . . most talked-about groups in L.A. . . . and perhaps the most commercial," acclaiming their "exceptional material" and their "exciting and fun" music.[34] With a nine-album deal with Epic, Pogo looked forward to a bright future.

Problems

Pogo entered the studio confident that they could get their pioneering sound onto tape and vinyl. However, that would prove difficult. Jim Messina, a trained engineer and the sole producer of *Pickin' Up the Pieces*, had problems with the assigned engineer, Terry Donovan, and his crew, who had little experience with rock music. As Messina explains, "What happened is they would hear distortion coming out of a guitar and they thought we were overdriving their speakers, which we weren't." When Messina tried to clarify or show them how to capture the proper sound, he heard an all-too-frequent response: "That's not how we do it here." Messina was further exasperated by not being able to adjust the faders: "I was not allowed to touch the board because even though I had been a recording engineer and I was an IBEW [International Brotherhood of Electric Workers] union member, once we signed with CBS we had collective co-bargaining agreements which disallowed me to touch the board." Messina was hobbled and the "union guys wouldn't listen" to him. The album never sounded the way he had planned. "I couldn't get what I heard out of the speakers until the second album when I could change engineers."[35]

More problems followed. With the recording completed, Messina and Furay set about mixing the album, i.e., blending the sounds, in this case, of eight tracks to create the versions of the songs that listeners would hear on vinyl. Mixing is the final step before the production of the master tape. The process is labor intensive, painstaking, and highly focused, and a well-mixed album requires a sonic vision for a cohesive sound to emerge. The slightest increase or decrease in the volume of a track can have a huge impact on the sound of a particular song. It is not unusual to leave the musicians out of the process, as musicians often have a tendency to focus on their particular instruments. "I had told Richie," remembered Messina, "I need to really listen and not be distracted so let's just limit the number of visitors that we have. . . . And then I remember mixing one night, somebody was at the door, and then Richie came back and didn't say anything and we just continued to work." The knock on the door had come from Randy Meisner, anxious to hear the progress. "I like engineering and mixing. I had done some recording myself, real small time but I was interested in it."[36] Furay denied Meisner access. Meisner was outraged: "'Wait a minute, I made the music too. . . . If you're not gonna let me down there I'm just gonna quit.' And it was as simple as that." Furay may have been impatient and short with Meisner, but he never expected him to quit. "Well . . . here we go again," thought Furay. For the immediate present, Pogo performed as a foursome with Messina returning to bass.[37]

"We were all in shock," said Messina. Breaking up before the release of a first album is, as Messina put it, "the dumbest thing any band could do and the greatest fear of every record company. . . . Everyone loses their investment of time, money, and energy. . . . It's kind of like being at the Kentucky Derby and having your horse sit down at the gate as it opens." Dickie Davis said, "I remember being totally blindsided by Randy's leaving. Totally blindsided. I can remember the whole night after that happened, where I was and what I was thinking. I was devastated. And I'm pretty sure Richie was too. . . . It was Neil all over again."[38] Everyone may have been devastated but no one tried to talk Meisner into remaining, and he found work quickly as the first recruit for Rick Nelson's Stone Canyon Band. Meisner performed on and coproduced Nelson's *In Concert at the Troubadour, 1969*. After a year, he quit and returned to Nebraska and worked at Frank Implement Company, a John Deere dealership owned by a friend and his father. "Yeah, [my friend] gave me a job as a part's man. . . . These farmers would come in and start yelling at me. 'Get the part! Come on!'"[39] It was a job similar to Furay's at Pratt & Whitney. Meisner worked there for a few months until Nelson asked him to rejoin the Stone Canyon Band. In 1971, Meisner left to join Linda Ronstadt's backing band and then, later that year, formed the Eagles with Don Henley,

Glenn Frey, and Bernie Leadon. In 1975, Meisner wrote and sang lead on a #4 hit for the Eagles, "Take It to the Limit."

Clive Davis was upset not only by Meisner's departure but also by Davis's and Furay's insistence on re-recording parts of the album. "That set off fireworks between us and Epic. . . . From then on . . . there was so much politics that was going on [between us and Epic]. It was exhausting."[40] While it would require too much time and effort to remove and re-record Meisner's bass parts and all his vocal harmonies, Poco did remove his lead and colead vocals. Grantham replaced Meisner on the colead to the title track, the lead on "Calico Lady," and prominent high supporting vocals on "First Love" and "Short Changed." While he cannot be certain, Messina thinks Meisner may have sung lead on "Tomorrow" as well, with Richie taking over the vocals on re-recording. No one clearly remembers, in part because during their prerecording days, in rehearsal and on stage, Poco would often shift lead vocals on songs, from night to night, to determine who sang which song most effectively. Meisner, for instance, remembers singing "Anyway Bye Bye" on stage, a song on Poco's second album.[41] The liner notes for *Pickin' Up the Pieces* give Meisner minimal credit: "Supporting vocals and bass by Randy Meisner," which, Messina says, "is really downplaying his contribution."[42]

Dickie Davis and Furay approached an increasingly frustrated Clive Davis about redoing the cover art for the album. They reasoned that it would be damaging to feature someone no longer in the band. To keep costs down, the art department erased Meisner's image from the illustration and, to retain the balance and composition of the picture, added a dog. Since the image has a Western motif with the four members casually talking, the dog works. Significantly, most of the country-rock bands of the time adopted a Western, rather than Southern, motif in their imaging. Olivia Carter Mather argues that the Western imagery deflects assumptions of racism by directing the audience "toward a mythologized region that represented a set of widely accepted American values," like free-spirited individualism, staunch independence, a strong work ethic, and steadfast morality. In addition, by presenting themselves as Western, the bands, Mather continues, tap "into cultural icons accepted almost universally by the baby-boom generation," who were children during "the golden age of the Western movie, Western television serial, and cowboy and cowgirl products such as toys and dress-up clothing."[43] True enough. However, as protests developed against the Vietnam War, for example, the imagery might have lost its appeal, as cowboy icons like John Wayne became associated with American conservatism.

On Poco's first album cover, Richie, the only one standing, relaxes in jeans and a fringed Western shirt against a window frame. Grantham, with a vest and Kentucky colonel tie, looks like a TV Western saloonkeeper. Messina, with his vest and seemingly open Kentucky colonel tie, sits in the foreground turned toward Young and the dog, who is placed slightly in front of Young's right side. Young, top left, seems to be dressed in a leisure suit jacket, the kind that would become popular in the 1970s. Opening the gatefold reveals, on the left sleeve, the song listing and liner notes with a sketch of four cowboys before their campfire, with coffee brewing and food cooking, their wagon behind them. On the right gatefold sleeve are four baseball cards, one for each smiling band member, autographed and with information on his hometown, principal instrument, and date of birth. This was not very hip in 1969, the year that saw millions of young people demonstrate against the Vietnam War and saw Jefferson Airplane release *Volunteers*, #13 on the album charts, whose opening track proclaimed "we are forces of chaos and anarchy . . . Up against the wall, motherfucker" and whose gatefold featured an absurdist photograph of two giant halves of a peanut butter and jelly sandwich. The artwork on Poco's debut seems a throwback to teenybopper magazines and album covers from the mid-1960s. Behind the image of the cards is a partially blocked lasso encircling a smiling quarter moon, stars, a silhouette of a cowboy on a horse, and a large star. Inside the star are the words "Now Playing." The back cover features an image of the four members in a large circle. Furay is in the foreground with the others around him. The track listing appears on the left side, the album title on the bottom left, and "Starring Poco" on the bottom right. Under the circle picturing the band, on the bottom center, is an image of an old radio with a ribbon of notes extending under the band portrait, emerging on the top left, and continuing off the cover. The cover art suggests cheerful old-time country-Western music, which is accurate enough but maybe not in stride with the growing restlessness of youth culture in 1969.

During the recording of *Pickin' Up the Pieces*, Pogo faced still another problem. The band had ignored a cease-and-desist order from Walt Kelly, who demanded the band no longer use the name Pogo. Just prior to taking the stage on April 10, at the University of California at Santa Barbara, Pogo was served with court papers notifying them that Kelly was suing the band for "trademark infringement" and unfair "competition," and directing the band to answer the complaint within twenty days of the April 8 date on the document. Clive Davis suggested changing the name immediately. But Dickie Davis disagreed: "It's a name. . . . It's a pogo stick. It doesn't have to belong to Walt Kelly. . . . You can't copyright a title. You can copyright a character but we're

FIG. 8 Poco (*from left to right*): Paul Cotton, Timothy B. Schmit, George Grantham, Richie Furay, and Rusty Young. Photo by Howard Zryb.

not that character." He flew to New York, where some of his former school-mates worked in publishing, and he asked them to arrange a meeting with Kelly. No such meeting resulted, but he did meet with Clive, who was losing patience. "Clive was pretty contemptuous of me, you know. He was running things and I wasn't. So I went back to Los Angeles," said Davis. "I think we gave [Kelly] $100 in liquidated damages or something for using his name. I disagree with that to this day, but we had to do it. We were stuck. They weren't going to release the album with the name Pogo on it."[44] Depending upon whom you ask, either Meisner or Young suggested Poco, a name Furay preferred to Pogo and all it required was changing the *g* to a *c*.[45]

Pickin' Up the Pieces

What seems to differentiate *Pickin' Up the Pieces* from other progenitors of country-rock, like *Safe at Home* or *Sweetheart of the Rodeo*, is that Poco's effort lacks self-consciousness. Under Furay's and Messina's leadership, Poco does not restrict itself by being overly earnest or overly respectful of the country music tradition the way Gram Parsons and other members of the Byrds seemed to be. Poco was comfortable enough to meld country with rock or other forms, or just play straight traditional country, or experiment with the Bakersfield Sound. They did not feel the need to prove their country chops. While Poco certainly wanted to reach a country music audience, they were not desperate to do so. As Furay said, "We wanted to be a crossover. . . . We're a rock-and-roll band but we would sure like to make inroads into country music and let people know that we're just like you. We're just making music."[46] If Poco's main objective had been to reach a country audience, Rusty Young would not have worked his pedal steel to sound like an organ as it does, for example, in "Nobody's Fool." The Byrds, on the other hand, yearned for the approval of a country music audience. On March 15, 1968, they played Ryman Auditorium, the home of the Grand Ole Opry in Nashville, and were not well received. They "elicited boos, catcalls or indifference, depending on who's telling the story."[47] Skeeter Davis, a country music singer with crossover hits, consoled the Byrds backstage. As Byrds leader Roger McGuinn says, "There were indeed some folks attending . . . who didn't seem to appreciate how sincere we were in doing country music."[48] It is doubtful that the Byrds got a fair hearing in Nashville. Country music fans and industry executives were put off by their long hair, hippie clothing, association with California folk-rock, and assumed liberal politics.

Pickin' Up the Pieces begins with an under-a-minute foreword, a poem by fan Kathy Johnson that Furay set to a melody, and twelve tracks of various tempos, rhythms, and themes. But all this is unified by the Poco sound—songs rich in melody, vocal harmonies, and instrumental interplay, which, in concert, could break into extended jams grounded in country, rock, or country-rock. All songs are written or cowritten by Furay except Rusty Young's "Grand Junction" and can be categorized this way: traditional country, like "Tomorrow" (well suited for George Jones), "Pickin' Up the Pieces," and "Oh Yeah," sung by Messina and not dissimilar to "Carefree Country Day" from the Springfield's *Last Time Around*; country love ballads, like "First Love" and "Make Me a Smile"; songs inspired by the Bakersfield Sound, "Just in Case It Happens, Yes Indeed" and "Consequently, So Long"; country-rock songs like "What a Day" and "Calico Lady"; straight-up rock, like "Short Changed"; or the country-rhythm-and-blues of "Nobody's Fool," which was performed, but not released, by the Springfield in a rhythm-and-blues arrangement with Dewey Martin singing lead.

The music may not "pop" out of the speakers the way Messina had hoped—"It's dead," he overstated[49]—but *Pickin' Up the Pieces* is nonetheless an innovative debut that demonstrated the possibilities in the fusion of country and rock. There are several standout tracks, including the title song, which has been a mainstay in Furay's setlist since its release. "Pickin' Up the Pieces" begins with Furay's quick acoustic guitar riff, which ends with a lilt. The same brief riff introduces just about every chorus. Throughout, Furay strums only major chords (B, E, F#) until the end, when he concludes with a minor chord (G#m). The major chords, along with Grantham's steady backbeat resembling handclaps, contribute to the brightness of the tone. The track also features Young's gentle pedal steel underneath the melody, with his solo from 2:16 to 2:28 followed by Messina's lead solo from 2:32 to 2:46. There is a seeming simplicity and casualness to the arrangement, which—accompanied by lyrics and cheerfully relaxed lead vocals shared by Furay and Grantham in an easily sing-alongable melody—conjures images of a backyard summer jam session where all is smiles and troubles are far removed. The track embodies the "positive feelings" that Messina hoped Poco's music would emit:

> Well, there's just a little bit of magic
> In the country music we're singin'
> So let's begin
> We're bringin' you back down home where the folks are happy
> Sittin', pickin' and a-grinnin'
> Casually, you and me will pick up the pieces, ah-huh.

While the title indicates that the singer has in some way been broken, he finds healing and renewal in simple but nurturing pleasures: "home," "picnic lunches," "Sunday afternoon[s]," "singin'" songs, "sit[ting] down strum[ming] on our guitars," family and friends, and making new friends, who will "see I really am a lot like you." The singer is recovering his strength and identity and moving on with hopefulness, contentment, and confidence. The acknowledgment of the singer's recent misfortune, whatever it may be, and the laid-back vocals and tone keep the song from being Pollyannaish.

Like most of Furay's lyrics on the album, "Pickin' Up the Pieces" reflects on his time in Buffalo Springfield. "If you look into the songs I wrote on the first Poco album . . . I was still trying to figure out what happened and express my feelings on those two years in the Springfield."[50] Additionally, he said, "We were starting a new thing, and we were leaving an old thing," which is to say that the songs are about moving on, renewal, and new beginnings. As a result, the songs express Furay's hopefulness and excitement, but also his sadness, anger, and confusion. And, yes, Furay's songs are autobiographical: "I think most of the time [the 'I'] is me. . . . It's my own experiences that I'm writing about. So, yeah, the 'I' is me."[51]

One of the most optimistic songs on the album is the opening track, "What a Day," which was recorded by the Springfield with Stills on lead vocals but not released until *Box Set*. After the Foreword, lower in volume than the other tracks—as if to literalize that the music is coming from deep in "the backwoods" of both rural America and the "memories" of individual psyches— "What a Day" blasts out (but not as much as Messina had hoped) to celebrate a new day: "It's a good morning and I'm feeling fine / Hey, it's such a lovely day / Smile!" The rhythm and lead vocals of Furay and supporting vocals of Grantham are not just up-tempo but positively jubilant and feature Rusty Young's dobro and banjo breaks, suitable for a hoedown or jamboree. By contrast, "Short Changed," the final track on the original side 1, grinds on in anger with fuzztone riffs and bursts by Messina. "Short changed," an irate Furay screams, "I've got to hand it to you. . . . Bloodstained, my hands were tied 'cause of you." It is a bitter expression of Furay's feelings at sometimes being bypassed in the Springfield's creative mix. I commented to Furay that it might be his most aggressive lyrical and vocal attack on record. He looked over the lyrics: "Yeah, yep, yeah. A little bitter." He laughed. He has not performed the song in decades. "I'm way past that now, and there are some songs I wouldn't even think about doing now."[52]

The most perplexing lyric on *Pieces* is the beautifully wistful ballad "First Love," which in form and tempo is similar to "Sad Memory" and features Young on an effectively mood-creating steel guitar. "Today my first love has arrived," Furay sings with nervous, rather than joyful, anticipation. He asks an indeterminate listener, "Did you see her? / Did you approve? What if I asked this of you?" He then sings about his childhood and playing with toys before recognizing that "older people play little games in another way." In the final line, Furay sings, "Today my first love is alone." Does the singer love his "first love"? I asked Furay about his lyrical intention. He looked the song over: "I don't know. . . . I probably was just struggling on how to make something flow [*Laughs*]." I mentioned that that is not his usual process, that he would not let the lyrics stand if they only flowed. He thought further: "What was I thinking? . . . I haven't a clue." He said it was not about his wife, Nancy, or the young woman in "Sad Memory." Then he realized, "It must have been a reflection back again on the Springfield. . . . You know, you're in a band and it's all working and it's all good. 'My first love has arrived.' And then by the third verse, you know, it's just like, it's gone"—as he sings, "castles crumble to sand."[53] While the lyrics may be as inaccessible or obscure as any Furay has written, "First Love" captures his confusion and bewilderment over the chaos that was Buffalo Springfield.

For three songs—"Calico Lady," "Tomorrow," and "Consequently, So Long"—Furay wrote the music to Skip Goodwin's lyrics. Goodwin, whom Furay met while working at Pratt & Whitney, tends to write lofty, almost pretentious lyrics that contrast with Richie's direct, plain style. "Silken-soft, she rises from the dawn," sings Grantham on "Calico Lady." On "Tomorrow," while Furay sings of "darkened clouds" releasing "fears," which "clean the festering earth . . . fortell[ing] of a Renaissance," Messina adds further grandiosity, not unlike "The Hour of Not Quite Rain," with strings and brass. However, the song remains at least somewhat grounded by Furay's sad but energetic vocals and Young's plaintive and countryish pedal steel. Closer to Furay's colloquial lyrical style is "Consequently, So Long": "It's been a long-time a comin' but I have to carry on." The final track on the album, it serves as Furay's farewell to the Springfield. Along with "Just in Case It Happens, Yes Indeed," Furay finds inspiration in the Bakersfield Sound.

A subgenre of country music, the Bakersfield Sound emerged out of what Merle Haggard called "the redneck honky-tonks" and what Glen Campbell termed "the fightin' and dancin' clubs" in Bakersfield, California.[54] Its two most famous practitioners were Buck Owens and His Buckaroos and Merle Haggard and the Strangers. The sound springs from the Depression-era children of the Okies, who escaped the dust bowl of Oklahoma to migrate to the San Joaquin Valley in search of work. By the late 1950s, a Bakersfield Sound had developed that contrasted with the sweet countrypolitan sounds coming out of Nashville. Nashville musicians, instead of incorporating rock and roll or rockabilly rhythms into country, as musicians in Bakersfield did, opted for more pop sounds, lush orchestrations, and smooth melodies and vocals. This was intended "to revive country sales, which had been devastated by the rise of rock 'n' roll."[55] Instead, Bakersfield musicians played a rough-hewn music, performed loudly on Fender Telecaster guitars, and picked more than strummed, effecting a cutting sound that interplayed with pedal steel guitars, fiddles, and a strong drum backbeat. In a sense, Nashville was minimizing the twang as Bakersfield was emphasizing it. As Buck Owens said, "I couldn't stand all the silky, syrupy stuff that was coming out of Nashville. Everything was oh, so sweet. 'Don't play too loud there, Harry, somebody might think you have some personality!' It was awful to me."[56] The Bakersfield Sound would be a major influence on country-rock and outlaw rock as played by Willie Nelson and Waylon Jennings. Asked if the Bakersfield Sound influenced the album, Furay responded, "Absolutely!

'Consequently, So Long,' 'Just in Case It Happens,' and even 'Pickin' Up the Pieces' to a certain degree." Owens, with his guitarist Don Rich's high harmonies, especially grabbed Richie: "I always liked Buck, Don Rich, and that whole sound."[57] Both songs would be featured in a medley, captured on *Deliverin'* with Rusty Young's "Grand Junction." Nestled between the other two songs, "Grand Junction" is an energetic instrumental, a kind of electric bluegrass. This provides dynamic interplay between Young's dobro and steel and Messina's lead.

In "Just in Case It Happens," another breakup song about the Springfield, Furay announces that "the heartache is gone, yes indeed." Yet despite the blithesome melody, uplifting harmonies, and upbeat music, Furay seems to protest too much. "What does it matter to me," he sings casually, "for lovin' you I have been such a fool / Hardly knowin' the game or the rules." He admits he was a "dreamin'," and believing "promises" and the "teasin'." But, he proclaims, the disappointment, pain, and frustration are over; "the memory's all in a dream" with the experience reduced to a boring "goodnight's yawn." But "just in case *it* happens" (the "it," according to Furay, representing future success[58]), be assured, he tells us, he deserves it, having "paid all [his] dues faithfully." Yet the cheery singer strains credibility by being too cheery, too quickly dismissive. Is the "heartache" really gone?

One of Furay's common songwriting strategies, as in "Just in Case," is to set sullen or angry lyrics in nimble, if not bright, melodies and arrangements, often misleading listeners into thinking Furay has no sense of despair or suffering, a lightweight among other songwriters. In his review of *Pickin' Up the Pieces*, for example, Robert Christgau called the album "nice and happy," rating it a B.[59] But as Peter Knobler has said, "If you listen to Richie sing, it's happy, happy, happy. If you listen to the words, it's not so happy."[60] Record producer Jim Mason once told Richie, "You can write a sad song and still make me feel good about it."[61] For Furay, it seems to be a form of therapy to transcend any personal sadness or disappointment and to transform the negative into a positive—not unlike Walt Whitman, who wrote, "The pleasures of heaven are with me and the pains of hell are with me, / The first I graft and increase upon myself, the latter I translate into a new tongue" (*Song of Myself*, #21). Like Whitman, Furay uses this process to reflect his generally hopeful spirit and his need to "keep on believin'." "That may be subconscious," he explained, "that when I am frustrated or whatever, one other side of me says, unconsciously, again, 'Hey, it's not the end of the world.'"[62] We see this strategy at work in songs like "Child's Claim to Fame" and Poco songs like "I Guess You Made It" and "A Man Like Me."

Reviews

Poco, who had received glowing live reviews, had expected *Pickin' Up the Pieces* to lift them into pop's stratosphere. For the most part, reviews were positive, and if they were not, they still predicted great success for the band. In *Billboard*, the reviewer wrote that "Poco is destined for big things and this album should propel them to stardom . . . a program of country and country rock that should score well." Similarly, in its lukewarm review, *Variety* thought that Poco's "wholesome-hip image could make a heavy market score." In the *Los Angeles Times*, Robert Hilburn wrote that the album "has some strong points" noting that "on their best songs (particularly the title track), the group carries the best and charm of its country roots [and] features good harmony and instrumental work." Later that year, Hilburn commented, "It seems only a matter of time before Poco is one of the nation's headlining attractions."[63] Missing, however, was a review in *Rolling Stone*, which by 1969 carried substantial authority with rock music fans.[64]

To promote the album, Poco played approximately a hundred live shows from May until early January, with the majority in California. On June 28, Poco arrived late from a Denver festival for a headlining gig at the Troubadour. As the band entered the club, they heard the supporting act. The then unknown comedian and musician Steve Martin, who had opened for them on several occasions, was entertaining the waiting audience by playing Poco songs on his banjo. But one performance Poco did not make that summer was at the Woodstock Music & Art Fair, August 15–18, in Bethel, New York. Davis had rejected an invitation for Poco to play the festival. Of course, Davis could not have predicted that Woodstock would become the defining moment of a generation, an event of epic proportions captured in films and albums. Having a performance on the hit film *Woodstock* or on its soundtrack (which went multiplatinum and held the #1 album spot for four consecutive weeks in the summer of 1970) could have led to a far different career trajectory for Poco. *Woodstock* launched the careers of acts like Santana and Joe Cocker, turned the Who and Sly & the Family Stone into major live attractions, and awarded novelty acts like Sha Na Na counterculture credibility. Davis explained the rejection: "We had played one or two 'festivals' before Woodstock, and they were horrible experiences. The audiences were treated like shit. There weren't enough bathrooms; there wasn't enough water; everybody was caged into these big dirt areas." Fairly or not, a manager needs to recognize potential career springboards, and here Davis failed. "You know, I do feel responsible," he said.[65] At the time, Grantham said, "We kind of thought it was a bad choice, taking this high school gig over a huge festival." Poco actually played California State University, Fullerton, that weekend. "It was a huge mistake," Grantham continued. "My God, you can't do a bigger mistake than turning down Woodstock."[66] In 2015, as Furay prepared to take the stage at the Canyon Club outside Los Angeles, Davis approached his old friend, whom he had not seen in years, and apologized for his decision some forty-five years earlier. "I think that it just gnawed at him for forty years," said Furay, "and he didn't ever say anything. . . . 'Let that go, man. For goodness sakes, don't hang on to that.'"[67]

Pickin' Up the Pieces peaked at a very disappointing #63 in September, and the title track failed to chart as a single. "The only thing keeping Poco . . . from being one of the nation's highest level groups is the absence of a couple of strong identifiable hits," wrote Hilburn.[68] That "identifiable" hit would elude Furay throughout his career. With *Pieces*, Furay said, "We were too rock for country and too country for rock."[69] Thus the album had experienced the same plight as *Sweetheart of the Rodeo*. Over the years, like *Sweetheart*, *Pieces* has established itself as a groundbreaking recording. In his study of country-rock, John Einarson called the album "wholly unique, fresh, effervescent . . . a major statement of the genre." In 2001, in the *All Music Guide: The Definitive Guide to Popular Music*, Bruce Eder called the album "one of the strongest debut records of its era, a blend of country and western influences, Beatlesque harmonies, and mainstream rock, all within one cover . . . a startlingly great record, as accomplished as any of the Buffalo Springfield, and also reminiscent of the Beatles and the Byrds . . . a landmark in country-rock."[70]

In the late summer of 1969, however, Poco needed to prepare for a second album and find a new bass player.

CHAPTER 7

"C'mon"

Hope and Frustration

Throughout most of the summer of 1969, Poco performed as a foursome. In June, they had auditioned Timothy B. Schmit again, but Rusty Young was still uncertain. Again, Schmit returned to Sacramento. At the end of July, the bass player and his girlfriend were visiting her parents in Southern California. One morning her father asked him, "Whatever happened to that band you were trying to get into down here?" The twenty-one-year-old reported that he had thought the audition had gone well but they still hadn't called him. "Then," Schmit continued, "her father said the greatest, simplest thing to me: 'Did you try calling them?' It had never occurred to me to call them." Poco was performing for a few days at the Golden Bear in nearby Huntington Beach. Dickie Davis arranged for Schmit and his girlfriend to be on the guest list. As he and his girlfriend were enjoying the show, Furay suddenly invited a shocked Schmit onstage. "This is a song that Timothy wrote," announced Furay. Schmit joined in for "Hear That Music," which he had composed after seeing Pogo at the Fillmore in late December 1968 and shared with the band during his most recent audition. "They brought me backstage after the show . . . and Richie said, 'Can you stay?' 'What?' 'Can you stay?' And I said, 'Yes! I can stay.' . . . 'I want you to be in the band.' . . . It was truly a dream come true."[1]

Schmit traveled and rehearsed with the band for over a month before his first official Poco performance. However, the tension between Young and Schmit was "thick enough to slice," wrote Furay, and mostly caused by Young, who did not wholeheartedly welcome the newest member. "Rusty was very chilly toward him," continues Furay. "For example, if there was only one chair available at a table, but it was next to Timothy, Rusty wouldn't sit in it."[2] Young said the tension resulted from Schmit's musicianship. "[Jimmy is] a brilliant bass player, but Tim's not. He's adequate. As an instrumentalist, I really missed having that bottom. Everything came off of that and when it wasn't there anymore it really bothered me and I let him know it."[3] However, Grantham said Rusty did not give Schmit "enough credit as a musician," and quickly added, "They just didn't get along very well."[4] Messina called Schmit "a great player" who, when he joined Poco, just did not have the experience yet. The cofounder also said, "Tim was a great addition. . . . He brought in a spark of life that was very important and very needed."[5] Schmit believed the tension had nothing to do with the music: "He was a jock and I was a hippie. That was more of the vibe. He was more of a slick guy. He despised marijuana but he would drink a cocktail. And I was a pot smoker."[6]

One night in mid-November, probably at Thelma's on Sunset Strip, it looked as though Schmit would be fired. There were equipment problems, but after the set Dickie Davis pulled Schmit into a tiny dressing room and told him that he was not working out. "He indicated," recalled Schmit, "that Rusty didn't think I was cutting it." Before he left that night, Schmit talked to Furay: "Hey, no, no. You are staying. You're the guy that should be here. . . . You're in the band. You're gonna stay. And I'll make sure that happens."[7] "Timmy was on the receiving end of that probably more than he deserved," said Davis.[8] Over fifty years later, Schmit and Furay have remained close. "Richie is always my champion," said Schmit. "A real mentor of mine. He taught me a lot, not by telling me this or that, just by example, as far as being a musician, as far as being onstage, and as far as singing goes. I just soaked it all in."[9]

Schmit played with Poco and Young until 1977, when he replaced Meisner again, this time in the Eagles, with whom he still tours. He and Young never grew close: "Rusty and I coexisted, but we weren't the best of friends. We were just really different from each other in a lot of ways."[10] In 2018, Young said that Schmit "was [Richie's] guy" and added, "he's a great guy and I love him to death, a really cool guy, has a great voice and it was neat to have him in the band."[11]

Preparing the Second Album

Disappointed with sales of *Pickin' Up the Pieces* and its appeal to the country audience, Furay felt the need to adjust Poco's sound, "just tinker a little bit."[12] The country-rock movement had not taken off as forecasted. None of its innovative artists, like Poco or the Flying Burrito Brothers, could find a place on AM radio. It would not be until 1972, with the Eagles, that country-rock found a short-lived AM audience. The Eagles scored three hit singles from their first album with "Take It Easy" (#12), "Peaceful Easy Feeling" (#22), and the not very country-rock "Witchy Woman" (#9). But these hits did not open the door for other country-rock songs, and the Eagles veered into a more pop-rock or eclectic sound for their greatest commercial success. For the most part, country-rock remained mostly a regional success, thriving in Southern California from the late 1960s until perhaps the late 1970s.

In a 1969 interview, Furay and Messina indicated only a lukewarm commitment to country-rock. "This country thing won't last too long, but we're interested in it," said Furay. "Country will have its day," said Messina, "and then something else will replace it. We're not worried about the change because as we said, we're doing the music we want."[13] More recently, Furay commented, "I really did feel like we had to compromise this somehow."[14] Of course, to rock fans a band's sound is sacred; to "compromise" the sound is to sell out or become inauthentic. Rock audiences have embraced what Keir Keightley calls a "romantic authenticity," which privileges "tradition, continuity, community, *a core sound*, gradual stylistic change, directness, and hiding musical technology," as opposed to a "Modernist authenticity," which privileges "radical shifts, openness regarding sounds, obliqueness, and the celebration of technology."[15] "The myth of authenticity," as Simon Frith declared, "is . . . one of rock's own ideological effects, an aspect of its sales process: rock stars can be marketed as artists, and their particular sounds marketed as a means of identity."[16] As if to join in the debate, Furay added, "But in the real world, musicians want to reach as many people as possible, and sometimes making changes—even small ones—can help them achieve that goal. It's entirely possible to broaden your appeal without tarnishing your art or minimizing your creativity."[17] Had critics known the shift was more calculated than organic, Furay believes that Poco would have been excoriated. The nineteenth-century myth of the committed but starving artist lies deep in the trenches of rock music sensibilities—ironic given the financial stakes.

For their second album, Poco, therefore, decided to emphasize the *rock* in their country-rock sound. However, during rehearsals they ran into problems with Clive Davis—again. When Poco returned to the studio for rehearsals, they discovered they were locked out. The tension between Clive Davis and Dick Davis had escalated to the point that Clive, who had signed Poco to a nine-album deal, would not sign off on the studio time. "There was so much drama going on between the two Davises." Richie sighs.[18] "Clive didn't like me. Plain and simple," said Dickie. "And he made no bones about it. I don't know why. [*Laughs.*] He was a powerful businessman and I was a freakin' hippie as far as he was concerned. This is total speculation."[19] More probable, the label executive may not have appreciated the manager's explosiveness or his lack of negotiating skills. Timothy Schmit remembers: "I heard Dickie several times on the phone. I think people stopped taking his calls."[20] Reportedly, Dickie had problems with other industry insiders like Ahmet Ertegun, Jerry Moss (the M in A & M Records), and promoter Bill Graham. Jim Messina said, "On one hand you can say that Dickie was very protective of the band and fought on our behalf. But sometimes it's better to avoid conflict in the discretion of diplomacy."[21] Davis has always been well liked by band members in Poco and Buffalo Springfield; neither band ever doubted his good intentions. However, Neil Young's biographer Jimmy McDonough described Davis as "energetic, gung ho and a bit of a hothead"—it was the "hothead" that generated most of the problems.[22] The Turtles' Mark Volman, who lived with Furay for a time, offers insight into Davis: "Dickie was well-meant; he knew what he was capable of doing and he just got in over his head. . . . All of that stuff that was going on with Dickie was just the fact that he was a young fella who just really loved the music, loved the band, [and] loved the guys he was with; you couldn't say that about a lot of managers."[23]

With an album awaiting rehearsal, Furay sought help from a friend and a Poco fan, then-agent David Geffen. With Furay in his office, Geffen called Clive Davis and stunned Richie with his profanity-laced rant at the head of Columbia Records. At first, Furay thought Geffen's strategy, seemingly the same as Dickie's, would only lead to further ostracism for the band. However, he soon realized that Geffen was "so forceful, so relentless, so unstoppable, that even this legendary music executive couldn't resist his will for long."[24] The difference, too, was that Clive respected Geffen. Even though Geffen was only twenty-six, he had proven his musical acumen with Laura Nyro and Crosby, Stills & Nash—unlike Dickie, who had not proven anything yet. The next day Poco was back in the studio. In his autobiography, Clive wrote, "No one is more persuasive than David."[25]

At Clive's insistence, Dickie was replaced. Furay again turned to Geffen for advice: "'You don't need a manager,'" said Geffen. "He was telling us in a very subtle way that he would take care of it." But Furay missed the subtlety. Instead, Poco hired Schiffman / Larson Management. "David got contrary over that and I think our relationship got hurt."[26] Todd Schiffman, a former musician and bandleader, was not yet thirty when he signed Poco. He had been working as an agent for the Contemporary Music Division of the Ashley Famous Agency (later ICM), where he represented Jefferson Airplane, the Doors, Janis Joplin, Steppenwolf, and others before beginning his own management and music publishing company with Larry Larson. Schiffman had known Furay for a couple of years. After the Springfield broke up and Pogo began, Schiffman lived next to Richie and Nancy in Laurel Canyon. They became friendly. "They wanted my opinion of what I thought of a rock band that did country," said Schiffman. "They played me some songs, and I thought it was great. . . . I kept in touch with them over a long period of time. When it came to them getting a manager, they went with a lunatic friend of Richie's (Dicky [sic] Davis), but they wanted me to be the agent, [but] I didn't get along with [Davis]." For his new firm, Schiffman said, "Poco was an important act and gave us credibility."[27]

Schiffman and Larson, who managed Poco until the very end of 1972, brought stability to Poco's managerial process. "They were absolutely the best managers that we had," said Richie. "They were very good at what they did: getting us gigs, keeping us on tour, and taking care of business."[28] However, they never garnered needed favor for Poco with Epic. "My opinion," said Furay, "is that Clive's a great big guy in the music business, but I never felt we got the [necessary] support from him," not only for *Pickin' Up the Pieces* but also for any future Poco albums featuring Furay. "We had no one really supporting us. We had only Clive Davis fighting us all the way. For some reason or another, he hated Dick Davis and it was just a fight from the beginning. . . . At the Troubadour we were knocking them dead. We were filling the house. We were a big deal. We had momentum, and Clive was definitely a momentum breaker when he didn't get behind us."[29] In 1973, Schmit put it another way: "Epic just doesn't know what to do with us."[30]

Poco

With a new bass player, new management, a more rock sound, and problems with Clive Davis at least on hold, Poco entered the studio in late 1969 to record their second album. We were "starting at square one," declared Richie and "what better way to do it than to make our name the only word on the record jacket"[31]—hence the eponymously titled album.

Jim Messina, serving again as producer, was determined to improve the sonic quality of *Poco* over that of *Pickin' Up the Pieces*, which frustrates him to this day. Hired as head engineer was Alex Kasanegras with Terry Dunavan, who was second engineer on *Pieces*.[32] With sixteen tracks to work with and a fully cooperative engineer, Messina had more flexibility than he did with the first album. He placed each vocalist, even those singing harmony, on a separate track. "Then if we wanted to overdub and double those parts, we could double them. . . . Generally, we might have anywhere from three to six vocal tracks on a song. . . . The voices were the most important thing in terms of giving the song its identity and its life. The drums and bass were the second, and then the guitars."[33] Messina insisted, and Kasanegras readily agreed, on separate drum tracks: one for the bass, one for the snare, and another for the high hat. Messina then used one track for the bass and two or three for the guitars with a few tracks left for whatever the song needed, like a piano on "Anyway Bye Bye."

For Messina, Kasanegras represented "the changing of the guard." He knew rock and roll, and he liked Poco's music. "He wanted this new music to sound good and he knew how to work those boards and consoles." Messina especially appreciated his cooperative spirit: "When I would ask him about something, he would say, 'Yeah, absolutely,' or 'Yeah, I could do that, but maybe we should do this.' And, I'd say, 'Yeah, that's better.' We had a working relationship." By padding the microphone, Kasanegras helped Messina get the fuzztone guitar distortion on "Hurry Up," and with proper balancing of sound, he caught the exciting interplay of two percussionists on "El Tonto de Nadie, Regresa." "It became really wonderful to be back in the studio with an engineer who understood."[34] The overall result is that the music on *Poco* explodes from the speakers—clear, rich, and urgent.

The Songs

On *Poco*, the tilt toward rock may have led to more vehement lyrics. On the first album, songs with angry and confrontational lyrics and aggressive rhythms and bitter vocals were few—only "Short Changed" and "Nobody's Fool." On *Poco*, the balance shifts with "Keep on Believin'" as the only unequivocally sunny and cheerful song. In fact, of the seven tracks, four, including "Believin'," are titled with commands: "Hurry Up," "You Better Think Twice," and the love song, "Don't Let It Pass By." Other titles do not suggest rosy situations: "Anyway Bye Bye," "Honky Tonk Downstairs," and the re-recording of "Nobody's Fool" bleeding into the jam "El Tonto de Nadie, Regresa" (Nobody's Fool Returns). The urgency in these titles matches the band's desperation for success and reflects their anxiety and dismay over the events of the past year, which included their name change, the loss of Meisner, tensions between Young and Schmit, problems with Epic, and the exit of Dickie Davis. However, no Poco album could ever sound too bleak or despairing. Whatever the song titles or lyrics, the boyish tenor of Furay and the uplifting harmonies will lighten almost any lyrical darkness—but not on *Poco*'s opener, "Hurry Up," a mid-tempo, muscular rocker.

With no musical intro to "Hurry Up," Furay's voice bursts out: "Here I sit with you like the day has got no hour." This is not the relaxing "good morning" of "What a Day" or the summer afternoon lovefest of "Pickin' Up the Pieces." Furay is tense and confrontational, reflected in Messina's scorching fuzz-toned solo from 3:00 to 3:24. Furay demands an explanation from his silent addressee (possibly an imagined Meisner) and seemingly mocks his silence with a stutter: "Hurry up, now tell me . . . my, my my . . . yeah!" When Furay sings, "I've been a-tellin' you, I'm feelin' just fine," his snide tone signals he is hardly fine. He preaches to his addressee about the virtue of patience, "as rewarding as a new love in spring." But then he attacks his listener for being "caught in his own dream," which destroys patience and group unity. "Hurry Up" marks one of the few Furay songs in which dreams are destructive. Along with images of love and home, dreams—a recurring theme in Furay—are usually favorable, as in, for example, "What a Day," "Believe Me" (1974), and "We Were the Dreamers" (2015). Dreams, for Furay, generate vision, motivation, hopefulness, and love.

One of the strongest cuts on *Poco* is "Anyway Bye Bye," the closing track to the original side 1. Inspired by Buffalo Springfield's disbandment, Furay fills the song with anger (references to "words [being] meaningless"), frustration ("tossin' in my sleeplessness"), fear ("changes that I dread"), and sarcasm ("anyway, bye, bye"). The music combines country-blues, light jazz, and rock and features Furay's effectively stylized singing that, with Messina's soaring lead guitar runs and Young's "organ" riffs and solos, delivers a riveting performance, all enhanced by Poco's harmonies with Grantham's high voice adding a touch of lightness. Furthermore, the track reveals how much Furay has developed as a vocalist from his mannered vocal tones and enunciations with the Au Go-Go Singers and some early Springfield tracks like "Clancy." Here, Furay holds, cuts, twists, elevates, and drops notes, effortlessly and gracefully. It takes twenty seconds, for instance, for Furay to cry out, "Baby, bye byes aren't always pleasin'." In addition, Messina's production skills lead to a clean sound with instruments and vocals that resonate. In Poco's earliest days, Randy Meisner sang lead on "Anyway Bye Bye," which remained a favorite of his. He recorded a bluesy, almost gospel, version of the song on his second post-Eagles solo album, *One More Song* (1980).

"Don't Let It Pass By," a country-blues ballad, marks another powerfully tender vocal performance by Furay. The singer and his beloved have just settled a dispute over "something silly, something trite," and the singer reproclaims his love and commitment, which seems mutual. The last verse is particularly moving as the singer laments the passing moment. Their bliss, he acknowledges, can only be fleeting, as "Monday morning ... comes too soon" and time moves us. However, the singer leaves nothing "half done" or "half said" and ends the song with a dramatic "I love you," seeming to hope that the intensity of the declaration will evoke recollections and, like the song itself, preserve the delicate scene. Many of Furay's songs focus on a brief dramatic scene, like "Hurry Up," or a fleeting emotional moment, like "Sad Memory." "Don't Let It Pass By" does both. As a potent lyricist, Furay has long been not only underrated but also unacknowledged. Songs like "Hurry Up," "Anyway Bye Bye," and "Don't Let It Pass By" indicate his ability to be succinct and crisp as well as dramatic and emotional, especially combined with the clarity and command of his vocals.

The lone traditional country song on *Poco* is a cover of Dallas Frazier's "Honky Tonk Downstairs." It was first recorded by George Jones as a B-side to "If My Heart Had Windows" (1967, #7 US Country) and appears on his album *George Jones Sings the Songs of Dallas Frazier* (1968). Poco slows slightly the melody and rhythm, adding a more bluesy effect, with Young's pedal steel punctuating lines, and taking a sad, high-register solo. Furay's voice holds up well next to the usually imposing vocals of Jones in what is not a classic Jones performance. The song tells of an alcoholic singer, ashamed that his wife supports him by working as a barmaid in the honky tonk below their apartment. Interestingly, Furay remembers talking with George Strait backstage after one of Strait's concerts: "He said that when he heard that song [by Poco], that was one of the songs that prompted him to pursue the career he had."[35] Strait recorded the song in 1981 on his debut album, *Strait Country*.

"Think Twice," the energetic country rocker by Jim Messina, was a good candidate for a hit single. The song begins with Messina slashing two chords, followed by a brisk electric guitar run leading to the first verse. Messina, in largely understated but mildly intimidating vocals, sings to a woman who contemplates "leaving [him] behind." He advises her to "take her time ... to think twice." The song is about an old girlfriend of Messina's. "It was a little bit of a love song," Messina said, "but also a little bit of angst and frustration about somebody not wanting to necessarily be with me."[36] The high harmonies of Furay, Schmit, and Grantham contrast poignantly with Messina's restrained lead vocal lines. About this time Messina was gaining confidence as a vocalist. "I was just getting my voice in those days, and those guys were very good. . . . 'You Better Think Twice' was the first time I began to feel like I could do this. I could stand up here with these guys."[37]

Inexplicably, the single, the first from *Poco*, was not released until the early fall, five months after the album's release. Usually, the single is released slightly ahead of the album to promote anticipation. Entering the charts at #93 in early October, "You Better Think Twice" stalled at a disappointing #72 in late November. Furay commented: "It was a good song with a nice melodic part. It was probably as AM-ey as any song on the album." However, he added, "I think 'Don't Let It Pass By' could have been an AM radio song at the same time."[38] Poco gained television exposure for "Think Twice" on both *American Bandstand* and *Something Else*, hosted by John Byner, where the song was introduced via a silly skit on a docked boat.[39]

"Keep on Believin'"

Furay is well known for his fast-paced songs of jubilation, proclaiming hopefulness and glad tidings. Most famous is "A Good Feelin' to Know" (1972), but there are many others: "What a Day," "C'mon" (1971), "Let's Dance Tonight" (1973), "Fallin' in Love" (1974), right up to "Dean's Barbecue" (2005) and "Someday" (2016). "Keep on Believin'" is another high-spirited performance of unwavering optimism. In 1967, Jim Delehant wrote that Furay "smiles a lot, and is always in a good mood," while in 2020, author Peter Knobler said "Richie is one of the real goodhearted people on this earth. He's a lovely guy, who has a rosy view of the world and he wants to have people feel that way too. 'Good Feelin' to Know'—'somebody loves you'—that's Richie in a nutshell." Furay is, indeed, generally upbeat and good-natured with a resilient optimism and welcoming geniality, "a people-person," as his sister said.[40] Of course, his expressions of hopefulness and good cheer, musical and otherwise, make his occasional outbursts of temper all the more surprising and hurtful.

Furay wrote "Believin'" with Timothy Schmit. Neither cowriter remembers what Schmit contributed to the song, but Furay sought to make the newest member of the band feel wanted and needed—especially necessary with Schmit given his tension with Young. Schmit remembers Furay's invitation to write with him, which came one afternoon while he and his girlfriend visited the Furays. Richie suggested the musicians withdraw to work on a song. "We went into the dining room or somewhere with the guitars and started kicking this thing around," recalls Schmit. "All I can tell you is that it was very awkward. First of all, I wasn't a seasoned songwriter. . . . I just kind of faked it, but I did my best to contribute. . . . Richie was being generous."[41] It was their only attempt at writing together.

"Keep on Believin'" is Furay's State of the Band Address. After all their recent problems, Richie calls on Poco to "keep on believin', keepin' it clear, [and] good times will finally arrive." The song is a pep talk to the band, Furay said, "about getting creative, of being able to get into the studio and do the work again. . . . It was like a song of 'Yeah, man, let's keep focus. Let's keep going ahead. . . . Let's keep our hand to the plow.'"[42] In rhythm and verse, the song references Poco's new direction, leaning more toward rock, "to find ourselves a new way," and to pursue it in full force without being "stranded in fear." The song features screeching and grinding guitars, Grantham's driving backbeat, Schmit's basslines with patterns resembling Bill Haley's "Rock Around the Clock" and the Four Tops' "I Can't Help Myself," energetic harmonies of Grantham and Schmit with Schmit breaking out from the confines of the chorus for a solo line ("It's been so long"), some carefully placed Beatlesque *oohs* (like in "Twist and Shout"), and a trademark Furay scream of joy eight seconds into the track—almost all of Furay's jubilation songs feature a similar scream. "Keep on Believin'" is a blistering and exuberant three minutes.

However, the song that marked Poco's biggest shift in sound consumed almost all of the original side 2 of *Poco*.

"Nobody's Fool / El Tonto de Nadie, Regresa"

During the daytime in the summer of 1969, Poco rented the Troubadour, where they worked out new material and broke in Schmit. "We were trying to find our identity," said Grantham, "and we just got into this jam [on 'Nobody's Fool']. . . . It just started, and all of a sudden it was, 'This sounds kind of neat.' . . . Everybody just stretched out."[43] At the time, jams were a key feature of bands from San Francisco, like the Grateful Dead and Jefferson Airplane, but country-rock bands were not playing long improvisations despite the rising popularity of jam bands. "In-A-Gadda-Da-Vida," the title track on Iron Butterfly's 1968 album, occupied all of side 2, at slightly over seventeen minutes, and became the top-selling album of 1969. "We wanted to keep up with the times," said Furay.[44] By the end of June, Poco began including "Nobody's Fool / El Tonto" in their setlist. Robert Hilburn, in his review of a late-1969 Poco performance at the Troubadour, called the ten-minute jam "probably the most impressive portion" of their set.[45] Coincidentally, Todd

Schiffman managed Iron Butterfly, but he had no influence on Poco's decision to feature the lengthy jam on their upcoming release.

When Poco entered the studio to record "El Tonto," Messina had hired percussionist Milton Holland to add texture. Holland, who was some thirty years older than most of the band, had worked with Duke Ellington, Ella Fitzgerald, Frank Sinatra, the Beatles, and the Rolling Stones. Ringo Starr had called him "a legend," and Bob Dylan called him "one of the greatest drummers in the world."[46] Grantham, who had played jazz in high school and considered Buddy Rich and Joe Morello of the Dave Brubeck Quartet among his influences, remains excited about his experience with Holland: "He was great. I loved playing with Milt Holland. . . . He filled in stuff like crazy. I didn't have to feel like I was filling everything in. He really added a lot. A lot!"[47] Holland, with his tablas, congas, and bongos, added a Latin flavor to the jam, hence the Spanish title. That August, Santana had released their first album, which rose to #4 on the album charts by mid-November. However, Furay did not think that had influenced "El Tonto."

"Nobody's Fool / El Tonto de Nadie" takes several twists and turns and mood swings. It begins with a light jazz riff from Messina's guitar and Young's organ-sounding pedal steel. At about the twenty-second mark, Messina fires off a rock riff, Furay screams, and "Nobody's Fool" begins with harmonies from Furay, Schmit, and Grantham. Different from the recording on *Pickin' Up the Pieces*, "Nobody's Fool" is shortened to just over two minutes with horns removed and a more prominent "organ." At approximately 2:10, Schmit's bass redirects the song back to its jazz leanings, and Young plays what could be a Hammond B3 solo, extending to almost the 4:00 mark. After a slow percussive transition from Grantham and Holland with Schmit's bass, Messina takes over the next two minutes, blasting rock riffs and leads until about the 6:30 mark. Holland dominates the next two minutes on percussion before, at 8:20, Messina reemerges with his rock guitar. The song moves forward, shifting the spotlight from Messina to Young to Holland and Grantham. Holding down the groove are Furay on rhythm guitar and Schmit on bass, sometimes using a walking bass line. There are surprises along the way, like Messina's jazzy blues solo at 10:40, with its rounded, high-register notes, lasting for almost ninety seconds before Young's squawks and sputtering bursts rise above Messina's solo to try to steal center stage. At 15:44, Messina introduces a catchy riff, which a few seconds later is mirrored in vocal harmonies of logatomes (*doo-doo-doo . . . dup*). After another scorching run from Messina, the song draws to a close at 18:25 after Furay, Schmit, and Grantham, in high harmony, deliver an enigmatic single line: "'Cause I got the same from you." The "completed" recording clocked in at over twenty-seven minutes, which Messina cut and spliced to its released length.

It was a daring release for Poco, for its length, its Latin underpinnings, and its shifting directions from rock to blues to jazz with little reference, if any, to country or country-rock. However, it gave the band an opportunity to stretch and showcase their substantial abilities, especially as soloists. Poco's fans, or Poconuts, liked it, then and now, especially in live performance, where it has always been greeted with enthusiasm. However, the jam, as powerful and intricate as it is, did not seem to attract many new fans to Poco.

Released on May 6 and dedicated to David Geffen, *Poco* introduced not only the band's tweaked sound but also its tweaked image. Gone was the cowboy imagery from *Pieces* with its campfire scene, lasso around the playing card portraits, and silhouetted cowboy on horseback. Instead, the cover for Poco, designed by the innovative Gary Burden with a drawing by Morris Ovsey, features the five members in the foreground of a brightly colored painting of an orange grove in a valley. Two disproportionately large oranges hang on each side—just above Young's head on the left, and Messina's on the right—hence its designation among Poconuts as "the Orange Album" or "Oranges." The band members are casually dressed, with the closest to cowboy imagery being Schmit's leather vest under a fringe jacket or Messina's apparently vintage black jacket, perhaps velvet, with a large white collar and what looks like a white ascot tie. Like Young and Schmit, Furay is in casual attire, in jeans and a brownish wool vest above a yellow shirt with multicolored polka dots. *Poco*, in large bright yellow letters, appears on the top of the jacket, above a white mountain peak, and stretches from one orange to the other. The colors could have been inspired by a colorful fruit crate from the San Joaquin Valley. The playful Wild West imagery on the first album has thus been replaced with an image of lush and prosperous California, suggestive of a band fresh, new, and bountiful.

Frustration

Poco entered the *Billboard* charts in early June 1970 and peaked two months later at a disappointing #58, five spots ahead of *Pickin' Up the Pieces*, a negligible rise and not enough to expand their fan base. Meanwhile, that same summer, Furay's former bandmates scored a #1 smash with Crosby, Stills, Nash & Young's *Déjà vu*. Furay was frustrated but has never begrudged any of his former bandmates their success.

FIG. 9 Poco at the Festival for Peace, Shea Stadium. *Left to right*: Timothy B. Schmit, Richie Furay, and Rusty Young. Copyright Ken Davidoff / Vintage Rock Icons.

To try to compensate for lack of airplay and to take advantage of their exciting live show, Schiffman and Larson constructed a relentless touring schedule. "I got involved and I got them the right agent," said Schiffman, "and we got the right venues and the right packages to put them on. Lo and behold, they became a huge act. They could go into five-, ten-thousand-seat arenas and pack them."[48] Schiffman exaggerates. On their own, Poco could not fill ten-thousand-seat arenas. But the manager crafted combinations that sought to introduce Poco to different audiences that might not otherwise find them. He scheduled dates with Van Morrison, Rod Stewart and the Faces, Buddy Miles, and Elton John. "[Elton] opened for us on a couple of shows," remembered Grantham, "and he was just incredible. We thought, 'Oh my God, this guy's gonna be huge.'"[49] Schiffman's strategy worked but only to a limited extent. Without a hit single or album, Poco never developed a large national fan base. Instead, they had strong followings in pocket areas, with perhaps none stronger than Boston and New York City.

On August 6, 1970, Poco played the Festival for Peace at Shea Stadium, then home of the New York Mets. (See fig. 9.) Sharing the stage with Janis Joplin, Creedence Clearwater Revival, Steppenwolf, Dionne Warwick, Paul Simon, and many others, Poco performed in the bright heat of the early afternoon and earned a tremendous ovation. Music critic Jerry Gilbert said it was "of enormous significance and considered by speculators to be an automatic springboard to the top for Poco."[50] Pete Fornatale, a deejay at the influential free-form rock station WNEW-FM in New York, missed the performance but wrote in the liner notes to *Deliverin'* that he "began hearing what knockouts they were in person," reporting that "eyewitness accounts" told how "they literally rocked Shea Stadium." As an eyewitness, who had his introduction to Poco that day, I can corroborate that tiers indeed shook from the foot-stompin' and dancing crowd. Fornatale championed Poco on the airwaves and is a significant reason for Poco's large New York City following. Backstage at Shea, Schmit remembers an impressed Paul Simon approaching the band. "He told us that he wanted to use us on a song," but nothing materialized. Furay said that the Shea Stadium performance "just really blew the whole thing right up." Afterward, he said, "[We] really saturated the East Coast . . . and that [became a] really great market for us." If people saw Poco, they liked them. The problem, as Young said in 1971, "is getting to the majority of the people . . . our problem is making everyone aware of us"—hard to do without a hit record. Schmit summarizes Poco's frustrating situation in the early 1970s: "You know, we would go to New York and people would come in droves to see us play. I remember them sprawled out over Central Park's little hills and streets, and I would walk down the streets and people would recognize me. . . . And then we would go somewhere else . . . Detroit or something and nobody knew shit about us. It was very hit and miss."[51]

When bands do not meet their commercial expectations, tensions develop. Furay and Messina did not quarrel or verbalize their discontent, but both were increasingly uneasy with one another. Messina felt Furay was exerting too much control, moving the band further in the rock direction. "Richie wanted to do tunes like John Fogerty—that kind of hard rock—and I wasn't into doing songs like John Fogerty; I didn't want to be a Creedence Clearwater." Curiously, Furay, who had written "Pickin' Up the Pieces" and "Just in Case It Happens," claimed that "Jimmy made the group more country than I had ever envisaged it. I wanted it more rock 'n' roll right at the beginning."[52] Late in 1970, after Messina had left, a college journalist reported, "One thing that the group made clear to me, when I talked with them, was that they don't like to be termed a country-rock band, even if part of their sound is in this bag."[53] Messina was upset with Furay's rejection of two songs that he had written for the band. He played Furay "Same Old Wine" and "Golden Ribbons," which he had hoped Furay would sing. "I thought that after Richie rejected a couple of songs, the best thing was not to submit any more material."[54] Messina withheld "Peace of Mind," the third song, which became a favorite among Loggins and Messina fans and which Messina still regularly performs today.

In the summer of 1970, Messina decided to leave Poco during a recording session, probably for "C'mon." Furay was doing take after take as he strove to reach a "very high note that was just at the end of his range," explains Messina. Again, the console board was controlled by an IBEW union engineer, and Messina was not allowed to touch the board:

> I would have to look at the engineer and say, "Roll in. Punch." Now this happened about 8, 10, 12 times. "Punch, punch, punch." Every time we did Richie didn't quite hit the note. So, on this one occasion, I said, "Punch," and the guy was reading a book at the same time. I mean he was looking at a comic book or something. I don't know what the hell he was looking at. And he was late. Richie thought he hit the note. He said, "I got it! I got it!" I said, "Well, you may have, but I'm not sure we did."

Messina understood Furay's frustration, but, nonetheless, found his response unsettling. "He threw his headphones down and said, 'Let me hear this.' He pushed me out of the way and said, 'Play it back.'" The engineer was too late. He did not record the note. Furay was enraged. "'I guess if I'm going to get this,'" the singer yelled, "'I'll need to do it myself.' . . . He grabbed my wrist and started gritting his teeth, and I thought to myself, 'Calm down. . . . Let him go through what he needs to go through.' At that moment I thought, 'This isn't working for me anymore.' That's when I decided I needed somebody to replace me as a musician, someone who's going to keep the band moving in the right direction."[55] One musician told me, off the record, that the incident inspired the Loggins and Messina song "Angry Eyes": "You try to defend that you are not the one to blame / But I'm finding it hard, my friend, when I'm in the deadly aim . . . I bet you thought you could cut me down with those angry eyes" (1972).

Messina telephoned Clive Davis to tell him that he was burned out with touring and wanted to spend more time with his wife, Jenny, whom he had just married, and that he and Furay were having difficulties. He asked to join Columbia's A&R department, where he would sign and produce bands. Davis suggested that they talk in person, which they did aboard a train from New York to Philadelphia, where Davis had a meeting. The label president hoped to dissuade Messina from leaving and asked Messina to think about it for a month. After the month, Messina was more determined than ever to leave, sending Davis a detailed plan and budget, including salary requirements, transportation, and rent. "I still wasn't sure he was making the right choice," said Davis, but "I figured why not give it a try?"[56] However, before he left, Messina followed Davis's instructions: "'Get this next album finished with Poco. Get yourself replaced. Leave in good spirits and be supportive of its success, and, once that's finished, we'll sit down and I'll contemplate what we might be able to do.' So that's what I did. I told the guys that I needed a change, and we need to find somebody to replace me that they're happy with."[57]

Furay found the news "discouraging" and "disappointing" and wondered if he were responsible for first Meisner's and now Messina's departure. "I didn't think so. . . . I considered myself to be easygoing, the sort of person who wants to make everyone around him feel comfortable and wanted."[58] But Furay also saw the opportunity to redirect Poco more fully into rock: "Jimmy is a great guitar player, and I think, whether he would admit it or not, that James Burton had a huge influence on him, who's, obviously, one of the most talented, creative, and innovative guitar players there ever was. But . . . Jimmy's guitar style was a lot more country than, say, a Paul Cotton," his replacement.[59] Cotton, whose voice resembles John Fogerty's, had been in the Illinois Speed Press, which released two albums and had played on several stages with Poco. Cotton had seen Poco in the earliest days at the Troubadour and followed their career as closely as he could. He jumped at Furay's invitation to join in September 1970. For approximately six weeks, he traveled with Poco and roomed with Messina, who reviewed guitar parts with him.

At the end of October, Poco was playing four nights at the Fillmore in San Francisco. On Halloween, the third of four nights, Furay decided to make the change and put Cotton on stage. Messina asked Furay if he could perform one last show, since Neil Young would be in the audience that night. "Neil had never been to a show. I really wanted to play because he was also a pal." Besides working with Young in the Springfield, Messina had played bass on Young's first solo album. Furay rejected Messina's request. Messina remembers the conversation: "Richie said, 'No. This is over for you.' I just felt so hurt by that. I had spent all that time getting Paul ready. I was extremely disappointed and extremely hurt. Not angry. Not vindictive. This was a guy who was my best man at my wedding, you know. I had been there in support of him all of his career from the Buffalo Springfield, wanting him to succeed, and leaving in a fashion where I didn't want to contribute to him not succeeding. It was another side of the man that I never expected to see."[60] Messina flew back to Los Angeles to work on production for *Deliverin'*. Then Clive Davis introduced him to Kenny Loggins, with whom Messina found his greatest success.

Deliverin'

"Everybody told us that we were a great live act and that we didn't capture that on record," said Rusty Young.[61] Therefore, the third album would be recorded live before audiences in Boston and New York, two cities with a copious number of Poconuts. *Deliverin'* included five new songs ("I Guess You Made It," "C'mon," "Hear That Music," "Hard Luck," "A Man Like Me") to go along with five songs from their first two albums, and Furay's two best-known Springfield songs ("Kind Woman," "Child's Claim to Fame"). The album also features the single from *Poco*, here titled "You'd Better Think Twice," and two medleys, the first featuring Schmit's humorous "Hard Luck" bleeding into "Child's Claim" and "Pickin' Up the Pieces," and another with "Just in Case It Happens," "Grand Junction," and "Consequently, So Long." *Deliverin'* is a rousing, high-octane set that captures Poco's passion, warmth, and jubilance in sprightly lead vocals, jaunty harmonies, energetic guitar interplay between Messina and Young, and startling sounds from Young's pedal steel guitar. In his positive review in *Rolling Stone*, Stu Werbin wrote, "Poco will always be better off keeping away from the studios and staying out in front of people." Of the songs re-recorded for *Deliverin'*, Werbin said that each "is infinitely more exciting and competent" than the originals.[62] It was a relatively easy production task for Messina: "It was pretty much live. I don't recall doing much at all. If anything, it might have been picking up a note here and there just to clean it up. . . . But I don't think any of those performances were changed from what I recall."[63]

Deliverin' begins with Furay's "I Guess You Made It," a seemingly joyous romp with Schmit on lead vocals. Grantham's percussion accelerates the song with his speedy cowbell taps, steady beat, cymbal washes, and charged rolls and fills. It seems a happy song until we listen to the lyrics, which are as bitter as "Short Changed." Furay was not sure of his target in "I Guess You Made It," but he did say it was probably Neil Young, as the title might suggest. "Neil had a way of bringing out the frustration in me."[64] The song takes no pity on its addressee, who stands with "feelings hurt," in denial that he has caused his own "scar" after rejecting the singer in his time of need. Instead of help, the addressee offered "a trick, then a smile" and "hurt." The singer calls on him to examine himself and confront his selfishness. The song ends with a sharp question: "Who's your next fool?" The well-dressed bitterness, clear in the lyrics and the snarky *guess* in the title, is lost in the camouflage of the music—especially in the harmonies, which sound particularly gleeful when Grantham and Schmit shout "surprise" five times from the 2:12 mark until

2:20, almost as if announcing a birthday party. The song never failed to ener-gize audiences. In a review of their show at the Fillmore East in early May 1971, "K.K." wrote, "The moment they are introduced, not a single person is left seated. Smiles began to appear as Richie says, 'Howdy, glad to be here tonight.' And then, 'I Guess You Made It'—a show stopper. An opening num-ber that leaves the audience screaming for more." In December of that year, in Poughkeepsie, New York, coreviewers wrote, "As soon as George Grantham began to beat out the introduction to 'Guess You Made It' on the cowbell, the audience was up and dancing. And they didn't stop bouncing and clapping as Poco sailed through joyous tunes like 'C'mon,' 'Hear that Music,' 'What a Day,' and 'A Man Like Me.'"[65] "A Man Like Me" is a companion to "Guess You Made It." Its performance might seem "joyous," but it is a stern rebuke of a hypocrite (Neil Young?) who "sang a sweet, sweet song" but took the singer "for a ride."

Released in mid-January 1971, *Deliverin'* fared far better than the first two albums, reaching a very solid #26; fifty years later *Mojo* called it "one of the landmark country-rock albums."[66] However, the album would have risen even higher had the single "C'mon" been given a full opportunity to succeed. Cam-eron Crowe reports that it was getting heavy airplay on the West Coast and "chances looked excellent for a nationwide hit." That is, until influential pro-gram director Bill Drake, one of the most powerful men in AM radio with ties, as a consultant and programmer, to stations around the country, misheard the song's chorus. In Drake's ears, "C'mon and *love* me," was "C'mon and *suck* me."[67] He immediately pulled "C'mon" from his playlists. Drake, with his partner Gene Chenault, had perfected the Top 40 format. He cut commer-cial time, hired deejays with strong personalities who talked less and played more music, and called his concept Boss Radio, with "boss" representing that which was "cool" or "groovy." When he pulled "C'mon," Drake was program-ming top stations in Los Angeles, San Diego, San Francisco, Tulsa, Memphis, Cincinnati, Boston, and New York. It was a blow to Poco.

But *Deliverin'*, with its very respectable showing and the addition of Paul Cotton, breathed new life and confidence into Furay. "We all felt pretty sat-isfied with that record," said Richie. "And, certainly, we were looking forward to the next project."[68]

CHAPTER 8

"What Am I Gonna Do"

Decisions

On September 7, 1970, Furay was home for the birth of the first of his and Nancy's four daughters, Timmie Sue. He would write the majestic "Sweet Lovin'" about the birth: "Tears runnin' down my face in ecstasy." Four days later, Furay played a date in San Diego, and then he was back to the East Coast for more shows, including the recording of *Deliverin'*.

Furay was never a drug-taking, groupie-enthralled rock star. He might indulge in beer, marijuana, amphetamines, and, on occasion, cocaine, but never regularly and never to the extent that it interfered with his work. As he checked in with Nancy from the road, he noticed that the phone calls were becoming shorter and shorter. Nancy talked more about their infant and the duties of new motherhood, seeming to care little about the latest Poco show. Furay began to feel neglected—foolishly, as he admits. "Hey, you get on the road and you get crazy. You're lost. . . . I didn't know what home was."[1] It was at this time that Richie met an attractive secretary and talented pianist who worked for an executive at Columbia Records. At first, it was friendship based on music, but, before long, the relationship evolved into a full-blown affair. "I thought that this secretary understood me and knew me better than my wife did. And I fell for it. I fell into the trap."[2] While Furay carried on his romance, his former bandmate and roommate released his smash solo album *Stephen Stills* (#3) and hit single "Love the One You're With" (#14), often interpreted as a paean to free love.

After some five months, the affair reached its nadir on February 12, 1971, when Poco headlined New York's Carnegie Hall, a prestigious and momentous event. They played two sold-out shows that night. (At the time, it was routine for rock bands to perform an "early" and "late show.") For the occasion

Nancy, with Timmie Sue, and Richie's mother flew in for the performance, attending with Richie's sister, Judy, who was then living in New York. However, after the midnight show, Furay did not return to the hotel where his wife and mom were staying. Instead, he stayed with his girlfriend in her apartment, explaining that he had to stay with the band as they had an early bus ride the next morning to Schenectady, New York. Looking back, Richie explained his mindset: "I thought I was taking care of [Nancy]; I was providing for her. She had everything I thought she needed, but she didn't have me."[3]

Soon, however, Richie found his double life disturbing. It was at odds with his Midwestern and middle-class upbringing, his sense of integrity, morality, and even pragmatism. "It was a very dark time in my life. Very dark," he explained. "It was a time when I was so consumed with things that I didn't know what reality was, 'upside down on a merry-go-round.' . . . To look back at it and to even think that I could have done what I did as far as even having them there for Carnegie Hall and then not even going to their hotel room or whatever, is just unbelievable. I can barely even think of it."[4] For a constantly touring musician, a failed relationship is an occupational hazard. It becomes difficult for the musician to relate to the problems and cares of his partner back home, who tries to maintain a stable lifestyle as the road is never stable and its problems seem so much more urgent.

About a month after Carnegie Hall, Furay called Nancy to confess. Nancy immediately asked her husband about the number of women with whom he had been unfaithful. Richie informed her that it was only one, which aggravated the situation. Nancy realized that her husband was not merely seeking physical gratification but also an emotional connection. The couple separated as Nancy moved in with her mom, found a job, and hired a divorce attorney. She was ready to move on. Richie continued touring with Poco, which included several dates in Texas that April. He took his girlfriend with him. In Texas, while not yet a born-again Christian, Furay had an epiphany: "I was making the worst mistake of my life. I was terrified and felt sick inside. . . . I know now it was the Holy Spirit stepping into my life."[5] At the first break, he returned to Los Angeles to try to reconcile with Nancy. After much humiliation and with much trepidation, Nancy decided to give the marriage another chance. In early May, Furay extended an invitation to Nancy and the other Poco wives and girlfriends to join them in Boston for a few days. Not all of Furay's bandmates were appreciative. Before the visitors arrived, Richie flew to New York and ended his relationship with his girlfriend. However, he did not return in time to meet an irate and suspicious Nancy, who had been expecting him upon her arrival.

From the Inside

In June 1971, Furay traveled to Memphis with Nancy and Timmie Sue for an expected three- or four-week stay. Richie had hoped to use the time in one location to record Poco's fourth album and repair his marriage. Neither the reconciliation nor the recording sessions went well. Soon after arriving, Nancy and Timmie Sue returned to Los Angeles after Furay continued to accept calls from his now ex-girlfriend in New York. Furay's distressed emotional state left its mark on *From the Inside*.

Furay wrote or cowrote six of the ten tracks on the album, with Cotton contributing three and Schmit the title track. It could be the strongest collection of songs that Poco ever assembled for an album, but they do not coalesce into a compelling whole. In addition, with Furay distracted by his marital problems, he could not be the leader needed at that moment. "He was going through a hard time in his life," said Grantham. "He was being torn left and right."[6] Furthermore, the band was road weary. Schiffman had kept them on tour nonstop. "We'd been on the road for six months straight," said Young, "and instead of going home, we went directly to Memphis to record that album."[7] However, on the surface, the fault for the lackluster performance on *From the Inside* lies with the production of Steve Cropper.

Cropper, the legendary guitarist of Booker T. and the M.G.'s, the house band at Stax Records, was not a good match for Poco. Recommended by Clive Davis, Cropper had previously produced *Them Changes*, a hit album for Buddy Miles, and the eponymous first album of Mavis Staples. He had, however, not produced a country-rock band. But Davis, who often relied on his musical instincts, perhaps felt Cropper's R&B energy could bring fuel to Poco's sound. It did not work. "We didn't really connect with him," said Young, "and he didn't connect with us."[8] In addition, Cropper's studio, Trans Maximus, was inadequate for Poco, who relied on multitracked vocals. "His tracks weren't all available," said Grantham. "We couldn't do all the recording that we wanted to do. We had to bunch it all together and mix it all down to make the album. . . . We had to do a lot of stuff on eight tracks!" The result is that the album, particularly its vocal harmonies, sounds bland. Jim Messina, who worked diligently on *Poco* to achieve a sound that pops from the speakers, would not have tolerated this. Grantham joked, "Jimmy would have definitely killed him."[9] Young noted that Cropper was having personal problems at the time, which caused him to miss sessions and to drink "pretty heavily."[10] According to Cotton, "He messed it up," before adding, "We were under great pressure and the album shows that."[11]

But the fault was not all Cropper's. "We still had influence on the record," said Furay, "and I think that's really wrong to [blame Cropper]."[12] *From the Inside* was not the record the band had intended to make. An un-Poco heaviness or, as band members suggest, a darkness soaks the album. Grantham and Schmit both acknowledge the album's "dark sound" and "dark energy."[13] Furay believes he brought the darkness with him: *"From the Inside* is a dark album and that has nothing to do with Steve Cropper. . . . I think it was an attitude that I brought to the record, not Paul, not Rusty, not George, not Timothy: me. I can do that. I can create an atmosphere. You can hear the darkness in the songs."[14] Poco wanted to re-record the album, but Clive Davis would have none of it, perhaps recalling the fiasco surrounding the release of *Pickin' Up the Pieces*. After all, a release date had been set and a tour scheduled.

The Songs

"Hoe Down," written by Furay and Young, welcomes us to the album by inviting us to a good old-fashioned country dance party. Accompanied at first only by handclaps, the vocalists shout with cheerful anticipation: "Well, I'm going to a hoe down / And kick up my heels / Go all night and never slow down / Yeah I love how it feels." Then with Schmit's pumping bass lines, a Furay or Schmit joyful *whew*, which recurs, and with occasional vocal breaks with Richie singing variations on the opening lines, the song showcases "country" Rusty on dobro and pedal steel (occasionally playing fiddle riffs) as he exchanges solos with Cotton on electric guitar. But "Hoe Down" encapsulates the problems with the album: the opening vocals sound lifeless. Because of the lack of tracks, Cropper was unable to place each vocalist on a separate track the way Messina had done on *Poco*. As a result, the song doesn't jumpstart the album. For comparison, listen to any live version of "Hoe Down" on YouTube or on *Poco: Live at Columbia Studios 9/30/71* (released 2010). Perhaps more problematic is that Poco seems confused over the kind of band it wants to be. With Messina's departure and Cotton's arrival, Furay planned to move Poco in a more rock direction. However, the opening track is not just country, but country hillbilly, complete with hoots and howls. Rusty Young is correct when he calls *From the Inside* "the most country thing we'd done."[15] The only unequivocal rock song on the album is Cotton's "Railroad Days," which he calls "my ode to Creedence Clearwater Revival"[16] and which features speedy and crinkly guitar parts similar to CCR's "Up Around the Bend" (#4, 1970) or "Sweet Hitch-hiker" (#6, 1971).

"Bad Weather," the following track, by Paul Cotton, and one of several high points on the album, is a country-blues song. Cotton auditioned for Poco with the song, of which he had recorded a far less bluesy version with his previous band, the Illinois Speed Press (ISP). The "bad weather" refers to ISP's impending breakup. Furay takes a rare guitar solo from 2:38 to 3:16, reprised, with some variation, from 4:18 until the song ends at 5:02. The solo, bluesy and melancholic, took Furay a while to craft: "Yeah, I'm not the guy that you call out to: 'Richie take it!' I'm not that schooled of a musician. . . . I've spent most of my time writing melodies . . . playing the chord progressions to those melodies and writing the songs." Of course, Furay never had to develop his lead skills. "I've always surrounded myself with great guitarists. It all started with Stephen [Stills] and Neil [Young]. . . . And in Poco we had Rusty Young and Jimmy Messina. . . . And then we had Rusty and Paul Cotton."[17] But Richie saw his contribution to "Bad Weather" as a sign of welcome to Poco's newest member. Furay would not play lead again until his first solo album, *I've Got a Reason* (1976).

Similarly, to fortify the band's chemistry, Furay chose Schmit's "From the Inside" as the title track. He wanted to let Timothy know that "we saw him as a full member, not a sideman or a Johnny-come-lately with lesser status than the rest of us. It was another example of my eagerness to make every member of the band feel like family."[18] The song marks a major step forward in Schmit's development as a songwriter, both lyrically and musically, from the simple good-time music of "Hear That Music" and "Hard Luck" to the more complex tonal shifts and heartfelt introspection of "From the Inside." Schmit dramatizes a tense situation: a couple struggling to "break our chains," "unwind," and talk it over "from the inside." The tender melody with emotional bursts reflects the singer's apprehension, fear, and confusion. "It was like a little page from my diary that you normally wouldn't share with people," says Schmit. "It had to do with the impending birth of my daughter and being twenty-two years old and having it happen the way it did, which . . . wasn't planned. . . . I wasn't making up a scenario; this scenario was happening."[19]

Furay's songs, except "Hoe Down," *seem* to be either about his marital crisis or pleas for reconciliation, as their titles suggest: "What Am I Gonna Do," "You Are the One," "Do You Feel It Too," "What If I Should Say I Love You," and "Just for Me and You." (Furay does not use question marks in these titles.) In the beautiful country-blues of "What Am I Gonna Do," featuring Young's weepy pedal steel, Furay voices his singer's dilemma and indecisiveness: "I'm locked in the middle . . . how can I choose?" Surprisingly, Furay wrote the song before his affair: "I was writing it about another person that I knew or that at least inspired it, and then I completed the tune and it didn't mean anything so it sat around for a year. Then all of a sudden I started living this situation and it really got scary. . . . I don't know how to explain it but . . . sometimes I write songs and then six months later I live 'em which is weird. . . . It really scares me at times."[20] The song may not have been written about Furay's affair, but it informed his performance. Furay's torture is evident in the delivery of the first two lines, especially the elongated *do*: "You've had me to love now / But what will you do?" The plaintive, mournfully painful vocals are especially forceful on the refrain of the title and lines like "Seems my whole life should be retraced" and "I should have seen a warning sign." It is one of Schmit's favorite Furay songs. "I still love that song. In fact, I used to sing it in my solo show. Richie told me that if I like it so much that he would let me sing it on the album." However, when Poco entered the studio, the bassist declined: "He actually lived this song, so I said, 'You gotta do it.'"[21] With its country flavor and its emotional and undulating melody line, the song would have suited George Jones, perhaps country music's greatest vocalist. Furay actually submitted the song to Jones around 2010, when the icon was planning a final album, but Furay never heard from Jones and the album never reached fruition.

"What If I Should Say I Love You," which Furay also wrote before the affair, blends country-blues and rock and features another especially expressive vocal performance from Furay, whose vocal tones shift from soft and tender to frustrated and threatening, and, when he sustains high notes, hopeful—the emotions of someone in a struggling relationship. The song opens with Cotton and Young trading bluesy-country-Western riffs for some sixteen seconds before a pause and Furay's wailing the title. The singer holds out his love to a listener who responds with ambiguity, irritating the singer. The tension rises until the one-minute mark when, for forty seconds, the music transitions to rock, complete with Richie playing a driving, thumping Chuck Berry rhythm: "I bet you know that you're breakin' my heart." The tension then eases but returns at 2:32, after the singer's unsuccessful proclamations of love. When the rhythm crashes just past 3:00, the singer delivers a veiled threat: "Maybe someday I would be gone / Then you'd be alone." Although he did not indicate what they were, Furay said that in the studio he added "clever little alterations" to this track and "Just for Me and You."[22]

"Do You Feel It Too," a song of new love, was written in 1966—soon after meeting Nancy. In July of that year, Furay recorded a demo version of the song, then titled "Can't Keep Me Down," on which he accompanied himself with acoustic guitar. (The verse with the original title was later dropped: "It's so great having you around / There's nobody can keep me down.") On the demo, he sings with the excitement of young love, as he does in the version he recorded with Poco for *Pickin'*, but omitted from the album—a wise choice as the track is too fast and cluttered with poorly arranged runs and fills by Young and Messina. A bluesy version, far superior to the others, appears on *From the Inside*. Furay's vocals are more passionate and convincing, the voice of one experienced in love and strained by its obligations and commitments. "Please remember," he pleads, "how I feel about you." Furay, it seems, reverses his usual practice of embedding sad lyrics in happy melodies. Here, the bluesy rhythms and tormented vocals undercut any of the glee in the previous versions and redirect interpretation, supported by the slow, staticky blues-rock intro and recurring riffs of Cotton and Young's "organ." As the song moves past the 4:00 mark, Cotton and Young take over the track with solos until, with the push of the rhythm section at approximately 4:50, the song hints at an extended jam like "El Tonto" but instead fades out.

Schmit may have passed on the lead vocals to "What Am I Gonna Do," but he accepts the lead on "You Are the One," one of Furay's joyful-sounding melodies with biting words. It seems as if Furay is pleading for his wife to return: "'Cause anyone who's turned around / And lost his way / Is looking for you / You are the one." I asked Richie if the song was about Nancy: "Nancy's not on that song at all." Then after some thought and after reviewing the lyrics, "I'm thinking that the second verse has Messina written all over it."[23] If that is the case, Messina is portrayed in the song as "shameless . . . tameless . . . aimless." Then, "You are the one who only needs to show a smile." It is a bittersweet summary of their relationship, suggesting that had Messina been a little more pleasant and optimistic ("wake up, the sun is shining") they might still be working together. The simple and lilting melody, the popping dobro runs, and the high harmonies of Furay and Grantham hide any anger or finger pointing—the title is repeated over a dozen times in the song. But any sarcasm is lost in the buoyant melody: "You are the one / Who can make any day seem worthwhile."

Knowing their need for a hit single, Clive Davis might have hoped that Cropper would "tweak" Poco's sound, helping them craft a hit. Certainly, Cropper had played or cowritten massive hits ("Sittin' on the Dock of the Bay" with Otis Redding, #1, 1968; "Time Is Tight" with Booker T. & the M.G.'s, 1969, #6). But new to production, he was more hands-off with the band. As Schmit said, "He kind of let us do our thing."[24] The single was Furay's "Just for Me and You," also written pre-affair and one of Furay's happy-in-love songs: "So let my heart go on a singin'." The quick-tempo, sing-alongable melody would seem to be AM friendly, but the single flopped. It's difficult to say why one

FIG. 10 Poco on the deck of the Furays' first Colorado home, March 1973. *Left to right*: Richie Furay, George Grantham, Rusty Young, Paul Cotton, and Timothy B. Schmit. Photo by Henry Diltz.

song is a hit and another isn't. Perhaps "Just for Me and You" was too country for the Top 40 with its pedal steel guitar and dobro, but the week before the September release of *From the Inside*, John Denver scored a #2 hit with "Take Me Home, Country Roads," which featured a banjo and pedal steel.

The reviews for *From the Inside* were lukewarm at best, some blaming Cropper for not capturing the sound of Poco, the way Messina had on *Deliverin'*. In his lukewarm review in *Rolling Stone*, Stu Werbin blamed Cropper for the album's "lack of inspiration and energy" and said that he missed the happier Poco, who could "actually write sad songs and perform them as if they were about something better than sorrow."[25] The album failed to build on the success of *Deliverin'*, petering out at #52 in late October—twenty-six places behind the previous album. This was not what Furay and the band had expected when they entered the studio with Cropper in May.

"Colorado Mountains I Can See Your Distant Skies"

For some time, Poco had discussed moving their "headquarters" out of Los Angeles. They had grown tired of the city and no longer needed the active club scene for gigs. "At that time," said Richie, "all that the band needed was an airport to get in and out of town." They discussed several locations. San Francisco seemed to be the favorite. Grantham was so sure they were moving north that he bought a house in the Bay Area. He was painting his house when, in late 1971, Furay flew up to deliver the final decision in person: "George," Richie told him, "we're going to Colorado."[26] George was upset at first, but easily appeased when he thought about Colorado, where he had lived before joining Poco. Richie, influenced by Nancy, was the prime initiator in relocating to Colorado, which Richie admits to deciding "practically on a whim."[27] Anxious to revive his ailing marriage, he thought a move away from a city would help. Besides, Nancy had read an article in the *Los Angeles Times* about the especially harmful effects of pollution on small children, and Timmie Sue had just turned one. Richie and Nancy settled in Nederland, a town some fifteen miles outside of Boulder. All the band members would be no more than a half hour apart from one another. (See fig. 10.)

After his disappointment with *From the Inside*, Furay was more determined than ever to score a hit record. He needed the right producer. Poco recorded a few tracks with Richard Podolor, who had a string of hits with Three Dog Night and Steppenwolf, but Clive Davis rejected the recordings and Furay's choice of producer with no explanation. Poco searched again and this time recommended Jack Richardson, who had worked with Alice Cooper and the Guess Who. Davis accepted Richardson, who brought along Jim Mason, who would work with Furay over the next several decades. After returning from their first European tour in early 1972, Poco began rehearsing new material at the Skunk Creek Inn, located in a Boulder shopping center. Richardson attended some of the rehearsals to prepare for the sessions and to gain an understanding of the band, their music, and their work habits. On a month-long tour beginning in late April, Poco road tested their new material in anticipation of their scheduled studio sessions with Richardson in June.

One new song, "Good Feelin' to Know," so excited the band that, as Paul Cotton said, "We opened with it, we closed with it, we encored with it. We thought that was the one." "People just flipped out before it was even recorded," added Young.[28] With audience response so effusive, Poco rushed into a Toronto studio, one with which the native Torontonian Richardson was familiar, to record "Good Feelin'." The sessions went well and Poco left confident, with a good song and a good record. "I was sure we finally had our radio song," wrote Furay.[29]

"Good Feelin' to Know" has an immediate and dramatic hook, opening with chords and crashing cymbals underneath zesty and sparkling harmonies—so unlike "Hoe Down": "When I need good lovin'/ I always [*Richie strikes an acoustic chord*] come home to you [*chords and cymbal crash*]/ You free my life [*chord and cymbal crash*] time of the blues." The vocalists sustain "blues" for some four seconds, as driving and grinding riffs emerge from Cotton's guitar and Young's "organ," before Richie's bright vocals, with Grantham and Schmit backing him, begin verse one. It is an explosive start, and the song maintains its high energy through up-tempo melody lines and an anthemic chorus, Grantham's speedy pounding, Schmit's tumbling bass lines, Cotton's rock riffs and solos, and Young's "organ" and steel guitar, which punctuates riffs and, at times, adds emotional depth as his notes soar, twist, and dip as Furay sings, "Colorado mountains, I can see your distant skies / You're bringin' me a tear of joy to my eyes." The concrete images and emotional urgency ("I got that old time feelin' burnin deep inside my soul") mirror the drive of the song. As the song approaches two minutes, when we might expect it to start winding down, Grantham accelerates the rhythm with 16th-note single-stroke rolls, with an accent on the 2/4 (quarter note backbeats). The long run, at some twenty-eight seconds, adds excitement without wearing out the listener, escaping any monotony as Furay sings verses three and four above the rolls. For the final minute of the 3:53 track, the enraptured band repeats the chorus to fadeout. It is a crowning achievement for Poco, their signature song. However, it failed to chart. Poco and Furay were devastated. "It was a blow to me that 'Good Feelin' wasn't a hit. . . . I thought it was a smash all the way."[30]

"Good Feelin' to Know" was released in June while Poco recorded the rest of the album. Richie remembers searching the Top 40 channels expecting to catch the song. Instead, he heard something else. "'Take it Easy' [by the Eagles] came out at the same time [actually a month after 'Good Feelin', on July 22]. We're driving around New York and all of a sudden I hear on the radio, 'I'm driving down the road trying to loosen my load.' I just threw up my hands and said, 'I'm out of here.' . . . Glenn Frey sat in my living room at 2300 Laurel Canyon Boulevard when I was rehearsing Poco for the first time. He definitely heard something there that he liked."[31] First Stills and Young had mega success, and now Frey and Randy Meisner, who played bass and sang harmonies as a founding member of the Eagles, were on their way to stardom. To increase his frustration, that spring Neil Young's success and acclamation grew with *Harvest*, a #1 and the bestselling album of 1972, and that fall Loggins and Messina scored a #4 hit with "Your Mama Don't Dance" and a #16 album with *Loggins and Messina*. Furay kept on believin' his turn was coming.

The Hit Single

On April 7, 1967, on KMPX-FM in San Francisco, Tom Donahue began broadcasting what most consider the first free-form rock music program. At that time the FM radio audience accounted for just 15 percent of the market share, which enabled Donahue to convince the station's ownership that a programming change directed at the growing youth movement, who yearned for a station to reflect its musical tastes, could be more profitable than the foreign language program he would be replacing. It was the beginning of a musical revolution. By the early 1970s, "serious" rock listeners shunned the Top 40, instead tuning into one of many FM progressive rock stations around the country where disk jockeys were largely free to program their own shows with their musical favorites. Leanne Meyers, who began her career at *Billboard* and went on to work in various capacities in the music industry, was typical: "I was a hippie. I moved down [from San Francisco], went to college [at the University of Southern California], and begged and begged and begged and finally got a job at *Billboard* in the chart department, and I remember going in and the retail coordinator said something to me about, 'Oh, so you must be really familiar with KFRC [the Top 40 Station].' I listened to KSAN," where Donahue had moved in 1968. "That's all I listened to. That was like the Bible."[32]

With the emergence of FM radio and the rock press, rock fans developed what might be considered a snobbishness, an elitist disdain, especially for the Top 40 and AM disk jockeys, often considered corporate hacks. Geoff Mayfield, a former director of charts and senior analyst at *Billboard*, and now a professor at the Los Angeles College of Music, commented on my inquiry into Furay and the Top 40. "It's interesting to me that you would even look at this. I was a fan of the Springfield and Poco. Fans of bands like that really didn't care about the charts."[33] In many ways, rock fans were so averse to the Top 40 that they preferred to, and sometimes would only, champion artists who *seemed* to avoid the Top 40, like the Flying Burrito Brothers or Leonard Cohen. As Mark Volman, who had plenty of hit singles with the Turtles, put it, "Among rock music fans, there is always the hipness factor. . . . If you were going to be a hip-music advocate you had to be careful about who you liked. That has always been a big problem with popular music."[34]

So why did Furay and Poco ache for a hit single? Peter Knobler, editor from 1972 to 1979 of the "hip" music magazine *Crawdaddy*, explained the importance of a hit: "One, it made you money; two, it gave you cachet in the music field; and, three, it gave you cachet among your peers. Everybody wanted a hit. There were great bands that never had hits, like Poco, Little Feat." He also discussed the benefits of increased attention, which led to a bigger budget for the next record and increased promotion. "It all snowballs. . . . Your whole livelihood and life will be advanced." A band like Poco could still earn a decent middle-class income, but as Knobler noted, they "fall to that second tier," which is where Poco landed.[35] "We thought," said Furay, "that a 'Good Feelin' to Know' was going to launch us into a different world. It was going to change us."[36] He thought they would be wealthy rock stars.

However, as Furay and many others have found, a hit single can be difficult to generate despite what cultural theorist Theodor Adorno famously suggested when, in 1941, he railed against the "pseudo-individualism" of pop music and its standardization, declaring that pop music listeners have "pre-digested" the latest hit. Adorno asserted that a hit song is similar to previous hits. "The ear deals with the difficulties of hit music by achieving slight substitutions derived from the knowledge of the patterns." For Adorno, pop songs follow a prescribed, standardized structure. To an extent, Adorno is correct, as pop songs are organized in sections (intro, verse, chorus, bridge, and outro), but Adorno's cynicism does not allow for much artistic or self expression within that structure. For Adorno, "Popular music becomes a multiple-choice questionnaire."[37] But a hit song is not so easily assembled. As Rusty Young said, "['Good Feelin'] had the energy, it had the hooks, it had everything."[38] Most hit songwriters have tried, without much precision, to explain what makes for a hit. Lamont Dozier, part of Motown's legendary songwriting team of Holland-Dozier-Holland, said, "I've written about 78 top 10 songs, and I still don't know what a hit is. I can only go by what I feel."[39]

Over the years as a record executive, Clive Davis has been responsible for a remarkable string of varied hit records and hit acts, from Tony Orlando, Janis Joplin, Bruce Springsteen, and Barry Manilow to Aerosmith and Whitney Houston. A graduate of Harvard Law School, Davis said, "[A hit single is] a combination of instinct and feel. You're really identifying the nature of the musical hook: How accessible is it, how memorable? Can you hum it or sing it back after you've heard it once or twice? You are appraising the lyric, and I am a very big lyric guy; you're considering their impact. So it's not a scientific thing, it's a visceral thing."[40] Meyers commented on Davis's musical instincts: "If Clive smelled a hit, whether he was involved in the creativity of that music or not, he would get [the hit] better than anybody else because he knew . . . the intuitiveness was in his blood."[41] Furay believes Davis never pushed Poco's records: "Clive's a great big guy in the music business, but I never felt we got the support from him. . . . I feel that he really compromised our career. It really disappointed me."[42]

Good Feelin' to Know

If *From the Inside* is Poco's most country album, *Good Feelin' to Know* is its loudest and most hard-rocking album, enabled by the production of Jack Richardson and Jim Mason, who captured the intensity, crispness, and excitement of Poco. Unlike Cropper, who provided little direction to Poco during the production of *Inside*, Richardson and Mason shared "tons of ideas" in what all considered a "give-and-take" collaboration.[43] Yet, as hard-rocking as *Good Feelin'* is, it does not neglect the band's country-rock roots or the established Poco sound of rich harmonies, guitar interplay, and Young's punctuating steel guitar and, with few exceptions, joyful images of picnics, new mornings, smiles, love, and singing. The album seemed primed to satisfy old fans while broadening Poco's appeal. In *Rolling Stone*, Bud Scoppa wrote, "I've always enjoyed Poco, but I didn't think they were capable of putting out this kind of power or intensity."[44]

Furay and Cotton each contributed three songs to the album, Schmit contributed two, and it included a Furay-suggested cover of Buffalo Springfield's "Go and Say Goodbye," which rocks harder than the original yet retains enough of the countryish Poco for older fans. In addition to the title track, Furay contributed the opener, "And Settlin' Down." It was a companion to "Good Feelin' to Know" and its expected follow-up single, designed to be similar in tone and sound.[45] While "Settlin' Down" is another upbeat sturdy rocker, although not as fast paced as "Good Feelin'," the song pulsates with Chuck Berry rhythms, Schmit's heavy bass, and Grantham's constant beat. These elements provide a solid setting for not only Furay's lead vocals and the vocal harmonies, but also the guitar interplay and solos of Young and Cotton. It is much different from Furay's third contribution, "Sweet Lovin'." The closing track receives a grand production, like "The Hour of Not Quite Rain" and "Tomorrow," but escapes the pretense of those two productions. The lyrical simplicity and graceful harmonies make the choirlike production majestic rather than ostentatious. This is helped along by producers Richardson and Mason's decision not to include strings—which some might think an obvious choice on a production like this. Celebrating the birth of Timmie Sue, Richie calls on himself and his wife, in a touching lyric, to give her "some lovin'/ Sweet, sweet lovin' . . . To light her way." He sings of love and responsibility, and the ecstasy and fears of new parents, as well as the prodigiousness of the occasion. In another outstanding vocal performance, Furay sings alternately with tenderness, sincerity, and the simplicity of a folk singer, never oversouling his voice and slipping into mawkish sentiment or effusiveness.[46]

Of Cotton's contributions, the best is "Ride the Country," with three movements that transcend the typical verse-chorus-bridge structure. The song begins as a slow, muscular rocker, with a melody line echoing the opening bars of Thunderclap Newman's "Something in the Air." The second movement begins at the 2:20 mark, when the song slips into a slightly more energetic country tempo before returning to the rhythm of the first movement at 3:40. At 4:52, the third movement begins as Grantham leads the band into a slightly faster tempo, featuring an extended Cotton solo, with the song fading out at 6:25. All movements are united by the low notes picked on Furay's or Cotton's rhythm guitar and the ephemeral notes of Young's pedal steel. "That one I thought was a good FM song," said Furay. "I love that. That's one of my favorite Paul Cotton songs of all time."[47] Cotton also contributed "Keeper of the Fire," a vaguely mystical, throbbing rock song, in which Cotton sings of seeing "a new light burnin'" and which features a neat release of tension on the second part of each verse. Cotton's "Early Times" emphasizes his slow, heavy guitar as he meditates on the demise of his previous band, the Illinois Speed Press, when "songs got to slippin'." Schmit submits two numbers to the album, a rather pedestrian ballad, "I Can See Everything," and a powerful slow rocker, "Restrain," which concerns a failing relationship and a singer frustrated by his lover's restraint: her failure to communicate and explain her dissatisfaction. The singer's frustration turns to anger: "Maybe discover what it feels like to grow." He calls on her to "restrain no more," supported by Cotton's stinging lead work at the song's end.

Although Furay may have complained of Davis's lack of support, *Good Feelin' to Know*, released in October 1972, was handsomely packaged with a portrait of the band consuming the inside gatefold cover and an eight-page booklet with credits, lyrics, and a full page left to the discretion of each band member. Grantham, for his page, used one large photo of himself feeding a small bird, while Richie seems to have chosen a wall from his home with several family pictures and a window looking out to a snowy Colorado landscape. Generally positive reviews welcomed the album. In *Rolling Stone*, Scoppa referred to its "hit record sound" and found the album "full of self-confidence . . . full of steam." In England's *NME*, Nick Kent wrote, "Richie Furay has never been more in control of his abilities as the title cut surely testifies—a nifty melody with vocals as clean as morning dew." Kent also singled out Schmit's compositions and then, in his typical snarly manner, wrote, "God knows, this band will be the very last to change the world. But the fact remains that good songs and tight fluid country-rock playing is still something worth pursuing and this is where the band tends to score." *Record World* listed the album under its

"Hits of the Week," stating that *Good Feelin'* "offers perhaps their best album ever" and celebrates it "as a clean, fresh breath of spring that will tide us all over through the winter."[48] Despite Poco's continued touring, *Good Feelin'* peaked at a dismal #69 in late February 1973, lower than any of their previous releases. Furay was confused: "An album like that shouldn't have to get lost in the shuffle. . . . It means we're still just reaching the same old ears. . . . Yet we turn more people on wherever we play. I just can't understand."[49]

Meeting with Geffen–Furay

Since their first performance at the Troubadour in October 1968, review after review, article after article predicted great and imminent success for Poco.[50] However, in April 1973, Cameron Crowe summarized the band's plight: "Poco is still on the verge."[51] By Christmas 1972, Furay had grown impatient. Poco was his "musical dream" and the "passion of [his] life," but it had begun to look like "a dead end."[52] When visiting his mother-in-law in Los Angeles in late 1972 or early 1973, Richie took a drive to the home of David Geffen, a friend and fan of Furay and Poco. Geffen, who was in charge of Asylum and pivotal in the Eagles rise, was always approachable and candid. He had an immediate solution for Richie: "Well, you know Chris Hillman's looking for something to do, and this singer-songwriter guy that works with the Eagles, J. D. Souther, is looking for something to do. Why don't we just put together another super group?" Richie was stunned. "You'll be as big as Crosby, Stills, and Nash," he told Furay. Furay's optimistic spirit was aroused. "I bought it hook, line, and sinker."[53] But, first, Furay had another album to record with Poco. He decided not to inform his bandmates of his impending departure.

Crazy Eyes

When Furay entered the studio with Poco in May 1973 to record their sixth album, he may have been less hopeful about its success, but he was also less anxious and self-pressured: "I wasn't a bundle of nerves wondering whether it would go gold. Mentally, I had moved on."[54] Furay would write only one new song for the album, "Let's Dance Tonight." He dusted off the title track that had been on his shelf for some four years and suggested a cover of "Brass Buttons" by Gram Parsons. Furay admits that he withheld songs: "I knew I would be needing tracks for my next group." In hindsight, he noted that it "probably wasn't the best thing to do, but I held on to some songs."[55] With less than Furay's total commitment—which the others did not perceive—*Crazy Eyes* would chart at #38, second only to *Deliverin'* during Poco's Furay era. In many ways the album returns to its country roots, closer in spirit to *Pickin' Up the Pieces* and closer to the country songs of *From the Inside* without that album's darkness and poor sonics. Interestingly, *Crazy Eyes* remains George Grantham's favorite Poco album.[56]

The opening track, "Blue Water" by Paul Cotton, joins an ever-growing list of environmental awareness songs, which had been proliferating since the late 1960s,[57] leading to the first Earth Day on April 22, 1970. The opening country-hillbilly rhythm with acoustic guitar, dobro, and thumping bass transitions into country-rock after about a minute with Paul Harris, soon to join the backing band of Souther-Hillman-Furay, adding an almost boogie-woogie piano underneath. "Blue Water" bleeds into "Fools Gold," keeping the listener in rural America with one of Rusty's trademark hoedown numbers like "Grand Junction," "Hoedown," or "Rocky Mountain Breakdown" from *Poco Seven* (1974). "Fools Gold" backed the single, Schmit's lovely ballad "Here We Go Again," which suffered a similar fate as previous Poco singles. Cotton also contributed "A Right Along," an out-and-out rocker.

Crazy Eyes features two covers; Cotton takes the lead on J. J. Cale's "Magnolia" and Furay on "Brass Buttons," a song Richie learned from Parsons while the two lived in Greenwich Village. "Brass Buttons" is a heartful ballad about Parsons's mother, heir to a citrus fortune, who suffered from depression and died of alcohol poisoning on the day of Gram's high school graduation in 1965. Several years earlier his father, also an alcoholic, had committed suicide. In the song, the singer contemplates his mother through ephemera and small possessions and recalls "warm evenings," "pale mornings," and "bottled blues," suggestive of her depression and alcoholism. In an especially touching image, he relates how he clings to her memory: "Her comb still lies beside my bed." I asked Furay if he identified with the song because of losing his father at a young age. "To tell you the truth," Richie said, "I didn't know until years later, that it was about his mom. . . . We were kids in New York. But I remember thinking, 'How in the world could this guy write a song [like this],' and I assumed it was about a relationship."[58]

In 1970, Johnny Rivers released the first recording of "Brass Buttons," which loses its emotional force in the heavy orchestration. Parsons included a quietly pained "Brass Buttons" on his posthumous album, *Grievous Angel* (1974), and the Lemonheads, an alternative rock band, feature a moving version on *Lovey* (1990). Poco's version eclipses these. Furay renders the slow ballad with sensitivity and compassion, and, characteristically, he never exaggerates the sorrow or oversouls the melody. The arrangement plays off the glittering images of "brass buttons, green silks . . . silver shoes" and "golden pins." The interplay of Richie's steel-stringed acoustic guitar with Harris's delicate electric piano and glimmering arpeggio runs, played with sustain peddle, creates a chimelike effect suggestive of the celestial and spiritual. The solos by Cotton and Young enhance the effect. Cotton's solo mourns in a high register with slow, rounded bent notes from approximately 1:48 until it gives way, at 2:08, to Young's pedal steel. Entering the song for the first time, Young's pedal steel delivers a frequently soaring solo until 2:28, after which it remains and plays above the vocals and other instruments. The song suggests that through her fanciful possessions, Avis Connor, Parsons's mother, appreciated beauty and the spark of life it induced within her. However, like Harris's delicate piano, she was too emotionally fragile for the world, and—more specifically, as her biography reveals—to cope with the suicide of one husband and the extramarital affair of a second. Thus, the song is her son's tribute and lament.

Richie wrote the album's title track about Parsons in 1969. The lyrics and performance convey mixed emotions about Parsons, suggesting the musician's lack of both honesty (" . . . who's been fooling who?") and perception (" . . . blind as you can be"). One biographer wrote, "By Gram's own admission, if his lips were moving and he wasn't singing, he was most likely lying."[59] Furay, who references "Brass Buttons" in the song, is tender as he sings about Parsons's youth among the "South Carolina pines" before mocking Parsons's "lifetime in deep thought," echoed later in his reference to Hamlet's self-inquiry: "So now to be or not to be is the question." Furay focuses on his mysterious "crazy eyes": "You could look into Gram's eyes, and you couldn't tell what was going on in that guy's mind." Furay's anger with his friend informs the sometimes biting vocal delivery. I asked Furay if he was trying to send Parsons a warning about his heavy drug use. "Eerie. You know, I think I was. I saw him as a very self-destructive person, a very talented guy, but never sure of himself in the way that maybe a lot of self-destructive people are. They go to extremes to be accepted. Gram had to go to the [Rolling] Stones and to keep up with some of the stuff that they were doing. He was trying to live the country image that he had of Hank Williams and George Jones, always just being inebriated."[60] Parsons spent the summer of 1968 living with Keith Richards, who wrote, "Gram taught me country music" and said that Parsons had "better coke than the mafia." Parsons could be difficult to work with, spending only brief stints in the Byrds, International Submarine Band, and the Flying Burrito Brothers. He may have gone "out of his way to please people," as Ben Fong-Torres wrote, but many recognized an underlying sadness and found him, as Mark Volman did, "dark" and "dangerous."[61]

Furay may have written "Crazy Eyes" as a kind of folk-country ballad, "a small piece," he says.[62] But producer Richardson had different ideas for the song and summoned Bob Ezrin, who had worked with Alice Cooper and Lou Reed, to rearrange and orchestrate the track. The result is a majestic almost ten-minute tribute to the complexity of Gram Parsons, his contradictoriness, his vast imagination, his frustrating behaviors, and his mystique. The production begins with a dire pound of a piano chord, which fades away behind the distant sound of erratic and ominous drumbeats. Thirty-two seconds later Richie strums his guitar and sings, holding "I" for four beats then "got a feeling about you," to seemingly unpatterned drumbeats. Furay is angry, reprimanding, "What had you to lose?" As the song progresses, the orchestra enters at about 1:26, then Cotton's electric guitar rumbles to support the eeriness. At 1:42, all slows down for Rusty's banjo, suggestive of Parsons's love of country music and his Southern roots. Richie strikes his acoustic guitar, almost dirge-like. The song moves on with bursts of guitars, solos from Cotton and Young, and multiple twists and turns, employing a full orchestra with brass fading out for several banjo solos and about a one-minute pedal steel solo set against high strings (4:44–5:40). The dark, somber, and harrowing tones are heightened at times by the rising and crashing sounds of the orchestra and Grantham's cymbal smashes, as well as the various movements in the song. All this indicates the drama, the inconsistency, and the intensity of Parsons. While in line with other lavish productions of Furay songs, like "The Hour of Not Quite Rain" and "Sweet Love," neither has the depth, the passion, or the complexity of sentiment of "Crazy Eyes." It's an epic achievement, one Furay found "really, really exciting."[63]

Parsons probably never heard "Crazy Eyes" or Poco's version of "Brass Buttons." The album was released on September 15, 1973, and Parsons died four days later of a drug overdose. Neither Poco's nor Furay's solo band dared to perform "Crazy Eyes"—until 2010. Scott Sellen, the multi-instrumentalist in the Richie Furay Band, approached Furay, who tells the story: "Scott said, 'Hey, you know what? We can do ["Crazy Eyes"].' I said, 'You're kidding.' He said, 'We can do it.' I remember I was on my way to Israel and, I made a road map of the song. . . . I came home and wrote out the timing on a napkin." During the performance, Sellen switched instruments, playing guitar, banjo, lap steel, and piano. "He was a one-man band doing that song," said Richie. A performance from Lafayette, Colorado, can be seen on YouTube.[64]

"Let's Dance Tonight" closes the album and the Furay era of Poco—until the 1989 reunion. The thirty-two-second intro begins with Richie slowly picking his steel-string acoustic guitar as if to introduce a lullaby, but, as the guitar pauses, Furay begins to sing and strikes a chimed harmonic. His soft voice escalates near a falsetto backed by an occasional guitar strum, quickly clipped piano runs, and what sounds like gentle feedback: "Slipping away heading out to L.A. / Gonna sing in the city tonight, tonight." The rhythm picks up, chugging along until the tension eases at the chorus: "Come on, let's dance." After the second verse and chorus, the rhythm picks up and rocks harder, with Schmit's bass and Young's fuzz-toned and gritty "Bear" leading the way. Young, always in search of new sounds, had been playing a new instrument, the Melobar guitar, invented by Walt Smith in the late 1960s. The Melobar combined a steel guitar with a standard guitar and would be played at a forty-five degree angle. Young's bandmates christened the instrument "the Bear" because of the deep growls and grunts Young coaxed from it. Curiously or perhaps fittingly, "Let's Dance" closes Furay's time with Poco much as it began, which is to say that the energy of "Let's Dance" was not captured on the recording. It is one of Richardson's rare misfires with Poco. The track pales, for example, next to "Good Feelin'" and "And Settlin' Down." Richie wrote bluntly, "It's an exciting rock-and-roll song that for some reason didn't get charged up to the degree it should have." Along with "Kind Woman," Richie said, "Let's Dance" is "one of two songs from my history that I always wanted to record again."[65] Furay got his chance on *The Heartbeat of Love* in 2006. A then sixty-two-year-old Furay drops the key, accents the rock guitar, and features a spitfire slide guitar from Dan Dugmore. While the song rocks with more vitality than the original, dropping the key cost it some energy. Somehow the music of the second needed to be combined with the vocals of the first. Live, the song has always been a fan favorite, and potent rock versions appear on both *Alive* (2008) and, in perhaps its best version, on *50th Anniversary Return to the Troubadour* (2021).

In 2001, in *All Music Guide*, Bruce Eder gave *Crazy Eyes* a five-diamond rating, the highest possible rating, and wrote that the album "contains some of [Poco's] most soulful music. . . . The resulting sound is richer than anything found on any other Poco album. . . . There's not a weak song, or even a wasted note anywhere on this album, and most bands would kill for a closing track as perfect as 'Let's Dance Tonight.'"[66]

Meeting with Geffen—the Band

In the late spring or early summer of 1973, David Geffen, who had been unofficially managing the band since Schiffman and Larson were let go, called a meeting in his Los Angeles office with Young, Grantham, Schmit, and Cotton. Geffen left two staffers, John Hartmann and Harlan Goodman, to break the news: Richie Furay was leaving Poco. The band had heard rumors while recording *Crazy Eyes*, but Richie had denied them. Furay was not present at the meeting.

The band was devastated. "This was a real shock to me," said Schmit. "They told us that Richie was quitting, that he was going off to do this other thing . . . the next big supergroup. . . . I was shocked that Richie wasn't there. He actually agreed to let management give us that news. I couldn't believe it. I couldn't believe that he wouldn't have said something to me, or any of us, or all of us. . . . I was a little bit hurt. Not because he was leaving, but because he wasn't there to tell us what he was doing. I would have said, 'This is really a surprise, but best of luck to you.'"[67] The others had similar reactions. They understood his decision to leave but felt betrayed by how he informed them of his departure. Grantham echoed Schmit: "Oh, I was disappointed, and I was hurt, more than angry. . . . I didn't know if we could go on. . . . But we had to go on, so we did."[68]

Richie regrets his handling of the situation. Indeed, it was cowardly and disingenuous. Furay had often talked about the importance of band unity, the band as family. As the leader of Poco, he had worked to make new members feel welcome and had initiated Poco's relocation to the Boulder area only eighteen months earlier. "I hurt people. I'm sure Rusty, George, Tim, and Paul were devastated that I could make that decision. It was like abandoning ship, leaving them out there. But I was focused, my mind was made up."[69] At the time, Furay was consumed by his quest for stardom, which would contribute to a second marital crisis. "I was consumed, driven [by the pursuit of stardom]. . . . Nothing was so important to me . . . nothing else really mattered in my life."[70] The band proved understanding, and any anger and hurt from his bandmates dissipated rather quickly; their friendships resumed, and Furay toured with Poco in the summer of 1973, performing for the final time with the band he had cofounded on September 4, 1973, at Worcester Polytechnic Institute in Massachusetts.

Poco continued on. They released three more albums with Epic, including a compilation, with similar results as the Furay-era albums: modest sales with chart positions above fifty. In 1977, Poco was seemingly dealt a knockout blow when George Grantham and Timothy Schmit left after *Indian Summer*, Poco's tenth studio album. Schmit once again replaced Randy Meisner, but this time in the Eagles, where Schmit remains as of this writing. Young and Cotton persevered, and in 1978, Rusty Young wrote and sang the band's first hit single, "Crazy Love," which rose to #17, followed by Paul Cotton's "Heart of the Night," peaking at #20. *Legend*, the album that featured the hits, rose to #14 and was certified a Gold record with sales of over 500,000, almost double that of any previous Poco album. Furthermore, at the end of 1979, *Billboard* declared "Crazy Love" the #1 Adult Contemporary hit for the year. Grantham would return in 1985 for another five years before returning again in 2000. In 2004, he suffered an onstage stroke that forced his retirement from music. Cotton left Poco in 1988 but rejoined in 1992 for another eighteen-year run. Poco continued under Young with various personnel, recording their last studio album of new material, *All Fired Up*, their nineteenth, in 2013. And, yes, until the end the band performed "Pickin' Up the Pieces," "Kind Woman," and "Good Feelin' to Know." Both Cotton and Young died in 2021. In tribute, Furay produced a video in which he called the pair "terrific guys" that he was "blessed to have been able to play music with." Then, accompanied by Dan Skarda on a second acoustic guitar and his daughter Jesse on backing vocals, he performed "Bad Weather" and "Crazy Love."[71]

In 1989, the original five members reunited for *Legacy*, an album that produced two popular singles: "Call It Love," #18, sung by Young and written by Ron Gilbeau, Billy Crain, Rick Lonow, and Jimmy Messina; and "Nothin' to Hide," #39, sung by Meisner and written by Richard Marx and Bruce Gaitsch. While the album reached #40 and scored Poco a second Gold record, *Legacy*, as the songwriting credits to the two hits suggest, had little in common with the Poco sound of 1969. Country-rock had been replaced with 1990s pop.

Thoughts on Furay and Poco

The Furay-Poco years were the band's most innovative. Poco were indeed, as Furay has stated and sung, "pioneers" ("We Were the Dreamers," 2015). Following Bob Dylan's lead, bands like Buffalo Springfield, the Byrds, and then Poco and the Flying Burrito Brothers introduced a new genre, country-rock. Each of those four bands featured one of two key musicians: Gram Parsons and Richie Furay. In the Springfield and the Byrds, Furay and Parsons were secondary members, not the leaders, although their contributions to those bands were major. However, when they formed their subsequent bands, they drew more fully from country music. But whereas Parsons was more interested in playing pure country, Furay experimented with the fusion of country and rock. In his six albums with Poco, Furay shifted the balance of sound, sometimes more country and sometimes more rock. Along with others, like

Parsons, Roger McGuinn, and Neil Young, Furay and his experiments with this crosspollination have inspired and influenced pop music ever since, contributing to the rise of country-pop, roots music, Americana, and alternative country and artists like the Eagles, Firefall, Vince Gill, Pure Prairie League, George Strait, Uncle Tupelo, Wilco, and many more. From the stage, at one Eagles show in Denver, Frey saluted Furay, who was in the audience: "If it wasn't for you, we wouldn't be here."[72]

Furay looks back with satisfaction at his years in Poco: "It was a great time in my life, a great time to be creative, a great time for me to search out and realize who I was as a musician and songwriter."[73] His years in Poco, I argue, mark the high point of his career.

CHAPTER 9

"On the Line"

SHF, Marital Problems, Conversion

On paper, Souther-Hillman-Furay (SHF) could not miss. The principals were all veterans of the LA music scene, all proven songwriters and vocalists, all stylistically similar, and all in their late twenties, still in the prime of their creative years. J. D. Souther had formed Longbranch Pennywhistle with Glenn Frey before recording his first solo album for Asylum in 1972. Chris Hillman was a founding member of the Byrds and cowrote the classic "So You Want to Be a Rock and Roll Star" before founding the Flying Burrito Brothers with Gram Parsons and joining Manassas, led by Stephen Stills. Hillman recruited former members of Manassas (1971–73) to support SHF: Al Perkins (guitar, steel guitar, dobro) and Paul Harris, who played keyboards on *Crazy Eyes*. Doug Altman, a friend of Perkins, was the first drummer for SHF.

In late 1973, SHF met for initial rehearsals in the studio above Furay's garage at his home outside of Boulder. The rehearsals were uncomfortable at first as each was cautious, apprehensive about making suggestions on each other's songs. There was not that immediate chemistry, that "magic," that had so inspired Furay in the earliest days of Buffalo Springfield and Poco, where band members felt safe to share musical ideas. The band was not jelling, musically or personally. J. D. Souther, said Mark Volman, "could be hard to like," and he did not seem excited about working in his first band—especially after Geffen "talked them into it." "I'm not a great team player under those circumstances," Souther admits. As Debbie Kruger writes, he "craves solitude."[1] Furay and Souther were especially different personalities. Richie is open, optimistic, and warm. As expected, Furay "made conscious attempts to get to know everyone in the band," wrote Peter Knobler, who was present at several of the early rehearsals.[2] Souther, on the other hand, has defined himself as "elusive and hard to find" and, when not working out one of his songs, was often "bored"—and let everyone know it. He can also be humorously cynical with a "jaundiced view of the world."[3] Whereas Richie strove to create a family atmosphere within his bands, Souther saw SHF as largely a business arrangement.

Hillman, who joked that SHF should be named Big Bucks, is somewhere between the two. He can be open and friendly, like Richie, and humorously cynical, like Souther. During one rehearsal, Souther whispered to Hillman, "We're the two assholes in the band." Hillman, whose previous experience had taught him the importance of good band chemistry, responded with what Knobler describes as "informed silence"—not wanting, perhaps, to offend either Souther or Furay.[4] On one occasion, Hillman served as an arbitrator when it looked as though SHF would not survive rehearsals. Furay had suggested different chords to one of Souther's songs as it approached the instrumental break. "It's my song!" J. D. shouted, clearly not interested in collaboration. "That does it." Richie yanked the chord from his guitar. "I quit." Al Perkins followed Furay into his house while Hillman coaxed Souther into pacifying Furay. Souther and Furay talked for over an hour at Richie's kitchen table and resumed rehearsals the next day.[5] A collaborative workmanship, however, never developed. As Hillman wrote, "It was as if we were three separate singer/songwriters performing with a backup band rather than functioning as a fully cohesive group." "It was just awkward," said Furay. "It just never felt right."[6] Rehearsals ended just before Christmas with plans to reconvene in the spring, in Los Angeles, to rehearse and record their first album.

Al Perkins

When SHF began rehearsals, Furay approached Hillman and was adamant that he did not want Al Perkins in the band. On his guitar, Perkins featured an image of a fish with the words "Jesus lives." Nothing, Furay thought, could turn off a rock music audience faster than a proselytizing Christian. "Rock and roll and Christianity," said Richie, "is like oil and water. It's not going to work." He told Hillman, "That's gonna definitely stop us from becoming big stars."[7] Hillman appeased Furay, for Richie did not know that Perkins, while on tour with Manassas, had led Hillman to a "foxhole conversion" during a perilous plane ride. That acceptance might have been temporary, but it increased Hillman's respect for Perkins. Some ten years later, well after SHF, Hillman, "with guidance from Al," would accept Christ more permanently.[8]

In those early months with SHF, Furay found himself getting along especially well with Perkins. One evening, he and Nancy invited Perkins and his wife, Debbie, over. After dinner, Al asked if he could play some tapes. Richie, thinking it would be music, agreed. Perkins, however, slipped on "The More Sure Word," a sermon from Pastor Chuck Smith of Calvary Chapel in Costa Mesa, California.[9] Richie was annoyed at first but obliged his guests. Before long, Richie found himself fascinated by Pastor Smith's discussion of the biblical prophecies fulfilled by Christ. After ninety minutes and a second recording, Furay had had enough, but as he writes, "Al had planted a seed."[10] That night had a more immediate impact on Nancy, who began consulting with Debbie. In a short time, Nancy made her commitment to Christ, but she did not discuss it with Richie, whom she saw as self-centered and obsessed with stardom. Nancy had also begun reading *Satan Is Alive and Well on Planet Earth* by Hal Lindsey, a gift from Debbie. Furay noticed the book: "Sakes alive! I didn't want to have anything to do with this."[11]

Los Angeles, Hawaii, Aspen

In the spring of 1974, SHF met in American Recorders studio in Los Angeles to record their first album. All agreed with Furay's recommendation to enlist producer Richie Podolor, whom Furay had wanted to hire for Poco. In addition, SHF decided to change drummers. Much to Furay's amazement, Hillman was able to recruit Jim Gordon, one of rock's premiere drummers. Gordon had recorded and toured with luminaries such as Delaney & Bonnie, Traffic, and Derek and the Dominoes and had cowritten "Layla" with Eric Clapton. He drummed for George Harrison's *All Things Must Pass*, and he was such an in-demand session player that he had drum kits set up in three different LA studios. "He would just go from one session to the next," said Furay.[12] Gordon was anxious to be part of a band and tour again, so he jumped at Hillman's invitation. Unfortunately, Gordon had psychological problems, later diagnosed as schizophrenia. On tour with SHF, he was prone to erratic behavior. On one occasion, while on Interstate 80 in Pennsylvania, he demanded that the van in which he was riding with Furay and others pull over before the next rest stop. They waited and waited for Gordon until they spotted him in a sprinter's stance, only to take off in a race with a passing semitruck. A few years later, as his condition worsened with mistreatment, he heard voices, which prevented him from eating, sleeping, and drumming. In 1983 he murdered his mother and, as of this writing, he remains in prison. "My heart just breaks for him today," says Furay, "but, man, he was one of the best rock-and-roll drummers ever."[13] Not many would disagree with Furay.

After the recording sessions began, Nancy and Timmie joined Richie in Los Angeles. One day Richie drove his Porsche to the studio, where SHF began the day by recording vocals to one of Hillman's songs. Richie, always trying to build positive band chemistry, did not want to seem as if he were in a hurry to move on to one of his songs, next on the schedule, so he left his Martin D-28 acoustic guitar in his car. The vocal session took hours, much longer than anticipated. Richie returned to his car to find the windshield smashed and his guitar stolen. Musicians build close ties to their key instruments, and the D-28 was the guitar Richie had had longest, taking it with him to college in the fall of 1962 and writing most of his songs on it. He was devastated.

With the sessions complete and some time off before the album's release and tour, Richie took his family to Hawaii for a month-long holiday. There, Richie noticed that Nancy was frequently reading the Bible while he focused on the upcoming release of *The Souther-Hillman-Furay Band* and the scheduled two-week residency at the Gallery in Aspen, Colorado, where SHF was to craft its stage show. The couple was drifting apart with neither much interested in the other's concerns. When they returned to Los Angeles, Richard heard from his business manager that a guitar, a Martin D-28, had been located in a pawn shop. As Richie rushed out, Nancy told him that she had been praying for its return. Flippantly, Richie replied that if it proved to be his guitar, he too would become a Christian. The guitar was his and had only slight damage. However, he was not yet ready to become a Christian. Their growing distance became clear to Richie when Nancy refused to accompany him in mid-June to Aspen.

The two-week run at the Gallery in Aspen went well enough, but SHF did not generate the passionate response of Springfield and Poco shows. "I don't think we ever did," said Richie.[14] There was much anticipation of these first shows performed by rock's latest supergroup. Furay remembers Poconuts traveling to Aspen for the show. One was Mitch Rose, who became a close friend of Richie in subsequent years. His motor home served as a hangout for the band, who were doing two shows a night. Rose remembers rafting down the Roaring Fork River with SHF, and, at the shows, he met Glenn Frey, Don Henley, and Dan Fogelberg. It was exciting for Rose the fan, but even after hearing a test pressing of the album, which he liked, and knowing that Geffen would promote it with full force, he could tell that "[SHF] were not going to be another Crosby, Stills & Nash; it wasn't going to be a big project like everybody thought."[15] Kenny Weissberg, a radio DJ at KRNW-FM, Boulder, who had interviewed Furay several times on his program and had become his friend, expected to write a rave review for *Cake Eaters*, an arts-and-entertainment magazine in Boulder. "Instead, I witnessed a band that lacked onstage chemistry and seemed more like three singer-songwriters showcasing their own material backed by indifferent sidemen. It was an anticlimactic performance that failed to live up to the hype."[16] His review seemed almost apologetic as he tried hard to be positive: "This should be a can't miss collaboration. The band's stage presence lacked flash, but was appealing anyway." He noted that Souther "was lackadaisical and seemed bored. His Fender Telecaster still had the price tag hanging from its neck, accidentally symbolic, perhaps, of Souther's discomfort with electric instruments. . . . The crowd was responsive, but nobody seemed overwhelmed." He concluded that "The SHF Band is overloaded with talent and if each individual ego can remain secondary and sedated, the three-part harmony club will have added a worthy charter member."[17] Weissberg avoided Richie for the next several months because of his tepid review.

After one show, two Poconuts approached Furay. After complimenting him on his performance, they rhapsodized about accepting Christ as a result of conversations with Al and Debbie Perkins. Richie was polite but dismissive. "That's good for you," he told them. "But I got a whole lot more to do with my life before I make a decision like that."[18] Even as Richie excused himself from the girls, he felt something happening to him. He was deflecting the call to Christianity, which seemed to surround him, first in his band, then in his home, and now with fans. He feared that being a Christian would change his fundamental self. The next day before the show he had dinner with the Perkinses. Al again played tapes of Pastor Smith and, once again as he had always done, Al asked Richie to pray with them. Rather than reject his offer, as he had always done, Furay accepted. It would mark a major turning point in his life. "I believe that at that moment in Aspen I was born again," he wrote.[19]

The next morning Richie eagerly called Nancy to inform her that he was ready to embrace Christianity. He expected an enthusiastic response, but there was only silence on the other end. "I was so upset," said Nancy. She had been thinking about divorce: "I can get out of this. I'm a Christian and he's not."[20] His becoming a Christian complicated the situation. A few days later Nancy headed to Aspen to drive Richie home. She did not want to hear about his newfound faith. The atmosphere in the car was decidedly frosty for the almost four-hour drive and did not warm up much after their arrival home. Within a day or two, and just before leaving for the first leg of the SHF tour, Nancy declared the marriage over. The marriage may have survived Richie's

FIG. II The SHF Band. *Left to right*: Jim Gordon, Al Perkins, J. D. Souther, Chris Hillman, Richie Furay, and Paul Harris. Photo by Henry Diltz.

infidelity, but it could not survive his ambition. In his quest for stardom, he had neglected his wife, failing to heed his own warning in "Hurry Up," which concerns the destructiveness of "a man [who] gets caught in his own dream." In tears and emotionally distraught, he called Perkins for advice, who invited him to fly to his home in California for a night before heading east to begin the tour. Furay struggled through an excruciating seven months before he and Nancy reconciled.

The Souther-Hillman-Furay Band

The Souther-Hillman-Furay Band was released in July to coincide with the band's first tour. As the tour rolled on and the Geffen-Asylum marketing team kicked into gear, the album raced up the charts, entering at #130 on July 20, shooting up fifty-four places the following week to #66, then peaking at #11 on September 7, the highest charting position of any album that featured Furay. By the third week in September, it had sold over 500,000 units and was certified Gold—Furay's first Gold album. It spent almost six months on the charts. The album, however, like the performances, did not spawn the kind of excitement that had been anticipated. Like the shows, the album is good, even very good, but hardly earthshaking or the immediate classic that other supergroups, like Crosby, Stills & Nash or Blind Faith, had released.[21] In fact, both Furay and Hillman have expressed incredulity about the legitimacy of the Gold certification. "Our debut actually shipped gold and probably came back gold in returns," remarked Hillman sardonically. "I'd like to think they're still in Geffen's garage." Furay simply said, "I'm not sure about all those sales."[22]

However, a #11 chart showing for SHF seems reasonable, given the hype surrounding the band. The position of an album on the charts was determined by sales as reported by select record stores and chains, not on albums shipped. It is possible that the Geffen-Asylum marketing team reported the number of shipped albums to a contact at *Billboard* in an effort to lobby for a higher chart position, and it is similarly possible that members of the team pressured stores to report higher sales. But the charts could only be manipulated to a limited extent, although label executives, often with great bluster, might have bragged otherwise.[23] Record labels reasoned that a high chart position would create buzz among consumers and thus increase sales; in addition, a high chart position assuaged artistic egos and complaints to the label about any lack of promotion.

The Souther-Hillman-Furay Band (SHF) is constructed very neatly, perhaps too neatly. Songs are alternated among the three principals. Furay and Hillman contribute three songs each, and Souther gets a fourth, with none having two consecutive songs. They take turns. This careful plotting, this politeness, results in an album that lacks attitude, an album that is always safe, never daring, but is, as one reviewer wrote, "pleasant" while another thought it demonstrated "competence" with "at least half" of it "very easy to take"[24]—not the kind of reviews earned by great rock-and-roll records.

Along with Souther's "Deep Dark and Dreamless" and Hillman's "Rise and Fall," Furay's three songs are among the album's best. The set opens with Furay's "Fallin' in Love," the single, which reached #27 and remains a mainstay in Furay's live shows. The band had struggled for a proper intro to the song until producer Podolor suggested the buzzing guitar lick that effectively kicks off the song and album and recurs during a later break. Unfortunately, the rest of the album lacks the vitality and muscular urgency of that riff. "Fallin' in Love"—a fast Poco-like rocker in the tradition of "What a Day" and "Good Feelin' to Know"—is pushed by Gordon's drumming, Hillman's percolating bass, the urgent lead vocals of Furay, including a Furay scream of jubilation at 2:15, and some carefully placed guitar fills from Perkins, who brings the song to a close with a staticky run. No other song on *SHF* rocks with as much enthusiasm or urgency. The other out-and-out rocker, Hillman's "Safe at Home," only approaches it.

Three familiar Furay lyrical motifs merge in "Fallin' in Love": love, dreams, and home. For Furay, love is the essence of existence and the fulfillment of a dream. As he sings, "nothing to love's like nothing to be"—not to love is not to exist. With love, one has a "lifetime" to realize "much of [one's] dream." Dreams in Furay have mostly positive or at least hopeful possibilities and implications (see "What a Day," "I Still Have Dreams" [1979], "We Were the Dreamers" ([2015]) but, on occasion, dreams can be destructive, as in "Hurry Up," or falsely optimistic as in "Just in Case It Happens." In "I've Got a Reason" (1976), Furay sings that he has been "a child in [his] dreams," alluding to his quest for stardom, which almost ended his marriage. The singer in "Fallin' in Love," like the voice in "Good Feelin'" and "Settlin' Down," is on the road and anxious to reunite with his beloved at home: "Turning home running free as the wind / Stretching my stride wanna hold you again." The singer here, like the singers in several Furay songs, expresses an intense desire to return home and is filled with happiness at the prospect of arriving soon. In song after song, from "Pickin' Up the Pieces" to "Hand in Hand" (2015), Furay idealizes "home" with images of marital and family love, backyard picnics with happy folks, beautiful weather, and music. At home his singers find comfort, relaxation, freedom, and empowerment. Home in Furay is never complicated. It is never entangled by duties and oppression; it is a place of catharsis, a place where all the complexities, pressures, uncertainties, and stress of a touring musician are relieved and cleansed. In 1981, "I realized that what I wanted most of all is stability," said Furay. And, in 2017, "I'm a homebody."[25]

One of the most underrated songs in the Furay catalog is "Believe Me," a love song to his wife, which he wrote after their reconciliation following his 1970–71 affair. The intro, which features a thirty-two-second solo from Harris on grand piano and Gordon's percussive taps low in the mix, gives the song an epic feel, similar to "Sweet Lovin'," which features an organ in the intro. Throughout the track, Furay's vocals are elegantly clear, intense, and never mawkish, as he sustains and bends notes. The rhythm builds and slows, only to rebuild and slow again. At the 2:20 mark Perkins sends out a heated guitar solo followed by Harris's speedy organ solo. The backing vocals, here as well as on other tracks, like Hillman's "Heavenly Fire" or Souther's "Border Town," add punch and reveal how flavorful SHF vocal harmonies could be. Furay had recorded a more rock version of the song with Poco but decided to hold it off *Crazy Eyes* and save it for SHF.

The song may be about Nancy and the couple's reconciliation, but the dominant image of light infuses the song with literary and religious intensity: "Her love light is shinin' on in the mornin', the glow is understood / Yes, it's been a long time with me feelin' this good." And, in one of Furay's most sublime lines, "I've got my warmest dream, your star in the sky, a light to go by." Comparing one's beloved to a "light" or "a star" has been well established through the centuries. In one famous scene from *Romeo and Juliet*, Juliet begs the night to "take [Romeo after his death] and cut him out in little stars / And he will make the face of heaven so fine" (3.2 22–25). For Richie the "star in the sky," Nancy, becomes his guiding light, "a light to go by," which will help lead him to Christ. In time, Furay would interpret retrieving his stolen guitar as evidence of the power of prayer. But, more so, that light that Furay sees emanating from his wife becomes a guiding star and, while not intentional in "Believe Me," Furay merges divine love with human love in much the same way Petrarch did in the 1200s when he wrote about Laura in his sonnets, particularly Sonnet XII: "Wherein he is brought by Laura's loveliness to the contemplation of the highest excellence." Petrarch celebrates Laura's "perfect beauty like a star [that] outshines the rest." Like Nancy's "glow," Laura's "golden glow . . . points to heaven . . . [and] the straight path to paradise." In the Bible, Jesus says in John 8:12, "I am the light of the world. He who follows Me shall not walk in darkness, but have the light of life." Furay has said that his songs sometimes foreshadow his life. "Believe Me" charts the course he followed. "[Nancy] was and she is my 'brightest star' and 'warmest dream.'"[26]

Richie's third song, "The Flight of the Dove," is a sturdy, thumping rocker with a touch of funk. After the first two verses at the 1:04-minute mark, the tension releases for the chorus, after which Harris takes an electric piano solo that slides right into a groove held down by the rhythm section of Hillman and Gordon. The song continues with Gordon pounding the backbeat and Harris's electric keyboard rumbling underneath. The song closes with an almost minute-long guitar solo from Perkins, who steps on a wah-wah pedal for cries and squawks. Lyrically, "Flight of the Dove" is elusive. Furay generally writes direct, accessible lines that have been well honed. Looking at the lyrics in "Dove," Furay found himself perplexed: "Let me see. . . . What was I getting at here? . . . What happens is that I'll start to write a song and I may not finish it for another six months to a year later. . . . I think this had to do with some issues in Poco. . . . I think the flight of the dove is me. . . . I don't sense that there was a bitterness. I just think there was just something that was . . . [*To himself*] Richie, what do you write these songs about? . . . There was something on my mind at that time because it's a pretty strong song."[27]

Indeed, it is a "strong song," musically and lyrically, despite being a bit obscure. It is not unusual for lyricists or poets to be confused about their own work. Sometimes the words are unclear because, when writing, the emotions are confused or the words spring from deep within. In early 1974, the latest Furay could have completed "Flight of the Dove," his life was in transition with major changes imminent. Lines in the song seem to hint at these changes—whether Furay intended to do so or not. Richie was struggling with SHF, his marriage was showing signs of renewed tension, and his faith in Christ had been stirred. It becomes possible, therefore, to read "apathy" in the following lines as a reference to Nancy's distancing herself from him or Souther's displays of boredom during rehearsals: "If I say to you I can't get through / Apathy, it's killin' me." At one point during early rehearsals, Furay became so frustrated that he exclaimed, "Why did I leave Poco? For this?"[28] In other lines, he might be expressing his fear that Nancy, his "star," might force a marital separation: "She's got a reason to fly like a star in the sky / Can't you hear her cry?" Furthermore, the dove, often a symbol in Christianity of the Holy Spirit (as in the 1960 #1 country hit by Ferlin Husky, "On the Wings of a Dove"), could refer to his imminent conversion: "Put nothing above the flight of the dove." The song could be about all these complex emotions fomenting in Furay at the time. As he said, "There was a lot going on in my life that I didn't even know about. . . . At the time, the Lord was really starting to tap me on the shoulder."[29]

Souther's standout moment on the album is the alliteratively titled "Deep, Dark and Dreamless," a tender ballad in which a compassionate singer expresses support for a friend who is depressed, lonely, and disoriented—as suggested by the mixed imagery in the opening line in which "the moon blows 'round your door and water burns like wine." Souther sings with convincing concern and emotion, trying to lift up the friend. But the singer has little success with lines like "You're not the only one" and "You're breaking my heart." However, at the 3:45 mark, the singer becomes less cliché-ish and more self-revealing, sharing his own battle with depression in a surge of emotion in which Souther hits high notes he hits nowhere else on the album: "You see, I know what it means to be all alone, and losing your dreams . . . Deep, dark and dreamless nights." It's a haunting performance, enhanced by the steel guitar of Perkins and the drum and cymbal crashes of Gordon. Of Hillman's songs, his most notable contribution to SHF is "Rise and Fall," which was written with LA drummer Len Fagan and is a bluesy bluegrass with dobro by Perkins, and Hillman on mandolin. He also wrote "Heavenly Fire" with Fagan, a beautiful elegy to his former bandmate Gram Parsons, who died only a few months earlier, which has an especially poignant second verse: "Lived the life you sang about / Carried me through when I had my doubts / Now there's an emptiness inside of me / All I've got left is your memory."

Album Art

For the album art, Geffen commissioned Jimmie Wachtel, who had designed covers for Joe Walsh and would go on to design covers for Crosby, Stills & Nash, Bruce Springsteen, and Bob Dylan. Oddly enough and unintentionally, the art reflects the contrived, inorganic formation of the band. The front cover features three large headshots of the principals, side by side, with the band's name overhead and stars between the performers' names. The supporting musicians are similarly profiled on the back cover. Each photo has been retouched and tinted—we might say photoshopped today—to appear as if all members were simultaneously present for a group portrait. Furthermore, if one looks closely, it is probable that Souther's head was pasted onto another neck and shoulders. Still, it is an effective cover, drawing attention to the stars and their supergroup.

In the gatefold, on the left quarter, are the song listings and credits. Three-quarters of the gatefold is consumed by a postcard, similar to Springsteen's famous cover for *Greetings from Asbury Park*, except here it reads "Greetings from Glamour City." Inside the card's pinkish orange borders are flashy images of Los Angeles and Hollywood, including the Capitol Records Tower, renamed, here, Geffen Records. Descending out of the bright night sky full of meteors and stars is a round disk resembling a poker chip with trailing streaks and with "The S.H.F. Band" printed inside. Playfully the artwork announces the expectations for the newest supernova. Souther-Hillman-Furay will be huge and catapult up the charts at lightning speed.

Tour

To promote *SHF*, the band took to the road from July through August and then again from October through November. Geffen saw that SHF was booked as both a supporting act for stylistically similar artists and as a headliner in smaller venues in cities where they could attract publicity. SHF played large outdoor spaces like Roosevelt Stadium, Jersey City, New Jersey (approximate capacity 30,000), in a one-day festival with Seals & Crofts, England Dan and John Ford Coley, and Maria Muldaur. They opened for the Eagles in the Memorial Coliseum in Ft. Wayne, Indiana (capacity 13,000), and headlined the Music Inn, in Lenox, Massachusetts, alongside Doc Watson and Steeleye Span (capacity 3,000). Perhaps the biggest venue they headlined was the Woolman Skating Rink in Central Park, New York City (approximate capacity 6,500), with many listening on the rocks and grassy areas surrounding the rink. The live shows, like the album, were good, mostly well received, but hardly spectacular, not what audiences might have expected of a supergroup. One reviewer in Phoenix asked himself if SHF was the next supergroup: "No way," he responded. Another reviewer called them "the poor man's Crosby, Stills, Nash and Young."[30]

The road did not reshape SHF into the tight unit that Geffen may have hoped. Their show, like the album, seemed more of an electric songwriter's circle with each principal getting approximately twenty minutes of the short one-hour set. By the second leg of the tour, it was clear SHF was not working out, either on or off stage. Like the show, the band remained fractured. They desperately needed a leader to steer them into a better musical and communal unity, but no one would take the challenge, and, in truth, no one would have succeeded. Souther, a loner, would neither have yielded to another member of the band nor have assumed leadership himself. Furay was not only distracted with his marital problems and his focus on Christianity, but he was also uncomfortable with Souther. In fact, his constant Bible reading and conversations with Perkins did little to develop the band's chemistry. "The band never felt cohesive," said Furay. "I never felt at home in that band. . . . Poco felt like a family. We did things together. We liked each other. SHF felt like three guys that were just trying to find a niche." The band created little excitement and, in October and November, despite a Gold album, ticket sales failed to meet expectations and resulted in the cancelation of a few gigs. Audiences perceived SHF as bland. As Furay said, "For all the personality there was in that band, there was no personality at all."[31]

Epiphanies and Conversion

One year after Al and Debbie Perkins played the Furays an audio recording of a Pastor Chuck Smith sermon, Richie completed his commitment to Christ. The Bible, prayer, conversations with Perkins and other Christians, and a series of epiphanies guided Furay to what he calls his conversion. The first epiphany occurred near the end of SHF's Aspen residency, when he willingly prayed with Perkins and, for the first time, felt Christ. A second epiphany occurred in September, after the first part of the SHF tour and during his separation from Nancy. Residing with the Perkinses in California, Furay decided to visit a Christian bookstore. As he drove north on the 605 Freeway, a torrential rainstorm broke out. He pulled to the shoulder of the road. "I just remember crying out to the Lord, 'I just want my family back.' I can see it vividly in my mind. It was raining so hard, and I was crying so hard, 'I just want my family back.' And the Lord said specifically to me, 'That's how much I want you to want me.'"[32] The voice caused Furay to contemplate his priorities and his relationship with God.

A few days later, on a particularly hot evening with the dry Santa Ana winds gusting, Richie was praying on the Perkins's balcony when suddenly he felt a chill and then a voice telling him to "go home." He went into the guest bedroom, where the voice got louder, "Go home." He had recently met Keith Ritter, a counselor at Calvary Chapel in Costa Mesa, California. "What should I do?" he asked Keith, who responded, "You should go home." Richie prayed with the Perkinses and the next morning left for Colorado with bad weather predicted for Denver. While boarding the plane, Richie, not eager to engage with anyone, heard a voice behind him singing, "There's just a little bit of magic in the country." Furay reluctantly turned to speak to "John," who volunteered his friend to give Furay a ride from the Denver airport to his Boulder home.[33] That September 12, Denver recorded its earliest snowstorm on record. John called his friend, DJ and music critic Kenny Weissberg, who had written an unflattering review of SHF in Aspen, to request the ride. Weissberg, under a deadline and unwilling to drive in the storm, refused—until he heard John's "new friend" was Richie Furay. Weissberg hurried to the airport. Like any rock journalist, he was full of questions for Furay, who answered politely but curtly. Weissberg remembered: "He's in the back seat. I'm driving a little station wagon and I look back. His eyes are closed and he's whispering to himself"—probably praying. Richie apologized for not being more communicative but explained that he was returning home to save his marriage. "It was eerie. Not another word was said for the rest of the car trip, another 20–25 minutes."[34]

Furay found himself at his front door with no key and no one home. He sat and waited until Nancy arrived. Stunned to see her estranged husband, Nancy allowed Richie to spend some time at home and then, in an effort to save the marriage, she somewhat reluctantly agreed to return with her husband to California, where he would prepare for the second leg of the SHF tour. A few weeks later, she informed him that she was pregnant with an abortion scheduled for the next day. After some discussion, Furay convinced her to cancel the abortion and to try marital counseling with Ritter. Richie remembers his wife's words at the first session: "I don't love him. I never loved him, and I'll never love him again."[35] Richie was dumbfounded but somehow remained hopeful. Nancy returned to Colorado after agreeing to bear their child but not to reconcile. Richie headed on the road with SHF and remained persistent in his phone calls. As he sings in "On the Line," on SHF's second album, "a dreamer will always try."

As the second tour drew to a close, in late November 1974, Furay and Perkins walked on a Florida beach: "I remember the Lord saying," Richie said, "'you made a commitment to me and now it's time we talk about it.'" From that point, Richie's commitment was total, and God became his first priority. "He had to be first in my life; everything else is secondary"—including family and music.[36] God's words made Furay more confident in reconciliation, and he continued to call Nancy. However, he had to record a second album.

Trouble in Paradise

By the time SHF completed their tour dates, they knew their days as a band were over. Yet in the spring of 1975, they reconvened to record *Trouble in Paradise* at Caribou Ranch in Nederland, Colorado, minutes from Furay's home, where they had first rehearsed in late 1973. To produce the album, Geffen had recruited the legendary Tom Dowd, who had produced Aretha Franklin, the Allman Brothers, Derek and the Dominoes, and many, many others. It was a difficult situation for Dowd. The principals wanted simply to fulfill their contract and move on. "We knew we weren't going on the road," said Hillman, "so . . . being quite honest with you, I just didn't bring out a couple of my songs. I think the other guys did the same thing."[37]

Furay should not have been anywhere near a studio. Immersed in religious examination and desperate to regain his family, he was not fully invested in the album. "I was there physically, but not emotionally. This is one of the only times in my career that I may have compromised the professionalism I've always prided myself on." He had written only two songs for the album. "Some artists become incredibly productive when they're in crisis," he wrote, "but I was so overwhelmed by the way my world was crashing around me that I couldn't concentrate on song writing."[38] Especially gnawing at Richie was that his home was about five miles from the recording studio. But since he was separated, he stayed in a cabin on the ranch's property. "Here we are, recording with one of the greatest sound engineers/producers of all time and I don't even remember the experience. It was just such a weird time in my life."[39] At one point, Nancy requested that he remove his belongings from their home. He obliged and rented a storage unit.

As a producer, Dowd was in a difficult predicament: "Richie was going through a religious transition. . . . Chris is a free spirit, a very happy and well-adjusted person who will go with anything and try anything, while J. D. has to have things his way, so you have a tough juggling act. . . . It's like a hot coal and an ice cube—you just can't get used to switching off one after the other. . . . I got the best out of them that I could. . . . I couldn't have wrung an ounce more out."[40] The end result was that these great talents combined to release a very mediocre album. In *Rolling Stone*, Bud Scoppa wrote that the "few moments of life contained on *Trouble in Paradise* are Souther's doing."[41] Indeed, the highlight of the album is Souther's "Mexico," which tells an engaging and humorous story about how a sly singer cheats with his girlfriend's friend while his girlfriend is in Mexico spending her "daddy's dough." The romance lasted a weekend. The singer gives his girlfriend hackneyed excuses: he was "sad and blue"; the affair was meaningless; "she gave me such a friendly shove"; the other woman knew "that I was yours" so "she didn't take a thing from you" or our relationship. As the song fades, he sings, "But I ain't mad about it" so "don't you be mad about it, baby / 'Cause it was just another night." The humor is enhanced by the pleasant breezy rhythm and the Mexican mariachi ambience created by the acoustic guitar riffs and Hillman's mandolin.

Furay's contributions are steeped in Christianity. "For Someone I Love" was written before he separated from Nancy and turned to Christ, but it was revised at the time of recording. Like several of his songs, it predicts his imminent future. In the heartfelt ballad, Furay pleads for the resurrection of his marriage, drawing on hopeful images of spring renewal ("when the winter snows melt" and "love is in bloom") and allusions to Christ, first suggested in a pun on *sun* and *Son* ("the sun is a shinin'"). The pun only becomes clear in the chorus as Richie sings, "Move over, give Him some room / Let Him take us to places unknown." Furay conflates trust in and love for the Lord with marital trust and love: "Lord, take us by the hand so we understand the meaning of love." Furay sings that despite having "grown so far apart," if "we really do believe in each other through You" that "we" will find "peace" and marital happiness. The simple arrangement, with Richie on acoustic guitar and his vocals high in the mix, with a quiet electric keyboard from Harris and an occasional riff from Perkins on electric guitar, reflects a glimmering brightness that underpins the singer's somewhat mystical and hopeful journey. "For

Someone I Love" marks a significant moment for the songwriter as he finds artistic inspiration in his Christianity, but the graceful ballad does not rank in the first tier of Furay ballads with "Kind Woman," "Sad Memory," "Believe Me," or "Don't Let It Pass By."

Furay's second contribution is "On the Line," a more upbeat mid-tempo rocker in which Richie, at first, seems to accept Nancy's ultimate rejection of him. He acknowledges her "free will," and he sings "maybe you will and maybe you won't [return to me]." But he questions her truthfulness to herself, and he believes she is "holding back." He confidently calls on her to "lay it out on the line" and reveal "the way that you love me." Again, he connects marital love with God's love, for by rejecting her husband she is "not receiving all of God's love," which will increase in the sanctity of their marriage. It is not one of his better vocal performances. Furay sings in a higher key than he would have liked. His voice strains ineffectively on the high notes in the middle of the long verse lines. Looking back, he wishes Dowd or someone else had recommended a different key.[42]

Despite poor reviews and no supporting tour, *Trouble in Paradise* had a fair chart showing, peaking at #39 in late July. Robert Christgau rated the album a C-, concluding that "this band usually goes by its initials because they stand for Shit Hits the Fan. Or do I mean fans?" In *Rolling Stone*, Scoppa ended his review with a question: "Why don't SHF redeem themselves while they still can and just forget the whole thing?"[43] The band agreed. Rumors circulated that a summer tour was on hold because either Hillman was ill or Richie had hurt his finger—which he did while splitting kindling. However, in truth, no tour was even contemplated. The members were relieved to be done with SHF. "We were awful," Hillman said. "We were never a band. We barely even knew each other. It had all the good ingredients, but boy, the cake turned out bad. S-H-F was three guys making minisolo albums on each record. The only advantage is that it got all three of our names around."[44]

Souther, Hillman, and Furay became better friends after the band ended. In 2012, improbable as it may sound, the three had lunch to talk about a possible reunion. As they tossed out ideas, they each began to realize it would not work. Souther was about to begin acting on *Nashville*, a television series, and as Richie said, uncharacteristically close-mouthed as his voice trailed off, "We had lunch together. It was a great time and I love 'em both. But the band, it just didn't seem . . ."[45] But Hillman asked a question that might have sunk any prospects: "I want both of you to go home and listen to the albums and tell me which songs you want to do? What songs do you do in your own shows? Because I don't do any of those songs." He added that he does sometimes perform "Rise and Fall" and "it comes off quite well," largely because "my musical partner Herb (Pedersen) is such a good singer."[46]

Reconciliation

As the sessions for *Trouble in Paradise* neared completion, Richie received a rare call from Nancy, informing him that their daughter was anxious to see him. Delighted, Richie raced over. That was followed by subsequent meetings and, on one occasion, he spent the night. Yet Nancy was not ready to take her husband back. With recording done, he had to vacate his temporary residence at Caribou Ranch and head back to California with the Perkinses. Shortly afterward, Nancy invited her husband to return home for an attempt at reconciliation. As in "For Someone I Love," the ice seemed to be melting in the Colorado mountains with love about to bloom. As if to signal his commitment to domesticity, Richie traded in his beloved Porsche and drove home in a newly purchased Chevrolet pickup. However, when Richie called Nancy to say he was on his way, she balked. Not yet, she said. She had reconsidered. Richie, who can be stubborn and persistent, hopped in the pickup with Steve "Bugs" Giglio, his road manager and friend, and headed off to Boulder. Nancy, who was well along in her pregnancy, was not pleased to see her husband. For several weeks, the couple shared the house as roommates, treating each other politely, distantly, and delicately.

On June 25, 1975, their second daughter, Katie, was born. "The next morning," Nancy remembered, "I'm holding her in my arms, and all of a sudden I feel this warm sensation come over me. . . . And I knew it was the Lord filling me with a love for my husband. I called him up, and I said, 'I love you.'"[47] Words Richie had not heard in months. From that moment, the Furays have remained together.

CHAPTER 10

"I've Got a Reason"

Going Solo

Richie Furay spent most of 1975 at home, working on his marriage, tending to his growing family, studying the Bible, and writing songs with some occasional backpacking and trout fishing. "Fishing is probably my #1 activity. . . . I love going up to those high mountain lakes. It's so peaceful up there. . . . We always pray: 'Lord, let us catch a little fish.'"[1] Furay would not return to the studio until the following spring and would not tour until late summer 1976. He did, however, accept the invitation of *Crawdaddy* editor Peter Knobler to write a reflective essay on turning thirty years old. (The June 1975 issue included other counterculture luminaries on the same topic, including Souther and Hillman.) Furay submitted more of a sermon, outlining his conversion in a passionate, humorless, and sometimes fire-and-brimstone statement of almost 1,500 words, a little more than a page, complete with over a dozen exclamation points and numerous biblical references. No doubt the feverish tone resulted partially from his continued anxiety over his marriage. He had not yet reconciled with Nancy when he wrote the piece.

In "A Good Feeling to Know"—he, or perhaps Knobler, dropped the apostrophe at the end of "feelin'," perhaps indicative of his earnestness and matured outlook—Richie declares that, until he found Christ, his life "had been one unfulfilled desire after another. Everything I thought I had ever wanted was covered with my ego and the lusts for it . . . cars, land, hit (Gold) records, possessions." He addresses the reader: "But what are *you* living for? If your sights aren't on the ultimate—Jesus Christ—then you're falling short of what life is all about! . . . If you don't have the love of God, you have no love at all." While not identifying his marital problems, he does write, "I'm going through the heaviest trial of my life right now while I'm stating my faith in

Him." He criticizes the emptiness of "cult" religions and states that the only way to heaven and eternal life is through Jesus. He urgently calls on readers to accept Christ into their lives: "Make that decision *now*." He warns that "The seven years following Christ's return are going to be years of hell. You better consider that alternative."[2] Knobler, Furay's friend, tried to caution him about publishing the jeremiad. "Richie, this is going to hurt your career. I really advise against it," he told him. "I care about you. This is not a good idea." But Furay was insistent: "Peter, this is important to me. . . . This is what I believe, so please print it."[3] As Knobler knew, this was not the Richie that fans loved, the vocalist with the beaming airy tenor who wrote joyful rhythms and constructed gorgeous harmonies, and the upbeat and energetic showman. The contrast in personas was sharp.

Since he prayed with the Perkinses in late July 1974 in Aspen, Furay has never wavered in his commitment to Christ. It has only intensified. His faith and, indeed, his life rest on six fundamental tenets that he, along with others, identified under a "Statement of Faith" when Furay served as pastor of Calvary Chapel in Broomfield, Colorado:

(1) We believe that there is one God eternally existent in three Persons: Father, Son, and Holy Spirit.
(2) We believe the Bible to be the inspired, the only infallible, authoritative Word of God, inerrant in the original writings.
(3) We believe in the deity of our Lord Jesus Christ, His virgin birth, His sinless life, His substitutionary-atoning death through His shed blood, His bodily resurrection, in His ascension to the right hand of the Father, His visible, personal return in power and glory and the establishment of His Kingdom on earth.
(4) We believe in the Holy Spirit, the third Person of the Godhead, Who came forth to convict the world of sin, righteousness and judgment; to regenerate, sanctify, to seal and empower for ministry, service, and witness all who believe in Christ. . . .
(5) We believe that all people are sinners by nature and choice and therefore are under condemnation; that God forgives those who repent of their sins and confess Jesus Christ as Lord and Savior, and that by the indwelling Holy Spirit God enables said believers to live a godly life.
(6) We believe in the bodily resurrection of both the saved and the unsaved; the final judgment and eternal blessing of the righteous and the endless suffering of the wicked.[4]

Furay's intense faith in these tenets, along with the necessity of reading the Bible daily and engaging in intense prayer, has led Richie to put his life in God's hands. In 1975, he told *Creem*, "Now I know I can't do anything on my own. The Lord directs my path."[5] A precept Richie still follows.

Christianity, Rock Music, and Furay

Furay's conversion came in the midst of another Great Awakening in America, the fourth in its history.[6] Beginning in the 1950s, a series of charismatic and fundamentalist preachers infused the nation with Christian fervor. Preachers like the Rev. Billy Graham gathered large crowds of worshippers at sports arenas and stadiums and warned young people about the dangers of rampant materialism and rock and roll, telling them that their insecurity and search for leadership have led them to false heroes like Elvis Presley and disk jockey Dick Clark. "I believe the leader should be Jesus Christ," Graham insisted.[7] On the cover of its June 21, 1971, issue, *Time* placed an image of Christ under the banner "The Jesus Revolution" and noted in the story that "the radical spiritual fervor of a growing number of young Americans . . . [has] proclaimed an extraordinary religious revolution in his name."[8] Over the years, Furay has performed at many Christian festivals, which have included preaching, music, and seminars. In 2018, one of Furay's most important spiritual mentors, Greg Laurie, said, "It's time for another Jesus Revolution."[9]

The Fourth Great Awakening was reflected in a number of Top 40 hits performed in a variety of genres: the gospel "Oh Happy Day" by the Edwin Hawkins Singers (#4, 1969); the fuzz-toned rock of "Spirit in the Sky" by Norman Greenbaum (#3, 1970), which was the bestselling single of the year; the gospel-rock of "Are You Ready" by Pacific Gas & Electric (#14, 1970); the pop-folk "Put Your Hand in the Hand" by Ocean (#2, 1971); hits from the Broadway plays, and later films, *Jesus Christ Superstar* (title track by Murray Head, #14, 1971, and "I Don't Know How to Love Him" by, first, Yvonne Elliman #28, then Helen Reddy, #13, both 1971); and *Godspell* ("Day by Day," cast, #14, 1972). At the end of 1971, George Harrison's spiritual "My Sweet Lord" hit #1, though the song is more vaguely mystical than Christian. Yet despite these incidental singles and a few excursions into Christian themes by rock elites—like Clapton's "Presence of the Lord" (*Blind Faith* 1969) and the Rolling Stones' cover of "Prodigal Son" (*Beggars Banquet*, 1968) and the Stones' own "Shine a Light" (*Exile on Main Street*, 1972)—there were no openly Christian artists who appealed to the hip rock crowd. The "hip" rock crowd can be described as music fans who bought albums, not singles, paid no attention to charts, and only reluctantly listened to AM radio. They might listen to AM radio in an automobile, since in the early 1970s few cars were equipped with FM transmitters. Many artists may have feared announcing that they were born-again Christians, especially after seeing the fate of Larry Norman. Norman, "the father of Christian rock," was dropped by Capitol Records when his first album, *Upon This Rock* (1969), failed to meet sales targets. Tellingly, Paul McCartney said, "Larry Norman could be a star if he'd just shut up about religion."[10]

When most rock musicians, like the Stones, performed Christian or gospel music, they did so as artists, cultural historians, or experimentalists and not as fervid Christians. Similarly, when Stephen Stills cries out that "Jesus Christ was the first nonviolent revolutionary" on the live CSN&Y's *4 Way Street* (1971), he is celebrating the historical Jesus rather than the divine Jesus. Bob Dylan, however, turned the first of his three Christian albums into a substantial commercial success. *Slow Train Coming* (1979) reached #3 on the charts and went Platinum with over a million sales within nine months of its release. His two follow-up Christian albums, *Saved* (1980, #24) and *Shot of Love* (1981, #33), are not included among Dylan's thirty-nine Gold and Platinum achievements—but neither of those albums is as musically successful as *Slow Train*.

There has always been a rift between Christianity and rock music, commonly called "the devil's music" and "jungle music" among conservative Christians.[11] Rock music and Christianity, "They're not going to work together," said Furay, like "oil and water."[12] John Thompson, however, argues that "Jesus and rock music are perfectly suited to each other."[13] Both, he argues, spring from gospel music (however indirectly) and from rebellious impulses—Jesus, the source of Christianity, was a revolutionary. However, Thompson overlooks centuries of history during which Christianity in the West became a dominant power or an ally to the empowered, so much so that Karl Marx warned of its oppressive effects on the working class. "Religion is the opium of the masses," he famously asserted in the 1840s, suggesting that religion, with its promise of a heavenly afterlife, sedated worshippers' impulse to effect social and economic change. Christianity, to Marx, had become another tool for governments and wealthy capitalists to keep workers in check. The hippie movement, for which rock music provided a soundtrack, sought, as Tom Wolfe said, "to sweep aside all codes and all restraints of the past and start out from zero."[14]

Rock music is rooted in angst, defiance, discontent, and hope—from Little Richard's sexual howls, Buffalo Springfield's more cerebral protest with

"For What It's Worth," and John Lennon's idealistic "Imagine" (1971) to the Clash's remake of the classic "I Fought the Law" (1979), Green Day's "American Idiot" (2004), and the Drive By Truckers' angry and ironic "Thoughts and Prayers" (2020). Rock music asserts the self and self-empowerment and encourages the self to be unyielding. "No retreat, baby, no surrender" sings Bruce Springsteen on *Born in the U.S.A.* ("No Surrender" 1984), a song covered as late as 2019 by Hawthorne Heights, and Tom Petty sings "I Won't Back Down" (1989), covered by Joshua Radin in 2019. Christians, particularly fundamentalist Christians, argue that true freedom comes in self-surrendering to the Lord. In his Holy Sonnet #14, John Donne called on God to "take me . . . imprison me . . . for I, / Except you enthrall me, never shall be free" (ca. 1609–10). Furay similarly addresses the Lord: "I'll give you my life, set me free" ("Mighty Maker," 1976).

How much Furay's evangelical beliefs have hurt his music career is debatable and unmeasurable. "I think it hurt it significantly," says Knobler. "I think record companies didn't know what to do with him."[15] Furay agrees, claiming that his solo albums were not adequately promoted.[16] However, the three Asylum albums, from 1976 to 1980, might not have been appealing to his fanbase as Furay moved away from his country-rock sound. In addition, as trends and consumer demographics changed, Furay may not have caught the era's zeitgeist—as Poco's music, perceived by some as overly happy, might have missed the spirit of rebellious angst a few years earlier. Wayne Robins, music journalist and editor at *Creem* from 1971 to 1975, believes Furay's religious leanings did not impact his popularity or sales of his records. "Anything and everything were acceptable in the mid-'70s," he said. "I don't think anyone really cared about his religious convictions. . . . Everyone seemed to be a spiritual seeker of some sort."[17] Certainly, Furay's Christianity has provoked responses that he had never previously experienced. It strained many friendships: "People, they just didn't even want to come near me. A couple of my friends were very fearful."[18]

I've Got a Reason

Furay signed a three-record deal with Asylum, which came with a warning from cofounder David Geffen: "'You're not going to give me any of that Jesus music, are you?' And, I said, 'David, you know, I'm going to write an album that you're going to be really happy with.'"[19] But for Furay not to write about his faith and conversion would have been disingenuous, if not impossible.

His songs have always been about himself. "My personal experiences were a creative wellspring, and . . . the more personal my lyrics were, the more the average listener could identify with them."[20] Throughout his career, the "I" in Furay's songs has been self-referent. He does not invent personae or heavily populate his songs as, say, Dylan does. In a sense, Furay writes autobiography, not fiction. On *I've Got a Reason*, he identifies himself as a singer-songwriter on several tracks. On "Starlight," he is "a singer of songs," and on "We'll See," he declares that "most of my life has been makin' music." He adds, "Some of the songs are very specific about Nancy and my struggle, and in others I'm reaching out."[21]

In the spring of 1976, Furay entered the studio with his first incarnation of the Richie Furay Band (RFB). He sought musicians who were both talented and Christian. "I wanted a team of people whose lifestyle was in synch with mine and who could identify with my new direction because they'd made their own choice for Christ."[22] From Calvary Chapel, Costa Mesa, he recruited Tom Stipe on keyboards, Jay Truax on bass, and John Mehler on drums. "They're all unknowns," Furay said at the time, adding that they used to call themselves A Wing and a Prayer, "but can they ever sing and play."[23] Furay also invited Al Perkins to join the band, but the guitarist, who agreed to play on the album, declined to tour. Steve Cropper, Stax guitarist and producer of *From the Insider*, participated in sessions for two cuts, "Starlight" and "Mighty Maker." It did not work out, however. "He had trouble, unfortunately, on both of them," said Furay.[24] As coproducers, Furay hired Bill Schnee, who had worked as an engineer for Richie Podolor on Three Dog Night sessions, and Michael Omartian, a keyboardist who had more experience as a musician than as a producer at the time. In future years, Schnee and Omartian would each be nominated for more than ten Grammy Awards.

Furay, with his personal and spiritual life in order, entered the studio confident and enthusiastic. "I was trying to get away from anything that sounded like Poco. I wanted to create a new sound for me, and so I went keyboard with Michael Omartian and Tom Stipe."[25] Overall, the music and production might have been too different for his fan base, not guitarish enough (despite some potent licks from Perkins), and, at times, overproduced with strings and disco sound techniques in an effort to sound contemporary, sometimes obscuring Furay's emotive tenor. However, the lyrics, as is typical of Furay, are well constructed, telling the story of his emotional journey to conversion, which we might chart with a jagged trajectory, moving ever upward but with dips along the way. Coming to the Lord, said Richie, "was a struggle and a half."[26] Furay is careful not to alienate either a secular audience or Geffen. The dominant tone is joy and thanksgiving. The opening track, "Look at the Sun," features a characteristic Furay howl of exhilaration. *I've Got a Reason*, even when proselytizing, never rants like Furay's fire-and-brimstone sermonizing in *Crawdaddy*; as he says, "you won't find the name of Jesus on that record anywhere."[27]

Furay reflects his newfound bliss and clarity of vision in images of light and the sun, which contrast with images of darkness and night. In the light is where God is present, providing love, hope, and renewal; in the dark is where God is absent and the devil dwells. (For Furay and other evangelicals, the devil is a real and active entity in the world.) On the album's second track, the slow rocker "We'll See," Furay sings, "Run for your life / Don't get caught in the night, turn on the light." Similarly, on "Getting Through," written with Stipe, Furay calls on the listener to welcome the Lord, who is omnipresent and available, "like the sun." With word play, this is suggestive of Jesus, the *son* of God. As Furay said to me, "Look at Christ, man. You can see it all. Look into the sun."[28] If God's "sights are on you," Furay sings, he will graft you in. "Like the dawn out in the desert, you can't make the darkness stay / Or live within a shadow tryin' to keep the light away." One of the highlights on the album, "Getting Through," is the only Poco-like track, featuring a fast-paced rhythm with banjo, high harmonies, and *ooohs* and Perkins's country-rock guitar riffs. It is easy to miss the proselytizing in the joyous melody and upbeat rhythm even as Furay subtly warns of "believin' in rock 'n' roll." He was more direct in a 1981 interview: "I personally believe that rock 'n' roll is the devil's playground. . . . There's so much destruction and people's lives can get so messed up in rock 'n' roll. It's a fantasy land."[29]

Furay mentions the devil twice on the album. "Still Rolling Stones," a pounding rocker with sizzling Perkins guitar, is a diatribe against the devil and his activities in the world: "The devil's a liar, the worst of his kind . . . So subtle, always disguised / The truth shakes him, his lies breaks him. . . . he's forsaken." The song is also, Furay said, a veiled attack on *Rolling Stone*, which "had started looking at my music differently ever since word of my Christian conversion began circulating. Many other publications followed suit to the point where my faith, not my music, was being reviewed."[30] "Mighty Maker," a prayer-song written before his reconciliation with his wife, asks God to restore his marriage and blames "the devil" and his temptation for driving "her away from me and our dream." The mediocre rocker is not improved by Omartian's addition of intrusive disco-like synthesized strings (irritatingly skittish on the chorus), the use of a cowbell, and some outer-space sound effects near the close. In "Starlight," another gorgeous Furay ballad, he thanks the Lord, who is "always there to let me know you care" and subtly attacks false idols and "cult religions . . . stars or books about how to free yourself," as he wrote in *Crawdaddy*.[31] But through the "sun" and in Christ there is always hope: "Good morning, sun / You've outlasted everyone." On the album cover, Furay stands tall, smiling, and casually dressed in a flannel shirt with a long-sleeved thermal shirt underneath. In the top left corner, the words "The Richie Furay Band" are encircled by sun rays.

Between "Mighty Maker" and "Still Rolling Stones" is the engaging calypso/reggae rhythm of "You're the One I Love," a celebration of his reconciliation with Nancy, who, as in "Believe Me," is likened to "a star . . . shining bright." Furay sets the jumpy, joyful rhythm with staccato strumming of his guitar; Traux plays percolating bass lines under the verses, which he releases at the chorus; and Stipe provides a soaring solo near the middle of the song. Schnee and Omartian contribute to the lightness of touch with various synthesized effects, including what sounds like steel drums (probably a cowbell). For Furay, conversion instilled a greater appreciation for his wife and natural surroundings: "I don't know how to explain it. Everything opens up. You see things differently. I saw my wife in a different way after I accepted Christ. I look at flowers as a color-blind guy—I'm not color blind but I'm color weak—I see beauty."[32] In the confessional title track, Furay outlines his life pre- and post-conversion. "Music *was* my life," he sings, "[but it] finally took everything." He appreciates that the Lord has given him "a gift [to] sing"— a gift for which he continues to thank God in his live performances—but has come to realize that his quest for stardom blinded him to the needs of his family and to the calling of the Lord. He acknowledges that he has "been a child in my life, a child in my dreams"—echoes of charges he made against Neil Young in "Child's Claim to Fame." Now, he proclaims, with faith in God and God's plan for him, "I've got a reason for living each day." However, the revealing ballad is marred by a bloated production, which features strings, arranged here by David Diggs, a sparkling keyboard, and a recurring riff on what sounds like a melodica. Furay seems to play into the production and perhaps tries too hard to deliver an emotional impact, reducing "I've Got a Reason," at times, to melodrama. Furay's voice, with its sterling clarity, is best in uncluttered settings.

"Look at the Sun," which Furay wrote with Stipe, is the album's supreme achievement. One of Furay's most underrated and underperformed songs, it captures the ecstasy of Furay the Christian. Furay's high tenor, contemplative and joyful, opens song and album, unaccompanied for four beats. "Look at the sun," he sings. A single note on Stipe's electric piano chimes as Richie holds "sun." Then, "Look at the way it comes down shinin'," followed by a rattle, rising strings, and vibration. Furay re-sings the two lines with his voice rising to a falsetto for the final "shinin'." After he sings "Just about," he pauses, chords crash, and the slow-to-medium-paced rocker begins. Those opening thirty-two seconds set a mystical tone that informs the album and introduces the *sun/son* pun as Furay's gaze at the sun signals his discovery and celebration of Christ. Furay experiences this rediscovery with each sunrise. He sings that until he came to the Lord he was "runnin' hard all night long . . . tossed to and fro . . . like a domino" in his quest to find "home," a home he hurried to in songs like "Good Feelin' to Know," "And Settlin' Down," and "Fallin in Love." But in those songs, he moves toward "home" without ever arriving. As he sings in "Sun," "Lord, by now you'd think I'd, I'd been home." It is only when Furay finds the Lord that he considers himself "home"—a concept "so blurred before I accepted Christ."[33] He can now proclaim, as he does in "Sun," "I laughed so hard I cried, I knew my old self had died." The song's title, written in present imperative tense, indicates his certainty and his desire for others to recognize salvation through Christ. After the three-minute mark of "Sun," the intro is repeated, followed by an almost ninety-second instrumental jam, much softer than the song's earlier rock feel. With its effective synthesized sounds and strings (arranged by Diggs), anchored by the electric piano, somewhat funky bass, and drums, "Sun" takes on a comfortably meditative tone, suggesting that the singer has escaped his darkness and left behind temptations and earthly pleasures for a superior state of fulfillment or, for Furay, "home." The song has a similar majesty and epicness to "Believe Me" and "Sweet Lovin'."

The album closes with "Over and Over Again." The lengthiest track, at over seven minutes, and the most explosive rocker on *Reason*, the lyrics exhort listeners to turn to the Lord. "Over and over again" nonbelievers miss the Lord's call, instead, "dancing with a stranger" (the devil) where it is "dark as night." But the good news is that all are "just a step away . . . come on and make [the choice] today." Then, "the mystery will unfold" and "the morning will come," presumably with the *sun/son*. Interestingly, Furay plays off Dylan's "Blowin' in the Wind." In Dylan's song the "answer . . . blowin' in the wind" is elusive, ambiguous, but when Furay sings in the concluding line, "Look to the wind to know what you must, the answer," there is absolute certainty as to Furay's "answer"— which is the final word for both song and album.

Taken as a whole, the nine tracks on *Reason* form a loosely structured song cycle. The songs combine to provide insight into the mindset and emotional life of its protagonist (Furay himself) over a couple of years, from just prior to his conversion to just after—although the tracks do not follow a linear progression. Still, the album tells the story of a singer who never found deep fulfillment, comfort, or a "home" until he escaped darkness and found the light of the Lord. The singer now lives confidently in the Lord's plan for him and continues to find renewal and even ecstasy in God's grace and love. Musically, *Reason* may draw from some of Furay's past forms, but the production is unlike his previous work. The more aggressive production leads to an uneven album, sometimes overly embellished. However, the vocals, the songs themselves with only a couple of exceptions, and especially the story of Furay's journey to Christianity infuse *I've Got a Reason* with urgency, resulting in a compelling listening experience—although the album remains underappreciated.

After *Reason*'s release in July 1976, Furay struck out on a three-month tour from mid-August to mid-November, playing some fifty dates. Along with Stipe, Truax, and Mehler, Furay added Diggs on second keyboard, Bob Wall on guitar, and Alex MacDougall on percussion, who appeared on a few tracks on *Reason*. RFB opened for headliners like the Beach Boys, the Band, Leon Russell, Marshall Tucker Band, and Hot Tuna. At first, the set included mostly songs from the new album supplemented by a handful of previous Furay songs, like "Kind Woman," "Good Feelin' to Know," "Fallin' in Love," "On the Line," and "Believe Me." As the tour went on, Furay decreased the number of songs from *Reason* and dipped into songs from Buffalo Springfield (e.g., "On the Way Home," "Sad Memory") and Poco ("Pickin' Up the Pieces," "Just for Me and You")—not a good sign. Reviews for RFB, especially as an opening act, were mixed. After the band supported Janis Ian in Edwardsville, Illinois, on the first night of the tour, the reviewer wrote that RFB sounded "like 1,000 other bands going right now." A month later, after RFB opened for Leon Russell, the reviewer found the set "overly long," bored by the lengthy drum and percussion solo. However, when RFB opened for the Band in Lenox, Massachusetts, the reviewer called Furay "impressive," noting how "one of rock's most distinctive high voices" had "more hard-edged power behind it now than ever before." He found "Over and Over Again" to be "particularly exhilarating."[34]

Enthusiastic reviews generally followed headlining performances. At the Bardavon Theater in Poughkeepsie, New York, RFB provided a "spirited evening of professional country rock . . . the highlight . . . was a twenty-minute collection of Poco's greatest hits." The reviewer noted that Furay "still displays one of the finest voices in rock and maintains a youthful exuberance on stage." At Dickinson College, Pennsylvania, the review reported that Furay "stunned the Dickinson audience . . . with an outstanding performance. . . . His last number left the audience in a frenzy." The review concludes, "Furay was magnificent—vocally crisp, clear and musically as tight as could be!"[35]

By October, Furay had replaced Wall with guitarist Virgil Beckham. Wall's stage antics may have irritated Richie. Onstage at Roosevelt Stadium, New Jersey, for instance, Wall took over the microphone to talk about his T-shirt, courtesy of the pretzel vendor; later, in the middle of "Over and Over Again," as the music slows, he leaned into the microphone, "Now you're going to get it." At times, he also shared Furay's microphone for his backing vocals. Although Furay demonstrated no reaction, many band leaders are unwilling to share the spotlight unless they extend an invitation. About Wall's departure, Furay would only say, "Bob was the odd man out. . . . He just didn't fit. There's no doubt about it."[36]

I've Got a Reason did not command much attention, although it did get some FM airplay. In its August 7 issue, *Cash Box*, a trade publication, listed it as #7 on its "New FM Action LPs" and noted that several FM stations around the country had begun playing it. However, it did not make its "National Breakout" list alongside Aretha Franklin, Average White Band, Rod Stewart, Crosby & Nash, the Commodores, and the Spinners. *Record World*, on August 14, reported much the same, citing airplay on select FM stations and ranking it ninth on its list of "Most Active on the FM Airplay Report" behind albums by Jefferson Starship, Rod Stewart, Crosby & Nash, and others. But the airplay did not escalate, and the album seemed to get lost amid new fall releases. It charted for just eight weeks, reaching a disappointing #130 on September 18, 1976, before disappearing the following week.

The Musical Soundscape

Always in a state of transition, the pop soundscape of the mid to late 1970s was particularly unstable. Since Furay's time in Poco and SHF, rock music had begun to lose some of its pop music dominance to disco. In the summer of 1975, Van McCoy's "The Hustle" rose to #1; that fall KC and the Sunshine Band scored a #1 with "That's the Way (I Like It)," and Donna Summer's "Love to Love You Baby" reached #2 in early 1976. In 1977, Studio 54 opened its doors and became one of the most famous nightclubs in the world with celebrities eager for photo opportunities and crowds lined behind velvet ropes entreating for admission. The Bee Gees, with a solid rock and pop back catalog, released the disco-driven soundtrack to *Saturday Night Fever*, which held the #1 position on the album charts for twenty-four consecutive weeks beginning January 21, 1978. To remain current, many rock artists appropriated disco rhythms and sonic effects. David Bowie combined disco with funk for his Top 10 hit "Golden

Years," and Paul McCartney garnered a #1 for his disco-affected "Silly Love Songs." The Rolling Stones and Rod Stewart drew heavily on disco for their respective international #1 hits "Miss You" (May 1978) and "Do Ya Think I'm Sexy" (November 1978). Not all rock fans or rock artists, however, welcomed the intrusion of disco. Stewart's fans were especially "dismayed" at the release of "Sexy" and questioned his authenticity. His disco phase sounded "more or less the final death knell for his image as a rock artist." The Stones had some internal conflict with "Miss You." Keith Richard, who grew to appreciate "Miss You" as it evolved in the studio, thought at first it was Jagger's "chasing musical fashion," which is "never the way we've worked." But the band agreed to "do some disco shit, keep [Jagger] happy"—especially since he frequented Studio 54.[37] "Disco sucks" became a mantra for hardline rock fans as anti-disco rallies and record burnings sprouted up around the country—the most famous of which was Disco Demolition Night in Chicago's Comiskey Park on July 12, 1979.

By the end of 1979, disco record sales were in decline,[38] but rock had other challengers. Punk had been gaining momentum since its emergence from a small club, CBGB, in New York City's East Village.[39] Bands like Blondie, the Patti Smith Group, Television, and, most importantly, the Ramones inspired worldwide punk scenes. Although it is a subgenre of rock, the punks nonetheless railed against what they saw as the self-importance and staleness of what today is called "classic rock." By the early 1970s, rock, for the punks, had lost its 1960s aggressiveness and edge and had become increasingly corporate. A few years later, in 1981, for example, the Rolling Stones accepted $1 million from Jōvan Musk to print the name of the fragrance company on concert tickets. As Joey Ramone of the Ramones said of the punk movement, "We were a reaction to all the pretentiousness, mediocrity, and superficialness that was going on at the time."[40] Formed in 1974, the Ramones released their debut and self-titled album two years later—fourteen high-octane tracks clocking in at a brisk time of 29:04 minutes. By the mid to late '70s, punk scenes and punk bands had formed around the world, attracting youth with their ferociously loud and speedy rhythms, stripped-down arrangements, and aggressive, unmelodic vocals. The Sex Pistols, the Slits, and the Clash stormed London, while on the US West Coast, bands like the Germs, Black Flag, X, and the Dead Kennedys raged. Punk, however, did not make inroads on the US charts until the latter part of the 1970s and then only moderately, but they did distract youthful potential consumers away from the more established and mainstream rock bands.

One of the favorite targets of the punks were the Eagles, the embodiment of "dinosaur rock" with their "peaceful easy feeling" and blockbuster success. "The entire punk movement," wrote Chris Willman in *Billboard*, "is oft remembered as a reaction to the Eagles and prog-rock," while Gersh Kuntzman in the *New York Daily News* termed the Eagles "easy listening . . . even too soft for an elevator."[41] In February 1976, the Eagles released their *Greatest Hits (1971–1975)*, the first album to be certified Platinum (sales of one million units) and, currently, the bestselling album of all time, immediately ahead of Michael Jackson's *Thriller* (1982) and their own *Hotel California* (December 1976). To punks, this represented rock star excess and pretentiousness. In 1989, *Rolling Stone* proclaimed the best album of the 1980s as the Clash's *London Calling*, which was released in the United States in January 1980 when "rock & roll needed a good boot in the rear."[42]

In addition, in the late 1970s, hip-hop began to realize its commercial potential. Previously confined to inner-city parks, recreation halls in apartment buildings, and a few clubs, hip-hop attracted the attention of music executives in 1979, when "Rapper's Delight" by the Sugar Hill Gang, on the independent Sugar Hill label, hit #36 in the United States, but #3 in the UK, #1 in Canada, and in the top 5 in several European countries, including #1 in Spain and in the Netherlands. Record labels ventured into inner-city neighborhoods to sign potential hitmakers, working from the premise that, as Richard Gottehrer, cofounder of Sire Records, said, "If you can be #1 somewhere, you can be #1 anywhere."[43] The following year Kurtis Blow earned rap's first Gold record with "The Breaks." Hip-hop, however, would remain largely on the margins until 1991, when *Niggaz4life* by N.W.A. reached #1 on the album charts, at which point hip-hop became "the defining genre on the Billboard charts."[44]

Dance a Little Light

Furay spent most of 1977 at home, where he and Nancy welcomed their third daughter, Polly, in December. Back in the studio shortly afterward, he released *Dance a Little Light*, his second of three Asylum albums and the weakest of his nine solo studio albums.[45] Released at the height of the disco craze, *Light*, like *Reason*, tries to be sonically current. However, while Schnee and Omartian have at least modest success on *Reason*, producer Jim Mason, who coproduced *Good Feelin' to Know*, fails on many tracks on *Light*. Songs like Furay's cover of "This Magic Moment" and his ballads "Ooh Dreamer" and "Bittersweet Love," a touching ballad of lost love, are overloaded with orchestration, smothering rather than supporting Furay's vocals and, on "Bittersweet," almost burying guest Jim Messina's almost minute-long guitar solo (1:48–2:43). In addition, Furay includes the charmless "Yesterday's Gone," which in its old-time soft jazz feel recalls the more effective "It's So Hard to Wait" from the Springfield. "I was thinking about a Beatle song," said Furay. "It had that kind of old timey thing."[46] Furay is probably referring to "When I'm Sixty-Four" or "Your Mother Should Know." Overall, *Light* lacks the musical and lyrical urgency and intensity of *Reason*, which was empowered by Furay's desire to tell his story of conversion, no matter how coded. "[*Light*]," Furay said, "was intended to be a little less open about my religion. It had its secular side"[47]— although religious expression comes through on several tracks. The result is a decidedly mediocre record, lacking in firepower, or as Mike Rimmer said tersely in his review of the 2003 re-release, "A workmanlike effort but it doesn't set my heart on fire."[48]

However, *Light* offers some very good tracks, like the bouncy cover of Dee Clark's "Your Friends" and "You Better Believe It," which features an incisive guitar solo from Virgil Beckham and is pushed by the horn section and Gabriel Katona's funky clavinet. Even better are the title track, "It's Your Love," and "Stand Your Guard," despite its passing resemblance to Argent's "Hold Your Head Up." Not coincidentally, perhaps, all three are more open about Furay's faith than the other tracks on the album. "Dance a Little Light," which Furay wrote with David Diggs, is a joyful rocker, not unlike "Let's Dance" in its rock-and-roll spirit, but harder rocking with a gospel feel. It opens with a crinkly guitar riff that recalls the opening seconds of "And Settlin' Down," and then Richie's vocals: "Shoutin' about it." "It" has several implications, but all Christian related. "It" may refer to the grace of the Lord or the "little light" that Furay hopes will "dance . . . on you"; "it" may also refer to the gospel as Furay slyly sings, "sounds a bit like good news"; and it could be eternal life for if one heeds the Lord's call, as Richie sings here, "You can live forever, forever and a day." The song rejoices in the Lord and his grace and presence, here and in the hereafter. "Light" could fit in a tent-show revival. Gabriel Katona plays a rockin'-and rollin' piano, the horns blast in celebration, and Beckham's guitar lends an edge. It is one of Furay's exhilarating and underrated rockers, perhaps not approaching "Good Feelin' to Know" or "Fallin' in Love," but it is equal to "Let's Dance Tonight" or "Keep on Believin'."

"It's Your Love" is the colorful opening track and Mason's high point. More funk than disco, the track has a brisk tempo, a fat bass line from Billy Batstone, perky congas from Victor Feldman, and lively horns. Furay plays a Nile Rogers–like rhythm guitar, and cowriter Beckham fires off wiry tight lead lines. The lyrics seem to celebrate Furay's love for both his wife and God. In

FIG. 12 Outtake from the photo shoot for *Dance a Little Light*. Photo by Henry Diltz.

the verses he proclaims, "I feel that my life has just awakened / It's your love that keeps me goin'." In the chorus, however, he sings, "Oh, little darlin', oh / I am goin' out of my mind . . . I just love this feelin' of me and you." I asked Furay about this, noting that he would not refer to the Lord as "little darlin'." The song "has a subtle message," he replied.[49]

"Stand Your Guard," the closing track, "is one of my favorite songs on the record," said Richie.[50] The anthem features a stomping, driving rhythm that marches forward with sometimes unnecessary strings. Like "Over and Over Again" on *Reason*, "Guard" concludes with a jam, which here lasts for four and a half minutes and has a country-rock flavor with Al Perkins on pedal steel and Rusty Young on electric slide and acoustic dobro. The song closes with repetitions of the chorus with Richie joined, as he was earlier on the track, by David Cassidy (of *The Partridge Family*) and Timothy Schmit. "'Stand Your Guard' dealt very specifically with what I was going through at the time. In it, I asked why some listeners were so put off by my faith. Many of them seemed almost wary of it, which perplexed me, since there's nothing to be frightened of. In the lyrics I try to examine this irrational fear."[51] There is anger and sarcasm in the song—although not as sharp as "Short Changed" or "I Guess You Made It." Ironically, Furay directs those who are intimidated by his Christianity to "Keep your distance and stand your guard / Though I never meant to threaten you." "It was also about the record company telling me I could do this and I couldn't do that. It was about articles in magazines. . . . So some of the song is talking to me and some of it is talking to them. I have to make my stand as well. . . . There's frustration in there too."[52]

Interestingly, in 2015, "Guard" came to life when interviewer Mike Greenblatt baited Furay. "Saturday nights you play rock 'n' roll to heathens like me and Sunday mornings you preach." Richie did not take the bait, noting he performed a limited number of devotional songs in his sets, and that the gospel and Jesus Christ are "my life . . . you don't have to believe it." Greenblatt then identified himself as "a godless, smoking, drinking, gambling Jew . . . [and an] agnostic." Furay's patience seemed tried, and he informed the journalist that *agnostic*, in Latin, means "ignoramus!" Greenblatt feigned fright: "Uh oh, here it comes." To which the interview closes with Furay cleverly telling Greenblatt "to think it over. And you better think twice." Three years later, Greenblatt, a generally excellent interviewer, admitted that he was "tweaking" Richie and "deserved" his harsh response.[53]

1978 Tour

Furay toured behind *Light*, playing some fifty dates in the spring and, after a break, the summer of 1978. Mostly performing as a headliner in clubs and smaller halls, Furay received reviews that ran from lukewarm to positive. But, as on the 1976 tour, the older, more familiar songs were better appreciated. Reviewing RFB at New York City's Bottom Line, Robert Palmer applauded Furay's "true, affecting tenor" after noting that "the strongest part of his set is his oldest/oldies medley." Nicolas Adde, reviewing Furay's Cellar Door show in Washington, DC, wrote that the new material played "well enough" but did not hold up to the Springfield and Poco songs, or what Furay called his "foundation set." In Dallas, Peter Oppel found Furay's new songs "far more appealing in concert [than on record]," singling out "Over and Over Again" and "Dance a Little Light." Still, Oppel wrote that "the highlight of the set" was "an 18-minute medley of songs he popularized with Poco." Oppel called the band "excellent . . . although the group seemed to lack that spark . . . that always drove Poco into being one of the best live bands this country has ever produced."[54]

As he did in 1976, Furay added more Springfield and Poco material as the tour went on. As he told the *Washington Post*, "We found when we began touring a year ago that fans came to hear the old stuff and were disappointed when they didn't hear the familiar songs."[55] This has long been a problem for touring musicians whose fans most want to hear, and sometimes only want to hear, a performer's older material, the songs to which fans came of age. Furay has found this "very frustrating." At his shows over recent years, he has made himself available to his audience:

> When some fans come, [I say], "Have you heard my new music?" "Uh, yeah, man, I heard your new music." "Yeah, well, which one do you like the best?" "Well, um, um," and then they hem and haw because they haven't heard it. They're lying to me—right to my face. But they want my autograph on all the old stuff. I've even gotten to the place that, sometimes, when they come with these stacks of records, seven or eight records for me to sign, I might sign two or three of them at the most, and say, "Look, listen to the new music. You can hear the new music and the new music is not gonna let you down."[56]

Playing the newer songs, Furay said, "keeps me going. . . . You write new music and you wanna play that. It's not that I don't want to play the old songs; I still enjoy playing the old songs, but I also have to be able to play the new songs."[57] Most touring artists have yielded to fans' demands for the hits and familiar material. On the North American leg of their 2019 No Filter tour, the Rolling Stones filled stadiums, typically performing nineteen songs, with usually one, and sometimes none, recorded after 1978. Doug Clifford, drummer in Creedence Clearwater Revival, explained why Creedence Clearwater Revisited did not play some of the more obscure CCR songs, specifically from *Mardi Gras*: "If we did those songs, we'd see the aisles fill as the audience heads to the restrooms."[58]

I Still Have Dreams

Furay never expected to record a third solo album for Asylum. Executives from the label informed Richie that they would be attending one of his shows at the Roxy in Los Angeles, May 11–13, and requested a backstage meeting afterward. Furay was certain the label would drop him. He would welcome the news. "All I wanted to hear was, 'It's been a good run, Richie. Thank you very much and we'll see you later.'" He believed he had delivered two commercially viable albums with little support. "Asylum expended little effort into promoting [*Light*] . . . poured precious few dollars into touring or promotion, and as far as I can tell, the staff hardly lifted a finger to get the songs on the radio."[59] One of the problems for Furay was that his friend and fan David Geffen, cofounder with Elliot Roberts of Asylum, had left the company shortly after Furay signed. Richie had no relationship with Joe Smith, who was now in charge. "Joe and I had never had any kind of rapport at all. I didn't really know Joe. I knew David well. David stayed in my house in Colorado."[60] Richie thought he would sign with a Christian label, where he could be open in his music, drop the codes of his conversion and devotion to Jesus, and find a new audience that would accept him for who he now was. Since the Jesus movement, the market for contemporary Christian music had expanded with new labels (Maranatha! Music, 1971; Myrrh, 1972) and a magazine (*CCM* or *Contemporary Christian Music*). However, the backstage meeting did not go as expected. "The show was a knockout," Richie explained. "The band was hotter than a firecracker. We blew everyone away. . . . Those guys came back after the concert and said, 'Oh man, we're ready. When you going to do that next record?' . . . That's how *I Still Have Dreams* came in."[61]

Never a fast or prolific writer, Furay hustled to work up ten songs for the album, got his road band together, and began recording at Caribou Ranch early in 1979, where he hoped for the "spontaneity" and "vibrancy" of live performance. The results, however, were stiff, "too studio bound."[62] He sought the advice of Charlie Reardon, who worked the Rocky Mountain region for Asylum and was a longtime fan of Furay. Reardon thought the songs had potential and gained approval for Furay to re-record the album in Los Angeles with different musicians and with Val Garay producing. Garay, who had worked with, among others, Linda Ronstadt, James Taylor, and Neil Diamond, liked the songs but thought some needed slight reworking. He recruited top LA session musicians: Waddy Wachtel and Dan Dugmore on guitars, Leland Sklar on bass, Russ Kunkel on drums, and Craig Doerge on keyboards. Furay recruited friends J. D. Souther, Randy Meisner, and Timothy B. Schmit to help with background vocals.

Recording with Garay and these musicians, Furay said, was "one of my greatest experiences" in music.[63] As Furay found, studio musicians can be amazingly efficient and effective. "It's a different mentality, a different way of thinking. . . . It's the difference between recording the song in three hours and maybe recording the song in one hour. . . . They have a strict sense of time and yet they have a strict sense of feel . . . and they are creative in different ways. A record is made and there's a simplicity to it. There's a lot less clutter. When you're playing live you can find clutter . . . overplaying because you get caught up in the moment. . . . But these guys are technicians." Yet,

Richie emphasized, they do not rush through songs: "It doesn't sound like 'next, next.' No, they put their heart and soul into the songs."[64]

Under Garay's supervision, *I Still Have Dreams* is the best sounding of Furay's Asylum albums. The production focuses on Furay's tenor and not on filling space with orchestration or sonic effects. The result is a clean and sparse recording, unlike *Light*. The contrast in sonics, epitomized by a comparison of "Bittersweet Love" from *Light* and "I Was a Fool" from *Dreams*, recalls the contrast between Poco's first two albums, *Pickin' Up the Pieces* and *Poco*. On *Dreams* and *Poco*, the songs pop from the grooves. Similar to *Light*, however, the Christian references are subtle and no songs demand a Christian interpretation—although, with a stretch, listeners could project Furay's religious fervor onto songs like "What a Fool" and "Headin' South," and even his zesty cover of the Rascals' 1960s hit "Lonely Too Long." *Dreams* might have been the album that Geffen expected from Furay when he signed him: solid songs, solid production, and no Christian references or proselytizing.

Furay wrote or cowrote six of the ten tracks on *Dreams*. The opening track, "Oooh Child," written with David Diggs, is a disco number and a love song. Furay saw the Bee Gees enjoying large success and thought, "You know what? I can do that, too." But he also expressed a common complaint among musicians, for which fans and labels might be responsible, however understandably: "I don't feel like I have to be put in a box. People say I only write in one style; well, take 'Yesterday's Gone' and compare that to 'Ooh Dreamer' and compare that to 'Island Love' and compare that to 'A Child's Claim to Fame' and 'Kind Woman.' I mean sometimes it's like a challenge for me: 'Can I write that kind of song?' . . . Don't put me in a box. I can write in whatever the musical styles are of the time." He joked, "I haven't tried rap yet though."[65] Along with the title track, "Oooh Child" introduces one of the album's dominant themes and one of his favorite lyrical motifs: dreams. Six of the ten tracks reference dreams. In the catchy chorus of "Oooh Child," he sings, "Baby, all my life I have been waiting / I see you in my dreams each night." On "Island Love," a bright calypso similar to "You're the One I Love," he sings about escaping to a tropical island with his love, where they will create "dreams that we'll share together." Island rhythms, particularly reggae, were trending since the rise of Bob Marley with *Catch a Fire* (1973); many rock artists, including the Rolling Stones, Paul McCartney, Eric Clapton, and Elton John, featured an island rhythm or two on their albums.

Billy Batstone, who played bass on the *Light* tour, wrote three songs for the album, including "Oh Mary," a slashing rocker in which the singer promises that, through his love, Mary's "dreams will come true"—the other two out-and-out rockers are written by Furay, "Come On" (not to be confused with Poco's "C'mon") and "What's the Matter Please?" which closes the album. "I Was a Fool," a ballad of lost love and a high point, is the closest the album comes to country or country-rock, with Richie's acoustic strums and Wachtel's countryish fills and solo. With "I Still Have Dreams," Batstone articulates Furay's "keep-on-believin'" attitude. The song, about a couple separating, resonates with Furay's marital problems. Not always communicative, Furay could identify with lines like, "We never talked at all about it. / Don't know why," or lines of sorrow, "left me here and cryin'." But always the optimist, Furay sings, "I still have dreams where you still love me." The ballad, which features a bass line resembling the dominant riff in the Temptations' "My Girl," showcases the emotive and crystalline vocals of Furay, who infuses all lines with pain, especially in the bridge (1:24–1:48), when he wails with high-pitched pain, like nowhere else in all his years of recording, "Is this goodbye? / I'll never know why, oh . . ." It is a powerful performance. Not so incidentally, Furay still considers himself a dreamer: "Sure! . . . as a person who looks forward I think [I am] going to dream. . . . Am I going to see all of those dreams fulfilled? I don't know, but it keeps the creative juices flowing."[66] In "Satisfied," a ballad written with Gabriel Katona and given a strong rock edge by Wachtel and drummer Russ Kunkel, Furay sings of a dream that came true: reconciliation with Nancy. In his live shows beginning in the early 2000s, Furay has turned the sturdy rock ballad over to his background vocalist and daughter Jesse, who gives it more of a country-rock feel. Jesse has recorded the song twice: on her father's live album *Alive* (2008) and on her excellent debut album *Jesse Furay Lynch* (2016).

Released in the early fall, *Dreams* did not sell well. It seemed to be off to a good start with the single, the title track, entering the *Billboard* charts in late October 1979 and peaking at #39 on December 15, where it remained for three weeks. That same week Furay noticed some old friends in the Top 10: the Eagles, who now included Timothy Schmit, were at #9 with "Heartache Tonight" (#1 a month earlier), and J. D. Souther was at #7 with "You're Only Lonely." After touring aggressively behind *Light* and *Reason* with little impact on sales and with audiences clamoring for his older songs, Furay decided to remain home with his family, which now included his fourth and final child, the above-mentioned Jesse, born on September 15, 1979. He did, however, lip-synch "I Still Have Dreams" and "Oooh Child" on *American Bandstand* in early January. His stint with Asylum was now over. For the rest of 1980, Furay made perhaps a dozen appearances, accompanying himself on acoustic guitar at Christian festivals, at special appearances with Pastor Greg Laurie, or in small venues on off days when traveling with Laurie.

United States Rock

At the end of 1980, Furay constructed a two-part strategy for his career in music. First, he signed with a Christian label, Myrrh and, second, he formed a band and signed with a secular label, Atlantic. Both companies agreed to the concurrent contracts. For Atlantic, Furay would record with United States Rock, composed of fellow born-again Christians Batstone, Beckham, Hadley Hockensmith on second guitar, and George Grantham, former Poco drummer. Furay and Atlantic agreed that USR would not play Christian music. Rather, Furay explained, the band would present testimony through the example of well-lived, contented Christian lives. "I viewed the band as a way to be more of a witness . . . being in the world, but not *of* it."[67] However, Atlantic balked after it heard the demo for the first album. They asked Furay to drop "Yellow Moon Rising," which included references to "angels in heaven," fallen angels, "the garden," temptations, paradise, and salvation. Furay refused. Atlantic relented but stipulated that it would not accept similar songs in the future. Furay envisioned similar problems as he had encountered with Asylum. At the Lord's direction, Furay said, he backed out of the contract, disbanded USR, and began crafting songs for his first unequivocally devotional album, *Seasons of Change.*[68]

"With My Whole Heart"

The Ministry and Devotional Music

Furay reached a new resolve after the Lord directed him to abandon United States Rock: "I *will* not compromise in *anything* I do. . . . I'm a servant of the Lord, and that's by *choice*."[1] I asked Furay how he could be sure that it is the Lord's voice he hears:

> Well, when you accept Christ, he lives in you. So my spirit and His spirit are then in communication. . . . The Scripture says, the voice of the Lord is first peaceful and gentle and easily entreated. You're not anxious. It brings a peace into your heart. . . . The Scripture says that it is like that still, small voice that Elijah talked about in the Old Testament. . . . You get that certain peace; it's gentle. . . . Can I misread [another voice for the Lord's voice]? Yeah. I can misread it, and that has happened too."[2]

With USR done, Furay focused on Christian service and on recording a new album for Myrrh, which had re-released *I've Got a Reason* in 1981. About that time, Richie and Nancy began hosting a weekly Bible study in their home. It began very small: "Nancy and me, this guy and his wife, and, and two other couples, we sat around that first night . . . just sucking our thumbs. 'Who's going to say something now?'" The next week Richie took some much-needed control: "I had Chuck Smith tapes and I got a book of commentary on the Book of John at the local Christian bookstore, and the next week I started teaching. I had only been a Christian for not that long, but someone had to take the initiative and go for it."[3] Before long the Wednesday evening group grew, and the Bible study moved from the Furays' home to Nederland Middle-Senior High School, where member Doug Gibney, later Pastor Doug, had connections. After two months in the school with a growing membership and the Furays' new home completed, the group decided to divide into two. Those who lived closer to Nederland continued to meet in the school under the guidance of Pastor Johnny Smith, and the other half, closer to Boulder, studied in Richie's new home, sitting atop a steep hill, where they still live.

On Easter Sunday, April 3, 1983, at the request of the group, Furay conducted service. By Mother's Day, the next month, Sunday services were permanent and held in a rented space in a Seventh Day Baptist Church in downtown Boulder. On October 13, 1983, Furay became Pastor Richie.

Seasons of Change

After the three Asylum albums failed to chart and after his dispute with Atlantic, Furay was eager to begin recording for Myrrh, where he could express his faith freely and directly. "I was going to offend people no matter what I did. So I figure, if I'm going to offend them, I at least ought to do what I want."[4] Above each lyric on the inner sleeve for *Seasons of Change*, Furay states his personal inspiration for the song and refers to a corresponding biblical verse. For example, above the lyrics to "Promise of Love," a song to his wife, Furay writes, "The Lord has blessed me with a beautiful family and a loving understanding wife. . . . As we love Him more, we love each other more." He then directs us to Ephesians 5:30–31: "For we are members of His body. . . . For this reason a man shall leave his father and mother and be joined to his wife, and the two shall become one flesh." In a sense, every song becomes a short sermon with an appropriate biblical reference, a brief explanation, and a personal application. But here, as opposed to his *Crawdaddy* statement, his sermonizing is never offensive or self-righteous, especially as Furay makes clear his convictions are hard-won and couched in some outstanding rock and roll and some melodic ballads.

The devotional songs on *Seasons* can be placed in the following categories:

1. Songs of celebration and joy in Christ and Christian fellowship: "Hallelujah," "Rise Up."
2. Christianity and Marriage: "Endless Flight," "Promise of Love."
3. Warnings, near jeremiad in tone: "Yellow Moon Rising," "Through It All."
4. Personal testimony: "Seasons of Change," "My Lord and My God."
5. Meditations: "Home to My Lord," "For the Prize."

Furay's lyrics, as expected, are precise and economical. He makes use of his favorite motifs and imagery as he sings of love (earthly and divine), home (shifted to heaven), and dreams, which, without Christ, can fast become "nightmares," as on the title track.

Furay coproduced the album with David Diggs, and, for the most part, the production is effective, not overly produced and not trying too hard to sound contemporary—although the opening track, "Hallelujah," seems to strive for that slick country-gospel sound of joyous affirmation that has long been a signature of contemporary Christian music. Similarly, "Endless Flight," with its use of the ubiquitous 1980s synthesizer and soft tenor sax solos from Jim Coile, strains to be danceable—although it remains an interesting track as Richie taps into the Philadelphia soul productions of Kenneth Gamble and Leon Huff. The lyrics to "Endless Flight" address Al and Debbie Perkins, whose marriage was in trouble. Furay challenges them to rediscover their love and continue their "endless flight" into eternity together. In the inscription above the lyrics, Furay writes that "the enemy seems to have been working overtime in creating havoc in Christian marriages." Furay was unable to help the Perkinses save their marriage. "What has really hurt me over the years," Furay said, "is that I've seen so many of my friends [divorce], even the person (Perkins) who has led me to the Lord . . . it became very disheartening to me that I couldn't help them."[5] Perkins plays steel guitar on the graceful country-rock ballad "Home to My Lord," a meditation on death in which Furay sings of his "mansion in the sky."

There are several outstanding tracks on *Seasons*. "My Lord and My God," a haunting ballad, adds strings and backing vocals for urgency. "Rise Up," a livelier and better produced "Hoe Down," has an old-time religion feel with Furay's coaxing vocals high in the mix and cowriter Diggs's gospel piano pushing the song, along with a pumping bass line, a pounding bass drum, and a tambourine. The lyrics, inspired by the wedding imagery in Matthew 22:1–14, call on listeners to attend the wedding feast in heaven, where Jesus is the groom and the saved are brides: "Rise up, in one accord . . . meet . . . down by the river . . . leave that picnic on the ground," images of baptism and earthly pleasures. As Furay writes in the inscription to the song, "That's a wedding I don't want to miss!" Furay re-recorded the song for *Alive* (2008), on which his vocals are even more charged.[6]

"Seasons of Change," the title track, is a sturdy, straightforward rocker with slashing guitar chords and a scorching guitar solo from Hadley Hockensmith. The "seasons of change" correspond to four general stages of Furay's life and the four States in which Furay has lived: Ohio, New York, California, and Colorado. His next residency, he is confident, will make him a "citizen of heaven." With the song's speedy rhythm and implicit reduction of his life to a year, Furay suggests the brevity and mutability of life and the importance of looking for the "living water of truth," which will lead to a "new life" and being "born again." The song's inspiration is John 3:3, in which Jesus said, "unless one is born again, he cannot see the kingdom of God." Not only does Furay draw on images of home and dreams, here broken dreams ("Hollywood seemed more a nightmare than a dream"), but also on "water," here and throughout the album, suggestive of rebirth and baptism ("Rise Up"; "My Lord and My God"). Additionally, in another image of life's brevity, he compares life to a "race," which he also does on the tumbling rocker "For the Prize," cowritten with Hockensmith, in which first prize is heaven.

"Yellow Moon Rising," cowritten with Tom Stipe, builds off an opening and recurring guitar riff, developed by Furay, that resembles the swamp rock riffs of John Fogerty and Creedence Clearwater Revival in songs like "Run Through the Jungle" (1970), which also references the devil, or "The Old Man Down the Road," which Fogerty recorded for *Centerfield* in 1984. "Yellow Moon" is what led to the controversy with Atlantic, for whom Richie agreed to record secular songs. He might have been testing the label, perhaps to see how much religion he could and could not include. The song has strong and obvious biblical overtones with references to paradise, the Garden of Eden, temptation, fallen angels, and heaven. For Furay, the devil is very real and active in this world. Here, he explains two similar verses from the Bible: 1 Peter 5:8 and Ephesians 6:11–17. In the first, Peter warns his audience: "Be sober, be vigilant; because your adversary the devil walks about like a roaring lion." In Ephesians, we are directed to "put on the whole armor of God . . . to stand against the wiles of the devil." In "Yellow Moon Rising," with only mild fire-and-brimstone images, like "a mighty long way to fall," Furay issues a stern but calm warning about yielding to temptation, for "the stakes will be high" and the "cost . . . heavy." Despite the serpentine riff and Hockensmith's solos, which seem to sound an alarm about the devil's approach, Furay emphasizes hopefulness in both his concern for the listener and in his sometimes folksy delivery ("Don't want to find you lost") and in his reference to his own struggle: "I crossed that line and lived a lie . . . suffered but didn't die," and found salvation. From approximately 2:44 to 3:28, Furay takes a vocal interlude, an absolute tour de force. His weaving, legato phrasing on "fallen," complemented by strings and piano, is more peaceful than terrifying, since, as the song proclaims, we can escape the fall. More than any of his other devotional songs, "Yellow Moon," more completely in both its music and lyrics, captures Furay's theology in its darkness and light, its struggle and joyfulness, its bleakness and yet hopefulness, and, perhaps most importantly, its mystery and faith.

Released in February 1982, *Seasons of Change* is a lively and satisfying album, energized by an unencumbered Furay, writing and singing openly of his conversion and faith. However, it failed to chart and received little attention—from either the secular rock/pop audience or the contemporary Christian audience. "I found myself in between a rock and a hard place. I was too Christian for the world and I was too worldly for the Christian market, so they did not accept me either. It was very frustrating."[7] Kalefa Sanneh calls this a "double helping of disdain—from inside and outside the church," not rare for Christian artists.[8] At the time of *Seasons*' release, evangelicals especially disavowed rock music as a means to express faith. In a 1981 interview, the Rev. Jerry Falwell, cofounder of the Moral Majority, thought it important for young people to engage in a "separation from rock music, separation from immorality, separation from Hollywood culture," and Jimmy Swaggart, then a prominent televangelist, wrote, "Religious rock does not offer hope. Since it is Spiritless, it can give none . . . the music within itself [is] full of sound and fury but no substance. . . . Its birth came from secular rock and roll which has no basis in God."[9] Prof. Randall Stephens summarized this view of rock music for many evangelicals: "Christian lyrics or evangelical messages could never redeem the loud, thumping beat or the droning of electric guitars." Besides, "rock music had far too many negative associations [and] was blatantly outlandish."[10]

In 2003, Wounded Bird re-released *Seasons of Change*. A few years later, writing in *Cross Rhythms*, a UK Christian magazine, Mike Rimmer finds it a "mystery . . . that [*Seasons*] isn't regarded as an absolute classic" and praises Furay's "distinctive" vocals with "tight harmonies and fabulous lead performances." He concludes his review by stating that *I've Got a Reason*, also re-released in 2003, "is a gem you need to discover."[11]

Pastor Richie Furay

In the Calvary Chapel movement, it is not unusual for Bible study groups to evolve into churches. In the early 1970s, Pastor Chuck Smith, who started the movement, asked Greg Laurie to lead a Bible group of thirty, which led Laurie to found the Harvest Christian Fellowship Church. In time, it became one of the largest churches in the United States. Furay traveled with Laurie in the early 1980s as the pastor promoted his radio ministry. Furay would talk of his experiences and conversion and sing a few songs, accompanying the minister to Hawaii, Alaska, Washington, DC, New York City, and many other places. By the 1990s, Laurie was attracting massive crowds in stadiums for his Harvest Crusades. Furay spoke and performed at several crusades in Anaheim Stadium during the 1990s. It was therefore no surprise when Furay and his study group founded Calvary Chapel Boulder on Easter 1983. Soon after, the church changed its name to the Rocky Mountain Christian Fellowship "because of some of the issues that were going on with different factions" in the Calvary Chapel affiliations and which Pastor Furay wanted to evade—although, as he emphasized, his church was always a Calvary Chapel ministry.[12] One reason Pastor Smith insisted on only a loose affiliation of churches, rather than founding a denomination, was to avoid bureaucracy and power struggles, which were happening and which Furay would experience within his own church. Smith preferred to say that Calvary Chapel was nondenominational, "just a Christian church."[13] The Calvary Chapel network has grown to well over 1,500 independent chapels.

Furay and his board of elders decided to rent space in the gymnasium of the Boulder Junior Academy, affiliated with the Seventh-day Adventist Church, where by then they had reverted to calling themselves Calvary Chapel Boulder. The congregation remained in the gym for eighteen years. Every Wednesday and Sunday, the members would set up and take down a sound system, banners, seating, and other components. In 2002, with the church having accumulated sufficient savings—including substantial contributions from Furay, partly from back royalties from his Springfield days paid him in the 1990s—the church bought property in Broomfield, less than fifteen miles southeast of the gym and with a second building they could rent to help with expenses. Calvary Chapel Broomfield was born. "We felt like, hey, we've arrived!" said Richie. "We're a real church now. We weren't renting from anybody."[14] For the first time, they had a permanent space. The building solidified their identity in the Broomfield community, within the wider network of Calvary churches, and within the congregation itself. It became a source of pride, a major accomplishment for the congregation, which never topped more than 225 members.

Pastor Furay had no formal training for the ministry, which was not unusual for Calvary Chapel pastors.

My teaching or my schooling, whatever you want to call it, was basically through Chuck Smith's Bible study tapes and then the pastors that we would be involved with when we would have pastor conferences: Dave

FIG. 13 Pastor Furay preaching in Calvary Chapel, Broomfield, CO, September 2015. Photo by Lisa Rosenberg.

Hunt . . . Chuck Missler, Gayle Erwin, lots of pastors would come along and [Pastor Smith] would just invite them to teach. I would also check out pastors who weren't Calvary Chapel pastors . . . John MacArthur [for example], but I would check that they were sound biblically in their doctrine—and that's what I was mainly concerned with."[15]

In addition, Furay could tap into his Calvary pastor-friends like Greg Laurie, Doug Gibney, or fellow musician Tom Stipe, who became a pastor just before Richie. According to Furay, his time in his college fraternity—Lambda Gamma Epsilon, or the Monks—with its large percentage of theology majors, had no influence on his conversion or his theology.

In 2015, Furay told *Rolling Stone* that his "main responsibility is to provide the Sunday morning sermon."[16] Furay might spend upward of twenty hours a week constructing a sermon of forty-five minutes or so. In preparation, Furay said, "I would just read the passage of Scripture over and over and over whether it was one verse or fifteen verses and read it [and] kind of wait for that still, small voice that's spoken of in the Old Testament, the Lord would start speaking to my heart. . . . Then I would listen to Pastor Chuck Smith's take on it and his message, and I would read different commentaries . . . Vernon McGee [and] Warren Wiersbe."[17] On Sunday morning, Furay would read the text, explicate it, and then apply it to contemporary life. Like his lyrics, his sermons are straightforward and accessible. (See fig. 13.) After service, Furay would reach out to individual members of the congregation during a light breakfast. One Sunday, in September 2015, I observed Pastor Furay and Nancy talking to just about all those present. All seemed comfortable with one another, and the pastor and his wife seemed much beloved.

Furay also provided counseling to those in need, but he made clear to those seeking his counsel that he had no formal training. "I never passed myself off as a professionally schooled counselor or marriage counselor," he said. "I would deal with the difficulties people were having in life [from] a Christian perspective. . . . I could never tell them what to do. I would always let them know that the Scripture has to be your guide. That's your manual for life."[18]

Poco Reunion

A couple of years after the aborted Buffalo Springfield reunion in the summer of 1986, Furay received a call from Rusty Young, who wanted to reunite the original members of Poco to record new music to mark their twentieth anniversary in 1989. Rusty said that pop star Richard Marx would work on the project with Marx's manager, Allen Kovac, who would negotiate a contract with RCA and arrange a tour in support of Marx. Marx, at the peak of his fame with bombastic and gushy pop hits like "Right Here Waiting" and "Hold on to the Nights," had nine top-twenty hits, with seven in the top five, between 1987 and 1990. On his debut single, "Don't Mean Nothing" (#3, 1987), Marx featured Joe Walsh of the Eagles on guitar and Timothy Schmit and Randy Meisner on backing vocals. Marx was so impressed with these backing vocalists that he purchased a Poco compilation CD.[19] He then implored Kovac to reunite the original members, which Kovac began by reaching out to Young. It took Furay some time and several conversations to agree to the reunion. He concluded that his church was stable and his participation would serve as "ministry outreach,"[20] not that he would preach in any way or sing his devotional songs, but his presence would prompt questions from fans and the media about his faith. Richie announced his plans to his board of elders and then to his congregation, all of whom seemed supportive.

The original members met for rehearsals at Jim Messina's studio in Nashville. Almost immediately there was tension. Richie's idea to include Schmit and Paul Cotton was rejected with no discussion. Kovac did not think George Grantham was the right drummer for the updated sound—"which really upset me," said Richie. "George is one of the greatest singing rock-and-roll drummers that there is. He could have done so well on this."[21] Instead, Kovac hired LA session drummer Gary Mallaber, who would be more efficient. Furay also explained that as a pastor he would not record any songs inconsistent with his faith or his pastorship, nothing about drugs and nothing overtly sexual—a tall order for a rock-and-roll band. And, as sessions progressed, Richie objected to several songs on the album. He was troubled by, for example, the blues rocker "The Nature of Love," one of three songs not written by Poco members but sung effectively by Randy Meisner, reminding us why Meisner once thought of himself as a blues singer.[22] Richie insisted that the song's writers, Jeff Silbar and Van Stephenson, change the following line: "Now some will find it on their wedding day / Some will find it on the back seat of a Chevrolet." The writers obliged Richie and changed the second line: "Some will never give their hearts away."

Furay also struggled with the "new-age philosophy" of Messina's "Look Within," an acoustic blues consistent with Poco's early albums and which does not seem remotely controversial. Messina calls on the listener, when "sad" and "blue," to "look within" for "a friend" and solace. The lyrics echo Emerson in "Self-Reliance," especially one of its most quoted lines: "Trust thyself: every heart vibrates to that iron string."[23] Furay objected as the song failed to recognize "the uniqueness of the God of the Bible, it seemed to say that all of us *are* God and that awakening the God-consciousness within is all one has to do to be on par with Him."[24] Furay refused to sing or play the song.

However, Furay's biggest objection was to "Call It Love," the #18 hit single, which Richie refers to as "Call It Lust." Written by Ron Gilbeau, Billy Crain, and Rick Lonow and sung by Rusty, the song, to Richie, was "pornographic" and "un-Poco." The writers tried to explain that they too identified as Christians and they did not think it offensive. "Look, guys," Furay responded, "it's not just that I'm a Christian, but I'm a pastor of a church. It puts me in a little different place, you know?"[25] Messina, who often served as a peacemaker between Richie and the others, stepped in; the writers capitulated and made minor changes.

Furay contributed two songs to *Legacy*. "If It Wasn't for You," which he wrote with Scott Sellen, his worship leader at Calvary, is an unexceptional ballad, despite the outstanding vocal performance. Its lyrics include thinly veiled spiritual implications—the "you" being the Lord. "I don't know how in the world we got 'If It Wasn't for You' on that record. It's probably the most spiritual of any of the songs that we submitted."[26] Perhaps the most traditional Poco song, "When It All Began," is largely Furay's; it has remained in his solo shows and he re-recorded it for *Alive* (2008). Furay and Sellen put the song together when they heard the music and melody by Nashville-based songwriters Steve Pasch and Anthony "M." Krizan. "All Began" is a bright, nostalgic country rocker, built on an allegro guitar riff of eight beats, in which Furay recalls Poco's "heart, rhythm and soul" and playing "summer nights in the park" in Boston and New York, locations, perhaps, of Poco's most enthusiastic audiences. "We had a huge following in New York and Boston too," confirmed Grantham. "We loved Central Park! . . . They were wonderful shows."[27]

Two of Furay's secular songs were rejected: "Heartbeat of Love" and "Forever with You"; both appeared on *The Heartbeat of Love*, his 2006 solo album. It is revealing that Richie, the cofounder of Poco, had two songs rejected— rejected definitely by Allen Kovac and high-profile producer David Cole and only possibly by Rusty and Messina.[28] In fact, *Legacy* hardly recalls the Poco of *Pickin' Up the Pieces*, the only album the original members recorded. The dominant sound of *Legacy* is late 1980s and early '90s pop with few exceptions, like "All Began," "Look Within," and Messina's "Follow Your Dreams." The two singles "Call It Love" and "Nothing to Hide" (#39) display the smoothness and sleekness of pop arrangements of the era. Young and Furay agree that the album and videos were attempts by Kovac and Cole to transform Poco into Richard Marx, or into the commercial style of Marx.[29] Writing in the *New York Times*, Stephen Holden called *Legacy* a "crisp, tuneful reunion album" while on *AllMusic*, Bruce Eder thought the singing "impeccable" and "the playing awesome," but found "the group's country-rock sound nearly compromised by the modern engineering." The result, Eder continues, is that the album sounds "mechanical and soulless compared with the group's old recordings."[30] It might be questionable how "Poco" the album is, but *Legacy* was certified Gold in January 1990.

Video

RCA planned a video for "Call It Love," the first single off *Legacy*, to be aimed at the audience of VH 1 (Video Hits One) with older viewer demographics than MTV, its sister station. Michael Bay, who went on to direct films like *Pearl Harbor* and *Transformers*, was hired to direct the video. Furay had immediate doubts. "I'd seen a lot of rock-and-roll videos at the time and I was concerned." Yet he participated in its filming since "we had in our contract that we had final say on everything." Bay tried to reassure the pastor: "'Oh, you're gonna love the video. I just did one with Donny Osmond and he just loved it'—trying to put me and Donny Osmond in some kind of a boat."³¹ Richie and Nancy watched what they thought was an advance copy. They were immediately appalled by the scantily clad attractive men and women who sweated and flirted in the heat of a very hot summer afternoon, drenching themselves in water to cool off. Interspersed and contrasted with the brightness of the day, the band played "Call It Love" on a dark rehearsal stage—the only part of the video the band had previously known about. Furay screened it several times, taking notes and jotting down over twenty offensive aspects of the video.³²

Furay called Kovac, who had had enough of what he interpreted as Furay's overbearing Christian morality. Kovac told Furay the video was finished, and Richie could call RCA executives with his complaints—which Richie did. An executive listened to Furay and promised changes that the pastor and his bandmates could approve in Nashville in two weeks at RCA's national convention, where the original Poco would perform for the first time in twenty years. However, when Furay arrived at the convention, the executive told him that no changes had been made. Furay called his manager, Mark Ferjulian, only to receive further bad news. A disappointed Pastor Greg Laurie had already seen the video on VH 1. Furay refused to perform and left the convention. He told his bandmates that he was not pulling a Neil Young, that he would tour with them, but that, out of principle, he had to leave the convention. Poco performed without him.

On Tour

Poco was scheduled for a three-week tour, opening for Marx, beginning near the end of January 1990, with a summer tour, mostly as a headliner, to follow. The setlist included several tracks from the new album; old Poco favorites; "Your Mama Don't Dance," Messina's hit with Kenny Loggins; and "Take It to the Limit," Meisner's hit with the Eagles. Richie did not hold back criticizing Marx for trying to sexually arouse teenage girls while also confronting Messina about a line in the bridge of "Your Mama Don't Dance." He asked the cofounder of Poco to change the wording of "You hop into the back seat where you know it's nice and dark . . . thinkin' it's a breeze." Messina explained that the police interrupted the couple before any sexual activity, but Furay was unmoved. Messina acquiesced and dropped the bridge from the performance. After a few dates, Messina approached Furay: "Look I cannot do this song without the bridge. I'm sorry but you're micromanaging my music now." He offered Furay an opportunity to change the wording, which Furay seized.

Richie's change was minute, substituting "back row" for "back seat." It would hardly seem worth the tension it caused. At Farm Aid, Messina said he went on autopilot and reverted to "back seat." Richie was "absolutely furious." Messina, who thought Richie "dogmatic and unyielding," commented, "It's one of those things where, in order to work with Richie, one had to really accept who he is, what he is, and how he feels, what he has to say, and whether or not it interferes with who you are. That's just something that comes with the territory."[33]

Richie abruptly left the summer tour soon after it began with over a month's worth of gigs remaining. His withdrawal added stress and caused problems for the band, who had to redo the setlist and, worse, explain his absence to upset promoters and disappointed fans. "A Poco reunion without Furay is something akin to a Beatles reunion without John Lennon. Why bother?" wrote Greg Haymes in his review of their performance at the Berkshire Performing Arts Center in Lenox, Massachusetts. As the review might be suggesting, many audience members thought the musicians were simply capitalizing on the Poco name. At the Circle Star Theater in San Carlos, California, just before the show, the promoter announced that Furay would not be part of the band, which prompted many in the audience to rise from their seats and request a refund. During another performance when an audience member shouted, "Where's Richie?" Young responded: "Richie's in church. . . . I hope that's OK?" The unimpressed reviewer wrote, "Unfortunately it wasn't."[34]

Messina was irate at Furay's departure: "It was like tearing the heart out of a brotherhood that supports you and suddenly you're adrift with all that unsold merch[andise], all those unsold CDs that we'd sell on tour, Poco got stuck with all that. Who's going to pay for that? We ended up paying ourselves. He just doesn't make good business decisions." Then he added, "That doesn't make him a terrible person. I loved working with Richie back in those days. He wrote good songs. We had fun together. But I cannot take that risk anymore of working with him again." Young was also upset with Richie, commenting, "A minister can't be in a rock 'n' roll band—it's too tense."[35]

"Looking back," says Furay about his experience in the Poco reunion, "who knows if I was a little rigid or not? I was probably a little more touchy than I should have been . . . a little overly sensitive."[36]

Problems with His Church?

Although Pastor Furay had informed his congregation that the Poco reunion would require him to be away for some ten to twelve weeks spread over the course of more than a year, there were rumblings almost immediately. One Friday night in August 1989, in Kansas City, where Furay was doing some pre-release publicity for *Legacy*, board member Glenn Watson contacted him to inform him that "the whole church is in an uproar" and "half the church" intends to leave. Watson gave the pastor an ultimatum: rock and roll or the ministry. Richie was dumbfounded. "The last thing I wanted to do was create a conflict."[37] He had sensed that a few members had concerns when he had discussed the Poco reunion, but not many, and he thought he had assuaged them. He was clear: the Poco reunion was a one-time event, and he was completely dedicated to the church. He flew back to Colorado the next day, and after a sleepless and prayerful Saturday night with Nancy, he decided to call a special meeting after Sunday service.

A nervous but resolved Richie addressed the congregation. He reviewed once again the time requirements of, and his reason for, participating in the Poco project. He then approached each member of the congregation to ask of individual concerns. However, what he heard pleasantly surprised him. Almost all expressed their support for Richie and their satisfaction with Furay's substitute pastor friend. The church was hardly in an "uproar." In fact, of the approximately one hundred members at the time, there were only three protesters other than Watson, all of whom left the church almost immediately. Relieved, Furay returned to his work with Poco. Had he left the reunion at that point, the lawsuits would have been financially and artistically crippling.

As the years passed, the church grew even more supportive of Furay's secular music career. "They get me," he said. "Whenever we play in town, they'll support us."[38] When I arrived at the church for an interview with Furay in September 2015, one of the church members, wearing a Buffalo Springfield T-shirt, warmly greeted me.

Humphrey's by the Bay

In 1995, Richie heard a message on his answering machine from Kenny Weissberg, the journalist and former DJ who drove Furay home from the Denver airport in a snowstorm in 1974 in Richie's quest to save his marriage. Weissberg was in San Diego promoting concerts at Humphrey's (later Humphreys) by the Bay, a scenic outdoor venue with, at that time, 1,300 seats. Weissberg had scheduled the Stephen Stills Band for July 6, 1995, and was asked by Gerry Tolman, Stills's manager, to find an opening act. Weissberg called Furay. However, when Richie did not respond in over a week, Weissberg took it as Furay's rejection. He hired Chris Hillman, another friend of Weissberg and Stills, to open. No sooner had the promoter hired Hillman than Richie called to accept the offer. Weissberg called Tolman, who he thought would bristle at a second opening act cutting into his client's time. But Tolman, according to Weissberg, "was a huge Richie Furay fan. 'We'll work it out,' he said."[39]

Furay took the stage at Humphrey's accompanied only by Scott Sellen. "He did a half an hour and sang hits, the songs people were familiar with, 'Kind Woman' and others. The audience went crazy for him." I asked Sellen about the performance: "It was fun. . . . Richie can be a lovable guy. He can still sing so great. The people were probably happy to see him because he hadn't been doing that kind of thing." Furay joined Hillman for the Everly Brothers' "Bye Bye Love," to which each forgot the words. Richie was overjoyed after the show. "Richie is a bear hug kind of guy, and he was so happy," reports Weissberg. Before the show, Richie had asked the promoter if he could talk about Jesus. "Well," said Weissberg, "it's Stephen's show and you can do what you want. But I'll leave that up to you." Richie decided against the idea.[40]

Inexplicably, Stills invited Hillman, but not Furay, to join him on stage for "For What It's Worth." "Maybe," suggests Weissberg, "he didn't call on him because Richie wasn't familiar with the way he had rearranged it." However, the two seemed glad to see one another. "I didn't have my Kodak instamatic with me," said Weissberg, "so I couldn't take a picture . . . but it was so amazing seeing the three of them talking backstage like old home week." Furay would play Humphrey's some half dozen times in future years as both supporting act and co-headliner. A few times, he opened for Poco with either Sellen or a four-piece band. "He would end his set and—it was all staged—Rusty would come on stage and say, 'Richie, Richie, wait a second. You're not going anywhere.' And then he sang maybe six or seven songs with Poco to start their show. And then he left and Poco finished."[41]

Two years later Furay found another exciting message on his phone. Neil Young informed Richie that Buffalo Springfield would be inducted into the Rock and Roll Hall of Fame, class of 1997.

In My Father's House

Like most Christian services, Furay's services always included music. Almost from the beginning, Furay teamed with worship leader Sellen to write original music. In the early days, the music was more bluegrass with the pastor on acoustic guitar and vocals, George Wargo on fiddle, and Scott on one of several instruments (guitar, dobro, piano, mandolin, banjo). Sometimes Scott would bring in a song, sometimes Richie, and each would contribute to the song or not. "We Lennon-and-McCartneyed everything," says Scott.[42] After a couple of years Wargo left Colorado.

In 1995, Pastor Tom Stipe, with the support of Pastor Chuck Smith, started a new record label for Calvary Chapel. Stipe, who had written and performed with Furay on *I've Got a Reason*, asked another musician, Randy Rigby, whom Richie also knew well, to put together an introductory compilation album for the new label. Richie was invited to contribute a new song or two. However, after Richie and Sellen played Stipe and Rigby a few songs, it was clear that the two had enough quality material for an album. Before long Furay found himself in Nashville with seasoned session musicians and Colorado producer John Macy, a pedal steel guitarist and engineer who has worked with a diverse group of musicians, from the Nitty Gritty Dirt Band, Los Lobos, and Ricky Skaggs to Gladys Knight and the Pips. Like Bob Dylan a few decades earlier, Richie was impressed not just with the talent and skill of the Nashville players, but also with their speed in learning the songs and developing their parts. "They would listen two or three times to a demo tape Scott and I had assembled, and then they would instantly write arrangements that would have taken most other performers weeks to produce."[43] The result was *In My Father's House*, ten original devotional songs, eight written by Furay and Sellen and two by Sellen ("Send Me Lord," "The Love I Will Possess"). Released in 1997, it was Furay's first solo album in fifteen years. Some of the songs had been used in church services as early as 1983.

As expected, the songs either celebrate the Lord and church fellowship or meditate on Christ's sacrifice, the glory of God, and salvation for true believers. As Furay says, "There's a specific chord that runs through them all and that's our relationship with Jesus Christ. A lot of them are very scriptural in the lyrical content and some of them are not as scriptural, but they're certainly relational."[44] Overall, there is a joyfulness, brightness, and country-rock tone to the album that recalls Poco more than any of Furay's previous solo albums. While his first four solo albums have their Poco moments ("Gettin' Through" on *Reason*, for example), none of those albums in its entirety recalls Furay's groundbreaking band. On *Father's House*, Furay recruited Rusty Young to play both dobro and steel guitar, along with a host of veteran country, country-rock, and bluegrass musicians, including Sam Bush and Hank Singer on fiddle with Bush doubling on mandolin, the rhythm section of Michael Rhodes on bass and Dennis Holt on drums, Pete Wasner and Steve Conn on keyboards, and, on guitar, Chris Leuzinger, who has played with Garth Brooks since 1989. Without question, it is an all-star band with each member delivering fitting solos. In addition, the production—by "Randy Rigby and John Macy with Richie," as the album says in its liner notes—sparkles in its clarity, with emphasis on the richness, depth, and range of Furay's vocals and on the musicianship, with no attempts to mimic the pop sound of contemporary Christian music or to suffocate the song with mood-setting strings. Instead, the sparse production creates an authoritative country-rock experience. In "We Have Come to Worship You," a song of somber intensity, Wasner and Singer on fiddle add not only texture but also meaning in their etherealness, while on "The Love I Now Possess," Leuzinger's bluesy fills and solos accentuate the singer's awe and humility.

Other extraordinary tracks include the opening track, "Hallel," a joyous celebration of Furay's commitment to the Lord, featuring Leuzinger on slide guitar and Steve Conn on Hammond B-3. "Wake Up My Soul," which Furay performs regularly and which appears in a live version on *Return to the Troubadour* (2021), is this album's "Hoe Down" or "Rise Up," but more bluegrass, featuring Sellen's banjo, Rusty's dobro, and Bush's mandolin. Self-identifying as a musician, as he did throughout *Reason*, Furay calls on God to "wake up my soul . . . wake up my hands and the instrument I play [and] my voice," so "the world" will hear him "worship" and "exalt" the Lord. "Peace That Passes All Understanding" (from Philippians 4:7) is a gentle country rocker with catchy guitar and steel guitar riffs and a popping, catchy chorus. Whereas "Look at the Sun" expresses Furay's ecstasy in his devotion to Christ, "Peace" emphasizes the mystical comfort and life confidence that comes with surrendering one's life to Christ. In "Peace," like the rest of the album, Furay does not so much proselytize directly or issue jeremiad-like warnings, but instead offers a living testimony to the benefits and beauty of living a Christian life.

Musically, *Father's House*, despite its Christian lyrics, would please most early Poco fans—that is, if they had the opportunity to hear it. As Darren Hirst wrote in his review, "This album deserves a much wider exposure than it will get on the small church-based label that Richie has chosen for its release."[45] The album failed to rank on even Christian charts.

Return to New York—September 11, 2001

Furay, like most Americans, was devastated and unnerved by the terrorist attacks of 9/11. "The tragedy," said Richie, "was very personal to me."[46] Furay has long had a special relationship with New York City. He began his career in Greenwich Village (about two miles from the World Trade Center), Poco had a large fan base there, and his daughter Jesse, studying music and drama, was living on the Upper West Side at the time of the attack. The previous year he and Nancy were visiting Jesse when they attended the ticker-tape parade for the World Champion Yankees. Very shortly after the attack, Richie called pastor friend Mike Finizio of Harvest Christian Fellowship, New York, located near Madison Square Garden, and volunteered his services.

Pastor Richie flew to New York City about three weeks after the attacks. During the day, Furay consoled firefighters and policemen as well as taking to the streets, not to proselytize, but to support, comfort, and encourage anyone in the shaken city who needed to talk. He made himself available in Midtown's Columbus Circle and in Washington Square Park, one of his former hangouts in the Village. In the evening, he joined other Calvary Chapter and Harvest ministers in a Midtown theater for a service, during which Furay played and sang. He also spent time in New Jersey ministering with Pastor Lloyd Pulley of Calvary Chapel Old Bridge before heading home in mid-October. "It was a powerful experience," summarized Furay.[47] He returned in December for a firefighters' appreciation breakfast.

I Am Sure

With Calvary Chapel Broomfield firmly established in its spacious setting and with thirteen new Furay-Sellen devotional songs, Furay reunited in Nashville with John Macy and the musicians from *Father's House*. To that core group, he added veteran guitar and pedal steel player Dan Dugmore from *I Still Have Dreams*; old friends Jim Messina, Rusty Young, Paul Cotton, Chris Hillman, and members of the Nitty Gritty Dirt Band (Jimmy Ibbotson, Bob Carpenter, and Jeff Hanna); and his daughter Jesse Furay Lynch. Like *Father's House*, *I Am Sure* is beautifully sung, expertly played, and crisply produced. The songs, like on the previous album, have their roots in country-rock but with more emphasis on rock. The difference between the two albums is like that between *Pickin' Up the Pieces* and *Good Feelin' to Know*. The lyrics, as on *Father's House*, all celebrate the Lord and Christian fellowship or meditate on Christ and his sacrifice. Again, like prayers, many songs address God directly (nine of thirteen here, eight of ten on *Father's House*), and many quote or paraphrase biblical verses, which Furay directs the listener to on the accompanying lyric sheet, just as he did with *Seasons of Change*. However, under the title track, Furay references Psalm 143, with which the song seems to have no relation. I asked Furay about this. He said, "I don't think that scriptural reference should have been there." He laughed.[48] It was a mistake. Overall, *I Am Sure*, self-funded and self-released, is both an intense and enjoyable album, even stronger than its predecessor. The deft interplay of the various instruments adds a dynamism to the album, particularly the electric guitars with acoustic guitars and the pedal steel, the fiddle with the banjo and, at times, with the Hammond B-3, as on "Most High."

"With My Whole Heart," the opening track, sets the more rockish tone of the album with the intro of Leuzinger's grinding guitar followed by the guitar interplay of Leuzinger and Dugmore, who create a riff that recurs in the song. Inspired by Psalm 138, Furay praises God and thanks Him for his support in troubled times with effectively understated vocals. More dramatic is the bluegrass "City of God," which opens with a brief, but low, bass vibration, as Furay sings, "His foundation is the Holy mountain / The Lord loves the gates of Zion." On *Lord*, we hear a subtle, single guitar note, which ushers in a contrasting, dramatic minor guitar chord four beats later on *Zion*. The minor key gives this celebratory song its seriousness if not somberness. Like many evangelicals, Furay has a special connection with Jerusalem and Israel. He first traveled there in the 1980s and, since then, has been there about a half dozen times, leading groups of forty or so through the Holy Land. "It becomes a very special moment in people's lives. It is so emotionally overwhelming sometimes that it's amazing."[49] He and Pastor Bob Probert had talked about leading a group of some ten backpackers in 2020, but the coronavirus pandemic halted their discussions. The other bluegrass track, "So Far to Go," is more sonically hopeful with Sellen's plucking banjo, Bush's sometimes sawing fiddle, and Young's dobro fills and solo. But the singer, as the title suggests, is desperate for God to "take my life in Your hand" and "lead me into the promised land." As another born-again Christian and one of pop music's great vocalists Dion DiMucci said, "If you had to retitle Psalms, you could call them the blues because they're full of brokenness and people maybe feeling apart from God . . . not feeling at rest." Then, as if addressing one of Furay's favorite themes, "They want a home and that's inside you, too . . . the idea of being at home and at peace within you. You could have a house that's not a home"[50] —as Furay experienced in the early to mid-1970s.

In "I Am Sure," another of Furay's extraordinary country-rock ballads, Furay expresses his confidence in his faith through his laid-back delivery and casual lyrics: "I'm sure of this thing." His faith, the song implies, is just an everyday "thing," an ordinary part of his life—although he never loses sight of its extraordinariness ("We are set apart . . ."). Underneath Furay's vocals and acoustic guitar, electric guitars and two steel guitars play off one another; at the midpoint of the track, the steel guitars play in unison (2:14–2:30). "I Am Sure" recalls the interaction of Young with Messina and Cotton. Another country-rock ballad with strong rock underpinnings is "Jesus, Eternal King," which features a trademark Furay falsetto of emotion, here a *whoa* at twenty seconds when the tempo picks up. The sturdy ballad combines Furay's tender vocals, worshipping "the light of the world" and the "righteous judge," with hard-edged, gritty guitar, and a pedal steel that at times recalls Young's "bear" or Melobar guitar. Sellen's banjo locks in the country roots to produce dramatic sound contrasts.

Along with "I Am Sure," the seven-minute "Father of Glory (Give the Glory to God)" is the album's strongest track. It begins slowly with an echoing, marching beat and clipped but ringing guitar notes, a sparse piano riff, and a vibrating jaw harp, over which Richie gently asks God to grant him "wisdom and revelation of what we're called to share . . . and [to] know the greatness of Your power." At 2:20, the pace picks up, dominated by gruff and earthy electric guitar riffs and Richie's jubilant "Hey" at 2:56, and a spirited Rusty Young lap steel solo from 3:56 to 4:24. Furay's vocals, while they pick up the pace, always remain in prayerful control. The tempo slows and returns to the meditative intro at 5:12 with variations and solos until the song's close. An anonymous reviewer in the secular *No Depression: The Journal of Roots Music* wrote, "For those who miss Furay's country-rockin' days of yore, 'Father of Glory' should bring a smile and jubilant shout to those who remember infectious rockers such as 'A Good Feelin' to Know' and 'Let's Dance' from Poco's mid-'70s heyday."[51] The song combines the meditative spirit with celebration, which summarizes both *Father's House* and *I Am Sure*. "Father of Glory" would seem to have been an effective close to the album. Instead, Furay closed with the pedestrian church ballad "Deep Within," which, along with "Wonderfully Praised," marks the album's only low point.

Overall, however, the album is excellent—arguably Furay's best solo studio album with the possible exception of *Heartbeat of Love*, which followed. The reviewer in *No Depression* agrees: "Over the past couple decades, Furay has occasionally recorded country-flavored gospel records, and his latest, *I Am Sure*, is arguably his best. What's readily apparent is the exceptional depth and range of his voice, which . . . if anything, [has] gotten stronger. . . . His soulfully expressive voice makes each syllable count." Similarly, Bruce Eder writes, "Furay knows how to wrap a melody around a psalm and make both of them count for something bigger than their individual parts. Even more important, this all works as music, too, at least from a traditional country-rock standpoint . . . in many ways this is a beautifully soulful follow-up to many of Poco's best moments from their early albums. . . . There are enough twists, including some pretty good rocking moments (especially on the guitars), sufficient to make this more than an exercise in latter-day folk-rock. [It] won't disappoint fans of Poco or any of Furay's other '70s-era musical ventures."[52]

In 2005, Furay played some twenty performances, Christian and secular, the most since 1982, and the first with a backing band since 1978—excluding the Poco reunion tour. The new Richie Furay Band, or his "family band," as Furay called it, included multi-instrumentalist Sellen and his son Aaron on bass, along with drummer Alan Lemke and Furay's daughter Jesse on background vocals, all of whom performed at Sunday Service at Broomfield. Until 2018, this incarnation of RFB would take to the road for stints of fifteen or so dates a year, with as few as four, in 2012, and as many as twenty or more, in 2006, 2007, 2009, and 2015, when he added Jack Jeckot on keyboards and harmonica. "[We] get in my little van. . . . my Sprinter, and [we] see how tough the road is. But I always give thanks to the Lord and glory to Him because if it were not for him, I wouldn't be doing it."[53]

CHAPTER 12

"Still Deliverin'"

Into the Twenty-First Century

On May 20, 2004, at the Belcourt Theatre, Nashville, Furay reunited with Poco, which then featured Rusty Young, George Grantham, and Paul Cotton, for a filming of a DVD released later that year.[1] During the rehearsals, Furay's good friend Peter Van Leeuwen told Richie that his favorite Poco song was "Let's Dance Tonight." "I told [Van Leeuwen] that if I ever get a chance to do another secular project, I want to re-record that song because I just love it too."[2] With a few phone calls and Van Leeuwen's financial support, Furay was in Quad Studios, Nashville, with John Macy, the musicians from his last two albums, and some old friends, including Stephen Stills, Neil Young, Mark Volman, Rusty Young, Timothy Schmit, Kenny Loggins, Mark Oblinger, and others.[3] "Though I'm a pastor now and most of the music I've been making for the past 10 or 15 years has been devotional," Richie explained, "along the way I've been writing a lot of mainstream songs. I decided to record them."[4] The result was *The Heartbeat of Love*, self-released in the spring of 2006, his first collection of secular songs since *I Still Have Dreams* in 1979.

The Heartbeat of Love

In his first four albums—*I've Got a Reason* (1976) through *Seasons of Change* (1982)—Furay experimented, more or less successfully, with different sounds and genres (e.g., disco, reggae, calypso, hard rock). But with *In My Father's House* (1997), he returned to his country-rock roots, where he remained for *The Heartbeat of Love* and his subsequent albums. As with the previous two devotional albums, the production by Macy and Furay is sharp and precise, emphasizing clear and uncluttered arrangements with Furay's tenor high in the mix. As the title and the CD's cover with its scarlet heart and attached Cupid wings indicate, *Heartbeat* represents Furay's most comprehensive collection of love songs. The word *love* appears in eleven of the twelve songs and *heart* in nine songs. With some overlap, songs can be placed into five categories:

1. Marital love, specifically, the wedding day: "Forever with You," "Only to You."
2. Songs for Nancy (including themes of love at first sight and enduring love): "Crazy for You," "Kind Woman," "Heartbeat of Love," "In the Still of the Night," "You and Me," "Real Love."
3. Troubled love and heartbreak: "My Heart's Cryin' Tonight," "Callin' Out Your Name."
4. Love for friends and community: "Dean's Barbecue."
5. Celebration: "Let's Dance Tonight."

Furay wrote or cowrote all the songs: five by himself, five with Scott Sellen, one with Jim Mason, and one with Sellen and Mason.

Interwoven into the love songs is the familiar Furay motif of dreams, which appears in half the songs. As in several songs, love or marriage in "Forever with You" marks the fulfillment of a dream: "So many nights I held you in my dreams / That they ever came true is amazing to me." In "Only to You," Furay sings, "I wasn't sure if my dream would come true / But you're a treasure from heaven." "Heaven," in post-conversion Furay, is never a vague reference to an abstract, idyllic place where fate or luck sends gifts. To Furay, heaven is where the Lord dwells and where true believers in Christ dwell in the afterlife, and, yes, the Lord might or might not intervene in human activities. If we look at only the lyrics to these songs and others on the album, they could seem mawkish and trite. However, the lyrics take on life and sincerity when set to rhythms and delivered by Furay. "Forever with Love," cowritten with Sellen for the wedding of the Furays' oldest daughter, Timmie, to Dave Aragon and rejected for Poco's *Legacy*, is a lively country rocker with a spirited, recurring eight-beat dual guitar riff from Chris Leuzinger and Dan Dugmore. Furay's daughter Jesse joins her father on the chorus, which makes the track feel like a duet.

Furay focuses on his marriage and his enduring love for Nancy on half of the twelve tracks. He recalls their earliest days in "Kind Woman" (the "definitive" version for Furay[5]) and "In the Still of the Night." In the Furay tradition of melodic country-rock ballads, "In the Still of the Night" establishes an ease-ful, swaying groove, for six-and-a half minutes, behind the rhythm section of bassist Michael Rhodes and drummer Dennis Holt. The track features a guitar solo and fills from Paul Cotton and includes cowriter Sellen on banjo, Macy on pedal steel guitar, and Pete Wasner's piano and organ, all adding to the track's rich texture. In the song, Furay mentions some past marital turmoil ("storms of life," "hurtin' each other") but explores his love at first sight for Nancy when he recalls seeing her "from the stage above" on "that summer night" at the Whisky a Go Go. He also sings of "love at first sight" in "Heart-beat of Love," cleverly evoking the Whisky with a sonic reference to Buffalo Springfield through the song's falsetto *whew-whew-whews*, with only a slight variation from "On the Way Home," a Springfield classic by Neil Young. In the almost pure country "Real Love," Furay celebrates his love for Nancy. He seems to sing from the perspective of pastor-counselor Furay, frustrated with a couple: "They don't know about love . . . lookin' for some way out." The mistake, he sings, is that they only "give each other half [their] lives . . . half a heart . . . and wonder why . . . they're fallin' apart . . . cryin' all night." "Real Love," like most of the album, is about pledging one's full heart, making a commitment to the other that will help solidify the relationship through the inevitable "storms of life" and "pourin' rain." He sings about these "storms of life" in "Callin' Out Your Name." He also sings about disappointments, hurt, and "cryin'" ("My Heart's Crying Tonight"). Love, for Furay, may be a mys-tery, "an ageless old rhyme" ("Kind Woman"), but it is fragile and ethereal, a "dream [easily] lost forever" as he warns to the light jazz-blues of "My Heart's Crying Tonight," which features saxophone work from Wrecking Crew vet-eran Jim Horn.

The more effective heartbreak song is "Callin' Out Your Name." It was written with Mason, but Furay could have written the lyrics in 1971 or 1974, when Nancy left their marriage. The song, which features Stephen Stills on backing vocals, begins with Furay tenderly pleading, "You know I want to be close to you." Then with the melody picking up the pace, pushed by Holt's drums galloping to the chorus, Furay blurts out in anger and frustration: "I can't believe you would turn your back and just walk away." Then, perhaps appealing to her sense of guilt, he questions her commitment: "Is my love for you just a choice between pleasure or pain? . . . Callin' out your name." As the chorus closes, the singer resumes his earlier tone and mentions his tears and desire "to work it out." After the second verse and chorus, Leuzinger's sharp and pointed twenty-eight-second solo leads to a defiant Furay, who increases the tension in the bridge:

I'm not gonna stand here and let you convince me
We haven't got reason to try
Either we learn to forgive and forget
Or all we've got left is good-bye
Good-bye, Good-bye!

The song, with Furay's fierce delivery and the musicians' raw performances, adds credibility to *Heartbeat*'s more uplifting commentaries on love, while creating the album's most dramatic moment.

Furay has long sung of the simple pleasures in life, from pleasant mornings ("Good Morning") and warm afternoon gatherings ("Pickin' Up the Pieces") to fun-filled evenings ("Hoe Down"). In the sprightly "Dean's Barbecue," Furay celebrates friendship, music making, and food in a 4:15 jam or, as Furay calls it, "a hoe down,"[6] recalling Poco's "Grand Junction" and "Fools Gold" and complete with a Furay *whoo* at the thirty-two-second mark. "Dean's Barbecue" maintains its brisk tempo through Holt's steady drumbeat, Rhodes's pumping-country bass line, Sellen's banjo, and Furay's electric guitar, all of which set the table for soloists like Sam Bush on both fiddle and mandolin, Jim Horn with an R&B sax solo, Rusty Young on dobro, Mickey Raphael (of Willie Nelson's band) on harmonica, old friend Al Perkins on guitar, Pete Wasner on piano, and Dan Dugmore on slide guitar. The song, like the barbecue, "turns up that July Texas heat."

"Dean's Barbecue" was inspired by Furay's participation in four of renowned chef Dean Fearing's barbecues, from 2002 to 2005, at Rosewood Mansion on Turtle Creek, Dallas. Fearing would invite musicians to perform and renowned chefs to cook for guests during his annual fundraiser to benefit various causes, from Dallas art groups to aid for those living with serious illnesses. One day photographer Andy Katz, who used to live in Boulder, told Richie that he had just met Fearing, who was a huge Furay fan. Katz asked Richie to send him a copy of *For What It's Worth: The Story of Buffalo Springfield*, which Furay had cowritten with John Einarson. Fearing responded with an invitation: "Hey, man, I've got a barbecue going on down here and I wanted to know if you wanted to come down." Richie, not a "foodie," was not familiar with Fearing's reputation as a star chef or his star-studded barbecues: "I'm thinking, oh my gosh, is this a backyard barbecue? I kind of hem-hawed around." Then Fearing told Furay that another musician had accepted his invitation: "Look, man," said Fearing, "I want you to come. . . . I was just in Nashville and I met this guy who loves American barbecue and he's gonna be there. You may know him, Stevie Winwood." Richie was floored. He then accepted the invitation from the "father of Southwestern cuisine." At Richie's first appearance, he sang "Kind Woman." Winwood approached him: "Aw man, I just love that song." Richie told the founder of Traffic, "If I record it again, I sure would love to have you." Winwood was excited: "Call me, man! I wanna play on that song." Some three years later Richie arrived in Nashville to re-record his classic. He reached out to the legendary English musician, who has a home in Nashville, but Winwood was in England.[7]

The album closes with another celebratory track, the re-recorded "Let's Dance Tonight," which in the context of the album celebrates love in all its forms. The song poses a rhetorical question and then a proclamation: "Ain't love grand? . . . so come on, let's dance."[8]

What few reviews *Heartbeat* garnered were all positive. Steve Stockman wrote, "If this was released in the early seventies it would have been a major release . . . maybe the best Richie Furay album with or without a band since [Buffalo Springfield]." Terry Roland called it "straight forward country-rock," noting the "fresh, energetic, passionate [vocals from Furay who] sound[s] like he's still 22" while Chet Flippo said the album "is a treasure . . . a joyous experience [and] great music . . . [that] it's not at all dated is something I would never have predicted."[9] Yet the self-released album largely went unheard with no label to promote it.

Autobiography, *Alive*, and Busy Times

In 2006, besides *The Heartbeat of Love*, Furay also released his autobiography, *Pickin' Up the Pieces*, written with Michael Roberts. The book is a straightforward narrative of his life, from his earliest days in Yellow Springs through his years in New York, Los Angeles, and Colorado. He is open about his music, his marital struggles, his conversion to Christianity, and his purpose for writing his life's story: "to share the love I have for Jesus Christ, my family, and you." He also hopes the reader will be "challenged to look deeper into your life" and "receive Christ."[10] He closes the book with a prayer to help readers in their spiritual journeys. To be clear, however, while Furay sprinkles his faith throughout the book, his proselytizing is never offensive and never overdone— at no point does he echo the tone of "Good Feeling to Know" in *Crawdaddy*.

Similarly, Furay never proselytizes from the stage. To this day he might play, depending on the length of the set, from one to four of his devotional songs, introducing them by simply thanking the Lord for his musical gifts. However, promoters and fellow artists for whom he has opened have been concerned, especially when he resumed playing secular venues as a solo artist in 2005. In 2006, he opened a few shows for old friend Linda Ronstadt, but Furay was bothered by her phone call to check on his setlist. The following summer Furay and his band performed at some fifteen shows with Chris Hillman and Herb Pederson. In Portland, at a show sponsored by Nike, a corporate representative called Mark Ferjulian, Furay's manager, to request a setlist. "'May I ask why you're asking for the setlist?'" asked Ferjulian. "'Well, we know that Richie is a Christian and we just wanted to make sure we weren't coming to a Christian concert.'"[11] Furay explained, "We weren't using that as a platform to proselytize and preach to people because people were paying money for that, and I understand that when you're paying money for a concert you're not paying money to hear about the politics or the religion of the performers."[12]

As if in response to those frightened by Furay's potential setlist, he released *Alive* (2008), a two-CD live set recorded over two shows on Richie's home turf, on December 5, at Boulder Theater and, on December 9, 2007, at Denver's Bluebird Theater. While the sonic quality is disappointing, the performance by Fury and his "family" band is not. They deliver impressive renditions of songs, spanning Furay's forty-year career, with approximately two-thirds of the set coming from his Springfield and Poco days. The album put an end to those fearful of Furay's setlist being overstocked with devotional songs. Only four of the album's twenty-nine songs are devotional. In addition to Furay, whose voice, one reviewer wrote, "has lost none of its range, clarity and . . . depth of emotion,"[13] *Alive* shines a spotlight on multi-instrumentalist Sellen, who plays an exquisite guitar solo on the extended "Just for Me and You" and a delicate piano on "Believe Me."

Two years after the release of *Alive*, Furay reunited with Buffalo Springfield for two benefit concerts for the Bridge School in October 2010 and then a highly successful seven-date tour in the summer of 2011. The Springfield had scheduled some thirty additional dates, but Neil Young abruptly opted out and those dates were canceled.[14] On September 18, 2013, at the request of Stephen Stills, Furay flew to Nashville to present his former roommate with the Spirit of Americana Freedom of Speech Award at the Ryman Auditorium. Furay had prepared a few words for the occasion, but he never delivered them. "Some other guy weaseled his way to being part of it," says Richie. "I think he was a radio guy."[15] Furay joined Stills and Kenny Wayne Shepherd on stage for a bluesy version of "For What It's Worth."[16]

On January 9, 2014, Poco was inducted into the Colorado Music Hall of Fame, along with Manassas (who backed Stills for tours and two albums from

1971 to 1973 and featured Furay friends Chris Hillman, Al Perkins, and Paul Harris), Firefall, and the Nitty Gritty Dirt Band, whom Furay joined in 2017 for a rendition of "Run for the Roses," released on *A Tribute to Dan Fogelberg*. RFB supported Rusty Young, Paul Cotton, and Timothy Schmit through seven Poco songs. Schmit remembered a backstage conversation: "Paul, Rusty, Richie, and I were in one of the little dressing rooms, just kind of reminiscing and talking, and Richie at one point said, 'You know, I'm the only one here in this room that has never had a hit record.' And, I thought, God, that's unbelievable. . . . If anybody should have had a string of them, it should have been him. . . . I also heard a sadness in his voice."[17]

Hand in Hand

Playing again with Buffalo Springfield ignited Furay's creativity. He wrote several new songs that might have found their way on a new Springfield album, any possibility of which disappeared with Young's withdrawal from the tour. In early 2014, with several quality new songs and a demo, Furay and manager David Spero began to hunt for a record label in Nashville. It did not go well. One response to Spero was representative: "I was going to cancel this meeting," said the executive, "but out of respect for Richie I came. But what am I going to do with a 70-year-old Richie Furay [and his] album?"[18]

On May 19, 2014, RFB was playing B.B. King's, a thousand-seat club in New York's Times Square. "I went around shaking hands [before the show]. It was a Monday night and people were [there] because they wanted to be." At one table sat Chuck Oliner and Allan Leighton from Entertainment One Music (eOne) in Nashville, who told Richie, "We're thinking of signing your record."[19] The following year eOne released *Hand in Hand*. For the recording, Furay assembled his usual team of Nashville musicians, who had been with him since *In My Father's House* in 1997, and some old and new friends, like Keb' Mo.' The music, similar to his last three studio albums, is steeped in country-rock and Americana. There are the familiar Furay themes and motifs, but now addressed from the perspective of a septuagenarian aware of aging, his own mortality, his legacy, and America's political health. However, despite the somberness of these themes, the overriding tone of the album is bright and vibrant as Richie rejoices in his spirituality, his love for his wife and family, his pride in his and Nancy's personal accomplishments, and his pride in his professional accomplishments. *Hand in Hand* includes twelve tracks: nine new recordings, two of which are covers, and three bonus tracks, including the "definitive" "Kind Woman" from *Heartbeat*, a live version of "Good Feelin' to Know" from *Alive*, and an alternate version of "Love at First Sight" with Jesse on lead vocals.

On April 18, 2015, *Billboard* reported that Furay "graces a *Billboard* chart for the first time in more than 35 years as *Hand in Hand* enters Heatseekers Albums at No. 12 and Folk Albums at No. 15. He last appeared on the Jan. 5, 1980 Billboard Hot 100 with 'I Still Have Dreams,' which peaked at No. 39."[20] More widely reviewed than *Heartbeat*, *Hand in Hand* was very favorably received by critics. In *Goldmine*, Michael Greenblatt raves that *Hand in Hand* came "seemingly out of nowhere . . . an absolutely gorgeous and rockin' album . . . featuring the kind of deeply introspective acoustic and electric Southern LA country-tinged rock 'n' roll that [Furay] himself pioneered." Hal Horowitz in *American Songwriter* notes that "it's great to hear Furay's immediately distinctive tenor voice on a batch of well-produced, catchy tunes played and especially sung with heart and a passion that recalls his salad days," and hopes that "if this album does nothing more than inspire some younger folks to search out his Poco and Springfield work, it has done its job." Horowitz does add that there were too many love songs to his wife and a couple of weak moments, like the "clumsy" "Don't Tread on Me." In *No Depression*, Mary Catherine Reynolds praises Furay's vocals: "It's the authenticity of his voice that makes *Hand in Hand* such a pleasure. His voice is in full force, driving the melody and the rhythm through familiar territory and into the rough terrain of life today. Not so young anymore, but quite a bit wiser, he is always ready to rock."[21] But this initial fever was not caught by fans, who failed to seek out the album, instead replaying Poco and Springfield albums, a source of endless frustration for Richie, who has told fans, "'You can hear the new music and the new music is not gonna let you down.' I've even gone so far in some places to tell people, 'If you don't like it, you write back and let me know, and I'll refund your money.' 'Cause if they like anything that I did in the past, if they like the Springfield, Poco, or SHF, the new music is not going to . . . let them down."[22]

Hand in Hand opens with "We Were the Dreamers," a companion piece to "When It All Began" from *Legacy*. Both songs are driven by a legato riff with a lilt, but the "Dreamers" riff is effectively scratchier. In both songs Furay reflects fondly on his time in Poco. However, whereas "When It All Began" looks back with joy and nostalgia, "Dreamers" is more concerned with Poco's unrecognized achievement. Using his familiar dream motif, Furay seems to question why Poco's dreams, at least when he was with the band, have gone unfulfilled: no smash singles or albums, no arena tours, no Rock and Roll

Hall of Fame. Poco, Furay sings proudly and correctly, were country-rock "pioneers" with a "sound all its own. . . . We blazed a trail for generations to come." Yet "others would claim their day in the sun" while, "today," the music "out of Nashville . . . echoes the sound." There is no bitterness or anger in the song as the lilt in the recurring riff adds an uplifting, almost quixotic, feel and Furay's vocals are prideful not scornful—although Furay would welcome more acclaim for Poco. As he told *Billboard*: "['Dreamers' is] the story of Poco. . . . Not that I sit around and dwell about Poco, but the lyrics began to tell that story and I just went with it. It was one of those natural things that just had a flow to it, and the (music) reminded me of what we were trying to do back in 1969."[23]

Love songs dominate the album. Excluding the bonus tracks, Furay includes four love songs: "Hand in Hand," "Love at First Sight," "Still Fine," and Dan Fogelberg's "Don't Lose Heart." Richie addresses his wife in the songs that he wrote or cowrote with Sellen with the exception of "Love at First Sight," which was to be a wedding song for Jesse's marriage to Tom Lynch, who performed with his father-in-law in two livestreams during the coronavirus crisis in 2020. Furay had the lyrics to "First Sight" rather quickly, but not the music. Finally, the music came to him in the shower one morning—in time for the couple's tenth wedding anniversary. One of the bonus tracks, another version of the song, features Jesse on lead and her husband on backing vocals. Richie's version is more old-school country with the dominant riff played on his acoustic guitar with performances by Dugmore on pedal steel guitar and Sam Bush on mandolin. Jesse's version is more pop-country with the dominant riff on Wasner's piano, an electric guitar solo, probably by David Snider, and strings.

Furay's two songs to his wife are country-rockers in the tradition of Poco, but it is doubtful that Furay could have written the lyrics at the time of Poco. Both have a persistent sense of mortality, a sense that time is running out. On the title track, he pleads, "Baby, don't ever let go / Hold me tight 'til the last dance we know . . . we won't worry about losing time. . . . But hand in hand we keep going on and on. . . . And so we run, hand in hand we run." There is a not-so-subtle acknowledgment that their lives are in their final stage, much like the "setting sun" in the lyrics. The music, especially through the interplay of acoustic and electric guitars, pushes on like Furay and Nancy, who run, much like the lovers in Andrew Marvell's famous carpe diem poem "To His Coy Mistress": "Thus, though we cannot make our sun / Stand still, yet we will make him run."[24] "Hand and Hand," said Richie, "it's not about puppy love. It's about 'here we are,' you know. We've had our struggles. We've had our ups and downs. But I would say we're more in love with one another today than we were when we were kids on the front of that album."[25] Furay is referring to the cover of *Hand in Hand*, which features a dual headshot of a young Richie and Nancy, ca. 1968, and which reinforces the theme of life's brevity.

In "Still Fine," the closing track, i.e., before the bonus tracks, Furay celebrates his enduring marital love with the enduring rhythms of Chuck Berry, as if to imply that he feels like a teenager around his "still fine" wife. Furay sings happily, but understatedly, similar to Ricky Nelson in "Hello Mary Lou." To the rock-and-roll piano and guitar, Richie sings of his appreciation of Nancy and "all [their] years together"—forty-seven at the time of the recording—and of small, playful moments of mature love: "My belt's a little tighter cause you cook so well / You just seem to turn an eye and say you can't tell."

One of the most revealing songs on the album is "Let It Slide," written by Ernie and Earl Cate, who as the Cate Brothers recorded the song in 1977 (*Cate Bros. Band Album*). The easeful ballad, says Furay, "sums up a lot of my life. . . . I feel very, very deeply moved by and identify with [it]."[26] (Reminiscent of the *Legacy* days, Furay did object to one line, for which the Cate Brothers provided an alternative. They changed, "Steel lovers I could not hold," to "Tough times, truth be told" in the second verse.) Through "Let It Slide," Furay suggests that he has found contentment with both his professional and home life. He sings of once "chasing rainbows" and "broken dreams," and the "hard luck and crooked schemes" entrenched in the music industry, which he has decided to "let . . . go" and "let . . . slide"—at least for the duration of the song. Now, he can be found "sitting in [his] easy chair," no longer caring if he is "ever rich or famous." Instead, he would "rather hang around home" and if he should "roam . . . it would be for a walk down by the river." In the context of Pastor Furay, "river" is suggestive of baptism, Christ, and church, especially given the choirlike intro of *ooohs*, which recur, and Wasner's churchlike organ prominent throughout the song. The relaxed melody and music reflect the mindset and emotion of someone willing to "let it slide." Furay, it seems, has arrived at the *home* he has long been heading toward in songs like "Good Feelin' to Know," "And Settlin' Down," and "Fallin in Love."

However, Furay's discontent reveals itself in his trilogy of political songs in the middle of the CD: "Don't Tread on Me," "Wind of Change," and "Someday." They are the first political songs he has written. "I like to think of them as patriotic, although," Richie conceded, "they are political." Previous to Pres. Barack Obama's administration, Furay was only marginally interested in politics. However, he believed President Obama divided the country and failed Israel. "We are polarized left and right," said Furay in 2015. "It's very, very sad. It's because of a lack of communication." He went on to say, "I have a certain position. I'm a right-leaning guy in a left-leaning world, and a lot of people don't like that."[27] In "Don't Tread on Me," Furay builds the song on a portentous six-beat guitar riff, on which he sings with pride and defiance that his "heart bleeds red, white, and blue." The song reveals some of Furay's anger at the left: "You wanna play / You're gonna pay." While the lyrics are often vague, the title and his tone reveal his conservatism. "Don't Tread on Me," a motto from the iconic Gadsden Revolutionary War flag, was adapted in the early 2000s by conservative movements, like the Tea Party, as well as by far-right militia groups. Furay used the song and video, with its magnificent images of the American landscape, to rally support for Pres. Donald Trump in 2020, although he showed no images of either Trump or Democratic contender Joe Biden. On the re-released video, the song closes with a slow electric guitar playing the melody to "God Bless America" for some thirty seconds. In 2020, with Tom and Jesse Lynch and Dan and Deb Skarda, Furay released a home recording on YouTube of "America, America." The four-part harmony accompanied only by Furay's acoustic guitar is a moving tribute to the country.

The second track of the trilogy, "Wind of Change," uses an effective metaphor of a traveler, an embodiment of America, who is lost in a snowstorm but who presses on through the "hazy forecast" and the "storm clouds . . . out east," indicating what Furay sees as the nation's problems emanating from Washington, DC. In the slow country-blues rocker, complete with banjo, fiddle, and pedal steel, Furay is at least somewhat confident that "the traveler" will see "the dawn of a brand new day" when "we can set things straight again." In both "Don't Tread on Me" and "Wind of Change," large choral groups add backing vocals, suggesting that many others share Furay's concerns. In "Someday," the third part of the trilogy, the "keep-on-believin'" Furay emerges more fully along with the Furay who can deliver angry messages in gleeful country-rock rhythms. Here it is energized by vigorous and dazzling guitar work from both Dugmore and Leuzinger, particularly in the last-minute jam. The track also features a surprising guest appearance from bluesman Keb' Mo', who was recording in a studio across the hall from Furay. "Every time we were working on that song," recalls Furay, "mixing it, tweaking it, or whatever—he kept coming over. 'Man, I wanna play on that song! I wanna play on that song!' And I'm thinking to myself: I've got Chris Leuzinger; I've got Dan Dugmore. Where am I gonna find a place for Keb' Mo'? No, where am I not going to find a place for Keb' Mo'? . . . Keb plays in the very beginning of the song when he plays that kaCHINK, kaCHINK."[28]

"Someday" is as much a love song as a political song. Richie sings, once again, of seeing Nancy for the first time when his "heart stopped beating," before he expresses his gratitude for having her by his side during these "troubled days." He reflects pleasantly on his love, but sadly on the nation:

> I'm disappointed and hurt at the direction that this nation has taken. I'm looking discouragingly a little bit at society. I talk about it in the second verse, particularly, "I been thinking a lot about life and love and things / I have a lot on my mind these days, troubled days. . . . It sure is good to have you here, / Just to know that you are near." I'm glad that I have someone that's going through this with me. I kind of sum all that up in "today, yesterday seems like a long time ago / . . . I hardly recognize the things that I used to know / Yes, there's a tear, a tear in my eye." . . . It's kind of discouraging to me.[29]

But Furay finds hope in love and the future. He expects "someday down the road, I don't know exactly when," he will see brighter days and realize that "all we needed was a place to start." For Furay, Donald Trump was that starting point, the reason to keep on believin'.

Hal Horowitz called "the driving rocker 'Someday' . . . and the lovely, harmony laden 'Wind of Change' . . . as good as some of [Furay's] best earlier work, which is a high compliment indeed."[30] Horowitz might be overrating "Wind of Change," but not "Someday," the strongest track on the album and one that stands up in live performance with "Let's Dance Tonight" and "Fallin' in Love."

Politics and Facebook

"I'm conservative in my thought," Furay said. "I'm conservative in my theology. I'm conservative in my politics. . . . My worldview is seen through the lens of the Bible and the things that [Pres. Donald] Trump supported: the first amendment, freedom of speech, the second amendment right, [and opposition to] abortion."[31] While Furay has never used a concert performance on a secular stage to preach either his religion or his politics, he has been very open and direct in expressing pro-Trump politics on Facebook. His loyalty to Trump has been unflinching. He has never contested any of Trump's falsehoods, large or small, from the size of the inaugural crowd in 2016 to his assertion of a stolen election in 2020.[32] On the contrary, Furay reposted Trump's speech of

December 22, 2020, in which Trump presented unsubstantiated and quickly debunked claims of election fraud.[33] Similarly, Furay condoned Trump's call to Brad Raffensperger in which Trump asked the attorney general of Georgia to overturn the state's election results. Furay directed his followers to an article in *American Thinker*, which justified Trump's arm-twisting since the president was acting honestly and with "massive amounts of evidence" that he had won the state.[34]

What troubles many friends and fans and what costs Furay political credibility are his news sources. He consistently references highly biased publications with low credibility, like *American Thinker*, *The Federalist*, *The American Spectator*, and *WorldNetDaily* (WND). He seems never to consult less biased and far more credible sources like the *New York Times*, *Washington Post*, or *Wall Street Journal*.[35] Richie's confirmation bias, which is to say that he only seeks sources to confirm his preconceived views, was apparent on January 6, 2021. During the attack on the Capitol Building, Furay watched coverage on the conservative Fox News cable network. He was irate that the newscasters used the "catchword 'mob'" for "these people who have come to DC with their families and kids" and for "putting the blame of these 'riots' on Trump supporters as the instigators." He implied that other protesters, like those in the Black Lives Matter movement or Antifa, had infiltrated the crowd and were responsible for the destruction. He then announced that he was turning to Newsmax TV "for truthful reporting."[36] To date, Furay has not retracted or modified his positions on the insurrection or on the 2020 election results.

In my conversations with Furay, he has always been respectful of our political differences. "You are entitled to your opinion," he said sincerely, shortly after the announcement of Joe Biden's presidential victory. "You're not a robot and I'm not a robot." He knows that many longtime friends and fellow musicians avoid him because of his political views: "Am I not allowed . . . to have another view? I mean Jackson Browne and David Crosby and all these guys . . . they have different views than me, and I can talk to them and not have a problem. What's the problem with these people that said you can't have a different view?"[37]

Pastor Furay Retires

One morning, a few days before Christmas 2016, as Furay sat across from his wife at the breakfast table, Nancy noticed that the side of his face was drooping. They went immediately to Furay's doctor, who sent him to the emergency room. After numerous tests, Furay was diagnosed with Bell's Palsy, a temporary facial paralysis that lasts up to nine months but rarely recurs. Richie's lasted about six weeks. However, it made Richie take notice: "I just got to thinking that Nancy and I put in all this time, year after year [at the church]. We avoided doing things for ourselves, and we don't have a time schedule on when or how long we're going to be here [on this earth] or not be here, and it just seemed like it was the time . . . to move on. . . . I do not have serious health issues . . . all kinds of arthritic things happen, surgeries [hip replacements in 2004 and 2008], this that and the other. . . . I was thinking maybe we should take some time just for ourselves. . . . We're getting old and we're both in our seventies. . . . It was just time."[38] He announced that he would retire as pastor at the end of 2017.

As leader of the search committee for his replacement, Furay tapped into the Calvary Chapel network. Recommendations led him to Kevin Utile, who had served as an associate pastor at Calvary Chapel San Juan Capistrano and had relocated to Boulder, where he took work as a digital marketing consultant. He joined the church on April 17 to work under Furay. "By July [2017]," Utile said, "both me and Richie knew this is what God has [for us]."[39] After thirty-five years, Furay conducted his last service at Calvary on Christmas Eve. On New Year's Day, the Furays with daughter Jesse, Scott Sellen, and keyboardist Jack Jackot boarded a five-day Caribbean cruise during which they would perform with the Moody Blues, the Zombies, Jefferson Starship, Dave Mason, the Little River Band, the Strawbs, and others.

Upon his return Richie found Pastor Utile different from the candidate Utile. "It was like two different guys," Furay said. In just one week Utile had made sweeping changes. Richie felt deceived. He had prayed and thought long and hard during the search process and had believed the Lord had directed him to Utile. "This was one of those times," Furay acknowledged, "when I didn't hear the Lord correctly. I also thought I had certain spiritual gifts—wisdom, discernment, knowledge. They're all listed in Ephesians. . . . I thought that I had the gift of discernment of spirit in protecting our church from false teachers and people that would come in to disrupt [us]. I missed it with this guy as did the rest of our board."[40] It was devastating for Furay, who had worked for thirty-five years to develop a church from a living-room Bible study group. He tried to be patient with Utile, but when he insulted Nancy before other congregants, Richie left the church and asked Utile to remove any mention of Pastor Furay from the web page for Calvary Chapel Broomfield. In January 2020, Utile changed the name of the church to Reach Church, Colorado.

Friendship with Sellen and *Return to the Troubadour*

When Richie left the church, he asked Sellen to leave with him. Scott refused, telling Richie, "Until the same things happen to [my wife] Carolyn and me that happened to you and Nancy we're staying." Furay told Sellen "your decisions have consequences." Scott was confused by what seemed like a veiled threat. Things worsened between the two when, a few months later, Sellen sent an email to church members that Furay paraphrased for me: "Well, Richie isn't what he always seems to be. If you really want to know who he is, read this article."[41] Attached was "More Messina," an interview article in the July 2018 issue of *Goldmine* in which Jim Messina blasted Furay for his bad business decisions, his volatility, his narrow-mindedness, and his "dogmatic and unyielding" character. But Messina did add "I love him like a brother."[42] Furay reached out to Messina in 2019 to talk and to invite him to play on *In the Country*, an album of country covers Richie was recording in Nashville, where Messina lives. Furay's three messages went unanswered.

Furay was not so conciliatory toward Sellen, calling his email, "a betrayal of thirty-five years of friendship."[43] Indeed, they had worked together in the church, cowritten many songs, recorded thirty-one of them, toured, and shared a close friendship. The Sellens met the Furays for lunch. "I apologized for sharing the *Goldmine* article," said Scott. "I had tears in my eyes."[44] But for Furay the friendship was irrevocably broken, especially when the Sellens continued to worship at Calvary Broomfield, not leaving until sometime in 2019.

With the friendship between Furay and Sellen ending, it would not be long before the Richie Furay Band, his family band, would also break up. Tension had been building in RFB for the last few years. The band was not always content with their pay, their meal stipend, and the small number of annual gigs, especially wanting to play more weekend dates in Colorado, where they could enjoy performing and not miss time from their day jobs. The major source of friction, however, was the recording of *Hand in Hand*. The band, with the exception of Sellen, believed Furay had promised them that they would back him on the album. Furay rehearsed the new songs with RFB, but, from Furay's perspective, the rehearsals did not go well. "I could see this was not going to happen," said Furay. "Whereas we had worked two weeks or more . . . trying to work out 'Don't Tread on Me,' these guys [in Nashville] had it recorded in two hours. So there's a difference. . . . I'm spending money, and, listen, I'm just going to say that . . . life changes."[45] Creating parts for a song, even one with a simple structure, is a far more complex process than reprising those parts on stage. Quality studio musicians, like those Furay has used in Nashville

The Richie Furay Band at the Troubadour, November 2018. *Left to right*: Scott Sellen, Alan Lemke on drums, Furay, and Jesse Lynch. Photo by Christinna Guzman.

since 1997, are adept at efficiently creating those parts, including the drumbeat and bass lines, the fills, and the solo, intros, and outros. For Furay, RFB, an excellent stage band, was not up to the task.

Scott and Furay honored RFB gigs scheduled until mid-November 2018. (See fig. 14.) In 2021, Furay released one of RFB's last performances: *50th Anniversary Return to the Troubadour*, a two-CD set with DVD, recorded that November at Los Angeles's famed club, where both the Buffalo Springfield and Poco debuted. The album and video serve as both a retrospective of Furay's career and a testament to the onstage excitement that RFB could generate. The first CD, called *Still Deliverin'*, runs through ten songs from Furay's years with the Buffalo Springfield and Poco through *Hand in Hand*. The renditions are all carefully crafted and fresh, with all songs longer than the original studio versions, allowing the musicians to stretch. The opening track builds anticipation with an airy two-minute intro in which each instrument introduces itself with a short, delicate riff above Alan Lemke's rapid cymbal taps before breaking into the recognizable chords and *whew-whew-whews* of "On the Way Home." In the penultimate track, RFB delivers a remarkably bluesy performance of "Anyway Bye Bye," featuring Sellen on guitar and Jeckot on piano. The first disk concludes with a rousing seven-minute performance of "Someday," which includes Jeckot's sizzling harmonica break.

The second CD, *Deliverin' Again*, reprises Poco's *Deliverin'*, a risky choice, for as Furay said, "There aren't that many groups that have done a live album of a live album!" It took manager David Stone about two years to convince Furay to undertake the re-recording of Poco's third album, which Bruce Eder noted was "about as perfect an album as they ever made."[46] *Deliverin' Again* may not have the youthful energy of the original, but RFB offers enjoyable and, in some ways, more illuminating and mature versions of some songs. On "I Guess You Made It," Furay's vocals, more deliberate than Schmit's on the original, reveal more of the singer's vulnerability and bitterness, while, on several tracks, his daughter's sterling backing vocals seem to inspire her father to keep high and sharp, as on "C'mon." In addition, the improved sound technology allows listeners to hear more clearly the instrumental fills, like the dobro of RFB newcomer Dave Pearlman on "Pickin Up the Pieces" and the interplay of instruments as on "Grand Junction" or "Consequently, So Long." But the success of the reprisal lies in Furay himself, who is not overly respectful to the original recording, granting his band flexibility and showcasing his lively stage persona, especially obvious on the video but also in his untiring and enthusiastic vocal performances. He is having fun. He may lower the key on some songs, like "Consequently, So Long," but none of his vocal magic is lost. As Doug Collette writes in his positive review of the CD, "this man's happy-go-lucky persona has never sounded more well-earned or worthy of admiration."[47]

Richie Furay: In the Country

On February 17, 2018, Furay with Sellen and Jesse Lynch traveled to Los Angeles to perform some ten songs with the Wild Honey Orchestra during an evening of Buffalo Springfield music to benefit the Autism Think Tank. Backstage, Furay reunited with two old friends from his days in Laurel Canyon: Val Garay, who had produced *I Still Have Dreams*, and his partner Michael Miller, who had helped convince Nancy to marry Richie. Miller had the idea that Richie should record an album of "iconic country songs" since Richie was "at the forefront of the country-rock world."[48] But Furay was unsure—that is, until a few weeks later when Garay and Miller sent Furay a list of three hundred possible songs for the album. Furay saw some of his favorites and agreed to the album after expanding the list with additional songs.

After much discussion, the list was pared down to twelve songs with, later, two added bonus tracks: "I Cross My Heart," a duet with Jesse, and "Pickin' Up the Pieces," recorded at the end of the fourth and final day of sessions at Blackbird Studio in Nashville in November 2019. "We did ["Pieces"] Bakersfield," said Richie. "We didn't do it Nashville . . . so there's a different feel, a different twang to the guitar than Nashville stuff."[49] Additional sessions were held in Los Angeles and Boulder in 2020 and 2021. Throughout the sessions, Garay and Furay wanted to put their mark on the songs. "We didn't do karaoke on these songs," said Richie. "We did our own arrangements and stuff."[50]

Richie Furay: In the Country was released by BMG Records in June 2022. Four features stand out: the vocals, the production, the musicianship, and the song selection. The clarity, emotion, and precision in phrasing in Furay's tenor is astonishing. "He sounds like he's thirty years old," said Grammy-winning Garay, who has worked with Linda Ronstadt, James Taylor, Dolly Parton, Sarah Brightman, and Santana, among many others. "He's an amazing vocalist. . . . He grew up in Ohio. He's got a kind of countryesque thing to his voice because he's from that kind of space. He has incredible range and incredible power. Just a great vocalist."[51] Furay commented, "I mean this was a performance. You can hear the emotions, but I mean if there was a little flat or sharp note Val went and tweaked them, but 90 percent of the vocal was [done] live [during those four days in Nashville]."[52] Indeed, on *Country*, Furay sings emotionally but never yields to sentimentality or melodrama, which less skillful singers might slip into, especially on tracks like Lee Ann Womack's "I Hope You Dance," a song with life advice like "I hope you never lose your sense of wonder," or John Denver's "Country Roads," in which Furay merges longing, excitement, and nervous anticipation in lines like "Drivin' down the road, I get a feelin' / That I should've been home yesterday." In the three country-rockers—Keith Urban's "Somebody Like You," Sammy Kershaw's "She Don't Know She's Beautiful," and Alabama's "I'm in a Hurry"—Furay sings with potency and animation.[53]

As expected, Furay and Garay recruited top session players like Chris Leuzinger and Tom Bukovac on guitars and Dan Dugmore on guitar and pedal steel, Glenn Worf on bass, Steve Nathan on keys, and Victor Indrizzo on drums, whom Garay flew in from Los Angeles and who made an immediate impression in Nashville. He became "the new rage drummer in Nashville," according to the producer, and was subsequently hired by Rascal Flatts and Hank Williams Jr.[54] Similar to his work on *I Still Have Dreams*, Garay never overloads the tracks. His emphasis is on Furay's voice. Any sonics added to what the core lineup produced are supportive of the voice and mood of the song, like the gospel choir in Cohn's "Walking to Memphis" or the strings on "In This Life." He also held guest musicians to a minimum, like Timothy Schmit and Perry Coleman, who sing backup on "She Don't Know," and Waddy Wachtel, who takes a solo on "I'm in a Hurry." "He kept saying to me," said Furay, "that this is a solo project. And I would say we should do harmony here or we should add this there." But, as Richie acknowledged with great satisfaction, "the voice stands out. . . . You can hear it and understand every single word."[55]

In an odd way, *In the Country*, with no Richie Furay original songs (except the bonus track remake of "Pickin' Up the Pieces"), serves to define or summarize Furay's career. He sings the music he sings best: country and country-rock ballads, country-rockers, country-blues, and country-gospel. Furthermore, Furay sings his familiar themes and motifs. There are several love songs ("Somebody Like You," "She Don't Know She's Beautiful," John Berry's "Your Love Amazes Me," Collin Raye's "In This Life"), songs of marital discord (Buddy Miller's "Chalk"), and songs of heading home ("Country Roads") or homelife ("I Hope You Dance," Lonestar's "I'm Already There" with Jesse's strikingly tender background vocals). There are songs about aspiring to dreams (Garth Brooks's "The River"), fulfilled dreams ("In This Life"), and broken dreams (Ricky Nelson's "Lonesome Town"), as well as references to finding comfort in music and music making ("Walking to Memphis") and songs that recognize, a more recent Furay theme, life's fleetingness, as in "I Hope You Dance" or the more humorous "I'm in a Hurry," in which the singer sees life as "a race," as Furay does in "Seasons of Change" and "For the Prize." "That [Alabama] song," said Furay "just resonated with me . . . simply because I've always been 'Man, I gotta get this done.'"[56] In the context of Richie Furay, many other songs take on stronger Christian overtones than the originals. The following songs, for instance, all reference God, the Lord, Jesus, or being Christian but take on more than passing significance when delivered by Pastor Furay: "I Hope You Dance," "Walking to Memphis," "In This Life," "The River," and "Chalk." Songs like "In This Life" and "Your Love Amazes Me," performed originally as love songs to wives,[57] in Furay's hands, can be interpreted as songs of Thanksgiving to the Lord for love and freedom from "the emptiness" and "imprison[ment] by the power of gold" ("In This Life"). The reference to unanswered prayers in "Your Love Amazes Me," in Furay, takes on irony: the prayers were, indeed, answered, but the singer just did not realize it. Furay was surprised when I mentioned the album's reprisal of his favorite themes: "Well, you know, these were songs that somehow just touched me. Maybe because of similar themes that I would write . . . maybe that's what it was subconsciously. . . . They were certainly songs that I identify with. . . . I think that your assessment is accurate and right on."[58]

Furay approached *In the Country* with all the excitement of a young artist. "I'm doing a project with Val Garay," he told me. "And it's really going to be good. It's amazing how good it's certainly going to turn out. I'm getting ready to go to LA tomorrow to finish up some vocals and then we go to Nashville again in March to finish up some more of the background vocals and then he'll be mixing it." A few months later, he said, "I can't wait for you to hear it." And then a year later, "I'm so proud of it. I just don't have words."[59] This kind of boyish enthusiasm and optimism has sustained his keep-on-believin' spirit for over five decades of music making and recording, which for a period in the 1980s was transferred to his pastorship, which always included music. The youthful joy and vivacity in his voice electrifies *In the Country*. "Once music gets in your blood, it's hard to get it out," Richie explained.[60]

Epilogue

As studies proliferate on the top tier of rock music artists, like the Beatles and Bob Dylan, there is a danger that lesser but still significant artists, like Richie Furay, will be marginalized and their contributions to the rock music era overlooked. *Keep on Believin'* argues for the importance of Richie Furay, his music, and his story, a long struggle with the intricacies and fickleness of music making and the music industry.

Besides contributing to American folk-rock with Buffalo Springfield, arguably the greatest American band of the 1960s, he helped usher in country-rock with, first, the Springfield and then, more fully, with Poco. When Furay cofounded Poco with Jim Messina, the pair decided to recruit Rusty Young, a pedal steel guitarist. Along with the Flying Burrito Brothers, Poco became the first rock-centric band to add a full-time pedal steel guitar, a staple in country music. With that addition, country-rock was born.

Furay is at his best when performing country-rock, or what today can be called Americana and roots music. From time to time, his artistic curiosity has led him to explore new trends, like disco in the late 1970s, but he has never been as artistically successful as he has been with country-rock. From songs like "Child's Claim to Fame" (1967) to "I Am Sure" (2004) and from "Good Feelin' to Know" (1972) to "Some Day" (2015), Furay consistently brings a vitality and freshness to the country-rock form, expanding its boundaries with loud rock riffs or ethereal church organs. In the music and words of his impressive body of work, Furay tells a very American story. He has tapped into the richness of the American soundscape and into what perhaps is the core of the American spirit—the quest to fulfill dreams, to keep on believin'.

FIG. 15 Richie Furay. Photo by Howard Zryb.

Notes

PREFACE

1. Knobler, in discussion with the author, July 13, 2020; Garay, in discussion with the author, July 7, 2021.
2. Schmit, in discussion with the author, April 8, 2020; Grogan, "'If It Wasn't.'"
3. Furay, in discussion with the author, August 24, 2020.

CHAPTER 1

1. Owen, a Welshman who made his fortune in textile mills, and his son William sailed to America in 1824 to realize his utopian vision of "an entirely new system of society [which] will gradually unite all individuals into one and remove all causes for contest between individuals" (Chiddister, "Owenites," 8). Owen established over a dozen such communities, including one in Yellow Springs, which collapsed after six months.
2. In 1630, John Winthrop sought to establish a model Christian community in New England. His phrase "city upon a hill" was inspired by Christ's Sermon on the Mount, Matthew 5:14: "Ye are the light of the world. A city that is set on a hill cannot be hidden" (King James Version).
3. Yellow Springs was incorporated as a village in 1856.
4. Heaton, "William Mills," 3.
5. In discussion with the author, September 23, 2019.
6. Heise, "William Mills."
7. Ibid.
8. Chiddister, "Full of Ideas," 17.
9. Ibid., 21.
10. Bradford, "Portrait," 110.
11. "Barbershop Color Line," 16.
12. Heaton, "Massive Demonstration," 172.
13. In discussion with the author, September 23, 2019. Furay got another taste of tear gas in Washington, DC, probably in August 1972, after a Poco concert when "something broke out and the police were clearing M Street." Furay, email message to author, March 29, 2022.
14. "Decennial Census of Population and Housing."
15. Heaton, "Arthur Morgan," 103. Throughout its history, Antioch has periodically closed to reorganize its finances. Bankrupt in 1858, Antioch struggled until 1862, when it closed and reopened after the Civil War. It closed three other times as well: from 1881 to 1882, from 1919 to 1921, and, most recently, from 2008 until 2011.
16. "Arthur Morgan," *Community Solutions*.
17. Chiddister, "Arthur Morgan."
18. Miller, *Quest*, 163.
19. Furay, *Pickin'*, 12.
20. Judith Furay Hugli, in discussion with the author, January 14, 2019.
21. Lithgow, *Drama*, 20.
22. Judith Furay Hugli, in discussion with the author, January 14, 2019.
23. In discussion with the author, January 14, 2019.
24. In discussion with the author, September 23, 2019.
25. "Brief History," *World House Choir*.
26. Vaccariello, "Long Weekend"; Williams, "Day in Yellow Springs"; "Reasons to Love"; "Yellow Springs: Cutest Hippie Town."
27. "Anderson Cooper."
28. "Statements of Votes."
29. In discussion with the author, January 14, 2019. According to Judy, Naomi was born with one tooth and nicknamed after Baby Snookums, a comic strip character depicted with one tooth, first featured in George McManus's *The Newlyweds*.
30. In discussion with the author, September 23, 2019.

31. In discussion with the author, January 14, 2019.

32. Kleiman, "In a Time."

33. In discussion with the author, January 14, 2019. Created and played by Bob Keeshan, Captain Kangaroo was the title character in the children's television series, which ran from 1955 to 1984.

34. In discussion with the author, September 23, 2019.

35. In discussion with the author, January 14, 2019.

36. Ibid.

37. Furay, *Pickin'*, 23.

38. In discussion with the author, September 23, 2019.

39. Ibid.

40. Furay, *Pickin'*, 17.

41. Dregni, "Scotty Moore's Gibson." Elvis's first four Sun singles: "That's All Right" backed with "Blue Moon of Kentucky"; "Good Rockin' Tonight" / "I Don't Care If the Sun Don't Shine"; "Milkcow Blues Boogie" / "You're a Heartbreaker"; "Baby Let's Play House" / "I'm Left, You're Right, She's Gone."

42. Judith Furay Hugli, in discussion with the author, January 14, 2019.

43. "Richie Furay Profile," 1:25–1:35.

44. Furay, in discussion with the author, September 23, 2019.

45. "Richie Furay Live," 5:28–5:53.

46. Furay, in discussion with the author, September 23, 2019.

47. In discussion with the author, January 14, 2019.

48. In discussion with the author, September 23, 2019.

49. Till, "Tales." In Yellow Springs, Fisher began his own record label, Spangle Records, which lasted for two years, until 1959. In time, he relocated to Nashville and, in 1977, scored big with his production of "Heaven's Just a Sin Away," a #1 country hit and Grammy winner for the Kendalls. In total, Fisher went on to produce twenty Top 10 hits.

50. Cody, "Country Rock Pioneer."

51. In discussion with the author, September 23, 2019.

52. Kitts, "'And Settlin' Down,'" 240–41.

53. Judith Furay Hugli, in discussion with the author, January 14, 2019; Furay, in discussion with the author, September 23, 2019.

54. In discussion with the author, January 21, 2020.

55. In discussion with the author, June 16, 2020.

CHAPTER 2

1. All quotations in this paragraph from discussion with the author, September 23, 2019.

2. In discussion with the author, January 11, 2019.

3. In discussion with the author, September 23, 2019.

4. Both quotations from discussion with the author, January 11, 2019.

5. In discussion with the author, September 23, 2019.

6. Harmelink, in discussion with the author, January 11, 2019.

7. In discussion with the author, January 10, 2019.

8. In discussion with the author, January 11, 2019.

9. Furay, *Pickin'*, 29.

10. In discussion with the author, January 10, 2019.

11. The Monks performed at a third club, but none of them remembers its name. For Dylan's firing, see Sablich, "From Macdougal Street."

12. Furay, *Pickin'*, 37.

13. Harmelink, in discussion with the author, January 11, 2019.

14. In discussion with the author, September 23, 2019.

15. In discussion with the author, January 10, 2019.

16. In discussion with the author, January 11, 2019.

17. Petrus and Cohen, *Folk City*, 293.

18. In discussion with the author, September 23, 2019.

19. Petrus and Cohen, *Folk City*, 188.

20. In discussion with the author, January 10, 2019.

21. Einarson and Furay, *For What It's Worth*, 24.

22. Nelson, "Bunky & Jake."

23. Shapiro, "Talk," 23.

24. Furay claims the Port Authority in Furay, *Pickin'*, 38, and Grand Central Station in Einarson and Furay, *For What It's Worth*, 23. Neither Harmelink nor Gustafson remembers.

25. Previously, Furay has written that the apartment was on the fifth floor, but he now believes it was probably on the sixth, as Bunky said—see Nelson, "Bunky & Jake"; Furay, *Pickin'*, 38. Furay, email message to author, November 20, 2020.

26. Harmelink, in discussion with the author, January 11, 2019.

27. Ibid.

28. Sietsema, "Farewell."

29. Einarson and Furay, *For What It's Worth*, 28.

30. Gustafson, in discussion with the author, January 10, 2019; Furay, *Pickin'*, 42; Harmelink, in discussion with the author, January 11, 2019.

31. In discussion with the author, January 11, 2019.

32. Ibid.

33. For years, Furay has said the address was 171 Thompson Street. Harmelink gave the address as well—see Einarson and Furay, *For What It's Worth*, 37, 51; Furay, *Pickin'*, 47. However, a handwritten note from Nels "Bones" Gustafson in Harmelink's collection, written in November 1964, gives the address as 175 Thompson, Apt. B, first level.

34. In discussion with the author, January 11, 2019.

35. Zimmer, "Stephen Stills."

36. Einarson and Furay, *For What It's Worth*, 27.

37. In discussion with the author, January 11, 2019.

38. Furay, email message to author, November 13, 2020.

39. Hoskyns, "Soul Stirrer."

40. "Jesse Fuller."

41. Harmelink, in discussion with the author, January 11, 2019.

42. Ibid.

43. Einarson and Furay, *For What It's Worth*, 32.

44. Furay, *Pickin'*, 44.

45. "Au Go-Go Singers Hit at Tidelands."

46. Einarson and Furay, *For What It's Worth*, 32.

47. "Au Go-Go Singers Hit at Tidelands"; Einarson and Furay, *For What It's Worth*, 32.

48. In discussion with the author, September 23, 2019.

49. Zimmer, "Stephen Stills"; "Stephen," 12.

50. Mesinger; G. C.

51. Einarson and Furay, *For What It's Worth*, 35; Gustafson, in discussion with the author, January 10, 2019.

52. Bustin, "Au Go-Go Singers," 20.

53. In discussion with the author, January 11, 2019.

54. Au Go-Go Singers, Letter, December 2, 1964.

55. Gustafson, in discussion with the author, January 10, 2019.

56. In discussion with the author, January 11, 2019.

57. In discussion with the author, January 10, 2019.

58. Einarson and Furay, *For What It's Worth*, 37.

59. Gustafson, in discussion with the author, January 10, 2019.

60. In discussion with the author, January 11, 2019.

61. Roberts, *Stephen Stills*, 85.

62. Furay, *Pickin'*, 49–50.

63. In discussion with the author, September 23, 2019.

CHAPTER 3

1. Kitts, "'And Settlin' Down,'" 245.

2. Ibid.

3. Einarson and Furay, *For What It's Worth*, 76.

4. In discussion with the author, September 23, 2019.

5. In discussion with the author, April 4, 2020.

6. Judy Furay Hugli, in discussion with the author, January 14, 2019.

7. Einarson and Furay, *For What It's Worth*, 76.

8. Greenblatt, "Fire in Furay," 42.

9. In discussion with the author, January 11, 2020.

10. In discussion with the author, April 4, 2020.

11. Kitts, "'And Settlin' Down,'" 246.

12. Ibid., 245.

13. Friedman, "Part 8."

14. In discussion with the author, September 23, 2019.

15. In discussion with the author, April 4, 2020.

16. Furay, *Pickin'*, 65.

17. Young, *Waging Heavy Peace*, 130; Friedman, "Part 8"; "Bruce Palmer." For other versions of the meeting, see McDougall, "Conversation," 7; "Various Accounts"; Einarson and Furay, *For What It's Worth*, 83–84.

18. Kitts, "'And Settlin' Down,'" 243–44.

19. McDonough, *Shakey*, 158.

20. Young, *Waging Heavy Peace*, 131.

21. McDonough, *Shakey*, 157.

22. Clipping, booklet, *Buffalo Springfield, Box Set*, 9, from Kassy Gerrick, "Good Ol' Dew," *Teen Set*, February 1968.

23. Buffalo Springfield, *The Missing Herd*, 1994, bootleg.

24. McDonough, *Shakey*, 156–57; "Who named Buffalo Springfield?" See also "In Search of a Name"; Einarson and Furay, *For What It's Worth*, 89–90.

25. Kubernik, "Buffalo Springfield."

26. *Waging Heavy Peace*, 393; McDonough, *Shakey*, 158.

27. Martin, "Elmer Valentine."

28. Furay, *Pickin'*, 76.

29. McDougall, "Conversation," 7; Etchison, "Buffalo Springfield," *Los Angeles Herald Examiner*; Einarson and Furay, *For What It's Worth*, 102; McDonough, *Shakey*, 159.

30. Weissberg, "Richie Furay," 34.

31. Davis, in discussion with the author, April 4, 2020.

32. Kubernik, *Neil Young*, location 468.

33. In discussion with the author, April 4, 2020.

34. Hodenfield, "As Bare as You Dare."

35. Einarson and Furay, *For What It's Worth*, 111.

36. Friedman, "Part 8."

37. Einarson and Furay, *For What It's Worth*, 98.

38. Young, *Waging Heavy Peace*, 393.

39. In discussion with the author, June 16, 2020.

40. College student Paul Williams started *Crawdaddy!* In February 1966, with its masthead proclaiming, "the first magazine to take rock-and-roll seriously." The inaugural issue of *Rolling Stone* appeared in November 1967, and Tom Donahue introduced freeform rock radio in April 1967 in San Francisco.

41. Willman, "Buffalo Springfield."

42. Furay, *Pickin'*, 154.

43. Clipping, booklet, *Buffalo Springfield, Box Set*, 35, from Jeffrey C. Alexander, "Buffalo Springfield Message," *Los Angeles Times*, September 17, 1967.

44. Allen, "Day."

45. Kitts, "'And Settlin' Down,'" 244.

46. In discussion with the author, September 23, 2019.

47. Young, *Waging Heavy Peace*, 390.

48. O'Rourke, "It Was 50," *Rebeat*.

49. Kitts, "'And Settlin' Down,'" 245.

50. Atlas, "Neil Young."

51. Young, *Waging Heavy Peace*, 336.

52. Atlas, "Neil Young."

53. Smith, "Off the Record," 11:31.

54. Smith, "Off the Record," 12:12.

55. Young, Liner notes for *What's That Sound?*

56. In discussion with the author, April 4, 2020.

57. Greene, "Stephen Stills Looks Back."

58. Silsbee, "R.I.P."

59. Williams, "Buffalo Springfield."

60. Greene, "Stephen Stills Looks Back."

61. Wouters, Comment on *What's That Sound?*

62. "AOTY . . . 1966."

CHAPTER 4

1. McDonough, *Shakey*, 173–74.

2. Durchholz and Graff, *Neil Young*, 28.

3. Greene, "Readers' Poll"; "Popdose 100"; Phull, *Story Behind the Protest Song*, 57–61; Browne, "For What It's Worth."

4. Einarson and Furay, *For What It's Worth*, 126.

5. Einarson and Furay, *For What It's Worth*, 127; Browne, "For What It's Worth."

6. Einarson and Furay, *For What It's Worth*, 156.

7. In discussion with the author, September 23, 2019.

8. Einarson and Furay, *For What It's Worth*, 155; McDonough, *Shakey*, 202.

9. McDonough, *Shakey*, 204.

10. Kitts, "'And Settlin' Down,'" 243.

11. In discussion with the author, September 23, 2019.

12. Einarson and Furay, *For What It's Worth*, 186.

13. In discussion with the author, April 4, 2020. See video, "Buffalo Springfield–For What It's Worth."

14. Young, *Waging Heavy Peace*, 391.

15. Davis, in discussion with the author, April 4, 2020; Young, *Waging Heavy Peace*, 391.

16. Young, *Waging Heavy Peace*, 391.

17. "Buffalo Springfield," *World Countdown*; Furay, in discussion with the author, January 21, 2020; Davis, in discussion with the author, April 4, 2020.

18. Kitts, "'And Settlin' Down,'" 244; Young, *Waging Heavy Peace*, 392.

19. Einarson and Furay, *For What It's Worth*, 185; Delehant, "Buffalo Springfield"; Davis, in discussion with the author, April 4, 2020.

20. McDonald, "Yorkville Kid."

21. Kent, "I Build Something."

22. Crowe, "Neil Young"; Williamson, *Journey*, 10.

23. In discussion with the author, April 4, 2020.

24. McDonough, *Shakey*, 221.

25. Furay, in discussion with the author, September 23, 2019; Einarson and Furay, *For What It's Worth*, 185.

26. Emerson, "Self-Reliance," 154.

27. Kitts, "'And Settlin' Down,'" 244.

28. Williamson, *Journey*, 16.

29. "Buffalo Springfield Again," *Rolling Stone*; Bouchard, review of *Buffalo Springfield Again*, 27; Gabree, in Silsbee, "R.I.P."; Phillips, "Rock Speaks," 130.

30. White, *Nearest Faraway*, 252.

31. Marcus, *Old Weird America*.

32. Christgau, "Basic Record"; Larkin, *Virgin*; Dimery, *1001 Albums*; "AOTY . . . 1967."

33. In discussion with the author, July 13, 2020.

34. Kitts, "'And Settlin' Down,'" 248.

35. Furay, *Pickin'*, 107.

36. Kitts, "'And Settlin' Down,'" 248.

37. In discussion with the author, September 23, 2019.

38. Kitts, "'And Settlin' Down,'" 245.

39. "Buffalo Springfield–Fox Theater," 59:30–1:03:45.

40. A live performance of the Springfield performing "Nobody's Fool" August 11, 1967, at the Teen and Twenty Club in Huntington Beach, California, is captured on *Buffalo Springfield: The Missing Herd*, 1994, a bootleg.

41. Silsbee, "R.I.P."; Delehant, "Buffalo Springfield"; Volman, in discussion with the author, 2020.

42. Gormley, "Neil Young"; Furay in Silsbee, "R.I.P."

CHAPTER 5

1. Einarson and Furay, *For What It's Worth*, 241.

2. In discussion with the author, April 4, 2020.

3. Kitts, "'And Settlin' Down,'" 243.

4. Greenblatt, "More Messina," 27.

5. Sweeting, "CSNY's."

6. Yorke, "Stephen Stills."

7. Furay, *Pickin'*, 109.

8. Gilbert, "Kenny Loggins."

9. Roberts, *Stephen Stills*, 77.

10. Crowe, "Neil Young."

11. Furay, *Pickin'*, 115.

12. Johnson, "Rock Show," 61.

13. In discussion with the author, April 4, 2020.

14. Ibid.

15. At one show, Palmer was so upset with the tuning that he usurped the microphone: "Will you guys get those fucking guitars in tune?" When they continued tuning, he slammed down his bass and walked off stage. McDonough, *Shakey*, 226.

16. "Buffalo Springfield—May 5, 1968," 9:54–10:00.

17. In discussion with the author, January 21, 2020.

18. Childs, "Neil Young."

19. In discussion with the author, January 21, 2020.

20. In discussion with the author, April 21, 2020.

21. Gifford, review of *Last Time*, 21; Sander, "Sweet Country," D31; Christgau, "Secular Music."

22. Einarson and Furay, *For What It's Worth*, 267; in discussion with the author, January 21, 2020.

23. Messina, in discussion with the author, April 21, 2020.

24. Gifford, review of *Last Time*, 21.

25. Zimmer, "Stephen Stills."

26. The number of draft dodgers and military deserters during the Vietnam War is difficult to determine as neither the United States nor Canada kept exact records. A low estimate is that there were 20,000 to 30,000 draft dodgers and 4,000 military deserters. Stewart, "'Hell, they're your problem,'" 68.

27. Varga, "Summer of Love."

28. Ostapiuk, "Beatles Said."

29. "Stephen Stills Quotes."

30. Furay, *Pickin'*, 112.

31. In discussion with the author, January 21, 2020.

32. Furay, *Pickin'*, 112.

33. In discussion with the author, January 21, 2020.

34. Willman, "Buffalo Springfield."

35. Gifford, review of *Last Time*, 21.

36. Kitts, "'And Settlin' Down,'" 246.

37. Ibid., 255.

38. Greenblatt, "More Messina," 23.

39. In discussion with the author, April 4, 2020.

40. Einarson, *Desperados*, 83.

41. Einarson and Furay, *For What It's Worth*, 262, 191.

42. Furay, *Pickin'*, 118.

43. Kitts, "'And Settlin' Down,'" 256.

44. Ibid.

45. Ibid., 256–57.

46. Ibid., 256.

47. Ibid.

48. "Tom Petty Inducts."

49. Kitts, "'And Settlin' Down,'" 246–47.

50. Pareles, "Rock-and-Roll Laureates," 15; Hilburn, "Rock Hall of Fame."

51. Kitts, "'And Settlin' Down,'" 247.

52. Furay, *Pickin'*, 231, 230.

53. In discussion with the author, January 21, 2020.

54. See Part 1, "Neil Young, Stephen Stills"; Part 2, "Exclusive."

55. Blinder, "What's That Sound?" 40.

56. "Super Seventies."

57. Orshoski, "Buffalo Springfield," 11.

58. Edmonds, "Box Set"; Unterberger, Review.

59. Sharp, "Buffalo Springfield."

60. Fricke, "Buffalo Springfield"; Harrington, "Review"; Wood, "Live Review."

61. In discussion with the author, September 23, 2019.

62. Greene, "Stephen Stills Breaks"; Kitts, "'And Settlin' Down,'" 247.

63. Greene, "Neil Young"; Greene, "Stephen Stills Breaks"; Greene, "Richie Furay."

64. In discussion with the author, September 23, 2019.

65. Kent, *Dark Stuff*, 306–7.

66. In discussion with the author, April 4, 2020.

67. Kent, *Dark Stuff*, 306.

CHAPTER 6

1. Greenblatt, "More Messina," 22.

2. In discussion with the author, April 21, 2020.

3. Einarson, *Desperados*, 109.

4. Back, "New 'Poco' Group."

5. Landau, "Country & Rock," 24.

6. Einarson, *Desperados*, 89.

7. Zimmerman, "Poco's Rusty Young."

8. Furay, *Pickin'*, 122.

9. In discussion with the author, January 21, 2020.

10. In discussion with the author, July 13, 2020.

11. Ibid.

12. In discussion with the author, April 8, 2020.

13. In discussion with the author, March 30, 2020.

14. Schmit, in discussion with the author, April 8, 2020.

15. Young, "Gregg Allman."

16. In discussion with the author, January 21, 2020.

17. Ibid.

18. Young and Messina, in Meyer, *Twenty Thousand Roads*, 266.

19. Kitts, "'And Settlin' Down,'" 248.

20. In discussion with the author, July 13, 2020.

21. In discussion with the author, April 21, 2020.

22. Meisner, in discussion with the author, May 6, 2020; Messina, in Greenblatt, "More Messina," 22.

23. Einarson, *Desperados*, 109.

24. In discussion with the author, May 6, 2020.

25. In discussion with the author, January 21, 2020; Kitts, "'And Settlin' Down,'" 250.

26. In discussion with the author, April 4, 2020.

27. *Pogo*.

28. Back, "New 'Poco' Group"; Gressel, "Poco Plays"; Fong-Torres, *Hickory Wind*, 61.

29. Etchison, "Harmonies."

30. Crockett, "Poco's Steel Guitarist."

31. Johnson, "Pogo and Biff."

32. Furay, in discussion with the author, January 21, 2020; Grantham, in discussion with the author, July 13, 2020.

33. Davis, *Soundtrack*, 140.

34. Hopkins, "Hollywood Hillbillies," 1, 4.

35. In discussion with the author, April 21, 2020.

36. Messina, in discussion with the author, April 21, 2020; Meisner, in discussion with the author, May 6, 2020.

37. Sharp, "Catching Up"; Furay, in Kitts, "'And Settlin' Down,'" 249.

38. Messina, in discussion with the author, April 21, 2020; Davis, in discussion with the author, April 4, 2020.

39. In discussion with the author, May 6, 2020.

40. Kitts, "'And Settlin' Down,'" 249.

41. In discussion with the author, May 6, 2020.

42. In discussion with the author, April 21, 2020.

43. Mather, "Taking It Easy," 29.

44. In discussion with the author, April 4, 2020.

45. Dickie Davis says it was Meisner who suggested Poco—in discussion with the author, April 4, 2020. Grantham says it was Young, who was interested in Spanish, who suggested the name—Flans, "George Grantham." It's more likely Young as Meisner might have been gone by then.

46. In discussion with the author, January 21, 2020.

47. Edgers, "It Was the Byrds."

48. Betts, "Byrds Flip."

49. In discussion with the author, April 21, 2020.

50. Einarson, *Desperados*, 150.

51. In discussion with the author, January 21, 2020; Kitts, "'And Settlin' Down,'" 240.

52. In discussion with the author, January 21, 2020.

53. Ibid.

54. Campbell and Haggard, in Rubin, *Merle Haggard's* Okie, 19.

55. Dawidoff, *In the Country*, 48.

56. Clay, "Twang 101."

57. In discussion with the author, January 21, 2020.

58. Ibid.

59. Christgau, "Consumer Guide."

60. In discussion with the author, July 13, 2020.

61. Furay, In discussion with the author, March 30, 2020.

62. Ibid.

63. "*Billboard* Album Reviews," 51; "Hartford," 54; Hilburn, "Four Springfields," 33; Hilburn, "Poco Highlights."

64. A few websites refer incorrectly to a *Rolling Stone* magazine review, which called the album "perfect." It was not the magazine, but Charley Walters's five-star review in the 1979 *Rolling Stone Record Guide*, edited by Marsh.

65. In discussion with the author, April 4, 2020.

66. In discussion with the author, July 13, 2020.

67. In discussion with the author, January 21, 2020.

68. Hilburn, "Poco Highlights."

69. In discussion with the author, January 21, 2020.

70. Einarson, *Desperados*, 149; Eder, "Poco," 309.

CHAPTER 7

1. Schmit, in discussion with the author, April 8, 2020.

2. Furay, *Pickin'*, 136.

3. Einarson, *Desperados*, 184.

4. In discussion with the author, July 13, 2020.

5. Einarson, *Desperados*, 184; in discussion with the author, April 21, 2020.

6. In discussion with the author, April 8, 2020.

7. Ibid.

8. In discussion with the author, April 4, 2020.

9. In discussion with the author, April 8, 2020.

10. Ibid.

11. Derrough, "Rusty Young."

12. In discussion with the author, January 21, 2020.

13. Back, "New 'Poco'"; Ferguson, "Country-Rock."

14. In discussion with the author, January 21, 2020.

15. Keightley, "Reconsidering Rock," 137, italics mine.

16. Frith, "Towards an Aesthetic," 261.

17. Furay, *Pickin'*, 139.

18. Kitts, "'And Settlin' Down,'" 249–50.

19. In discussion with the author, April 4, 2020.

20. In discussion with the author, April 8, 2020.

21. In discussion with the author, April 21, 2020.

22. McDonough, *Shakey*, 162.

23. In discussion with the author, June 20, 2020.

24. Furay, *Pickin'*, 138.

25. Davis, *Soundtrack*, 131.

26. In discussion with the author, March 30, 2020.

27. Cline, "Interview of Todd Schiffman."

28. In discussion with the author, July 13, 2021.

29. In discussion with the author, January 21, 2020.

30. Crowe, "Poor Poco."

31. Furay, *Pickin'*, 139.

32. On *Pieces*, Terry's surname is spelled Donovan, while on *Poco* it is spelled Dunavan. Such errors are commonplace on album jackets. *Kasanegras* appears as *Kazengras* on *Loggins and Messina* (1972) and as *Kazanegras* on Loggins & Messina's *Full Sail* (1973). Messina was listed as engineer Jim *Mecina* on Lee Michaels's *Carnival of Life* (1968). We might also note the inconsistent use of the ampersand in just about every group that has *and* in its name.

33. In discussion with the author, April 21, 2020.

34. Ibid.

35. In discussion with the author, January 21, 2020.

36. Morsch, "Looking Back."

37. In discussion with the author, April 21, 2020.

38. In discussion with the author, March 30, 2020.

39. "Poco–You Better Think Twice."

40. Delehant, "Buffalo Springfield"; Knobler, in discussion with the author, July 13, 2020; Judith Furay Hugli, in discussion with the author, January 14, 2019.

41. In discussion with the author, April 8, 2020.

42. In discussion with the author, March 30, 2020.

43. Flans, "George Grantham."

44. In discussion with the author, January 23, 2019.

45. Hilburn, "Poco Highlights."

46. "Milt Holland."

47. In discussion with the author, July 13, 2020.

48. Cline, "Interview of Todd Schiffman."

49. In discussion with the author, July 13, 2020.

50. Gilbert, "World."

51. Schmit, in discussion with the author, April 8, 2020; Furay, in Gilbert, "Poco: Interview"; Young, in Scoppa, "Poco."

52. Messina, in Gilbert, "Kenny Loggins"; Furay, in Gilbert "World."

53. Fishel, "Rock Revival."

54. Gilbert, "Kenny Loggins."

55. Messina, in discussion with the author, April 21, 2020.

56. Davis, *Soundtrack*, 141.

57. In discussion with the author, April 21, 2020.

58. In discussion with the author, March 30, 2020; Furay, *Pickin'*, 141.

59. In discussion with the author, March 30, 2020.

60. In discussion with the author, April 21, 2020.

61. Ruhlmann, Liner notes, 24.

62. Werbin, Review of Poco's *Deliverin'*, 52.

63. In discussion with the author, April 21, 2020.

64. In discussion with the author, March 30, 2020.

65. K.K., "Poco," 28; Kimmel and Lawrence, "Poco Delights."

66. Mojo Staff, "Richie Furay."

67. Crowe, "Poor Poco."

68. In discussion with the author, March 30, 2020.

CHAPTER 8

1. Greenblatt, "Fire," 42.

2. In discussion with the author, March 30, 2020.

3. Adams, "Story," 9.

4. In discussion with the author, March 30, 2020.

5. Furay, *Pickin'*, 144.

6. In discussion with the author, July 13, 2020.

7. Ruhlmann, Liner notes, 25.

8. Einarson, Liner notes, 1.

9. In discussion with the author, July 13, 2020.

10. Einarson, Liner notes, 1.

11. Gilbert, "Poco," 11.

12. In discussion with the author, March 30, 2020.

13. Grantham, in discussion with the author, July 13, 2020; Schmit, in discussion with the author, April 8, 2020.

14. Kitts, "'And Settlin' Down,'" 242.

15. Gilbert, "World."

16. Einarson, Liner notes, 3.

17. Kitts, "'And Settlin' Down,'" 242–43.

18. Furay, *Pickin'*, 150.

19. In discussion with the author, April 8, 2020.

20. Gilbert, "Poco."

21. In discussion with the author, April 8, 2020.

22. Furay, *Pickin'*, 149.

23. In discussion with the author, March 30, 2020.

24. West, "Timothy."

25. Werbin, Review of Poco's *From the Inside*, 49.

26. Kitts, "'And Settlin' Down,'" 239.

27. Furay, *Pickin'*, 152.

28. Cotton and Young, in Ruhlmann, Liner notes, 27.

29. Furay, *Pickin'*, 154.

30. Crowe, "Poor Poco."

31. Kitts, "'And Settlin' Down,'" 250.

32. In discussion with the author, March 12, 2021.

33. In discussion with the author, March 4, 2021.

34. In discussion with the author, March 16, 2016. The Turtles had five top-ten hits, including "It Ain't Me Babe," "Happy Together," "She'd Rather Be with Me," "Elenore," and "You Showed Me."

35. In discussion with the author, July 13, 2020.

36. In discussion with the author, March 30, 2020.

37. Adorno, "On Popular Music," sections #21, #14, #27.

38. Ruhlmann, Liner notes, 28.

39. Lindvall, "Behind the Music."

40. Milano, "Legendary."

41. In discussion with the author, March 12, 2021.

42. In discussions with the author, January 21, 2020, March 30, 2020.

43. Furay, *Pickin'*, 153.

44. Bud Scoppa, Review of Poco's *Good Feelin'*.

45. With perhaps an unknowing nod to Adorno, labels have had artists follow up hit singles with similar sounding records: Elvis followed his first RCA release, "Heartbreak Hotel" (1956), a blues song and his first #1, with another blues ballad, "I Want You, I Need You, I Love You" (#1, 1956); in early 1964, the Beatles followed their first US #1, "I Want to Hold Your Hand" (released 1963) with "She Loves You," another high-energy joyful rocker, with the same result, another #1; the Kinks rocked hard with power chords on first "You Really Got Me" (#7, 1964) and then with "All Day and All of the Night" (#7, 1964); Three Dog Night had their first top ten with the ballad "One" (#5, 1969), followed by another, "Easy to Be Hard" (#4, 1969). Genre notwithstanding, consider Madonna's first two top ten hits, the dance pop of "Borderline" (#10, 1984) and "Lucky Star" (#4, 1984), and in 2010 Adele had her first two #1s in the United States with two bluesy songs concerning failed relationships, "Rolling in the Deep" and "Someone Like You."

46. Schott, "Oversouling." Melisma, or what Jerry Wexler called "oversouling," occurs when singers supposedly demonstrate passion but fail the song with gratuitous and misfired vocal pyrotechnics.

47. In discussion with the author, March 30, 2020.

48. Scoppa, review of *Good Feelin'*, 51; Kent, "Poco"; "Hits of the Week," *Record World*, cover.

49. Crowe, "Poor Poco"; Gilbert, "World."

50. See, for example, Hilburn, "Poco Highlights"; Dachis, "Poco"; "Poco, Carnegie Hall"; Provost, "Folk Songs"; Scoppa, "Poco."

51. Crowe, "Poor Poco."

52. Furay, *Pickin'*, 155.

53. Kitts, "'And Settlin' Down,'" 251; Furay, *Pickin'*, 155; in discussion with the author, March 30, 2020.

54. Furay, *Pickin'*, 158.

55. Furay, *Pickin'*, 157; in discussion with the author, March 30, 2020.

56. Grantham, in discussion with the author, July 13, 2020.

57. To name just a handful, Pete Seeger's "My Dirty Stream" (1966), Jefferson Airplane's "Eskimo Blue Day" (1969), Joni Mitchell's "Big Yellow Taxi" (1970), Marvin Gaye's "Mercy Mercy Me (The Ecology)" (1971), the Beach Boys' "A Day in the Life of a Tree" (1971), and John Denver's "Rocky Mountain High" (1972).

58. In discussion with the author, March 30, 2020.

59. Meyer, *Twenty Thousand*, xx.

60. Kitts, "'And Settlin' Down,'" 248–49.

61. Richards, *Life*, 248; Richards, in Meyer, *Twenty Thousand*, xx; Fong-Torres, *Hickory Winds*, 61; Volman, in discussion with the author, July 20, 2020.

62. Kitts, "'And Settlin' Down,'" 249.

63. Ibid.

64. Kitts, "'And Settlin' Down,'" 249; "Crazy Eyes."

65. Furay, *Pickin'*, 157, 153.

66. Eder, "Poco," 309.

67. In discussion with the author, April 8, 2020.

68. In discussion with the author, July 13, 2020.

69. Einarson, *Desperados*, 259.

70. Adams, "Story," 9.

71. Furay, "Tribute."

72. Grogan, "'If It Wasn't.'"

73. In discussion with the author, March 30, 2020.

CHAPTER 9

1. Volman, in discussion with the author, July 20, 2020; Geffen, in Knobler, "So You

Wanna Be," 48; Souther, in Kruger, "J. D. Souther."

2. Knobler, "So You Wanna Be," 52.

3. Kruger, "J. D. Souther"; Knobler, in discussion with the author, July 13, 2020.

4. Knobler, "So You Wanna Be," 52.

5. Ibid., 53.

6. Hillman, *Time Between*, 157; Furay, in discussion with the author, June 16, 2020.

7. In discussion with the author, September 25, 2015; Kitts, "'And Settlin' Down,'" 251.

8. Hillman, *Time Between*, 173–74.

9. Pastor Smith, founder of the Jesus People and the Calvary Chapel movement, has been called one of "the most influential figures in modern American Christianity" by Donald E. Miller, a professor of religion at the University of Southern California. Goffard, "Pastor Chuck Smith."

10. Furay, *Pickin'*, 164.

11. Furay, in discussion with the author, June 16, 2020.

12. Ibid.

13. Furay, *Pickin'*, 174; in discussion with the author, June 16, 2020.

14. In discussion with the author, June 16, 2020.

15. In discussion with the author, October 12, 2020.

16. Weissberg, *Off My Rocker*, 216.

17. Weissberg, "SHF Band Debuts," 10.

18. Furay, *Pickin'*, 168.

19. Ibid., 169.

20. *Life Off Screen*, 22:14, 21:09.

21. In 1989, Furay received a second Gold and a Platinum award for *Retrospect*, a compilation of Buffalo Springfield songs released in 1969, and in 1990, his third Gold album for *Legacy*, Poco's reunion album.

22. Wasserzieher, "This Byrd"; Furay, in Einarson, *Desperados*, 262.

23. See "HBO Vinyl." To be clear, many chart watchers were suspicious of the chart rankings in *Billboard* before the introduction of Nielsen SoundScan in 1991. Derek Thompson presents a common view: "[The charts were] warped by label preferences and record-store inventories. It often over-counted songs that labels preferred (like rock) and under-counted genres they were indifferent toward (like country and rap)." Thompson, "1991."

24. Hartenbach, Review of *SHF*; Nolan, "Souther-Hillman-Furay Band."

25. Sowa, "Richie Furay"; Kitts, "'And Settlin' Down,'" 240.

26. Kitts, "'And Settlin' Down,'" 241.

27. In discussion with the author, June 16, 2020.

28. Knobler, "So You Wanna Be," 53.

29. Kitts, "'And Settlin' Down,'" 251.

30. Price, "SHF Band"; Lomax, "Threesome."

31. Kitts, "'And Settlin' Down,'" 251; Weissberg, "Richie Furay," 34.

32. In discussion with the author, June 16, 2020.

33. Furay tells the story, *Pickin'*, 180–81, and in discussions with the author, June 16, 2020, July 13, 2021.

34. Weissberg, in discussion with the author, June 19, 2020.

35. Furay, *Pickin'*, 182.

36. In discussion with the author, June 16, 2020; Furay, *Pickin'*, 177.

37. Crowe, "Early Bird."

38. Furay, *Pickin'*, 184, 183.

39. In discussion with the author, June 16, 2020.

40. Grundy and Tobler, "Tom Dowd."

41. Scoppa, Review of Souther-Hillman-Furay's *Trouble in Paradise*, 56.

42. In discussion with the author, June 16, 2020.

43. Christgau, "Consumer Guide '70s"; Scoppa, review of Souther-Hillman-Furay's *Trouble in Paradise*, 56.

44. Crowe, "Early Bird."

45. Kitts, "'And Settlin' Down,'" 251.

46. Zimmerman, "Time Flies," 46.

47. Adams, "Story," 10.

CHAPTER 10

1. In discussion with the author, August 24, 2020.

2. "Good Feeling," 52, 53.

3. Knobler, in discussion with the author, July 13, 2020.

4. "Statement of Faith," received as an email attachment in a message from Furay to the author, May 1, 2021.

5. Weissberg, "Richie Furay," 90.

6. America's First Great Awakening occurred between 1720 and 1745, led by preachers and theologians like George Whitefield and Jonathan Edwards. The Second Great Awakening, 1795–1835, was led by, among others, James McGready, Timothy Dwight, and Charles Grandison Finney. The Third Great Awakening, 1855–1930, featured prominent preachers and theologians like Dwight Moody, Charles Spurgeon, and Mary Baker Eddy. The Fourth Great Awakening, 1960–1980, was energized by Billy Graham, Jerry Falwell, Chuck Smith, and others.

7. "'Live Clean,'" D22.

8. "New Rebel Cry," 56.

9. Laurie, "It's Time."

10. McCammon and Baker, "'Father of Christian Rock'"; McCartney, in Thornbury, *Why Should the Devil*, 3.

11. See Thompson, *Raised by Wolves*, 17, 71.

12. In discussion with the author, September 25, 2015.

13. Thompson, *Raised by Wolves*, 12.

14. Wolfe, "Great Relearning," 14.

15. In discussion with the author, July 13, 2020.

16. See Kitts, "'And Settlin' Down,'" 252.

17. In discussion with the author, February 6, 2020.

18. Hibbard, "Ex-Rocker Furay," 3.

19. Kitts, "'And Settlin' Down,'" 252.

20. Furay, *Pickin'*, 188.

21. In discussion with the author, June 16, 2020.

22. Furay, *Pickin'*, 187.

23. Weissberg, "Richie Furay," 90.

24. In discussion with the author, June 16, 2020.

25. Kitts, "'And Settlin' Down,'" 253.

26. In discussion with the author, June 16, 2020.

27. Kitts, "'And Settlin' Down,'" 252.

28. In discussion with the author, June 16, 2020.

29. Hibbard, "Ex-Rocker Furay," 3.

30. Furay, *Pickin'*, 189.

31. Furay, "Good Feeling," 52–53.

32. In discussion with the author, June 16, 2020.

33. Ibid.

34. Lambrecht, "Ian Theme"; Davenport, "Once Again"; Marks, "Rock 'n' Roll Spirit."

35. Remsynder, "New Furay"; Frisch, "Experienced Furay.'"

36. In discussion with the author, June 16, 2020. See "Richie Furay–Full Concert," 9:45, 21:55.

37. Giles, "Why Rod"; Richards, *Life*, 456, 401.

38. Fuchs, "Drop in Album Sales," 6, 31; Grein, "1979," 3.

39. In December 1973, Hilly Kristal opened the club with the awkward name of CBGB and OMFUG, which stood for Country Bluegrass Blues and Other Music for Uplifting Gourmandizers.

40. Robins, *Brief History*, 189.

41. Willman, "Why Are"; Kuntzman, "Glenn Frey's Death."

42. Clark, "Best-Selling Albums"; "100 Best Albums," 54.

43. Gottehrer was referring to the surprising success of Blondie's "In the Flesh" in Australia. "The song got to #1 in Australia," he said, "which at that time might as well have been the moon to most Americans." *NY 1977*, 34:59–35:10.

44. Thompson, "1991."

45. I'm including *Richie Furay: Into the Country*, released in 2022.

46. In discussion with the author, June 16, 2020.

47. Sowa, "Richie Furay."

48. Rimmer, Review, *Dance*.

49. In discussion with the author, June 16, 2020.

50. Ibid.

51. Furay, *Pickin'*, 192.

52. In discussion with the author, June 16, 2020.

53. Greenblatt, "Fire," 42; Greenblatt, "Return of Furay," 18.

54. Palmer, "Rock," C21; Adde, "Furay Brings"; Oppel, "Richie Furay."

55. Hershberg, "Richie Furay's," B5.

56. Kitts, "'And Settlin' Down,'" 260.

57. In discussion with the author, June 16, 2020.

58. Telephone conversation with the author, September 23, 2014.

59. Kitts, "'And Settlin' Down,'" 252; Furay, *Pickin'*, 193.

60. In discussion with the author, June 16, 2020.

61. Kitts, "'And Settlin' Down,'" 252; in discussion with the author, June 16, 2020.

62. Furay, *Pickin'*, 196.

63. In discussion with the author, June 16, 2020.

64. In discussions with the author, June 16, 2020, August 24, 2020.

65. In discussions with the author, June 16, 2020.

66. Kitts, "'And Settlin' Down,'" 240–41.

67. Baker, "It's No," 10.

68. Furay said, "The Lord told me to go to L.A. and tell [Atlantic] 'No.'" Baker, "It's No," 12.

CHAPTER II

1. Baker, "It's No," 12.

2. In discussion with the author, August 24, 2020.

3. Kitts, "'And Settlin' Down,'" 252.

4. Sowa, "Richie Furay."

5. Kitts, "'And Settlin' Down,'" 241.

6. The printed lyrics on the inner sleeve repeat the chorus as "Rise up, we'll *have* a picnic on the ground." But on both the studio and live recordings of the song, Furay changes *have* to *leave* near the end.

7. Kitts, "'And Settlin' Down,'" 252.

8. Sanneh, "Unlikely Endurance of Christian Rock."

9. "Interview with the Lone Ranger of American Fundamentalism," 23.; Swaggart, *Religious*, 113. In the late 1980s, Swaggart lost most of his following after a sex scandal involving a prostitute.

10. Stephens, *Devil's Music*, 191.

11. Rimmer, Review, *Seasons*.

12. In discussion with the author, August 24, 2020.

13. Vitello, "Chuck Smith."

14. In discussion with the author, August 24, 2020.

15. Ibid.

16. Greene, "Richie Furay."

17. In discussion with the author, August 24, 2020.

18. Ibid.

19. Britt, "Re-Formed Poco."

20. Furay, *Pickin'*, 216.

21. Kitts, "'And Settlin' Down,'" 254.

22. Meisner modestly told me, "Maybe I considered myself [a blues singer] but I don't think I sang the blues very well." In discussion with the author, May 6, 2020.

23. Emerson, "Self-Reliance," 151.

24. Furay, *Pickin'*, 220.

25. Kitts, "'And Settlin' Down,'" 254.

26. Ibid.

27. In discussion with the author, July 13, 2020.

28. Furay, in discussion with the author, August 24, 2020. Furay said that Young and Messina may have found the early versions of these songs too proselytizing.

29. Rockin' and Rollin' Dentist, "Poco."

30. Holden, "Pop Life," C14; Eder, review of *Legacy*.

31. Kitts, "'And Settlin' Down,'" 254.

32. Furay reported twenty-three offensive aspects in Kitts, "'And Settlin' Down,'" 254, and twenty-one in Furay, *Pickin'*, 224.

33. Greenblatt, "More Messina," 26, 27.

34. Haymes, "Leader's Departure"; *Deliverin'*, July 11; Varga, "Without Furay."

35. Greenblatt, "More Messina," 27; Young in Brown, "Poco Survives."

36. Kitts, "'And Settlin' Down,'" 254.

37. In discussion with the author, August 24, 2020; Kitts, "'And Settlin' Down,'" 254.

38. Kitts, "'And Settlin' Down,'" 255.

39. Kitts, "Chasing," 9.

40. Weissberg, in discussion with the author, June 19, 2020; Sellen, in discussion with the author, October 10, 2020.

41. Weissberg, in discussion with the author, June 19, 2020; see also Weissberg, *Off My Rocker*, 218–20.

42. In discussion with the author, October 2, 2020.

43. Furay, *Pickin'*, 228–29.

44. In discussion with the author, August 24, 2020.

45. Hirst, Review, *Father's House*.

46. Furay, *Pickin'*, 233.

47. In discussion with the author, August 24, 2020.

48. Ibid.

49. Ibid.

50. Wilcock, "Dion," 10.

51. Review of Richie Furay–*I Am Sure*.

52. Review of Richie Furay–*I Am Sure*; Eder, review of *I Am Sure*.

53. Kitts, "'And Settlin' Down,'" 255.

CHAPTER 12

1. The DVD, featuring Poco songs from various periods, is clumsily titled *Poco: Live from the Belcourt Theater, Nashville, Tennessee, Pickin' Up the Pieces*.

2. In discussion with the author, September 25, 2015.

3. Some of these friends, like Stills and Young, recorded their parts separately and sent Furay digital files.

4. Caligiuri, "Spotlight."

5. Kitts, "'And Settlin' Down,'" 256. For discussion of the re-recording of "Kind Woman," see chapter 5.

6. Kitts, "'And Settlin' Down,'" 257.

7. Ibid.

8. For more discussion of "Let's Dance," see chapter 8.

9. Stockman, Review; Roland, "Richie Furay Returns"; Flippo, "Nashville Skyline."

10. Furay, *Pickin'*, 240.

11. Kitts, "'And Settlin' Down,'" 253.

12. In discussion with the author, August 24, 2020.

13. Roland, review of *Alive*.

14. See chapter 5 for more information on the Springfield reunion.

15. In discussion with the author, November 12, 2020. Most likely the presentation was by Ken Paulson, president of the First Amendment Center and dean of the College of Mass Communication at Middle Tennessee State University. It is possible that Furay was misinformed about what his role would be.

16. See "2013 Official Americana Awards."

17. In discussion with the author, April 8, 2020.

18. Kitts, "'And Settlin' Down,'" 260.

19. Ibid., 260–61.

20. Trust, "Chart Beat," 55.

21. Greenblatt, "Fire in Furay," 40; Horowitz, "Review: Richie Furay"; Reynolds, "For Richie Furay."

22. Kitts, "'And Settlin' Down,'" 260.

23. Graff, "Exclusive."

24. "To His Coy Mistress" was published posthumously in 1681; Marvell lived from 1621 to 1678. The purpose of the song and poem are very different. Furay proclaims his eternal love to his wife while Marvell uses the concept of life's brevity to seduce a young woman.

25. Kitts, "'And Settlin' Down,'" 258.

26. Ibid., 259.

27. Ibid., 258.

28. Ibid., 259.

29. Ibid.

30. Horowitz, "Review: Richie Furay."

31. Greene. "Richie Furay"; in discussion with the author, November 12, 2020.

32. The *Washington Post* charts 30,573 false or misleading claims over Trump's four years. Kessler, Rizzo, and Kelly, "Trump's False."

33. On December 30, 2020, Furay wrote on Facebook: "There's no doubt the American people have been had; corruption, collusion, whatever you want to call it." Under which he posted a link to what he considered the truth, "Statement by Donald J. Trump, the President of the United States." Trump, "Statement."

34. Widburg, "Media Are Lying."

35. *The Federalist, American Spectator, American Thinker*, and *WorldNet-Daily* receive very weak scores on their factual reporting and objectivity from journalism watchdog organizations. Ad Fontes scores publications for reliability on a scale of 0–64. Scores above 24 are generally acceptable with scores of 32 being very good. On reliability, *The Federalist* scores highest with only a 25.38; *American*

Spectator 19.32, *American Thinker* 19.87, and *WorldNetDaily* 20.84. In contrast, the *New York Times* scores 45.19; *Washington Post* 44.27, and *Wall Street Journal* 47.11. Bias scores are on a scale of -42 to +42, with higher negative scores being more left, higher positives scores being more right. Scores closer to zero indicate more neutral or balanced reporting. On bias, *The Federalist* scores 20.66, *American Spectator* 24.15, *American Thinker* 23.49, and *WorldNetDaily* 22.44. In contrast, the *New York Times* scores -8.23, *Washington Post* -7.25, and *Wall Street Journal* 5.81. All scores as of July 3, 2021.

Another media watchdog, Media Bias/ Fact Check (MB/FC), rates publications on factual reporting, scoring them under one of six categories: Very High, High, Mostly Factual, Mixed, Low, Very Low. *WND* is rated low in factual reporting and "extreme right" in bias. *American Spectator* is "mixed" on factual reporting and "right" on bias. *The Federalist* is "mixed" on factual reporting and close to "extreme right" on their scale; *American Thinker* is "low" on factual reporting and "extreme right." In its conclusion, the site states that *American Spectator* is of "mixed credibility" and *The Federalist*, *WND*, and *American Thinker* are "low credibility." MB/FC rates the *New York Times* "high" on factual reporting, "left-center" on bias; *Washington Post* "mostly factual" and "left-center" on bias, and *Wall Street Journal* "mostly factual" and "right-center." In conclusion, MF/BC states that all three newspapers are of "high credibility."

36. Furay, "FOX," January 6, 2021.

37. In discussion with the author, November 12, 2020.

38. In discussion with the author, August 24, 2020.

39. Utile, "3rd Year," 13:05.

40. In discussion with the author, August 24, 2020.

41. Furay, in discussion with the author, August 24, 2020. Sellen confirmed the conversation and email. Sellen, in discussion with the author, October 2, 2020.

42. Greenblatt, "More Messina," 27, 26.

43. In discussion with the author, August 24, 2020.

44. In discussion with the author, October 2, 2020.

45. In discussion with the author, August 24, 2020.

46. Mojo Staff, "Richie Furay"; Eder, Review of *Deliverin'*.

47. Collette, "Richie Furay."

48. Garay, in discussion with the author, July 7, 2021.

49. In discussions with the author, June 16, 2020, July 13, 2021.

50. In discussion with the author, January 21, 2020.

51. In discussion with the author, July 7, 2021.

52. In discussion with the author, July 13, 2021.

53. Rather than identify the songwriters, I identify the recording artists most associated with the songs.

54. Garay, in discussion with the author, July 7, 2021.

55. In discussion with the author, July 13, 2021.

56. Ibid.

57. "Your Love Amazes Me" "speaks to [John Berry] about his wife Robin and her never-ending love and support" while Raye's "In This Life" has been called an "ideal wedding song." Dauphin, "John Berry"; Moore, "Country Rewind."

58. In discussion with the author, July 13, 2021.

59. In discussions with the author, January 1, 2020, June 16, 2020, July 13, 2021.

60. Caligiuri, "Spotlight."

Bibliography

Adams, Stephen. "The Story of a Rock 'n' Roll Life." *Focus on the Family*, August 2007.

Adde, Nicholas. "Furay Brings a Mixed Evening to the Cellar Door." *Washington D.C. Evening Star*, April 25, 1978. http://www.angelfire.com/rock3/deliverin/Furay/Review4-24-78.htm.

Adorno, Theodor W., with the assistance of George Simpson. "On Popular Music." Originally published in *Studies in Philosophy and Social Science*, Institute of Social Research, 1941, 17–48. Accessed April 4, 2021. http://www.icce.rug.nl/~soundscapes/DATABASES/SWA/On_popular_music_1.shtml.

Allen, Jim. "The Day Buffalo Springfield Played Their First Show." *UCR* [Ultimate Classic Rock], April 11, 2016. https://ultimateclassicrock.com/buffalo-springfield-first-show.

"Anderson Cooper Andy Cohen Dave Chappelle New Year's Eve 2019." BEST-NEWSUSA!!! YouTube. December 31, 2018. Video, 7:54. Accessed September 10, 2019. https://www.youtube.com/watch?v=cXfSVrS_T6E.

"AOTY: Highest Rated Albums of 1966." *Rolling Stone* online. 2020. Accessed March 3, 2021. https://www.albumoftheyear.org/ratings/35-rolling-stone-highest-rated/1966/1.

"AOTY: Highest Rated Albums of 1967." *Rolling Stone* online. 2020. Accessed March 3, 2021. https://www.albumoftheyear.org/ratings/35-rolling-stone-highest-rated/1967/1.

"Arthur Morgan." *Community Solutions*. Accessed November 1, 2020. http://www.communitysolution.org/aboutus/ourfounderaem.

Atlas, Jacoba. "Neil Young: His Solo Odyssey." *Circus*, June 1970. Rock's Backpages. Accessed December 7, 2020. http://www.rocksbackpages.com/Library/Article/neil-young-his-solo-odyssey.

The Au Go-Go Singers. Letter to Howard Solomon, December 2, 1964. From the collection of Robert Harmelink.

"Au Go-Go Singers Hit at Tidelands." Clipping, ca. late November 1964. From the collection of Robert Harmelink.

Back, Ann. "New 'Poco' Group May Be on Its Way." *Dallas Morning News*, July 17, 1969. http://www.angelfire.com/rock3/deliverin/PocoFtWorth1969.htm.

Baker, Paul. "It's No to USR, but Richie Rocks On." *CCM*, February 1982.

"Barbershop Color Line: Ohio Man Guilty of Refusing to Cut Negro Hair." *New York Times*, August 25, 1960.

Betts, Stephen L. "Flashback: The Byrds Flip the Opry Script." *Rolling Stone*, March 15, 2016. https://www.rollingstone.com/music/music-country/flashback-the-byrds-flip-the-opry-script-186608.

"*Billboard* Album Reviews." *Billboard*, June 7, 1969.

Blinder, Elliot. "What's That Sound? It's Neil Young." *Rolling Stone*, April 30, 1970.

Booklet. *Buffalo Springfield, Box Set*. Atco R2 74324, 4-disc set. 2001.

Bouchard, Albert. "Review of *Buffalo Springfield Again*." *Crawdaddy!* February 1968.

Bradford, Gamaliel. "Portrait of Margaret Fuller." *North American Review* 210, no. 764 (July 1919): 109–21.

"A Brief History of the World House Choir." *World House Choir*. Accessed March 22, 2020. https://worldhousechoir.org/history-of-world-house-choir.

Britt, Bruce. "Re-Formed Poco Takes to the Studio for New Album." *South Florida Sun Sentinel*, April 8, 1989. https://

www.sun-sentinel.com/news/fl-xpm
-1989-04-08-8901180614-story.html.

Brown, G. "Poco Survives Musical Fest Sound Woes." *Denver Post*, July 7, 1990. http://www.angelfire.com/rock3 /deliverin/Review7-7-90.htm.

Browne, David. "For What It's Worth: Inside Buffalo Springfield's Classic Protest Song." *Rolling Stone*, November 11, 2016. https://www.rollingstone.com /music/music-features/for-what-its -worth-inside-buffalo-springfields-clas sic-protest-song-106435.

"Bruce Palmer Recalls the Day That the Buffalo Springfield First Met in 1966." YouTube. January 11, 1986. Video, 1:40. https://www.youtube.com/watch?v= vTkgsGwqhcw&list=RD4IhUMy4aNnI &index=2.

"Buffalo Springfield." *World Countdown News*, 1967. Rock's Backpages. Accessed December 7, 2020. http:// www.rocksbackpages.com/Library /Article/buffalo-springfield.

"Buffalo Springfield Again." *Rolling Stone*, December 14, 1967. https://www.roll ingstone.com/music/music-album -reviews/buffalo-springfield-again -191036.

"Buffalo Springfield—For What It's Worth & Mr. Soul—Medley." Hollywood Palace, 1967. YouTube. April 8, 2011. Video, 3:54. https://www.youtube.com/watch ?v=3V8VvEzuQ6Y.

"Buffalo Springfield—Fox Theater—Oakland, CA—6/2/11." YouTube. June 22, 2011. Video, 1:32:35. https://www.youtube .com/watch?v=4dmZe2igiMQ&t= 3342s.

"Buffalo Springfield—May 5, 1968—Long Beach Sports Arena—Long Beach, California." YouTube. November 13, 2020. Video, 56:05. https://www.youtube .com/watch?v=etVvULGC0eE.

Bustin, John. "Au Go-Go Singers Have a Sure Winner—Music." *The Austin American-Statesman*, December 2, 1964.

Caligiuri, Jim. "Spotlight: Richie Furay." *The Austin Chronicle*, March 17, 2006.

https://www.austinchronicle.com /music/2006-03-17/348324.

Chiddister, Diane. "Arthur Morgan Started Antioch School in 1920s." *Yellow Springs News: Installment 6: 1913 to 1928*. Accessed October 31, 2020. https://www.ysnews.com/old/stories /2003/july/history_06.html.

———. "Full of Ideas: Antioch Struggled from Its Start." In *Two Hundred Years of Yellow Springs: A Collection of Articles First Published in the "Yellow Springs News" for the 2003 Bicentennial of Yellow Springs, Ohio*, 17–23. Yellow Springs: Yellow Springs News, 2005.

———. "A History of Racial Diversity." *YSNews.com*. February 4, 2010. https://ysnews.com/news/2010/02/a -history-of-racial-diversity.

———. "The Owenites: The First Dreamers." In *Two Hundred Years of Yellow Springs: A Collection of Articles First Published in the "Yellow Springs News" for the 2003 Bicentennial of Yellow Springs, Ohio*, 8–9. Yellow Springs: Yellow Springs News, 2005.

———. "Phyllis Lawson Jackson: Deep Roots, and a Historian's Eye." *YSNews.com*. December 22, 2016. https://ysnews .com/news/2016/12/deep-roots-and-a -historians-eye.

Childs, Andy. "The Neil Young Story Part 2: The Lights Turned on and the Curtain Drawn." *ZigZag,* March 1975. Rock's Backpages. Accessed January 9, 2021. https://www.rocksbackpages .com/Library/Article/the-neil-young -story-part-2-the-lights-turned-on-and -the-curtain-drawn.

Christgau, Robert. "A Basic Record Library: The Fifties and Sixties." *Robert Christgau: Dean of American Rock Critics*. Accessed December 24, 2020. https://www.robertchristgau.com/xg /bk-cg70/basics.php.

———. "Consumer Guide Reviews: Poco." *Robert Christgau: Dean of American Rock Critics*. Accessed February 12, 2021. https://www.robertchristgau .com/get_artist.php?name=poco.

——. "Consumer Guide '70s: S." Review of *Trouble in Paradise. Robert Christgau: Dean of American Rock Critics.* Accessed April 26, 2021. https://www.robertchristgau.com/get_chap.php?k=S&bk=70.

——. "Secular Music." *Esquire*, November 1968. Accessed January 21, 2020. https://www.robertchristgau.com/xg/bk-aow/column5.php.

Clark, Travis. "The 50 Best-Selling Albums of All Time." *Insider*, September 17, 2020. https://www.businessinsider.com/50-best-selling-albums-all-time-2016-9#50-matchbox-twenty-yourself-or-someone-like-you-1.

Clay, Lev. "Twang 101: The Bakersfield Sound." *Premier Guitar*, November 24, 2018. https://www.premierguitar.com/articles/28225-twang-101-the-bakersfield-sound.

Cline, Alex. "Interview of Todd Schiffman." In Oral History Collection. UCLA Center for Oral History. 2004. Accessed October 5, 2020. https://oralhistory.library.ucla.edu/catalog/21198-zz000s93f2.

Cody, John. "Country Rock Pioneer Richie Furay's Many Claims to Fame." *JohnCodyOnline.com: Words & Music.* 2005. Accessed December 12, 2018. http://johncodyonline.com/home/articles/2007-02-RichieFuray.html.

Collette, Doug. "Richie Furay Delivers Fiery Career Retrospective on 'Deliverin': 50th Anniversary Return to the Troubadour (Album Review)." *Glide Magazine*, May 21, 2021. https://glidemagazine.com/257284/richie-furay-delivers-fiery-career-retrospective-on-deliverin-50th-anniversary-return-to-the-troubadour-album-review.

"Crazy Eyes—Richie Furay Band Feb. 2011." RFB. YouTube. February 28, 2011. Video, 9:38. https://www.youtube.com/watch?v=0tL1XVbrJnk.

Crockett, Jim. "Poco's Steel Guitarist Stretching Out: Rusty Young." *Guitar Player Magazine*. November/December 1972. https://www.calsharp.com/rusty.html.

Crowe, Cameron. "Early Byrd Finds His Wings: Hard-Working Chris Hillman Goes Solo." *Rolling Stone*, October 21, 1976. https://www.rollingstone.com/music/music-features/early-byrd-finds-his-wings-227480.

——. "Neil Young: The Rolling Stone Interview." *Rolling Stone*, August 14, 1975. https://www.rollingstone.com/music/music-news/neil-young-the-rolling-stone-interview-123513.

——. "Poor Poco: They Were 'The Next Big Thing' Four Years Ago." *Rolling Stone*, April 26, 1973. http://www.theuncool.com/journalism/rs133-poco.

Dachis, Ron. "Poco at the Depot." *Minnesota Daily*, ca. April 20, 1970. Accessed July 13, 2021. http://www.angelfire.com/rock3/deliverin/Review4-17-70.htm.

Dauphin, Chuck. "John Berry Tells the Tales Behind His Hits on 'Songs and Stories.'" *Billboard*, April 2, 2015. https://www.billboard.com/articles/news/6523944/john-berry-songs-stories-interview.

Davenport, John. "Once Again for Russells." *Houston Daily Cougar*, September 21, 1976. http://www.angelfire.com/rock3/deliverin/Furay/Review9-18-76.htm.

Davis, Clive. *The Soundtrack of My Life.* New York: Simon & Schuster, 2013.

Dawidoff, Nicholas. In the *Country of Country: A Journey to the Roots of American Music.* New York: Vintage, 1998.

"Decennial Census of Population and Housing." U.S. Decennial Census cited in "Yellow Springs, Ohio" Wikipedia entry. Accessed November 1, 2020. https://en.wikipedia.org/wiki/Yellow_Springs,_Ohio.

Delehant, Jim. "The Buffalo Springfield." *Hit Parader*, June 1967. Rock's Backpages. Accessed December 1, 2020. http://www.rocksbackpages.com/Library/Article/the-buffalo-springfield.

Deliverin': 1989–1990. July 11, 1990, entry. Accessed June 19, 2021. https://www.angelfire.com/rock3/deliverin/poco89-90.htm.

Derrough, Leslie Michele. "Rusty Young Still Has Stories to Tell." *Glide Magazine*, June 4, 2018. https://glidemagazine .com/207387/rusty-young-still-has-sto ries-to-tell-interview.

Dimery, Robert. *1001 Albums You Must Hear Before You Die*. London: White Lion, 2018.

Dregni, Michael. "Scotty Moore's Gibson ES-295: First Guitar of Rock and Roll." *Vintage Guitar Magazine*, March 2015. https://www.vintageguitar.com/22152 /scotty-moores-gibson-es-295.

Durchholz, Daniel, and Gary Graff. *Neil Young: Long May You Run; The Illus- trated History*. Minneapolis: Voyageur Press, 2012.

Eder, Bruce. "Poco." In *All Music Guide: The Definitive Guide to Popular Music*, edited by Vladimir Bogdanov, Chris Woodstra, and Stephen Thomas Erlew- ine, 309–10. San Francisco: Backbeat Books, 2001.

———. Review of *Deliverin'*. All Music, ca. 2000. Accessed July 10, 2021. https://www.allmusic.com/album/deliv erin-mw0000203944.

———. Review of *I Am Sure*. AllMusic, ca. 2005. Accessed June 15, 2021. https://www.allmusic.com/album/i-am -sure-mw0000701455.

———. Review of *Legacy*. AllMusic, ca. 2004. Accessed June 19, 2021. https:// www.allmusic.com/album/legacy -mw0000200446.

Edgers, Geoff. "It Was the Byrds Album Everyone Hated in 1968. Now 'Sweet- heart of the Rodeo' Is a Classic." *Washington Post*, August 16, 2018. https://www.washingtonpost.com /entertainment/music/it-was-the-byrds -album-everyone-hated-in-1968-now -sweetheart-of-the-rodeo-is-a-classic /2018/08/16/a2534a88-9a8f-11e8 -b60b-1c897f17e185_story.html.

Edmonds, Ben. "Box Set." *Rolling Stone*, June 25, 2001. https://www.rolling stone.com/music/music-album-reviews /box-set-87289.

Einarson, John. *Desperados: The Roots of Country Rock*. New York: Cooper Square Press, 2001.

———. Liner notes to *From the Inside*. Poco. Epic / Sony / Iconoclastic Records. Icon 1035. CD. 2013.

Einarson, John, and Richie Furay. *For What It's Worth: The Story of Buffalo Springfield*. New York: Cooper Square Press, 2004. First published as *There's Something Happening Here: The Story of the Buffalo Springfield, For What It's Worth*, 1997, by Rogan House.

Eligon, John. "A Small Ohio Town Clamors to Curb Aggressive Policing." *New York Times*, February 5, 2017.

Emerson, Ralph Waldo. "Self-Reliance." 1841. In *The Portable Emerson*, edited with an introduction by Jeffrey S. Cra- mer, 150–72. New York: Penguin, 2014.

Etchison, Michael. "The Buffalo Springfield– Harassed to Extinction." *Los Angeles Herald-Examiner*, September 15, 1968.

———. "Harmonies C/O R.F.D." *Los Angeles Herald-Examiner*, clipping, ca. October 25, 1968. https://www.angelfire.com /rock3/deliverin/DebutRev68.htm.

"Exclusive, Never Before Released–Seen Before Buffalo Springfield 1986, Rehearsal Part 2." YouTube. March 28, 2018. Video, 5:38. https://www.you tube.com/watch?v=4lhUMy4aNnl.

Ferguson, Jayne. "Country-Rock Oriented Group Raps of Changing Musical Times." *Dallas Morning News*, July 17, 1969. https://www.angelfire.com /rock3/deliverin/PocoFtWorth1969 .htm.

Fishel, Jim. "Rock Revival: Sly, Poco, Clas- sics IV Rip Up Miami." *Miami Hurri- cane*, December 8, 1970. https://www .angelfire.com/rock3/deliverin/Review 12-4-70.htm.

Flans, Robyn. "George Grantham–Dedica- tion." *Modern Drummer*, August 1985. https://www.moderndrummer.com/arti cle/august-1985-george-grantham.

Flippo, Chet. "Nashville Skyline: Coun- try-Rock Pioneer Richie Furay Is Back."

CMT, February 22, 2007. http://www
.cmt.com/news/1553094/nashville
-skyline-country-rock-pioneer-richie
-furay-is-back.

Fong-Torres, Ben. *Hickory Winds: The Life
and Times of Gram Parsons*. New
York: St. Martin's Griffin, 1991.

Fricke, David. "Buffalo Springfield Launch
First Tour in 43 Years." *Rolling Stone*,
June 2, 2011. https://www.rolling
stone.com/music/music-news/buffalo
-springfield-launch-first-tour-in-43-years
-233789.

Friedman, Barry, AKA Frazier Mohawk.
"Part 8: Buffalo Springfield Manager Frazier Mohawk." *Uncut*, March
5, 2009. https://www.uncut.co.uk
/features/part-8-buffalo-springfield
-manager-frazier-mohawk-37469
#LVVu6Q2G3t9TEIQ0.99.

Frisch, John. "An Experienced Furay Delivers Dynamite Music." *Dickinsonian*,
November 11, 1976. http://www.angel
fire.com/rock3/deliverin/Furay/Review
10-22-76.htm.

Frith, Simon. "Towards an Aesthetic." In *Taking Popular Music Seriously: Selected
Essays* by Simon Frith, 257–73. Alder-
shot, Hampshire: Ashgate, 2007.

Fuchs, Aaron. "Drop in Album Sales Points
to Dip in Disco's Popularity." *Cash Box*,
August 25, 1979.

Furay, Richie. "A Good Feeling to Know."
Crawdaddy, June 1975.

——. "14 minutes - take a listen . . . there's
no doubt the American people have
been had. . ." Facebook, December 30,
2020. https://www.facebook.com
/richie.furay.9/posts/pfbid0ejAaC1aX7
LPHifXTXLZZmQ8UZzshdaJV1TGWM
fD7cJPQrLEjZMbY83x9rQpQh8Eil.

——. "FOX (listen to you sounding like par-
rots using the 'catchword' phrase -
'mob'). . ." Facebook, January 6, 2021.
https://www.facebook.com/richie.furay
.9/posts/pfbid07AuvLGLSj3wJfMk11F
c76cQckEtrbavWpeWnR6vx7Th6SaY
BWtXQNMWiRK7EDorQl.

——. "Tribute Paul Cotton & Rusty Young
'Bad Weather' & 'Crazy Love.'"

YouTube. December 29, 2021. Video,
6:15. https://www.youtube.com/watch
?v=m2W4eZ-UsDc.

Furay, Richie, with Michael Roberts. *Pickin'
Up the Pieces*. Colorado Springs:
Waterbrook Press, 2006.

G. C. "Night Life: Cheery Sounds." Clipping,
ca. late November 1964. From the collection of Robert Harmelink.

Gifford, Barry. "Last Time Around." *Rolling
Stone*, August 24, 1968: 21–22.

Gilbert, Jerry. "Kenny Loggins (with Jim Messina Sittin' In) Talkin' 'Bout . . ." *Zig-
Zag*, January 1974. Rock's Backpages.
Accessed January 6, 2021. http://www
.rocksbackpages.com/Library/Article
/kenny-loggins-with-jim-messina-sittin
-in-talkin-bout.

——. "Poco: Interview with Richie Furay."
Sounds, February 19, 1972. Rock's
Backpages. Accessed February 27,
2021. http://www.rocksbackpages
.com/Library/Article/poco-interview
-with-richie-furay.

——. "The World Still Hasn't Caught Up
with Poco." *ZigZag*, September 1974.
Rock's Backpages. Accessed March
6, 2021. https://www.rocksbackpages
.com/Library/Article/the-world-still
-hasnt-caught-up-with-poco.

Giles, Jeff. "Why Rod Stewart Turned to
Disco with 'Da Ya Think I'm Sexy.'"
UCR: Classic Rock and Culture, February 12, 2016. https://ultimateclas
sicrock.com/rod-stewart-da-ya-think
-im-sexy/?utm_source=tsmclip&utm
_medium=referral.

Goffard, Christopher. "Pastor Chuck Smith
Dies at 86; Founder of Calvary Chapel
Movement." *Los Angeles Times*, October 3, 2013. https://www.latimes.com
/local/obituaries/la-me-1004-chuck
-smith-20131004-story.html.

Gormley, Mike. "Neil Young: On His Own in
His Own Special Way." *Detroit Free
Press*, February 28, 1969. Rock's
Backpages. http://www.rocksback
pages.com/Library/Article/neil-young
-on-his-own-in-his-own-special-way.

Graff, Gary. "Exclusive: Watch Former Buffalo Springfield Member Richie Furay Perform His New Song 'We Were the Dreamers.'" *Billboard*, March 13, 2015. https://www.billboard.com/articles/columns/rock/6502077/richie-furay-we-were-the-dreamers-exclusive-video.

Greenblatt, Mike. "The Fire in Furay." *Goldmine*, July 2015.

——. "More Messina." *Goldmine*, July 2018.

——. "Return of Furay." *Goldmine*, June 2021.

Greene, Andy. "Neil Young Explains Buffalo Springfield's Aborted Reunion." *Rolling Stone*, June 4, 2012. https://www.rollingstone.com/music/music-news/neil-young-explains-buffalo-springfields-aborted-reunion-116424/.

——. "Readers' Poll: The 10 Best Protest Songs of All Time." *Rolling Stone*, December 3, 2014. https://www.rollingstone.com/music/music-lists/readers-poll-the-10-best-protest-songs-of-all-time-141706/country-joe-and-the-fish-i-feel-like-im-fixin-to-die-rag-173632.

——. "Richie Furay on Buffalo Springfield, Life as a Pastor and Solo Artist." *Rolling Stone*, April 22, 2015. https://www.rollingstone.com/music/music-news/richie-furay-on-buffalo-springfield-life-as-a-pastor-and-solo-artist-47155.

——. "Stephen Stills Breaks Silence on Short-Lived Buffalo Springfield Reunion." *Rolling Stone*, November 5, 2012. https://www.rollingstone.com/music/music-news/stephen-stills-breaks-silence-on-short-lived-buffalo-springfield-reunion-236726.

——. "Stephen Stills Looks Back at Buffalo Springfield: 'I Have No Regrets.'" *Rolling Stone*, May 30, 2013. https://www.rollingstone.com/music/music-features/stephen-stills-looks-back-at-buffalo-springfield-i-have-no-regrets-630549.

Grein, Paul. "1979: The Great Rock/Disco Title Bout." *A Billboard Spotlight*, supplement of *Billboard*, December 22, 1979.

Gressel, Janine. "Poco Plays Pretty Music at Eagles." *Seattle Daily Times*, July 4, 1969. http://www.angelfire.com/rock3/deliverin/Review7-3-69.htm.

Grogan, Cindy. "'If It Wasn't for You . . .' Richie Furay." *Culture Sonar*, June 3, 2019. https://www.culturesonar.com/if-it-wasnt-for-you-richie-furay.

Grundy, Stuart, and John Tobler. "Tom Dowd." Excerpt from *The Record Producers*, 1983. Rock's Backpages. Accessed April 15, 2021. http://www.rocksbackpages.com/Library/Article/tom-dowd.

Gustafson, Nels "Bones." Letter to Mr. Wassem, ca. November 1964. From the collection of Robert Harmelink.

Harrington, Jim. "Review: Buffalo Springfield Reunion More Than Just Nostalgia." *Mercury News*, June 1, 2011. https://www.mercurynews.com/2011/06/01/review-buffalo-springfield-reunion-more-than-just-nostalgia.

Hartenbach, Brett. Review of *The Souther-Hillman-Furay Band*. Allmusic, ca. 2005. Accessed April 22, 2021. https://www.allmusic.com/album/the-souther-hillman-furay-band-mw0000221448.

"Hartford, Peggy Lee, Williams, Neil Young, Poco, Dick Gregory, Man, Charlatans, Lester Top LPs." *Variety*, June 4, 1969.

Haymes, Greg. "Leader's Departure Takes the Country Out of Poco." *Daily Gazette* (Lenox, MA), August 1, 1990. Accessed June 19, 2021. http://www.angelfire.com/rock3/deliverin/Review7-31-90.htm.

"HBO Vinyl: 1973 Shaping the Culture—Payola." *Rolling Stone*. YouTube. March 29, 2016. Video, 4:04. https://www.youtube.com/watch?v=nrMRYqMxi1U.

Heaton, Lauren. "Arthur Morgan Comes to Antioch." In *Two Hundred Years of Yellow Springs: A Collection of Articles First Published in the "Yellow Springs News" for the 2003 Bicentennial of*

Yellow Springs, Ohio, 102–6. Yellow Springs: Yellow Springs News, 2005.

———. "Massive Demonstration Shakes Town." In *Two Hundred Years of Yellow Springs: A Collection of Articles First Published in the "Yellow Springs News" for the 2003 Bicentennial of Yellow Springs, Ohio*, 169–75. Yellow Springs: Yellow Springs News, 2005.

———. "William Mills–'The Yellow Springs Man.'" In *Two Hundred Years of Yellow Springs: A Collection of Articles First Published in the "Yellow Springs News" for the 2003 Bicentennial of Yellow Springs, Ohio*, 10–16. Yellow Springs: Yellow Springs News, 2005.

Heise, Robin. Introduction to "William Mills–Obituary." *Yellow Springs Heritage*, May 17, 2015. Reprint of "Death of Judge William Mills." *Xenia Torchlight*, November 12, 1879. http://ysheritage.org/william-mills-obituary/#wp-comments.

Hershberg, Jennifer. "Richie Furay's Memory Lane." *Washington Post*, April 25, 1978, B5.

Hibbard, Cynthia. "Ex-Rocker Furay Finds Religion a 'Good Feeling to Know.'" *Orange County Register*, February 1, 1981.

Hilburn, Robert. "Four Springfields Return on Albums." *Los Angeles Times*, July 6, 1969.

———. "Poco Highlights Its Albums." *Los Angeles Times*, December 18, 1969. http://www.angelfire.com/rock3/deliverin/Review12-17-69.htm.

———. "Rock Hall of Fame Inductee Neil Young Boycotts Event." *Los Angeles Times*, May 7, 1997. https://www.latimes.com/archives/la-xpm-1997-05-07-mn-56356-story.html.

Hillman, Chris. *Time Between: My Life as a Byrd, Burrito Brother, and Beyond*. Los Angeles: BMG, 2020.

Hirst, Darren. Review of *In My Father's House*. *Cross Rhythms*, February 1, 1998. https://www.crossrhythms.co.uk/products/Richie_Furay/In_My_Fathers_House/9910.

"Hits of the Week." *Record World*, November 18, 1972.

Hodenfield, Chris. "As Bare as You Dare with Sonny and Cher." *Rolling Stone*, May 24, 1973. https://www.rollingstone.com/music/music-news/as-bare-as-you-dare-with-sonny-and-cher-177349.

Holden, Stephen. "The Pop Life." *New York Times*, February 7, 1990.

Hopkins, Jerry. "The Hollywood Hillbillies: What's Old Is New." *Rolling Stone*, February 15, 1969.

Horowitz, Hal. "Review: Richie Furay: *Hand in Hand*." *American Songwriter: The Craft of Music*, April 16, 2015. https://americansongwriter.com/review-richie-furay-hand-hand.

Hoskyns, Barney. "The Soul Stirrer: Sam Cooke." *MOJO*, January 1995. Sam Cooke. Rock's Backpages. https://www.rocksbackpages.com/Library/Article/the-soul-stirrer-sam-cooke.

"In Search of a Name." In booklet, 1, with *Buffalo Springfield, Box Set*. Atco R2 74324. 4-disc set. 2001.

"An Interview with the Lone Ranger of American Fundamentalism." *Christianity Today*, September 4, 1981.

"In the Hour of Not Quite Rain (Buffalo Springfield Cover)–Wild Honey Orchestra Feat. Our Truth." YouTube. August 3, 2018. Video, 3:51. https://www.youtube.com/watch?v=aosUIRanCXM.

"Jesse Fuller–'San Francisco Bay Blues' (1968)." YouTube. July 18, 2010. Video, 4:04. https://www.youtube.com/watch?v=uBME_J0pf3o.

Johnson, Pete. "Pogo and Biff Rose at the Troubadour." *Los Angeles Times*, clipping, ca. December 1968. https://www.angelfire.com/rock3/deliverin/Review11-68.htm.

———. "Rock Show Benefits Radio Strike Fund." *Los Angeles Times*, March 26, 1981.

Keightley, Keir. "Reconsidering Rock." In *The Cambridge Companion to Pop and Rock*, edited by Simon Frith, Will

Straw, and John Street, 109–42. Cambridge: Cambridge University Press, 2001.

Kent, Nick. *The Dark Stuff: Selected Writings on Rock Music.* Cambridge, MA: DaCapo Press, 2002.

———. "I Build Something Up, I Tear It Right Down: Neil Young at 50." *Mojo*, December 1995. Rock's Backpages. Accessed December 30, 2020. http://www.rocksbackpages.com/Library/Article/i-build-something-up-i-tear-it-right-down-neil-young-at-50.

———. "Poco: *A Good Feelin' to Know.*" *New Musical Express*, January 13, 1973. Rock's Backpages. Accessed February 27, 2021. https://www.rocksbackpages.com/Library/Article/poco-ia-good-feelin-to-knowi-epic.

Kessler, Glenn, Salvador Rizzo, and Meg Kelly. "Trump's False or Misleading Claims Total 30,573 over 4 Years." *Washington Post*, January 24, 2021, updated February 10, 2021. https://www.washingtonpost.com/politics/2021/01/24/trumps-false-or-misleading-claims-total-30573-over-four-years.

Kimmel, Michael, and Wendy Lawrence. "Poco Delights Crowd." *Poughkeepsie Miscellany*, December 12, 1971. https://www.angelfire.com/rock3/deliverin/Review12-10-71.htm.

Kitts, Thomas M. "'And Settlin' Down': An Interview with Richie Furay." *Rock Music Studies* 4, no. 3 (2017): 238–61.

———. "Chasing the Music: An Interview with Kenny Weissberg." *Rock Music Studies* 9, no. 3 (2022): 1–17. https://doi.org/10.1080/19401159.2022.2029168.

K. K. "Poco." *Cash Box*, May 22, 1971.

Kleiman, Dena. "In a Time of Too Little Time, Dinner Is the Time for Family." *New York Times*, December 5, 1990. https://www.nytimes.com/1990/12/05/garden/in-a-time-of-too-little-time-dinner-is-the-time-for-family.html.

Knobler, Peter. "So You Wanna Be a Rock 'n' Roll Star?! Souther, Hillman &

Furay . . . and Geffen." *Crawdaddy*, July 1974.

Kruger, Debbie. "J. D. Souther." *Goldmine*, October 9, 1998. http://www.rocksbackpages.com/Library/Article/j-d-souther.

Kubernik, Harvey. "Buffalo Springfield." *Record Collector*, September 6, 2018. http://recordcollectornews.com/2018/09/3548.

———. *Neil Young: Heart of Gold.* London: Omnibus, 2015. Kindle edition.

Kuntzman, Gersh. "Glenn Frey's Death Is Sad, But the Eagles Were a Horrific Band." *New York Daily News*, January 19, 2016. https://www.nydailynews.com/entertainment/music/glenn-frey-death-sad-eagles-lousy-band-article-1.2501461.

Lambrecht, Bill. "Ian Theme Kinky, Depressing." *Telegraph* (Alton, IL), August 18, 1976. http://www.angelfire.com/rock3/deliverin/Furay/Review8-17-76.htm.

Landau, Jon. "Country & Rock." *Rolling Stone*, September 28, 1968.

Larkin, Colin. *Virgin All-Time Top 1000 Albums.* 3rd ed. London: Virgin, 2000.

Laurie, Greg. "It's Time for Another Jesus Revolution." *CBNNEWS.com*, August 11, 2018. https://www1.cbn.com/cbnnews/us/2018/august/it-rsquo-s-time-for-another-jesus-revolution.

Life Off Screen with Dan & Peggy Rupple—Episode 4: Richie & Nancy Furay. MasterMedia International. Spring 2020. Video, 43:15. https://www.youtube.com/watch?v=f9v9AUby7fE.

Lindvall, Helienne. "Behind the Music: How to Write a Hit Song." *The Guardian*, July 14, 2011. https://www.theguardian.com/music/musicblog/2011/jul/14/how-to-write-a-hit-song.

Lithgow, John. *Drama: An Actor's Education.* New York: HarperCollins, 2011.

"'Live Clean,' Graham Tells Teen-agers." *Washington Post*, June 26, 1960.

Lomax, Michele. "Threesome Proves Twang Not Enough." *San Francisco Examiner*, September 2, 1974. https://www

.angelfire.com/rock3/deliverin/Furay
/Review8-31-74.htm.

Marcus, Greil. *The Old Weird America: The World of Bob Dylan's Basement Tapes.* New York: Picador, 2011. Reprinted and revised from *Invisible Republic: Bob Dylan's Basement Tapes*, 1997.

Marks, Ken. "Rock 'n' Roll Spirit with the Band." *Berkshire Eagle*, August 30, 1976. http://www.angelfire.com/rock3/deliverin/Furay/Review8-28-76.htm.

Marsh, Dave, with John Swenson. *The Rolling Stone Record Guide.* New York: Random House / Rolling Stone Press, 1979.

Martin, Douglas. "Elmer Valentine, Owner of Rock Clubs, Dies at 85." *New York Times*, December 9, 2008. https://www.nytimes.com/2008/12/09/arts/music/09valentine.html.

Mather, Olivia Carter. "Taking It Easy in the Sunbelt: The Eagles and Country Rock's Regionalism." *American Music* 31, no. 1 (Spring 2013): 26–49.

McCammon, Sarah, and Elizabeth Baker. "The 'Father of Christian Rock' Larry Norman's Battles with Evangelicalism." *NPR Music*, March 25, 2018. https://www.npr.org/2018/03/25/596450516/why-should-the-devil-have-all-the-good-music-larry-norman-s-battle-for-and-again.

McDonald, Marci. "A Yorkville Kid Is Coming Home and His Songs Are Sadder Now." *Toronto Daily Star*, February 1, 1969.

McDonough, Jimmy. *Shakey: Neil Young's Biography.* London: Vintage, 2003.

McDougall, Allan R. "A Conversation with Stephen Stills." *Rolling Stone*, March 4, 1971.

Mesinger, Maxine. "Big City Beat by Maxine." *Houston Chronicle*, section 2, November 18, 1964.

Meyer, David N. *Twenty Thousand Roads: The Ballad of Gram Parsons and His Cosmic American Music.* New York: Villard, 2008.

Mihalek, Robert. "Segregation at Little Theatre Ends Quickly, Quietly in 1942." In

Two Hundred Years of Yellow Springs: A Collection of Articles First Published in the "Yellow Springs News" for the 2003 Bicentennial of Yellow Springs, Ohio, 137–40. Yellow Springs: Yellow Springs News, 2005.

Milano, Brett. "The Legendary Clive Davis on Music, Law and Luck." *Harvard Law Today*, September 11, 2017. https://today.law.harvard.edu/the-legendary-clive-davis-on-music-law-and-luck.

Miller, Timothy. *The Quest for Utopia in Twentieth-century America: 1900–1960.* Volume 1. Syracuse: Syracuse University Press, 1998.

"Milt Holland: Biography." *All About Jazz.* Accessed February 18, 2020. https://musicians.allaboutjazz.com/miltholland.

Mojo Staff. "Richie Furay on RedeLIVErin' Poco." *Mojo*, June 10, 2021. https://www.mojo4music.com/articles/stories/richie-furay-on-redeliverin-poco/?fbclid=IwAR2uvtd8fOcn8hql_dmH_66fBjBWmYlJzhksbbJiDdacuG0t_ptDAp2UD30.

Moore, Bobby. "Country Rewind: Collin Raye Narrates Your Wedding Reception with 'In This Life.'" *Wide Open Country*, May 16, 2018. https://www.wideopencountry.com/in-this-life-song-collin-raye.

Morsch, Mike. "Looking Back 50 Years: Jim Messina Revisits a Better Sounding Poco Album." *The Vinyl Dialogues Blog*, June 12, 2020. https://vinyldialogues.com/VinylDialoguesBlog/looking-back-50-years-jim-messina-revisits-a-better-sounding-poco-album.

Mulvey, John. "Jeff Tweedy Interviewed: 'This Is the Biological Reason Why Hell Exists.'" *Uncut*, July 8, 2014. https://www.uncut.co.uk/features/jeff-tweedy-interviewed-this-is-the-biological-reason-why-hell-exists-6701.

"Neil Young, Stephen Stills, Richie Furay, Buffalo Springfield Rehearsal, 1986." YouTube. December 21, 2017. Video, 14:04. https://www.youtube.com/watch?v=fWMGFnXHk44.

Nelson, Paul. "Bunky & Jake: Ex-Fug and Folkie Form Blues-Rock Combo." *Rolling Stone*, April 19, 1969. https://www.rollingstone.com/music/music-news/bunky-jake-ex-fug-and-folkie-form-blues-rock-combo-191095.

"The New Rebel Cry: Jesus Is Coming!" *Time*, June 21, 1971.

Nolan, Tom. "The Souther-Hillman-Furay Band: *The Souther-Hillman-Furay Band*." *Phonograph Record*, 1974. Rock's Backpages. http://www.rocksbackpages.com/Library/Article/the-souther-hillman-furay-bandi-the-souther-hillman-furay-bandi.

Noyes, John Humphrey. *History of American Socialisms*. Philadelphia: J. B. Lippincott, 1870.

NY77: The Coolest Year in Hell. Directed by Henry Corra, VH1, 2007, 87 minutes. DVD.

"The 100 Best Albums of the Eighties." *Rolling Stone*, November 16, 1989.

Oppel, Pete. "Richie Furay Delights at Whiskey River Gig." *Dallas Morning Star*, May 28, 1978. http://www.angelfire.com/rock3/deliverin/Furay/Review5-28-78.htm.

O'Rourke, Sally. "It Was 50 Years Ago Today: 'Cherish' by The Association." *Rebeat*, October 2016. http://www.rebeatmag.com/it-was-50-years-ago-today-cherish-by-the-association.

Orshoski, Wes. "Buffalo Springfield Boxed." *Billboard*, July 7, 2001.

Ostapiuk, Peter. "The Beatles Said, 'It's Easy,' But the 50th Anniversary of the 'Our World' Broadcast Reminds Us That It Wasn't." *Intelsat*, June 20, 2017. Accessed January 11, 2021. https://www.intelsat.com/resources/blog/beatles-said-its-easy-but-50th-anniversary-of-our-world-broadcast-wasnt.

Palmer, Robert. "Rock: Richie Furay Sings with Country Influence." *New York Times*, April 24, 1978, C21.

Pareles, Jon. "Rock-and-Roll Laureates." *New York Times*, May 8, 1997, 15.

Petrarch. *The Sonnets of Petrarch*. Translated by Joseph Auslander. New York: Longmans, Green & Co., 1932.

Petrus, Stephen, and Ronald D. Cohen. *Folk City: New York and the American Folk Music Revival*. New York: Oxford University Press, 2015.

Phillips, Tom. "Rock Speaks Sweetly Now." *New York Times*, December 17, 1967.

Phull, Hardeep. *Story Behind the Protest Song: A Reference Guide to 50 Songs That Changed the 20th Century*. Westport, CT: Greenwood, 2008.

"Poco." *Sandspur* (Rollins College, FL), November 10, 1972. https://stars.library.ucf.edu/cgi/viewcontent.cgi?article=2428&context=cfm-sandspur.

"Poco, Carnegie Hall, New York." *Poco: Deliverin*, clipping, ca. February 1971. https://www.angelfire.com/rock3/deliverin/Review12-70.htm.

Poco: Live from the Belcourt Theater, Nashville, Tennessee, Pickin' Up the Pieces. Air Music and Media, 2004. DVD.

"Poco—You Better Think Twice." John Byner's Something Else, 1970. YouTube. October 16, 2006. Video, 5:06. Accessed March 6, 2021. https://www.youtube.com/watch?v=3CWpqJVg7MQ.

Pogo. Accessed February 5, 2021. http://www.waynecountry.net/Pogo/characters.html.

"The Popdose 100: The Greatest Protest Songs of All Time." *Pop Dose*, January 18, 2017. https://popdose.com/the-popdose-100-the-greatest-protest-songs-of-all-time.

Price, Hardy. "SHF Band Fails to Make Grade." *Arizona Republic*, August 31, 1974. https://www.angelfire.com/rock3/deliverin/Furay/Review8-30-74.htm.

Provost, Sarah. "Folk Songs of Paxton, Rock Sounds of Poco Delight SPAC Audience." *Gloversville* (NY) *Daily Leader Herald*, August 31, 1971.

"Reasons to Love the Artsy Town of Yellow Springs, Ohio." *Travel Hacks Guide*.

Accessed May 17, 2019. https://travel
.thefuntimesguide.com/yellow-springs
-ohio.

Remsynder, Rick. "New Furay Band Headed
Up." *Times Herald Record*, October
20, 1976. http://www.angelfire.com
/rock3/deliverin/Furay/Review10-15
-76.htm.

Review of Richie Furay—I Am Sure. *No
Depression: The Journal of Roots
Music*, November 1, 2005. https://
www.nodepression.com/album
-reviews/richie-furay-i-am-sure.

Reynolds, Mary Catherine. "For Richie Furay
Talent and Legacy Go Hand in Hand."
*No Depression: The Journal of Roots
Music*, May 23, 2014, published in
2015. https://www.nodepression.com
/for-richie-furay-talent-and-legacy-go
-hand-in-hand.

Richards, Keith. *Life*. New York: Little,
Brown, and Company, 2010.

"Richie Furay—Full Concert—08/28/76—
Roosevelt Stadium (Official)." You-
Tube. November 6, 2014. Video, 51:31.
Accessed May 23, 2021. https://www
.youtube.com/watch?v=BQoiWJnw
Wvs&t=2684s.

"Richie Furay Live from Stargazers Theatre." Colorado Music Network. You-
Tube. March 3, 2018. Video, 1:50:43.
Accessed November 1, 2020. https://
www.youtube.com/watch?v=
qM52lvLV0mM.

"Richie Furay Profile." Written and produced
by Robert Parish. Wild Field Features,
2007. YouTube. December 30, 2012.
Video, 4:07. Accessed October 5,
2019. https://www.youtube.com/watch
?v=GcfQ6poeeJw.

Rimmer, Mike. Review of Richie Furay—
Dance a Little Light (Reissue). *Cross
Rhythms*, January 1, 2004. https://
www.crossrhythms.co.uk/products
/Richie_Furay/Dance_A_Little_Light
_reissue/8280.

——. Review of Richie Furay *Seasons of
Change*. *Cross Rhythms*, March 3,
2010. https://www.crossrhythms.co.uk

/products/Richie_Furay/Seasons_Of
_Change/13726.

Roberts, David. *Stephen Stills: Change
Partners; The Definitive Biography*.
Kimbolton, UK: Red Planet, 2016.

Robins, Wayne. *A Brief History of Rock,
Off the Record*. New York: Routledge,
2008.

Rockin' and Rollin' Dentist. "Poco—The
Sound & The Furay." April 1, 2017.
Accessed June 19, 2021. https://
rocknrolldentist.wordpress.com/2017
/04/01/poco-the-sound-the-furay.

Roland, Terry. Review of *Alive*, *The Phantom
Tollbooth*, ca. 2009. Accessed June
16, 2021. http://www.tollbooth.org
/2009/reviews/furay.html.

——. "Richie Furay Returns to Re-Claim His
Fame with *Heartbeat of Love*." *Folk-
works,* November–December 2007.
https://folkworks.org/features/feature
-articles/67-2007-6/35346-richie-furay
-returns.

Rubin, Rachel Lee. *Merle Haggard's "Okie
from Muskogee."* New York: Blooms-
bury 33 1/3, 2018.

Ruhlmann, William. Liner notes to *Poco: The
Forgotten Trail (1969–1974)*. Poco.
Epic / Legacy / CBS Records E2K
46162. 2-disc set. 1990.

Sablich, Justin. "From Macdougal [*sic*]
Street to 'The Bitter End,' Exploring Bob Dylan's New York. *New York
Times*, October 18, 2016. https://www
.nytimes.com/2016/10/18/travel
/exploring-bob-dylans-greenwich-vil
lage-new-york.html.

Sander, Ellen. "The Sweet Country Sounds
of Buffalo Springfield." *New York
Times*, October 6, 1968.

Sanneh, Kelefa. "The Unlikely Endurance of
Christian Rock." *New Yorker*, September 17, 2018. https://www.newyo
rker.com/magazine/2018/09/24/the
-unlikely-endurance-of-christian-rock.

Schott, Ben. "Oversouling." "Schott's
Vocab." *New York Times*, February 14,
2011. https://schott.blogs.nytimes.com
/2011/02/14/oversouling.

Scoppa, Bud. "Poco." *Circus*, August 1971. Rock's Backpages. Accessed March 6, 2021. https://www.rocksbackpages.com/Library/Article/poco.

——. Review of Poco's *Good Feelin' to Know*. *Rolling Stone*, December 21, 1972.

——. Review of Souther-Hillman-Furay's *Trouble in Paradise*. *Rolling Stone*, July 17, 1975.

Shapiro, Fred C. "The Talk of the Town: Bedford-Stuyvesant." *New Yorker*, August 1, 1964.

Sharp, Ken. "Buffalo Springfield Again: A Conversation with Richie Furay." *Goldmine*. September 13, 2011. https://www.goldminemag.com/articles/buffalo-springfield-again-a-conversation-with-richie-furay.

——. "Catching Up with Eagles and Poco Co-Founder Randy Meisner (Interview)." *Rock Cellar*, November 10, 2016. https://www.rockcellarmagazine.com/randy-meisner-interview-eagles-poco-hall-of-fame-stories.

Sietsema, Robert. "Farewell to Tad's, Manhattan's Last Meat Honkytonk." *Eater New York*, July 9, 2014. https://ny.eater.com/2014/7/9/6190829/farewell-to-tads-manhattans-last-meat-honkytonk.

Silsbee, Kirk. "R.I.P. Buffalo Springfield's Dewey Martin." *Goldmine*, March 12, 2009. Rock's Backpages. http://www.rocksbackpages.com/Library/Article/rip-buffalo-springfields-dewey-martin.

Smith, Joe. "Off the Record Interview with Stephen Stills, 1987–11–25." Library of Congress. Audio Interview, 40:17. https://www.loc.gov/item/jsmith000226.

Snow, Mat. "Buffalo Springfield: Expecting to Fly." *MOJO*, September 1994. Rock's Backpages. Accessed January 7, 2021. http://www.rocksbackpages.com/Library/Article/buffalo-springfield--expecting-to-fly.

Sowa, Tom. "Richie Furay Sings Brand New Canticle." *Spokesman-Review* (Spokane, WA), clipping, ca. February 15, 1981. Accessed August 8, 2020.

https://www.angelfire.com/rock3/deliverin/Furay/FurayConcerts.htm.

"Statement of Votes Cast, General Election, Greene County, November 03, 2020." Greene County Board of Elections, Ohio. Accessed July 22, 2021. https://www.boe.ohio.gov/greene/c/elecres/20201103precinct.pdf?__cf_chl_jschl_tk__=pmd_481049b4b2b3c885ddd2c7a9c82224d6d18d514e-1626968711-0-gqNtZGzNAjijcnBszQdO.

"Stephen." In booklet, 12–13, with *Buffalo Springfield, Box Set*. Atco R2 74324. 4-disc set. 2001.

Stephens, Randall J. *The Devil's Music: How Christians Inspired, Condemned, and Embraced Rock 'n' Roll*, Cambridge, MA: Harvard University Press, 2018.

"Stephen Stills Quotes." Citatis.com. Accessed January 12, 2021. https://citatis.com/a21516/269073.

Stewart, Luke. "'Hell, they're your problem, not ours': Draft Dodgers, Military Deserters and Canada-United States Relations in the Vietnam War Era." *Études canadiennes / Canadian Studies* 85 (2018): 67–96.

Stockman, Steve. Review of Richie Furay's *Heartbeat of Love*. *Soul Surmise*, August 10, 2007. https://stocki.typepad.com/soulsurmise/2007/10/richie-furay--.html.

"Super Seventies Rock Site's Super Daily Music Chronicle: April 1973." Accessed January 21, 2021. https://www.superseventies.com/sdmc_40_Apr_73.html.

Swaggart, Jimmy. *Religious Rock 'n' Roll: A Wolf in Sheep's Clothing*. Baton Rouge, LA: Jimmy Swaggart Ministries, 1987.

Sweeting, Adam. "CSNY's Stephen Stills and Neil Young (1999)." *Rock's Backpages Audio*. Accessed January 9, 2021. http://www.rocksbackpages.com/Library/Article/csnys-stephen-stills-and-neil-young-1999.

Thompson, Derek. "1991: The Most Important Year in Pop-Music History." *The*

Atlantic, May 8, 2015. https://www.the
atlantic.com/culture/archive/2015/05
/1991-the-most-important-year-in-music
/392642.

Thompson, John J. *Raised by Wolves: The
Story of Christian Rock & Roll*. Toronto:
ECW Press, 2000.

Thornbury, George A. *Why Should the Devil
Have All the Good Music?* New York:
Convergent Books, 2018.

Till, Chris. "Tales of a Forgotten Music Star."
YSNews.com, June 7, 2018. https://
ysnews.com/news/2018/06/tales-of-a
-forgotten-music-star.

"Tom Petty Inducts Buffalo Springfield at the
1997 Rock & Roll Hall of Fame Induction Ceremony." YouTube. May 6, 1997.
Video, 1:45. https://www.youtube.com
/watch?v=6nsfAnLSewU.

Trump, Donald. "Statement by Donald J.
Trump, the President of the United
States." Facebook. December 22,
2020. Video, 13:53. https://www
.facebook.com/DonaldTrump/posts
/10166014477280725.

Trust, Gary. "Chart Beat: Richie Furay
Returns." *Billboard*, April 18, 2015.

"2013 Official Americana Awards—Stephen
Stills 'For What It Is Worth.'" YouTube.
September 18, 2013. Video, 6:05.
https://www.youtube.com/watch?v=
diVD6GWnDO8.

Unterberger, Richie. Review of *Buffalo
Springfield [Box Set]*. Fall 2001.
Accessed January 7, 2021. https://
www.allmusic.com/album/buffalo
-springfield-box-set-mw0000006966.

Utile, Kevin. "3rd Year—Reach Boulder."
Reach Church. 2018. Video, 26:00.
https://reachchurch.co/vision.

Vaccariello, Linda. "Long Weekend: Yellow
Springs, Ohio." *Cincinnati Magazine*,
October 5, 2015. https://www.cincin
natimagazine.com/daytripperblog/fall
-2015-travel-guide-yellow-springs-ohio.

Varga, George. "The Summer of Love,
An Epic Tipping Point for Music
and Youth Culture, Turns 50." *San
Diego Union-Tribune*, May 27, 2017.
Accessed January 14, 2021. https://

www.sandiegouniontribune.com/enter
tainment/music/sd-et-music-summer-of
-love-20170515-story.html.

———. "Without Furay, Poco Fall Short of Legacy." *San Diego Union*, ca. June 25,
1990. Accessed June 19, 2021. http://
www.angelfire.com/rock3/deliverin
/Review6-24-90.htm.

"Various Accounts of Their Meeting in Hollywood." In booklet, 2, with *Buffalo
Springfield, Box Set*. Atco R2 74324.
4-disc set. 2001.

Vitello, Paul. "Chuck Smith, Minister Who
Preached to Flower Children, Dies
at 86." *New York Times*, October 13,
2013. https://www.nytimes.com/2013
/10/14/us/chuck-smith-minister-who
-preached-to-flower-children-dies-at
-86.html.

Wasserzieher, Bill. "This Byrd Has Flown:
Chris Hillman Comes to the Coach
House." *OC Weekly*, August 1997.
Rock's Backpages. Accessed April
2021. http://www.rocksbackpages
.com/Library/Article/this-byrd-has
-flown-chris-hillman-comes-to-the
-coach-house.

Weissberg, Kenny. *Off My Rocker*. Boulder:
Sandra Jonas Publishing, 2019.

———. "Richie Furay: Hooked on the Holy
Ghost." *Creem*, November 1975.

———. "SHF Band Debuts in Aspen." *Cake
Eaters*, July 11, 1974.

Werbin, Stu. Review of Poco's *Deliverin.'
Rolling Stone*, March 4, 1971.

———. Review of Poco's *From the Inside. Rolling Stone*, October 14, 1971.

West, David. "Timothy B. Schmit: From the
Inside." *Pocketmags*, June 5, 2017.
Accessed March 2, 2020. https://
pocketmags.com/us/magazine-articles
/article/1569/timothy-b-schmit-from
-the-inside.

White, Timothy. *The Nearest Faraway Place*.
New York: Holt, 1994.

"Who Named Buffalo Springfield? Stephen
Stills and Van Dyke Parks Square Off!"
YouTube. June 3, 2013. Video, 3:16.
https://www.youtube.com/watch?v=
1Z0fphNakvM.

Widburg, Andrea. "The Media Are Lying About Trump's Phone Call with Raffensperger." *American Thinker*, January 4, 2021. https://www.americanthinker.com/blog/2021/01/the_media_are_lying_about_trumps_phone_call_with_raffensperger.html#ixzz6igrI9k8H.

Wilcock, Don. "Dion the Wanderer Comes Home to the Blues." *Blues Music Magazine*, no. 27 (Fall 2020).

Williams, Amanda. "A Day in Yellow Springs—Ohio's Hippie Enclave." A Dangerous Day Travel Blog. Last modified May 25, 2020. https://www.dangerous-business.com/a-day-in-yellow-springs-ohios-hippie-enclave.

Williams, Paul. "Buffalo Springfield: Everybody Look What's Going Down . . ." *Crawdaddy!* March 1967. Rock's Backpages. Accessed December 11, 2020. http://www.rocksbackpages.com/Library/Article/buffalo-springfield-everybody-look-whats-going-down.

Williamson, Nigel. *Journey Through the Past: The Stories Behind the Classic Songs of Neil Young*. San Francisco: Backbeat Books, 2002.

Willman, Chris. "Buffalo Springfield Fans Get Next Best Thing to a Reunion: A Richie Furay-Led L.A. Tribute." *Variety*, February 18, 2018. https://variety.com/2018/music/news/buffalo-springfield-tribute-1202703176.

———. "Why Are the Eagles So Hated? An Explainer on the Immensely Popular Yet Divisive Rock Band." *Billboard*, January 20, 2016. https://www.billboard.com/articles/columns/rock/6851078/eagles-hatred-explainer-defense-glenn-frey.

Winthrop, John. "A Model of Christian Charity." 1630. Hanover Historical Texts. Accessed October 31, 2020. https://history.hanover.edu/texts/winthmod.html.

Wolfe, Tom. "The Great Relearning." *American Spectator*, December 1987.

Wood, Mikael. "Live Review: Buffalo Springfield Finds That Old Spark at the Wiltern." *Los Angeles Times*, June 5, 2011.

https://latimesblogs.latimes.com/music_blog/2011/06/live-review-buffalo-springfield-finds-that-old-spark-at-wiltern.html.

Wouters, Patrick. July 7, 2018. Comment on *What's That Sound? Complete Albums Collections*. AllMusic, User Reviews. https://www.allmusic.com/album/whats-that-sound-complete-albums-collection-mw0003176316/user-reviews.

"Yellow Springs: Cutest Hippie Town Ever." YouTube. May 31, 2018. Video, 6:16. https://www.youtube.com/watch?v=oi2zZQCqvYc&t=273s.

Yorke, Ritchie. "Stephen Stills: An Interview in England—Part 2." *Circus*, September 1970. Rock's Backpages. http://www.rocksbackpages.com/Library/Article/stephen-stills-an-interview-in-england--part-2.

Young, Neil. Liner notes to *What's That Sound? Complete Albums Collections*. Buffalo Springfield. Rhino/Atco R2 566970. 5-disc set. 2018.

———. *Waging Heavy Peace: A Hippie Dream*. New York: Blue Rider Press, 2012.

Young, Rusty. "Gregg Allman Story from My Book." Poco Forum, May 28, 2017. http://forum.pocoband.com/viewtopic.php?f=3&t=6769&sid=10f6dda8e4e33ae4eec56f654f19d71c.

Zimmer, Dave. "Stephen Stills Carries On." *BAM*, April 6, 1979. Accessed November 17, 2020. https://4waysite.com/dave-zimmer-bam.

Zimmerman, Lee. "Poco's Rusty Young Looks at Retirement and Life After 'Crazy Love.'" *Goldmine*, April 14, 2014. https://www.goldminemag.com/articles/pocos-rusty-young-looks-life-45-years-crazy-love.

———. "Time Flies for a Byrd." *Goldmine*, December 2020.

Index

reviews (*continued*)
  Pogo, 96
  RFB 1976 tour, 175
  RFB 1978 tour, 181
  Seasons of Change, 191
  Souther-Hillman-Furay Band, The, 155
  Souther-Hillman-Furray (SHF), 153, 160
  Springfield reunion tour, 88
  Trouble in Paradise, 163–64
Reynolds, Mary Catherine, 214
Rhodes, Michael, 201, 209–10
Rich, Don, 106
Richards, Keith, 94, 143
Richardson, Jack, 135, 139, 144–45
Richie Furay Band (RFB), 171–82, 206,
  213, 221–23
Richie Furay: In the Country (album), 221,
  223–26
"Ride the Country" (song), 140
Rigby, Randy, 201–2
"Right Along, A" (song), 142
Rimmer, Mike, 179, 191
"Rise and Fall" (song), 155, 158, 165
"Rise Up" (song), 188–90, 202, 241n6
Ritter, Keith, 161–62
Rivers, Johnny, 40, 142
"Road of Plenty" (song), 86
Roberts, Michael, 211
Robins, Wayne, 170
rockabilly, 13–14, 105
rock and roll, 43–44
  and authenticity, 111
  Buffalo Springfield Again, 64
  and Christianity, 86, 150, 168–70, 172,
  191
  Good Feelin' to Know, A, 139–40
  and hit singles, 137–38
  I Am Sure, 203–6
  "Kind Woman," 83
  "Let's Dance Tonight," 145
  musical soundscape, 176–78
  "Nobody's Fool / El Tonto de Nadie,"
  119
  Poco, 114–15
  See also country-rock
Rock and Roll Hall of Fame, 85–86, 90, 200
"Rockin' in the Free World" (song), 88
"Rock & Roll Lullaby" (song), 84
"Rock & Roll Woman," 63–64, 70, 74
"Rocky Mountain Breakdown" (song), 142

Rocky Mountain Christian Fellowship, 192
Rodgers, Jimmie "Honeycomb," 25, 27
Roland, Terry, 211
Rolling Stone, 232n40, 236n64
  Buffalo Springfield, 51
  Buffalo Springfield Again, 63–65
  country-rock, 92
  Deliverin', 125
  "For What It's Worth," 53
  and Furay's Christian conversion, 172
  Furay's sermons, 193
  Good Feelin' to Know, A, 139–40
  From the Inside, 134
  "In the Hour of Not Quite Rain," 80
  Last Time Around, 75
  Pickin' Up the Pieces, 107
  on Pogo, 97
  Springfield reunion tour, 88
  Trouble in Paradise, 163–64
Ronstadt, Linda, 98, 183, 212, 224
Roosevelt Stadium, New Jersey, 159–60,
  176
Rosas, Rick, 88–89
Rose, Mitch, 152
Rosewood Mansion, 210
Roulette Records, 25, 27–28, 30, 31
Roxy, Los Angeles, 182
"Run for the Roses" (song), 213
Ryman Auditorium, 102, 212

"Sad Memory" (song), 12, 27, 48, 65,
  67–68, 79, 104, 116, 164, 175
Safe at Home (album), 92, 101
"Safe at Home" (song), 156
"Salt Creek" (song), 45
"Same Old Wine" (song), 122
Sams, Ronnie, 19–20
San Carlos, California, 198
Sander, Ellen, 75
San Francisco, California, 53, 73–74, 135,
  137, 232n40
  See also Fillmore, San Francisco
"San Francisco Bay Blues" (song), 26, 29
Sanneh, Kalefa, 191
Satan Is Alive and Well on Planet Earth
  (Lindsey), 151
"Satisfied" (song), 185
Saunders, Steve, 50
Schiffman, Todd, 112–13, 118–19, 121, 129,
  145–46